Feminism. Art. Capitalism.

Feminism. Art. Capitalism.

Angela Dimitrakaki

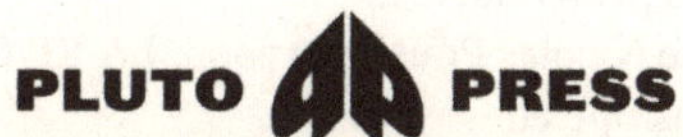

First published 2025 by Pluto Press
New Wing, Somerset House, Strand, London WC2R 1LA
and Pluto Press, Inc.
1930 Village Center Circle, 3-834, Las Vegas, NV 89134

www.plutobooks.com

British Library Cataloguing in Publication Data
A catalogue record for this book is available from the British Library

ISBN 978 0 7453 5124 7 Paperback
ISBN 978 0 7453 5126 1 PDF
ISBN 978 0 7453 5125 4 EPUB

Typeset by Stanford DTP Services, Northampton, England

Simultaneously printed in the United Kingdom and United States of America

EU GPSR Authorised Representative
LOGOS EUROPE, 9 rue Nicolas Poussin, 17000, LA ROCHELLE, France
Email: Contact@logoseurope.eu

Contents

Acknowledgements

As perhaps every feminist and Marxist piece of writing, this book is excerpted from a process of lifelong political learning. As such, the book is a reflective moment made possible because of, and in response to, the critical intellectual work of many in art theory and beyond. It is impossible to list these thinkers here or adequately express the gratitude due.

This book was written intermittently between 2015 and 2025, a decade in which much changed while remaining the same or getting significantly worse. In these ten years I had real-time dialogues on topics and questions picked up in the book with Kirsten Lloyd, Nizan Shaked, Victoria Horne, Angeliki Roussou, Elke Krasny, Ewa Majewska, Keti Chukhrov, Ana Teixeira Pinto, Giovanna Zapperi, and Marina Vishmidt, among others to whom I remain grateful. I thank them for their political alertness, the practice of comradely dialogue where disagreement is permitted, and the imperative to persist against the confusion generated by injurious historical forces. Marina's passing in 2024 brought on a permanent state of bereavement in the field, but the path carved for Marxist feminism by her brilliant interrogation has now been taken up by many. While there is no consolation for this tremendous loss, political judgement can be obtained even from imagining what Marina would have thought about oversights, simplifications, and shortcuts such as those encountered in this book. The numerous exchanges with comrades at the conferences of Historical Materialism in London, and eventually also in Athens, have informed the book's outlook beyond art theory in more ways than I could possibly acknowledge.

I am deeply thankful to all who practiced solidarity in the waged workplace — without it, without them, I would have abandoned the project (and not only that). I thank my students, especially those who asked 'when do we start the revolution then?' at the end of courses. I thank the doctoral researchers I had the pleasure to work with, and especially those who have been critical interlocutors in the fragile collectivity forming anew around Marxist feminism — in recent years, Fabiola Fiocco, Natassa Philimonos, Tobey Pan. I am grateful to all my colleagues, and especially Viccy Coltman, Heather Pulliam, Tamara Trodd, for understanding the clash between social reproduction labour and the waged workplace. The active support I received during the Covid-19 period was feminism in practice. In writing the book in such adverse conditions, their example has helped keep the crucial distinction between deeds and words in sight.

I thank the grassroots activist groups I have been involved with, some transnational, for complexifying the meaning of political belonging. Numerous collaborations with artists, curators, educators from Europe and beyond have also informed lines of argument and questions in the book. You know who you are, and thank you.

I am sincerely thankful to the team at Pluto Press, especially David Castle and Esther Leslie, and truly indebted to Naira Antoun for her advice and work on the manuscript. Part of Chapter Three first appeared in the article 'Feminism, Art, Contradictions', *e-flux journal* 92, June 2018, and I thank the journal for first providing me with the space to think on the depth of contradictions structuring the art field that feminism enters, as well as permission to include portions of the article in the book.

Above all, I am grateful to my wonderful friends for tolerating my absences and for sharpening the feeling called life, to my partner for the same, as well as for the shared learning and deepest possible intellectual comradeship, and to my all-women core — my strong, insightful, and kind feminist mother (1946–2022), my wild and generous daughter, and my sister with whom sisterhood becomes real. I will always be grateful to Maria and Daria (no words really), to my step-dad, my dad and his partner, and to Oskari, Tuula, and Timo for their precious help in the past difficult decade. Migrant, post-nuclear, expanded family bonds, not always organised by kin, give hope. And, dearest Jenny, you are always here, our conversations on art, life, labour, crisis, never over.

As I finish the book in June 2025, the Palestinian struggle continues being met with genocidal terror and tech-capital's weapons. This outrageous historical fact defines our contemporary in its abundance of many other horrors, including violence against women and girls. No more, never again, and all power to the humanity of Palestine, of refugees, of those who rise against the hegemony that is so injurious to life.

Introduction

In the twenty-first century it is apparent that feminism is one of humanity's long-term struggles. In the simplest possible terms, feminism is the struggle against the exploitation, oppression, violence, control, and discrimination that women suffer as social beings. This experience is not uniform; the lives of working-class women as highly exploited people are unlike those of women who benefit from exploitation, even if the latter may still face discrimination. The division of labour is indeed central to how women are persuaded or forced to live: women carry out most of the world's unpaid care labour, tend to be in the lowest paid jobs, and are subject to a gender pay gap globally. Refugee and migrant women — fleeing hardship unimaginable by the non-displaced — experience heightened gender violence, stigma, and isolation. Lesbians have been seen as threats to 'womanhood', as have trans women, depending on historically and contextually legible articulations and interpretations of sex and gender, while being a 'woman' remains tied to appearances, which, for many, is an unbearable burden. Women thus arise as a tentative political subject and a precarious collectivity in historical conditions that are not static but that are certainly divisive. Not all women are feminists — most are not, often because feminism is itself associated with the scorned and devalued realm of the feminine, femaleness, and feminisation, or with the difficulty of obtaining a subject coherent enough for political struggle in a society of acute antagonisms. Carried through generations, the feminist struggle has many dimensions and layers, is strewn with conflicts, and marked by setbacks and blockages. Feminism has not been a unified field — and though it is rare that a political cause enjoys unity, it is politically necessary not to normalise disunity (a desired outcome for the oppressors and exploiters) but to trace its roots in the trajectory of the political cause as part of a social history. This study engages feminism in these terms.

Feminism entered the art field in a notable way after World War II, and especially since the 1960s, when what is recognised as 'contemporary art' also emerged. In this study, 'art' comprises artworks and the socio-economic relations and intellectual paradigms that allow the categorisation of certain objects or actions as artworks. Today, the art field is sustained by a constellation of specialised forms of labour. In it, many workers can barely manage, many of them are women, and only some are feminists. The art field has its very own profit-led market but also comprises artistic, curatorial, theoretical, and peda-gogical efforts to oppose art's entrapment in commodification and all that comes with it. Art has institutions that employ or show the work of some women but leave most out, whatever their gender. This is a structural condition encountered, approvingly or resistively, by all. Benefits are accrued upwards, and what is called 'the public' expe-rience artworks (sometimes as their co-producers) not in a field of open possibilities but of known hierarchies: *ArtReview* publishes Power100, an 'annual ranking of the most influential people in art',[1] where mostly familiar names go up and down year after year. The relativised power of the West in an art world perceived as global for a few decades now has allowed individuals from other regions to be on the list. The list is significant, however, not as content but as form: metrics, contest, performance, levels. This is a form that makes sense to us because we live in a historically specific class society organised around the competition of capitalist markets.

The global art world marked the consolidation of global capi-talism in the late twentieth century. This (art) world is where an artwork that expresses risk (a core capitalist value aiding competi-tion), especially the risk to not count as art (say because it simply presents everyday objects), can sell for over \$6 million, as Malcolm Bull notes, while 44 percent of humanity falls under the poverty line and 24.3 million more women than men live in 'extreme poverty'.[2] Capitalism is a profit-led system of production relations and values, predicated on the enclosure of all that is vital for life and its repro-duction, where millions provide labour in exchange for wages so that they remain alive, along with millions whose unwaged labour is also essential. This is a complex and dynamic system, involving change, characterised by contradictions, but always recognisable in its abysmal socio-economic divides. To keep profits up, capitalism requires unstoppable 'growth' — meaning: extreme levels of competi-tion and environmental devastation — and its logic spills into society, exceeding what is more narrowly defined as the economy. Capitalism is thus the unavoidable terrain of the feminist struggle, and feminism in art is no exception.

This book navigates aspects of the entanglement of feminism, art, and capitalism as a lived reality with a history. When referring to 'historical circumstances', these have a specificity that compels reflection on what forces shape them. To address this specificity, I turn to historical materialism as a method of analysis practiced by Marxist feminism. Through this method — which sees capitalism as a mode of production and reproduction enabled by forces configured at a moment of human history rather than as an expression of 'natural' inequalities among human beings— I attend to issues that feminist art theory and history have sometimes overlooked or ceased to be preoccupied with, despite their disruptive knowledge. What has determined the omission, forgetting, and underplaying of these issues is part of the book's enquiry. Conclusions are not always possible, but posing questions is.

It can be said that the book constitutes an enquiry into the relationship between art and society, and yet this formulation may be misleading in presenting art and society as separate, connected tentatively through a choice in language. For Marxist feminism, social relations and forces do not arise in language, even if the concepts we use are important for what we see and what we don't. Writing about art is also labour, Carol Duncan argued in the 1980s: 'Like the art market itself, art history is always in flux as the dead and dying artefacts of other eras — works whose original meaning has faded — are given new use by the living labour of the critic-scholar'.[3] Historical materialism thus prompts us to look deeper into how our mode of production makes specific forms of living labour possible, as well as certain concepts dominant. What I hope the book offers is an elucidation of critical parameters in the entanglements it addresses and in confronting some of the contradictions and dilemmas faced by feminism. Although the book concerns contemporary art, it often returns to the past, in recognition that modernity, where various iterations of 'the contemporary' have emerged, is where feminism concretised into a political idea.

Modernity, as such, is intertwined with the contradictions of capitalism. How did capitalist modernity persist, delivering the art world of today, despite its contradictions? Across my undergraduate studies in archaeology and my later studies in feminism and art history, I was offered perspectives that paid cursory attention to how societies are reproduced from one day to the next over long periods of time. Answers to this 'how' I found in the writings of Karl Marx (with which I naively thought I was already engaging as a teenager) and the body of theory known as Marxism, riven by rich internal debates. Growing up as a girl in Southern Europe in the 1970s and 1980s, I also encountered feminism. It was in in the streets, and my mother, who did not go to university, brought it home in the form of the popular press after her waged working day. I could see why both Marxism and feminism were necessary simply by existing in the society I did. When I came to the UK as a postgraduate student in the 1990s, however, I realised that Marxism and feminism had a difficult relationship, which impacted the study of art. With few exceptions, a Marxist feminist art history was a spectral potentiality. Griselda Pollock would write: 'The project before us is therefore the development of art historical practices which analyse cultural production in the visual arts and related media by attending to the imperatives of both Marxism and feminism. This requires the mutual transformation of existing Marxist and recent feminist art history'.[4] But the end of the Cold War — the momentous geopolitical event that closed the 1980s — would be unfavourable for such a synthesis: this was when 'capitalism and the market could be declared the final form of human history itself', Fredric Jameson recollected in an essay about that period's obsessive end-ism.[5] Not so visible in feminist art history, the Cold War (and its outcome) is treated in this book as decisive for the shaping of both contemporary art and feminism.

The feminist scholarship available to me as a doctoral student might occasionally deploy Marxist concepts but largely within frameworks such as poststructuralism and phenomenology, which existed in evident tension with historical materialism, to say the least. Psychoanalytic concepts combined with strands of feminism and Marxism, but left many confused about whether the psychic structures described were changeable, despite refuting biological determinism. The issue is not one of methodological purity, of course, but rather what compelled a historically specific eclecticism and what processes this eclecticism could ultimately address. Important to feminist art theory and practice, 'deconstruction' referred to language and systems of thought, but what gave rise to (favoured) systems of thought, and who had access to them? More often than not, the emphasis was on signs and the function of everything, including the body, as text or code. The body at work and the unemployed body were discussed in the 1970s, but then appeared to fall off the grid.

To put it personally yet politically, the feminist readings available to me in the 1990s did not explain why I was fired along with other young women by a London museum that faced 'financial difficulties'; why a wealthy woman gallerist in Athens, where I briefly worked, was feared by women artists who had to sell work to survive; why so many — artists, curators, theorists — were forced to move continuously to secure temporary income; why suddenly everyone craved digital stuff while few asked what digitality required from nature; why 'community art', sustained by many women, was appearing in neighbourhoods described as deprived rather than working-class. Eventually, after I had read all about circulating signs, embodiment, textuality, everyone's 'decentred' subjectivity and what constituted 'privilege', and got an entry-level academic job, reality pressed questions such as: why were so many 'working mothers', me included, on overdraft at the end of the month, what dictated our endless working days, and why was I expected to compete for 'research funding' with feminist colleagues? What made everyone tolerate all this and a lot worse was unclear — yet this continued even after the 2008 global financial crisis revived interest in how the economy formed subjectivity and forced choices. This book addresses this damaging state of things, exacerbated in the 2020s by 'economic uncertainty', the unravelling of capitalist democracy, and the normalisation of inhumanity in accepting hyper-imperialism, genocide, and weapons factories as good for jobs and profits. We are told that no alternative to capitalism exists, while historical materialism is a theory that specifically addresses capitalism's mechanisms that keep us in place. This book observes some of these mechanisms, asking if and how art is implicated, and suggesting that feminism must not lose sight of the deeper layers of capitalist hegemony.

The first two chapters concern processes that exceed the art field. Chapter One examines what makes up capitalism in the first place and why feminism can never realise its emancipatory goals within it. I start by considering the historical relationship between capitalism and feminism. I then look at how some feminists deployed accumulation — a Marxist concept — to think about the condition of women in capitalism, but also the main contradiction that capitalist modernity generated for feminism. Following that, I describe the fundamentals of capitalism, and how it persistently hides the labour that sustains it. I also consider other processes of concealment organised by capital: global space and class confusion. I look briefly at how art tries to work against such concealment, and also at how an art world organised by the logic of capital can determine access to artworks of feminist intent.

Having presented how capitalism broadly works, in Chapter Two I turn to the role of ideology in its social processes. Ideology became an important concept for Marx, and later, in the 1970s and 1980s, for the feminist critique of the history of art. I am primarily concerned, however, with the ideological formation of feminism itself. I look at the 2010s, a decade largely defined by the global financial crisis of 2008, the ramifications of which are still unfolding. I trace the conflict between anticapitalist and neoliberal feminism, yet by thinking about ideas that were important to both. I ask why anticapitalist feminism encountered obstacles despite engaging class formation and providing an expanded view of the working class through social reproduction. To understand these obstacles, I turn to prior fragmentations of feminism under hegemonic ideology — feminism as personal choice, the dissensus structuring identity politics — which appeared at a moment in the history of capitalism when labour movements were defeated and postmodernism enacted the so-called 'cultural turn'. I conclude with some thoughts on Carla Lonzi (1931–82), an Italian art critic who left art for feminism, and ask if and how the radical independence she sought addressed but was also perhaps mediated by ideology.

Having examined capitalism in its broader material and ideological operation in relation to feminism, the remaining chapters focus more on art. Chapter Three is concerned with the contradictions that feminism faces in the capitalist art field, in an effort to show that such contradictions organise a wider terrain of contestations that feminism merely encounters in a specific way. To do this, I first reflect on why both the right and left think of art as important. I then look at curatorial projects from the fraught 2010s — a biennale and a Documenta — to present how 'the global' comes into conflict with 'the local' shaped through the geopolitics and biopolitics of capitalism, and the impasses that arise beyond the good intentions of curators and artists. The chapter engages the question of political judgement in art and its significance for art-based feminism.

Chapters Four and Five argue that modernity continues to be the matrix of our experience. I introduce the concept of the Long Modern to attend to how 'the contemporary' arises in this trajectory. I start by considering the ideological function of the artist in capitalist modernity and the equally ideological constitution of class-mediated femininity as its very antithesis. I then move to the more recent contemporary that gave us the feminist art movement in the 1970s and 1980s. Why did a feminist art movement arise then, and what historical conditions shaped it and its intellectual affiliations? I consider the Cold War, when postmodernism became hegemonic, and also the May 1968 uprising, that happened in France but had much broader relevance. Chapter Four concludes by examining why 'the contemporary' is a privileged temporality for feminism. Chapter Five argues for a feminist theory of the contemporary in art that disaffirms capitalism. I trace connections that I see as central in such an endeavour: between emancipation and limits; identity and economy; representation and performative prefiguration in political aesthetics, with performative prefiguration often attached to socially engaged art and commoning. My main aim here is to highlight how these practices approach but are also approached by capital.

Chapter Six, the last in the volume, addresses the beating heart of capitalist modernity: technology — its ubiquity much more conspicuous than capital's, its impact much greater than feminism's. Technology is encountered as progress but also as magic across the political spectrum. The chapter's anchoring question is how technology, where determinism and open-endedness meet, encounters feminist intent. I observe a difference in how technology functioned for feminism's second wave: whereas some artists used the camera as a tool separate from them, others sought a fusion with technology that implicated performance and performativity. In seeking new grounds for accumulation and value, but also to expel as much labour as possible from the production process, capital has consistently tried to enter the body and give us an entity known as the cyborg. In attending to this imaginary, taking us back to the 1920s, I revisit the work of artists that offer radically different takes on the very question of technology and where it is heading.

More broadly, the book asks: what can we learn from the half century separating the 1970s, the decade of feminism's revolt in art, from the 2020s, when this revolt is taught as a historical subject rather than lived as an ongoing collective commitment? The body of Marxist feminist scholarship that emerged after 2000 and picked up after the 2008 financial crash underpins my exploration of this question — and here the groundbreaking work of Marina Vishmidt (1976–2024) remains unsurpassable in the avenues it opened. In the ten years since this book's inception in 2015, I was motivated to keep this question in sight often by my students, to whom the book is dedicated. Thinking about how emancipatory knowledge comes into being in a society where university education is enclosed as a consumer good, and access to it is an investment, sets up a telling contradiction. The book is written for those who, like me and my students, can feel intimidated by the intricacy and range of social antagonisms and uncertain about how art is connected to them; those who may harbour awkward questions about feminism's trajectory and prospects, but who at the same time see feminism as indispensable to dismantling the hegemony — the consensus — that propagates and deepens the social injustices that capitalism generates and on which it thrives. Everything remains to be thought and done against this consensus.

1

Feminism Against Capitalism

All three words that appear in the title of this book — feminism, art, capitalism — refer to social processes with long, complicated, and intertwined histories. In this first chapter, I mostly focus on two of these words: feminism and capitalism. Feminist art history rarely has as one of its starting places an elucidation of the relationship between feminism and capitalism, which may obscure from view what makes up the crisis-ridden world that feminism addresses today. Both 'feminism' and 'capitalism' end with the infamous '-ism' but each word refers to a different *order of relations* in and about society. Capitalism is a historically specific way in which society produces what it needs; feminism is a historically generated political demand against the inferiorisation of about 50 percent of humanity in its concrete social conditions. 'Feminism' and 'capitalism' have not existed forever.

Some claim a history of feminism over the centuries. This is based on sporadic texts in defence of women's education and potential, such as Christine de Pizan's literary allegory *The Book of the City of Ladies* (c. 1405) or Sor Juana de la Cruz's celebration of 'woman as the seat of reason and knowledge rather than passion' in the seventeenth century.[1] The agitated late eighteenth century saw the publication of Olympe de Gouges's *Declaration of the Rights of Woman and of the Citizen* (1791) and Mary Wollstonecraft's *A Vindication of the Rights of Woman* (1792). As far as we know, however, 'feminism' in connection with women's liberation appears in the nineteenth century, occasionally credited to Charles Fourier, a French philosopher associated with Utopian Socialism.[2] In this century, which gave us feminism's first wave, we find socialist Flora Tristan's *The Workers' Union* (1843), which imagined 'a workers' international' and included a chapter on women's rights and the working-class family, while in 1851, African American Sojourner Truth, who survived slavery as forced labour, would ask publicly at a Women's Rights convention: 'Ain't I a woman?'[3]

Turning to capitalism as a concept, Adam Smith is credited with presenting key aspects of a market economy fashioned by capital in his book of 1776, *An Inquiry into the Nature and Causes of the Wealth of Nations.* The word 'capitalism' — suggesting that capital had generated a system — appeared in the nineteenth century when the industrial revolution consolidated a much longer process (including the preceding period of manufacture). Although the words 'capital' and 'capitalist' were already in use, the first written mention of 'capitalism' is attributed to Louis Blanc, a French socialist historian who used it in the 1850 edition of his book *Organisation of Labour.*[4] At that time, Karl Marx was exploring how capital had generated a historically specific mode of production. He also observed that 'the mode of production of material life conditions the social, political and intellectual life process in general'.[5] This is why Marx's interdisciplinary programme of research is called historical materialism — because he paid attention to the epochal changes that the material basis of society was undergoing at the time and, more broadly, he was able to see that the ideas and institutions marking a specific society were connected to how that society's material basis was organised. Marx sought to undermine the way capitalism can appear natural, without a beginning, without contradictions, without end. Indeed, looking back from the twenty-first century, 'capitalism surfaced just a few hundred years ago (i.e. in the last 0.25 percent of human history)' and so 'if human history took place over the course of a single day, capitalism only unfolded three minutes before midnight'.[6] Agricultural societies thousands of years ago developed property relations and stored surplus food while trade and social classes have existed since ancient times, but in these 'three minutes' of history, the possibility to produce commodities at a mass scale, obtain profit through squeezing as much labour as possible from low-waged bodies, and invest for the (endless) generation of capital have delivered a new way of life.

Both 'capitalism' and 'feminism' became concrete references during the industrial revolution, when specific social relations emerged as a new mode of production was being consolidated. Observing the formation of the new economy (capitalism) invited questions about how specific groups of people (collective subjects) fared in it. Here, we can consider how feminist perspectives that did *not* disregard the organisation of the economy explained women's relationship to capitalism.

ACCUMULATION AND WOMEN IN CAPITALIST MODERNITY

Marx's *Capital Volume I* (1867) connects the existence of capital with accumulation. The section 'The Accumulation of Capital' refers to how capital gets amassed once its systemic relations are established, while 'The So Called Primitive Accumulation' refers to the processes necessary for capitalism to arise. Referencing enslavement, the colonies, and expropriation, Marx summarised primitive accumulation as 'the historical process of divorcing the producer from the means of production'.[7] Some feminists of the second wave, which erupted in the 1960s, found the concept of primitive accumulation intriguing, and started to explore how it connected to women.

Capital's etymological connection with 'head' ('caput' in Latin), 'cattle' (animals as movable property), and 'chattel' (as in 'chattel slavery') already suggests that whatever made capitalism possible involved force and coercion. European expansionism and the 'discovery' of continents enabled the violent appropriation of land, raw materials for factory production, and racially inferiorised human beings to put to work as slaves in plantations. Meanwhile, the enclosure of common land in Europe forced peasants to become waged workers in the factories of the industrial revolution.[8] For feminists, there was more: in her influential study *Caliban and the Witch: Women, the Body and Primitive Accumulation* (2004), Silvia Federici argues that the witch became 'the embodiment of a world of female subjects that capitalism had to destroy [for its emergence]: the heretic, the healer, the disobedient wife, the woman who dared to live alone, the obeah woman who poisoned the master's food and inspired the slaves to revolt'.[9] Although the social relations described as patriarchy (literally meaning 'the rule of the father'/the patriarch/older men) predated capitalism, eliminating such women was important for the regime of obedience that capitalism would install around the division of labour.

This division of labour was organised by the bourgeoisie as the newly powerful class that owned the means of production and was refashioning the world around the flow of commodities. The emergence of a modern 'public sphere' where discussion and debate took place was tied to the bourgeois subject and originally referred to institutions overseeing capitalist trade;[10] capitalism would continue to prize communication and information, to the point of interpreting everything in terms of commodifiable data, as we know 200 years later. Production, labour, commerce, and exchange belonged to the public domain, as did what was considered 'the news'. This does not mean that women, and even children, did not work in factories: 'In contrast to popular conceptions of a male-dominated factory workforce, the Industrial Revolution in England was initially founded on the labor of women and children'.[11] Still, women had to come firmly under men's control in an economy where the generation and replenishment of armies of human beings capable of hard industrial labour was essential. Capitalism would oversee the transformation of the family from a production unit to a consumption unit relying on the wage,[12] and so who would bring in the wage and who would be devoted to producing the worker became pivotal. The violence against the 'world of female subjects' served to push women into the home consigning them — or at least the ideal of womanhood — to reproductive labour. Hence, Federici argues that the 'persecution of the witches… was as important as colonization and the expropriation of the European peasantry from its land were for the development of capitalism'.[13]

Not all feminists accepted Marx's distinction between primitive accumulation and accumulation as capitalism's unstoppable drive to break frontiers. In 1986, Maria Mies, following the communist revolutionary Rosa Luxemburg (1871–1919), saw 'the secret of modern capitalism' in continuous accumulation:

> Violence was the heart of what Marx had called the *primitive accumulation of capital.* But contrary to what Marx had believed, namely that this violence and this primitive accumulation had *preceded* capitalism proper, we saw that it continued up to our own day, with regard to women and to the colonies — now called developing nations — and with regard to nature, the foundation of all life and production. Nature was treated in the same one-sided, exploitative way — as a 'free good' — as women's labour or the colonies were treated. To put it the other way round: women and the colonies were treated as 'nature', they were 'naturalized'.[14]

The disagreement continued, and much has been written on what precisely is or is not accumulation as capitalism changes. What is undisputed is that the drive for accumulation was seen to justify a divide between a higher, dynamic order of activity called civilisation, including the production of culture and belonging to certain men, while a lower order of entities were perceived as passive and relegated to the realm of freely available nature. For Nancy Fraser, accumulation required brutal expropriation as 'the back-story' of capitalism that enabled its 'front-story' of exploitation.[15] The now ubiquitous and positively inflected term 'civilisation' made sense within capitalism: in the eighteenth century, the term was used to set up a system of international relations whereby 'civilised' nations could rule over 'uncivilised' or 'less developed' nations.[16]

This civilisation is known as capitalist modernity, and also gave us modern 'art' — expected to address and involve the sense or actuality of 'being of the times'. Although the world market appeared around 1500, it was in the nineteenth century, when capitalism had developed further, that 'the experience of modernity' matured and became 'translated into the various classical visions of modern*ism*'.[17] 'Modernity' connects to the Latin 'modus': way of doing/manner/ measure — the generation of a new 'now'. Change defined the nineteenth century, it was the century of inventions and also saw the emergence of several new concepts and '-isms', as we have seen already. Much of what shapes capitalist life today found form in the nineteenth century: the centrality of technology for production and population control (and it is then that we get both photography and film); the formation of nation-states and the consolidation of international law premised upon European racism and the characterisation of certain states that did not embrace capitalism as 'imbecile';[18] a modern imperialism that was the highest form of capitalism, as World War I (1914–18) would make clear at least to Lenin;[19] the *ideal* (not reality for many) of the home as a calm private sphere cared for by women versus a tense public life organised by and for men ('public woman' indicated saleability, not being a public figure); and, despite a prevalent attachment to occultism in that century, political ideas that prioritised human reason and self-determination over belief in an extra-human authority and sought to expand on or question the limits and blind spots of the Enlightenment in the seventeenth and eighteenth centuries.[20] Feminism was such an idea.

Yet a contradiction at the heart of capitalist modernity undermined political ideas like feminism. Karl Marx and Friedrich Engels indicated this conflict in *The Communist Manifesto* (also a nineteenth-century text, published in 1848) which asked of workers to throw off their chains and rise against their exploiters.[21] This radical possibility arose because in modernity, as Marx and Engels famously wrote, 'all that is solid melts into air' — this was, and is, the experience of modernity as such: development. On the one hand, *economic* development as understood by capitalism required ceaseless accumulation, and therefore an unprecedented scale of extraction and exploitation, achieved through processes of inferiorisation. On the other hand, development registered as the potential for *self-development*, which was not lost on those rendered inferior. The prospect of human equality arose — the meaning of equality is still debated of course — and the inferiorised would decry their dehumanisation. References in the twentieth and twenty-first centuries to human flourishing and human rights express and renew this will, with many still demanding to be treated as humans, while capital's catastrophic treatment of what came to be known as the environment would lead to multiple explorations of how humans, in their historical circumstances acting on and in the world through labour, connected to nature. This, then, is the contradiction that capitalist modernity entailed: it generated the idea, desire, and hope of equality but, on the material level, it required that most people remain subordinate, exploited, and oppressed.

One expression of this contradiction (self-development versus the reproduction of capitalist society) is that the exodus of some women from the home has meant their replacement with other women. In 2022, we were informed that 'demand for domestic services is growing worldwide due to the increases in women working outside the home, the aging of populations and the increasing need for long term care and the loss of extended family support' while, according to the International Labour Organization (ILO), 'of 5.6 million domestic workers aged 15 years and above globally 76 per cent are women'.[22] The gender division of labour appears to be structural in capitalism, and the conflict it produces in women's lives was one of second-wave feminism's central concerns.

This conflict found expression in the work of some women artists such as Mierle Laderman Ukeles in the US who, in the 1960s, felt trapped in the material conditions of the private family as a mother while she regarded herself as an artist making artworks and bringing them into the public sphere: 'I literally was divided in two... Half of my week I was the mother, and the other half the artist. But, I thought to myself, "this is ridiculous, I am the one".[23] This binary — mother/carer *or* artist — is one that is imposed by capitalism and its organisation of society's reproduction. The artist stated succinctly, and with exemplary clarity, how this binary became manifest in art as shaped by capitalist modernity in her now renowned *Manifesto for Maintenance Art 1969!*: on the one hand, you had 'development', the new, 'dynamic change', which would lead to death if no one was doing the necessary work that kept people alive; against it, you had 'maintenance' associated with 'perpetuation', repetition (rather than newness), stasis, but also essential for the continuation of life and even for preserving the new. The male-dominated historical avant-gardes of the late nineteenth and the first half of the twentieth century had invested in change and development. She, in turn, decided to change what art was about. Turning maintenance into art, as she proposed and practised in her 1970s performances, was meant to dissolve the conflict. In a sense, it did: Ukeles became a successful artist, which meant that she was able to exist in the public sphere as an artist. But one woman artist's liberation and success could not be translated into the liberation and possibility of success of all women artists, let alone of all women, in the capitalist context. The old conflict between the *idea* of equality and the *material* conditions generated by capitalism remains unresolved for most women.

If anything, this conflict has become more pronounced. Whereas modernity in the nineteenth century and until World War II entailed as a possible resolution the revolutionary overthrow of capitalism and the move to socialism as a socio-economic system that would eventually dismantle class, this prospect of total, transformative social change waned in the second half of the twentieth century. In the arts, the historical process of withdrawal from the revolutionary prospect was remembered after the Great Recession of 2008 (capitalism's most severe crisis since the crash of 1929). Curator Jorge Ribalta described it in an exhibition catalogue in 2015 as follows:

> The living conditions of the working class in the West during the 1970s were light years away from the conditions before the war. Eric Hobsbawm refers to the postwar period — principally the 1950s and 1960s — as the 'golden age' of capitalism, a time of unprecedented improvements in the living conditions of the

working classes. This improvement was based on a kind of pact between labor forces and capital, leading to the emergence of the 'welfare state'. *Capital renounced part of its profits in favour of workers. In exchange, workers renounced the revolution.* But this process reached a turning point in the 1970s. The financial crisis of 1972–1973 sparked a downturn that led to the start of the neoliberal era at the end of the decade.[24]

The 1970s proved to be a decisive decade for society, as much as for art, and while the decline of the revolutionary worker is not questioned, its causes continue to be debated and contextualised: was it that leftist political parties failed to represent the workers or that the role of the working class itself diminished as capitalism evolved?[25] Whatever the case, rather than considering revolution, workers, including many women in the 1970s, accepted being valued and valorised as 'human resources' (another late-nineteenth-century idea).[26] The workers that human resources departments manage perhaps feel lucky to have a job and accept pay according to the whims of the labour market, rarely asking: what is the actual value of our labour?

WORK, FREEDOM, CAPITAL

Capitalism does not rely on serfdom, requiring instead that human beings see themselves as free. As Marx described, presumably free persons enter the market where they sell their human capacity to work (labour-power) to other free persons who buy this capacity to make commodities. Those who sell labour-power are workers while those who can buy large quantities of it are capitalists *if* they manage to obtain from it value that exceeds what they paid for it. The capitalist invests money to buy raw materials, technology, and labour-power: these three things are already bought as commodities on the market, but only one of these commodities is 'special' — labour-power — because to extract raw materials and make technology already requires the realisation of human labour. Therefore, labour-power is the origin of all value. But how does the capitalist think about such value?

For Marx, workers are paid wages that suffice to keep them alive and able to work again the next day but that do not correspond to what the workers actually produce in the hours worked. The difference between the work done to cover the workers' own needs and the extra work the capitalist squeezes from the workers to generate more capital than that invested in them is called surplus value. As sociologist Alf Gunvald Nilsen puts it:

> This is the central hinge of Marx's argument: under capitalism surplus value accrues to the capitalist, and is thereby foundational to what exploitation is and how it works. And, crucially, inequality deepens whenever the difference between wages and the amount of value that workers produce increases. As such, deepening inequality is hardwired into the dynamics of capitalist accumulation.[27]

Capitalism is meant to be a transparent system. Marx showed that it is not. Positing both the worker and the capitalist as free generates a seductive symmetry, which cloaks the fact that their relationship is *not* one of equals. In jobs that appear to have greater autonomy and are felt as 'personal projects', additional exploitation habitually occurs: an artist is hired as university lecturer; she is contracted for 35 hours per week, but the work to be done typically takes 50 hours per week. The artist knows because she hires child care for 50 hours weekly to meet deadlines — not just marking assignments but also making her 'own' art for which she was hired in the first place. Meanwhile, she sees that the university makes enough profit to invest in real estate and new technologies, which are considered 'growth'. If she complains, she is told to improve her 'time management skills' or seek other employment that better 'suits her needs'. She is free to accept her over-exploitation or go.

For this economy to meet little to no resistance, the idea of freedom must become diffused in society. We hear about freedom all the time. The birth of the free worker also signalled the birth of the artist as free and autonomous. Capitalist societies are described as 'free societies'. In the 1960s, 'unfree production relations' in 'Third World nations' were seen as a key obstacle to their development.[28] Since the late twentieth century and in the context of neoliberalism, which refers to the deregulation (greater freedom) of capitalist markets, 'free choice' has been used to make palatable the increasing precarity of jobs (which are no longer meant to be for life) and to undermine workers' collective bargaining.[29] The contemporary 'gig economy' where workers (say, delivery couriers) are positioned as freelancers who possess the means of labour (say, bikes) and are called 'on demand' to be connected to customers via digital platforms is an extension of the free worker logic. This further freedom of the worker saves the capitalist traditional production costs — insurance, pensions, even tax. The 'gig economy', a term coined as the global financial crisis of 2008 was generating great unemployment, is where workers are persuaded that they are not workers at all, but rather self-employed freelancers enjoying freedom because they are in control of their hours — much like running their own business. The contemporary art field has been described as a gig economy — even as providing its prototype. A cursory look at how most artists fare in this economy suggests that the idea of the free worker hides a reality of exploitation:

> Artists have been working in the gig economy since long before there was a gig economy, but the casualisation of the arts, which transfers risk from the employer to the (self)employee has been on the increase. The entire cultural economy depends on self-employment; it is not the Arts Council that subsidises the arts, it is the artists.[30]

Thus, unlike preceding modes of production — such as feudalism, where the class structure was obvious as brutal hierarchy — capitalism hides its classed reality using the idea of freedom.

The capitalist is free to hire as few workers as possible so as to drive down the cost of production, which is why technological innovation has been important: technology absorbs skills, making part of the workforce redundant. Unemployment is essential to capitalism because it generates a 'reserve army of labour' or 'disposable workers',[31] keeping people competing for jobs and driving wages down, especially if unionisation and thus collective bargaining declines. In the 1970s, feminists wondered whether women 'are particularly useful to capital as a reserve army of labour',[32] to be called on when more labour is needed and then easily dropped, pushed back to their 'natural' sphere of the home should labour demand ease. Despite the fact that artists, unlike industrial workers, do not produce *directly* for a capitalist, the unemployment principle organises the art field too: theorists, curators, artists, students compete incessantly for teaching and research opportunities, residencies, commissions, and internships.[33] The prized autonomy of the artist, which becomes a feature of all 'creative' labour even beyond the art world, is a barrier to the standardisation that collective bargaining implies. In 2022, an *ArtReview* article suggested that unionising was a recent discovery in the arts: 'From the Whitney Museum to Tate Modern, workers at art and cultural institutions are discovering that unions aren't just for hard-hats'.[34] What we glean, however, from all this is that the art field displays structural features of capitalist society: individuals who perceive themselves as free, competition, reserve army of labour, attempts to unionise. What makes the art field special, perhaps, is confusion about what should be considered work, labour, employment. Greg Sholette observed in 2010 that a vast 'dark matter' of invisible human effort and hopeful participation (sometimes labour waiting to be realised) is integral to how the art field is sustained.[35] That year also, Hito Steyerl argued that 'this mess', contemporary art, 'is kept afloat by the sheer dynamism of loads and loads of hard-working women'.[36] The 1970s feminist project of enabling women *as a group* to realise their potential and be creative subjects in art did not ultimately overcome capital's operative logic: using the idea of freedom to harness the human capacity to work, much of which is freely given. Capital's worldmaking requires what has been called 'labour of love', unexpectedly connecting the raising of children to being in the art field.

The 'grow or die' imperative of capital means that the capitalist must acquire more and more companies, leading to monopoly or oligopoly — that is, a few mega-businesses eat up smaller businesses: bookstore and coffee chains replace independent bookstores and cafés. This tendency generates a logo-based homogenisation of everyday space, but its most important effect is extreme wealth concentration. In 2023, the richest 1 percent had 'nearly as much wealth as the rest of the world put together over the past two years'; in 2024, capitalism was preparing for its first trillionaires while the 'wealth of [the] five richest men' doubled 'since 2020, as five billion [were] made poorer in [a] decade of division'.[37] Concentrated wealth means concentrated political power, overt or covert. The burgeoning of finance at the turn of the century has coincided with the experience of a failing, eroded democracy. Finance is capital in circulation. Its money-based operations include hunting for new investment markets, mass debt as profit opportunity, and speculation as the investors' ultimate freedom.[38] The expansion of finance since the 'neoliberal decade' of the 1980s, often referred to as 'financialised capitalism', meant societal needs would further fade before the obsession with the circulation of capital. In 2018, Marina Vishmidt provided an elaborate account of how art both 'mediates and is mediated by the forces of speculative capital',[39] showing the art field's material and ideological dependence on capitalism's historical trajectory.

Contemporary accumulation combines production with finance, the operations of which appear more shrouded in mystery for the lay person than even how mobile phones are made. A system of desirable personality attributes is set in motion to perpetuate acceptance of the status quo, ensuring that exploitation is hidden behind notions of meritocracy: as everyone is free and in charge of her/his/their fate in capitalism, the wealthy are simply smarter, riskier, or more hardworking than those who remain in need because they are not good enough for such freedom of opportunity. Moreover, the argument goes, individuals and corporations with huge 'net worth' give back to society through philanthropy (literally meaning being a friend of humans). Connected to lower taxes (material harm) *and* presenting the exploiters as benefactors (ideological harm), philanthropy is widespread in the capitalist art field. Arts philanthropy generates social consent for the capitalist class while it also shapes trends by endorsing specific art practices.[40] Where the state and philanthropists co-fund basic social goods (housing, hospitals, museums, and more), this legitimises as much as it conceals of how capital profits *in the first instance*: by not paying for all the work it requires. Concealment is essential for capitalism, and what follows are merely two of several possible examples.

CASES OF CONCEALMENT:
GLOBAL SPACE, CLASS CONFUSION

Global Space

While we may live in environments of conspicuous consumption, accumulation is not always visible. This applies also to the art economy, which is where property (artworks) is subject to specific procedures of mystification. The art economy's use of freeports as storage facilities is a case in point — the point being that freeports are not merely spaces of storage but spaces of circulation patterned on finance. Freeports have a long history, but they have proliferated since the 1990s, when neoliberalism forged a kind of space known as 'global space'. This new conception of actually existing space on the globe helps capital hide not only assets, but also labour, in special 'autonomous' zones.[41] In 2020, John Zarobell offered a dizzying analysis of art freeports which 'represent a convergence of state interests and neoliberal market processes since they generate *exceptions* to state regulation that benefit the wealthy and allow them to deposit their investments in secrecy jurisdictions'. Numerous agents are involved in making this possible — the artist being the least interesting, as opposed to accountants, lawyers, and collectors. The conclusion that matters is that freeports 'demonstrate how even the most recondite and valuable things can be converted into capital and harnessed for their potential to generate more value through the novel instruments of financialization'.[42]

Stefan Heidenreich discusses the example of the Geneva Freeport that can 'hold up to one million artworks'. The mention of freeports is uncommon in feminist art history and yet, as Heidenreich observes:

> never before now have so many artworks been produced to remain hidden, all enclosed in disenchanted wooden boxes, suspended in a permanent circuit of exchange, in a place called a 'freeport' because it is free of customs duties and taxes of all kinds. Since no one is allowed to see the art, it is also free of audience and spectators, an anti-*theatron*; it is a place of un-seeing.[43]

Organised by the capitalist art market, this un-seeing is incompatible with the desire for visibility that was long a central concern for feminist art history in relation to women's work. We will return to the question of visibility later; for now, we note that art is not exempted from the general tendency of mystification and secrecy. This operation is both material and ideological. Freeports in relation to art indicate that, above all, art is an asset, immersed in practices of financialisation and understood through the vocabulary of finance capital — rather than, say, the methodological tools of feminist art theory and history: feminists cannot even know if and how many women artists' works are kept in the invisibility of freeports. Heidenreich suggests that storing art in freeports has become an investment that entails 'risk' whereby artworks function as 'derivatives' — that is, these works, made by artistic labour, promise a future realisation of value (thus profit) for the collector which is decided through 'benchmarking with other collectors'. This requires complex and exclusionary expertise quite different from the traditional connoisseurship that feminist art theory critiqued in the 1970s and 1980s as being biased against women artists.

What kind of institutional art space (and not just infrastructure) do freeports normalise? The Geneva Freeport is highly securitised: 'Artworks… are stored in hygrometry and temperature-controlled rooms conceived as impenetrable safes. They are locked behind nameless, armored doors built to hold out against explosives and equipped with biometric readers granting access to the lucky few—a James Bond-style place!'[44] A BBC arts editor who visited the Geneva Freeport in 2016 wrote: 'I found the visit a rather sad and bleak experience. If there are really a million artworks in there, all of which were created to [be] seen and enjoyed, it seems a travesty to the point of immorality'.[45] For feminists, the issue cannot be immorality. Rather, the opacity of capital's operations enabled by the freeport is a *political* issue, for if women and feminist artists are successful in the art market, the more likely it is that at least part of their work — converted to an asset — remains hidden and is thus prevented from contributing to anything akin to consciousness raising, critical agency, aesthetic rupture (to name just a few aspects of art's political communication). Freeports turn any art into a tool for exchange. Complaining that art is kept away from politically minded viewers can sound like a joke given that the freeport situates art in the labyrinth of offshore investment as tax avoidance for the wealthy.

Steyerl compares this hiding operation to how global space also serves to hide human beings designated as refugees.[46] They, and more broadly 'undocumented' migrants, are kept away from the spaces of visible citizen life in special 'hotspots'. Globalisation, which entered the art vocabulary in the 1990s, after the end of the decades-long Cold War between the USA and the USSR, has been marked by two seemingly antithetical and yet complementary spatial geometries: open and closed borders. The demand for open borders for the circulation of merchandise, or just capital, has co-existed with the demand for closed borders that seeks to regulate the flow of labour-power (often other reasons for such regulation are presented by capitalist governments). In 2025, the US government's experimental adoption of import tariffs in its trade war with China, referred to as 'Liberation Day' by President Donald Trump, was seen as an affront to 'normal' capitalist globalisation while the hounding of 'illegal' immigrants on US soil and building new detention centres was merely an intensification of established capitalist governmental practice — still, the closed and open borders' interplay, variable, competition-driven, and treading a precarious balance, continues to define global space's zones of invisibility.

When it comes to labour-power, capital must ensure it gets it as cheap as possible. The term 'post-industrial societies' partly describes societies that have experienced the flight of industries for geographies where labour-power is cheap (and, typically, those who sell it have fewer rights and more expendable lives). These tend to be the societies of the Global South or the so-called Third World, usually invisible to the core consumer nations of the imperialist Global North unless visited through the tourism industry, contributing to the destruction of local ecosystems. (Many variants of tourism exist, including art tourism and sex tourism: 'neo-colonial relations that are the hallmark of capitalist globalisation have systematically organised "sex tourism" for predominantly cis-men').[47] The people of the Global South can also appear to the Global North as 'flows' of migrants and refugees. The twenty-first century is defined by such movements of the dispossessed, and the response of wealthy nations has been to set up an intense and murderous border regime, complete with border walls and camps where people are held in conditions that the rest of society rarely witnesses first-hand. In 2022, Britain's plan to 'stop the boats' (as per the Tory party slogan) by sending asylum seekers to Rwanda, thus making them invisible to the public, was an expression of this logic of concealing the neocolonial relations that mark the articulation of global space.[48]

All this may seem odd given the presumed attachment of capitalism to free labour movement and dynamic change. But it is not. Rather, the concealment of the capitalist system's brutality in its efforts to regulate and manage exploitation is central to its reproduction. This came up in a series of letters between Nadya Tolokonnikova, a member of the Russian feminist punk and performance art group Pussy Riot and philosopher Slavoj Žižek in 2013. In one letter, Žižek says: 'It's no longer disciplinary institutional power that defines everything, it's capitalism's power to produce variety — because markets get saturated. Produce variety and you produce a niche market.'[49] Tolokonnikova, incarcerated in a women's labour camp in Russia at the time, disagreed, seeing brutal disciplinary institutional power as essential behind the façade of a 'free' society where new identities are shaped by market breakthroughs. She replied: 'Modern capitalism has a deep interest in seeing that you and I believe the system runs completely on principles of free creativity, limitless growth and diversity, and that the flip side — millions of people enslaved by all-powerful and... fantastically stable standards of production — remains invisible'.[50] Both are right. The clash between a perception of capitalism that engenders change as it seeks out new markets and cheaper production and a view that focuses on how capitalism uses global space to conceal its actual relations of production is ongoing.

Many of the things we consume are produced across multiple locations. Supply chains of dizzying perplexity form a map of the global economy that is near-impossible to figure out, making capitalism a real and yet elusive and unrepresentable totality. Rendering invisible the violence of this totality — against art and human beings — helps perpetuate the politically vital illusion that contemporary capitalism is a dynamic field of liberated creativity where fluid processes have replaced rigid structures. This makes it indeed hard, as Žižek notes, for many to understand what it is that we are protesting against and fighting for. Feminism is not exempt from the implications of this observation.

Class Confusion

Capitalism requires consumers: masses of people who buy its intangible and tangible commodities — that become an endless flow of sometimes toxic garbage through planned obsolescence. Only a few luxury markets, such as that of artworks, rely on non-mass sales (though in the case of artworks, we have different kinds of consumption, as we will see in later chapters). Here, I want to argue that consumerism has something to do with the concealment of the class relation: the basic antagonism between capital and labour. To whom would capitalists sell their commodities if *all* workers made just enough to literally keep themselves alive and continue working? Indeed, segments of the working class had to be allowed spending power, which appears as *privilege* — this was the essence of the American Dream that emerged during the economic boom after

World War II. Consolidating capitalism's transformation of the family from a unit of production to a unit of consumption was central to the American Dream. The capture of the family clinched consumerism as it made needs and desires increasingly impossible to tell apart — the needs associated with social reproduction blended with the desire to offer 'the best that money can buy' to loved dependents. Consumerism made capitalism *desirable* as such.

Besides giving some workers a degree of spending power, turning everyone into a waged worker would have been a source of instability for capitalism, as it must always press wages downwards. Despite capitalism's tendency to generate monopoly, small businesses had to be maintained, promising something different to their owners than a waged life. These small-business owners are part of the 'small' or petite bourgeoisie, always afraid of becoming proletarianised and dreaming that capitalism will afford them the opportunity to become more powerful exploiters (run a bigger business with more waged workers). Others are rentiers — investing, for example, in buying to rent flats or shops from which they get income — or better-off 'professionals'. These social strata live with the hope of upward mobility and are associated with a 'middle class', largely understood as an identity: one premised on manners, education, prospects, and consumer power. Yet whether the middle class actually exists as a class or whether this concept is deployed to cover the fundamental antagonism between capital and labour is harder to assert.

Hiding the antagonism between capital and labour has been a major victory for capital since the second half of the twentieth century, which is also when 'contemporary art' and 'second-wave feminism' both emerged. A salient development of contemporary capitalism is the concealment of the truth that you cannot have a capitalist class without a working class to exploit. That the working class is seen as elusive, and possibly as non-existent, offers a measure of the dominance of capital — especially given that political parties that supposedly exist for the benefit of workers also espouse this idea.[51] Socialists have struggled to understand why the working classes have lost sight of their own existence. In 2024, Bhaskar Shunkara summarised the relevant economic history, along with the left parties' responses that led to 'class dealignment', meaning the workers' abandonment of even reformist socialist parties. This happened because social democracy eventually responded to the *contradictions of capitalism* by choosing the interests of capital over those of workers. Given the asymmetric dependence of labor on capital, this response was rational in an economic sense. But one of its political consequences was the mass departure of workers from parties of the Left.[52]

Correct as this may be, it also means that workers themselves lost sight of the 'contradictions of capitalism'.

For Vivek Chibber, although belonging to a class has to do with one's *position* in production, class structure does not necessarily lead to the consciousness of class belonging and thus of having class interests to be pursued not individually, but collectively. The fact, then, that 'class structure' exists does not mean that 'class formation' will follow. Chibber argues that the extreme atomisation of life under capitalism in the second half of the twentieth century and the risks faced by those who enter collective struggle dissuade workers from acting as a class.[53] Yet this does not explain why other collective struggles have taken place in the very same period. This argument merely highlights that these other collective struggles, second-wave feminism included, unfolded in a historical moment when thinking deeply about class was discouraged or sidelined.

Class continues being sidelined — or not thought about deeply — even in cases where left activism addresses the economy. We hear, for instance, that as capitalism continues to invent technology to cut production costs, more and more people will be left jobless, and the introduction of Universal Basic Income (UBI) has been proposed as a solution. It is a popular idea in leftist art circles, with *Art for UBI (Manifesto)* published in 2022.[54] UBI for all art workers — effectively, state wages for art — might help alleviate the field's endemic precarity. Yet research indicates that the comfortable family (class) background of some artists mitigates against precarity,[55] which would make UBI for artists an unattractive proposal for taxpayers who are losing their national health systems. Equally important is that through UBI, 'the blue-chip gallery would have the state's collaboration in the branding of its roster as even more elevated from the grey mass of "Universal Basic Income Artists", whose work is deemed worthy of only the minimum wage'.[56]

Art-centred proposals for UBI have been shaped in a context where UBI is seen as a possible survival mechanism for populations *within* capitalism, the dismantling of which is not necessarily demanded. As capitalism is interwoven with imperialism and the Global South/ Global North divide, the class relation not only structures life within a nation-state but also the relationships of entire regions and continents. As value is transferred from the Global South to the Global North, 'the material benefits of living in an imperialist country accrue to all but the poorest and most oppressed sections of global North society'.[57] It is hard to see how implementing UBI in the countries of the capitalist core would not rely on this value transfer, not to mention that refugees and migrants are already seen as threats to state resources. Inequality (as both the foundation and outcome of capitalism) and the class relation would persist despite implementation of UBI.[58] UBI for artists could be supported by taxing millionaires and large businesses, but the capitalist state fears that doing so would lead to capital flight — it is the argument that even left-leaning capitalist governments typically make. In the example of UBI, we start observing a problem that finds many incarnations in our social reality: not studying the workings of class in its historical specificity can render social justice proposals vulnerable.

How capitalism prevents workers from acquiring consciousness of their collective social being remains, then, an open question while the class divide stands:

> anyone who holds economic control over the workplaces, has political power, dictates the terms of other's working conditions, or owns capital that can be invested in production, is part of the capitalist class. And anyone who must sell their ability to work for a wage and has no access to the ability to produce their own life's necessities for themselves is part of the working class.[59]

Obfuscating this fundamental divide — and generating confusion as to what class is — underpins consent for capitalism's reproduction, premised on the belief that capitalism's ills can be rectified. But actually existing capitalism is not a matter of 'ills'. Capitalism does not merely generate inequality as a by-product of capital's activities at the level of distribution. Rather, capitalism requires, presupposes, and ensures inequality in order to function. Because inequality is the ground rather than the mere outcome of capitalism, equality is contextual and lived as inequality by others in some part of the economy's cycle. A feminism that posits equality as its goal without rejecting capitalism must then clarify if what is meant by this is essentially gender equality within one class.

CAPITALISM AS FEMINISM'S PROBLEM

As we have now drawn a schematic picture of capitalism and how it generally functions, we can return to the specificity of women's condition within it. As recently as 2022, the International Labour Organization (ILO) stated that 'around the world, finding a job is much tougher for women than it is for men. When women are employed, they tend to work in low-quality jobs in vulnerable conditions, and there is little improvement forecast in the near future.'[60] A question for Marxist feminism has been how *not* to exclude from the exploited working class the masses of women who are not employed for wages but do not belong to the capitalist class either. The inequality on which capitalism relies does not merely exist in the space–time of waged labour, even as we know that the gender pay gap (women paid less than men and/or forced into part-time work or low-paid jobs) exists across the board.[61] And importantly, only *some* waged labour creates value for capital directly: a waged worker who makes mobile phones to be sold as commodities creates such value; a waged worker employed as a nanny in the factory owner's home does not. What is certain, however, is that to ensure the viability of its production arrangements, capitalism must appropriate the work that replenishes the waged workforce: the variety of care activities to *reproduce* the worker and the bringing up of children to become future workers, consumers, and soldiers (capitalism needs armies). Most of this is done by women: according to ActionAid, in 2024, women performed 75 percent of unpaid domestic/care work globally.[62]

There has been much debate on whether domestic care activities are work or labour, 'productive', 'unproductive' or 'non-productive', 'oppressive but not alienating', and how they are connected to the obtainment of surplus value.[63] Marxist and socialist feminists have argued that such work should be conceptualised as social reproductive labour. In doing so, they consider the questions: What is considered *direct* service to capital? And, how far back in the cycle should we go to distinguish between production and reproduction? As Tithi Bhattacharya puts it: 'Let us slightly modify the question "who teaches the teacher?" and ask this of Marxism: If workers' labor produces all the wealth in society, who then produces the worker?'[64] The question does not imply that women's unpaid work at home generates surplus value, but rather that capitalism is a *totality* sustained by various forms of interdependent labour. Capital as a social relation exceeds the direct production of value.

In the 1960s and 1970s, feminists who grasped the role of capitalism in shaping women's lives vehemently critiqued the idea that there was anything natural in so-called 'women's work'. This included the Wages for Housework Movement which highlighted the key processes through which women became disadvantaged. This movement was comprehensively reviewed by Louise Toupin after years of research, in the context of a general reappraisal of social reproduction as a key concept for contemporary feminist research and activism.[65] Since the early 2000s, there has been discussion of capitalism facing a 'social reproduction crisis', with some believing that technology can help alleviate it.[66] It is this crisis — note: a crisis of capitalism — that has prompted some feminists to focus both on capitalism and the concept of, and struggles around, social reproduction: the activities that keep people alive and thus society functioning on a basic level day after day. Yet such knowledge is not new. It predates even 1970s feminism: communist revolutionaries had persistently located the oppression of women in their exploitation in property and the family (Friedrich Engels published *The Origin of the Family, Private Property, and the State* in 1884) or, like Rosa Luxemburg, sought positions different to that of bourgeois interpretations of feminism.[67] Such insights came to be buried as revolutionary prospects were defeated.

Social reproductive activities can entail a degree of instability in terms of their socio-economic location and meaning. An image of a mother baking at home connotes family time, but this is relative. If she holds a waged job, baking for her child takes place in her leisure time; if the same mother bakes for a boss in a supermarket or does this as part of her small business, this is her paid work, her non-leisure time. Depicting the home as a site of non-work and repose is extremely important for capitalism: as long as this safe space exists, life under capitalism can be presented as 'normal', averting large-scale social unrest. That is, the middle-class fantasy of home life as time away from work is essential to the dominant ideas about what makes contemporary life tolerable. And yet, there is a sharp contrast between the persistent designation of the home as the safe place of positively inflected intimacy and the global data on femicides that show the home is a site of acute violence against women. In a stream of United Nations annual reports, the home is affirmed as the most dangerous place for women while 'violence against women and girls is the most pervasive human rights violation'.[68] Women victimised by domestic abuse may also die by suicide, and so the real count of domestic terror victims rises. Violence against women is right at the heart of the site associated with the organisation of social reproduction in capitalism.

There is, however, a broader question around gendering and the home. In heterosexual households, the few men who stay at home as carers may also face isolation, exclusion, and even depression stemming from not fulfilling gender role expectations (the expectation to be wage earners).[69] In the 1950s and 1960s, suburban American housewives did not turn to medication, as per the Rolling Stones' track 'Mama's Little Helper', because of having abstractly busy days (their husbands had busy days outside the home). Rather, the busy days of the private sphere are emptied of social worth. In the 1970s and 1980s, the will to achieve visibility for women artists contrasted with the invisibility of women as homemakers. Was this the reality of all women? No. For example, in core capitalist countries built on slavery, the working classes were (and are) significantly racialised, and being *just* oppressed homemakers was not the reality for all women. In these same societies, the abolition of slavery came with compensation for the class that lost its property of human slaves[70] — compensation essential to maintaining their class position and having servants dedicated to the labour of social reproduction. Today, studies of the Global South reveal how domestic gender violence produces defeated 'docile' women, essential to obtaining the 'ideal worker' in industrial production.[71] In the twenty-first century, the private family continues to function as the paradigmatic reservoir of invisible, 'worthless' work that is gendered. Gender is not just a matter of bodies or psyches *but also resides in social sites:* in 2020, even a shared belief in equality among heterosexual couples would 'not be sufficient to counter potential obstacles to equal sharing [of domestic chores] in the UK'.[72]

Gendering through various enactments of soft and hard violence is thus a key parameter of contemporary capitalism, not a relic of some past patriarchy. This gendering of the division of labour is best achieved when it is made *desirable*. Older women who have experienced stricter gender roles in the family caution younger women who may be contemplating an exodus from the public sphere of labour.[73] Underpinned by disillusionment with waged labour environments where most women are asked to throw away their lives and energies in conditions characterised by unequal pay and often sexual harassment, a 'new domesticity' became a fashionable *choice* at least since 2000. The trend carried on, re-affirming traditional gender roles, and in 2025 'working mothers continue to leave' the American workforce, impacting sectors central to social reproduction (health, education, and childcare) where women workers concentrate.[74] This tendency predates and exceeds the extremely conservative tradwives (traditional wives) movement, sweeping social media since 2022 and glamorising women's retreat to private service in the family.[75]

Artist Ursula Biemann commented on women willingly presenting themselves as obedient, traditional wives-to-be in her video essay *Writing Desire* (2000), which attended to the internet-based brides market in global capitalism. In the context of global competition among women for access to marriage security (economic security through a male 'provider'), traditional femininity is principally a promise of offering something akin to women's 'special' labour-power in the home. More broadly, the retreat to the home is fashioned as personal choice, appealing to conservative women committed to traditional family values *and* left environmentalists keen to grow organic vegetables for the family unit. And so, the private (family)/public (labour) divide established in the nineteenth century continues, despite notable changes in capitalism since. These changes include the way that the home can now be the workplace of the plugged-in, digital, casualised, often freelance worker, as artists and other 'creatives' know all too well, while at the other end of this, Global South industrial workers may be forced to use the factory as their sleeping place and women leave their children to other family members to work abroad and send back money. If ever an objective ('to demand wages for housework does not mean to say that if we [women] are paid we will continue to do it', Federici declared militantly in the mid-1970s),[76] wages for housework have not materialised; instead, social welfare as benefits to those families that capital constructs as 'needy' fuel constant debate. An outcome of this is that far-right political parties, indicative of the overall growth of the fascist tendency, argue that they alone can support families against mainstream capitalist governments which don't care — and so these parties present as 'anti-systemic' when they are anything but.

The gendering process that underwrites capitalism is thus quite complex: human beings, material sites, *and* abstract attributes and values are gendered in the economy of capital. The sphere of care is considered static, passive, and feminine whereas 'male' qualities are associated with the core values of capitalism. We see this in finance and markets as new frontiers to be conquered, where money-making is seen as creative and 'hunting' for profit is valued. In 2011, Vishmidt pointed to how finance hides even the question of how value is generated:

> The old idea of 'the worker as *the* producer of wealth' would be the classic figure of the programmatist workers' movement... In a number of historically and locally differentiated ways, this idea, and its associated political trajectories, runs from the mainstream of the social democratic or Labour left in the 20th century all the way to the discourse of the 'commons' today, and it inheres, albeit problematically, also in the 'negation' and 'refusal of work' tendencies.... Whether it's as producers, or as 'reproducers' performing unwaged or care labour, the idea is that we could run all this better ourselves. The question of social relations organised through the form of value does not come up. What financialisation shows us is that value is derived these days, and for the past few decades, from *the old capitalist dream of money making money*, and workers are a cost, unless they are debtors.[77]

Told and *represented* by finance, this lie that money makes money enables a trajectory where the denigration of work and labour in contemporary capitalism must be enacted time and again. Not only is housework not finding its place as labour, as feminists hoped, but so-called productive labour and waged labour at large are being undermined. The widely operating illusion that 'money makes money' further marginalises care and social reproduction, as this logic of the wealthy finds expression as the logic of the poor: scores of people hope to make ends meet by feeding the gambling industry, which has been on an 'upward trajectory for the last few decades' of globalisation and in 2023 of 'a value exceeding $540 billion'.[78]

All this said, in contemporary capitalism social reproduction is changing. Given capitalist technology's penetration into biological life today (not possible in the nineteenth or for most of the twentieth century), an urgent question for contemporary feminism concerns whether it is still meaningful to distinguish between 'production' and 'social reproduction'? Paul Cammack argues that this distinction may be heading to redundancy as 'the appearance of "contract pregnancy" or the "commodified womb" are significant aspects of the commodification of the human body, a trend which is just as evident in markets for organs, tissues, blood and stem-cells, and in the use of human subjects for large-scale drug trials'. As he further asserts, 'it is now clear, as it could only be in abstract prospect in Marx's time, that the historical-materialist framework does indeed encompass production in capitalist society in all its forms, including 'the production of life, both of one's own in labour and of fresh life in procreation'.[79] This undermines any notion of 'women's work' as untouched nature, but it does not change the fundamentals of how capital captures such work. The penetration of capital into the womb is where we are at — and it goes without saying that all subjects with a womb, including the vast majority of cis-women, are classed and their class plays a role in how capital can mine them for profit. Which aspects of social reproduction can be drawn into direct valorisation and profit-making and which should remain 'natural' is a fine balancing act for capital, its biopolitical imperialism, and the ideas it must make acceptable and even popular.

What the discussion so far indicates is that an *ideology of gendered values* is directly connected with the hierarchy of work (and jobs) in capitalism and what counts as labour — and that capitalism ultimately relies on a tremendous amount of unpaid work in order to exist. In 2016, the British press, carefully avoiding references to gender or sex, made public 'official government figures' demonstrating 'an extraordinary attempt to quantify the volume of work done in the home — and put a price on what it would cost if that work was paid': the figure for 2014 was an astonishing £1 trillion.[80] In 2020, women globally were doing '12.5 billion hours of unpaid care work every day. When valued at minimum wage this would represent a contribution to the global economy of at least $10.8 trillion a year, more than three times the size of the global tech industry'.[81] It is thus unsurprising to hear in 2023 that 'just 14 countries—all high-income economies—have laws that give women the same rights as men. Worldwide, nearly 2.4 billion women of working age still do not have the same rights as men'.[82] Formal rights hardly translate to emancipation, and yet a connection between women's rights and women's work must be made. Even if feminism would start with rights, it would end with work. Globalised capitalism and its efforts to capture 'human capital' for growth affords more data about women's place than ever before. The data hardly gives cause for feminist celebration.

THE DIFFICULTY OF LEARNING FROM HISTORY

One of Federici's arguments in *Caliban and the Witch* is that capitalism rescued a fundamental script of social relations relying on inequality, including, royalty, inherited wealth, access, and connections. Seen this way, capitalism was a lifeline thrown to an already extant class-based social reality to thwart the potential that common land offered to the peasantry. Some women were persecuted because of their potential role in the social shift to the commons that might have led to an alternative modernity. The art world compels us to consider the complex history of class power and its articulation in capitalism: the woman heading the *ArtReview* 'Power 100' in 2024 is described as 'royalty' in 'the real world' but also as 'a symbol of the increasing influence of the Gulf region in the spheres of finance, commerce, politics, sports and entertainment and… art', and she was offered the directorship of a biennial at the age of 22.[83] The opportunity to head an art biennial at such a young age exceeds the wildest career dreams of students in curating, no matter how much effort they put in. The art world appears to be where class power is affirmed, and perhaps especially when not represented by a white man.

As is well known, the subordination of women far predates capitalism. In 2011, David Graeber's *Debt: The First Five Thousand Years* indicated that economies structured through the entanglements of markets with war have required women's treatment as exchangeable objects, that is, their dehumanisation.[84] In grasping, however, that women's history *is also* a history of the transition from one mode of production to another, we can ask: did capitalism, at the point of its emergence, antagonise and suppress women's agency acting against the social contract of property? If so, capitalism managed to eradicate memory of this. Capitalism tied women's desired independence to their fashioning as consumers while it successfully retained them as family and community carers. In 2009, Hester Eisenstein described how the formal labour force in advanced economies was transformed upon women's entry since the 1960s: women's entry into the workforce became used to expand part-time, flexibilised, and ultimately precarious labour.[85] This was hypothetically how women could 'have it all': financial independence and families. Women did not, of course, have it all; rather, capitalism did.

Capitalism elaborated a gender-based norm around work and non-work from the outset. This involved class and the 'worth of individuals as human beings', in Sheila Rowbotham's words, who argued in the 1970s:

> The most crucial factor in deciding the peculiar helplessness of women was the exclusion of the privileged from production. As bourgeois man justified himself through work, asserting his own industry and usefulness against the idea of aristocratic leisure, his woman's life was becoming increasingly useless. Bourgeois women did not make capitalism, they merely attached themselves to its makers and lived off man's activity. Their dowry helped him to accumulate. Their bodies served him as ornament, toy, and mirror. Women were for relaxation.[86]

And as the bourgeoisie was able to embed its values as hegemonic (that is, to convince all classes that its values were common sense and indeed 'natural'), what women came to strive for was precisely to be 'useless' and exclude themselves from what counted as 'production'. A woman's greatest achievement in a process of upward social mobility was to be her withdrawal from the public sphere where the idea of labour was situated. This outlook is updated today:

> White working-class femininity is associated with failure, and as a result, working-class women increasingly feel they need to identify with a more aspirational and glamorous femininity made available in profusion across the world of media, on TV and in magazines in particular. To be properly feminine they must seek *middle-class respectability*, or else jeopardise their status and sexual identity as

modern working women. This shows clearly how gender is made to articulate directly with the wider individualisation processes so as to diminish or reduce the significance of social class in everyday political discourse of women.[87]

What Angela McRobbie observes is that not only has capitalism's dominant class shaped women's aspirations generally, but also that such aspirations lead many contemporary women to lose sight of their reality as classed subjects. If we read Rowbotham and McRobbie's nuanced assessments together, we see that 'being a woman' is constructed by capitalism as a paradoxical proposition: woman-ness is meant to be beyond class while it is formed through distinct class characteristics. The classed aspect of 'being a woman' must be concealed, as are so many other things in capitalism. This concealment of the ways that femininity is anchored in class has enabled perceptions of woman as appearance, image, mask — all of which have featured strongly in artworks by feminists and non-feminists alike: in the late 1970s, Cindy Sherman's distilment of femininity as code circulating in film is a famous example. Sherman's *Untitled Film Stills* (1977–80) demonstrated how pervasive the idea of woman as pure sign was: a simulacrum (a copy without an original) in the exchange circuits of technology-fuelled visual culture.

And yet class struggle has hardly been unrelated to women's history. The October Revolution of 1917, one of the formative events of twentieth-century history, is a case in point.

Six weeks after the October Revolution, marriage was replaced with civil registration and divorce became available at the request of either partner. These measures were elaborated a year later in the Family Code, which made women equal before the law. Religious control was abolished, removing centuries of institutionalized oppression at a stroke; divorce could be obtained by either partner with no reason given; women had the right to their own money and neither partner had rights over the other's property. The concept of illegitimacy was eradicated — if a woman did not know who the father was, all her previous sexual partners were given collective responsibility for the child. In 1920, Russia became the first country to legalize abortion on request.[88]

Despite all this, we rarely hear today about the October Revolution as part of women's history. Overall, the dominant narratives of women's histories in contemporary capitalism suppress experiences in which class struggle met demands for women's emancipation. The work done by Clara Zetkin, Alexandra Kollontai, and many other pioneers of socialist feminism has been consigned to oblivion, with most women today not even knowing the origins of International Women's Day or the radical politics of love and sexual freedom that inspired communist revolutionaries, let alone their focus on gender and work. Exhibitions such as *Red Love* (Testa Konsthall, Stockholm 2018), featuring artist Dora García who revisited Alexandra Kollontai's work and life, are rare, and a lot more is needed to challenge the suppression of this other history of women. What really comprises this history, and which aspects of it are deemed more acceptable perhaps than others by the art world? Curator Maria Lind wrote: 'García argues that in reading Kollontai we learn that the fight must still be fought, and that change will not happen without love and affect, regardless of how exploitative they can be.'[89] Although it is true that the fight must still be fought, communism as an alternative modernity that Kollontai worked for was not exhausted in love. Rather, it is capitalist ideology that constantly compels women's lives to be examined through the route of affect; 'affect' connotes 'femininity'. In order to not suppress the history of which Kollontai was part — the 'fight [that] must still be fought' — Kollontai needs to be named as a Marxist revolutionary involved in class struggle through strategy. This comes with baggage that must be addressed. A male revolutionary leader (namely, Lenin) would infamously ask of a woman revolutionary (Inessa Armand) to not engage the 'demand for freedom of love' on the grounds that 'in the present social conditions' it would 'turn out to be a bourgeois, not a proletarian demand'.[90] It is thus far from simple to remember, represent, and learn from the history made by Kollontai, and other communist women like her. And such remembering should not be scripted as a labour of love for contemporary feminism, but as the labour of history-making.

The suppression of this part of women's history does not just serve the propagation of the myth that it was capitalism's liberal societies that enabled women to gain whatever freedoms they currently enjoy, including the possibility of financial and sexual independence. Such suppression also serves to affirm a perception of modernity as a *singular* history tied to capitalism and its discontents. The rejection of so-called western epistemologies can be taken to be an outcome of this notion of modernity as singular. By referring to *Western* epistemologies, we lose sight of which epistemologies specifically served and serve capitalism in the historical conditions of its articulation and imperialist worldmaking. At present, historiographies of feminism need to consider the fact that 'non-Marxists or anti-Marxist Feminism is the dominant modus operandi of feminist theory in the Euro-Atlantic context' and that this 'is often not a clearly stated position, but rather a tacit presupposition of feminist theorising'.[91] The suppression of women's revolutionary history creates a public consciousness where this singular capitalist modernity is either hailed as a gift to women who should therefore tolerate its shortcomings or it generates narratives in which modernity is rejected as an evil that must be abandoned. In such cases, a recourse to a pre-modern, often idealised, past is invoked as a credible and desired alternative. Modernity however cannot be exited, as both those who strive for universal access to the capital-enclosed advances of medicine and those whose lives are destroyed by capital's military drones know too well — no one can actually be 'left behind' in the totalising synchronicity of capital. In the twentieth century, 'decolonization was not solely achieved with national independence. Economic control also had to be obtained but was not'.[92] Of course not — the miracles of capitalist technology need rare-earth elements.

As economic independence was unrealisable without overthrowing the globalising mode of production, decoloniality would sometimes find solace in the primacy of culture, with a particular focus on language. In language, the structure of a sentence permits the presentation of equivalents. This is often a limit of decolonial feminism: in 2010, Maria Lugones referred to 'ways of organising the social, the cosmological, the ecological, the economic, and the spiritual *non-modern*' as distinct from the 'premodern'.[93] From the perspective of historical materialism, this is both right and wrong. Such a view sees that the world operates in synchronous mode but fails to account for how capitalism benefits from the perpetual dichotomy between the material and the immaterial — say, by presenting the 'economic' and the 'spiritual' in an unjustified equivalence. Typing these words on a computer (or even writing them with a pen: an industrial object) and using modern academia's methods for disseminating them already locks Lugones, myself, and everyone reading the equiva-lence and objections to it firmly in modernity rather than in anything 'non-modern'. There is no political safety in the non-modern. After World War II, the quest for the not-modern found expression in post-modernism: a crucial concept in feminism's historical trajectory that we will examine later in this book. In 2002, Fredric Jameson asked whether modernity can be de-singularised.[94] The question remains open but responding to it requires that modernity is understood *not* merely as a narrative category. Deposing the category does not magically alter reality. As for the popular and populist notion that women's liberation could only be effected in capitalism, in 2017 an unapologetic defence of colonialism drew on such arguments while taking capitalism for granted; and in 2020 in France, an open letter signed by 100 scholars argued against the very legitimacy of post-colonial and decolonial critique calling it a 'sham'.[95] Such positions, not unusual in liberal feminism on the right, are but a justification of capital's hold on modernity.

Not naming the causes of modernity-as-disaster enables returns to idealised and idealist traditionalism, including the belief that women are innately predisposed or socialised to caring for the planet. Yet women also use the fossil economy. Upper-class women can launch their curatorial and artistic careers upon wealth accumulated through the fossil economy, not to mention that oil sponsorship is integral to the art institutions of capitalist modernity.[96] Historically speaking, the oil industry built capitalism, not patriarchy. It is unclear if this has been forgotten by those proliferating feminist eco-spiritualisms prioritising a universal non-masculine care principle. No such invo-cation can undo the colonial divides of capitalism: the postcolonial condition announced in the twentieth century has morphed into a neocolonial reality, generating a rift where universal feminist soli-darity and a common feminist cause can only sound hypocritical, as the pejorative, yet most accurate and illuminating term, 'imperial-ist feminism', reminds us. Whether the contemporary art field can disidentify from imperialist feminism *in practice* rather than simply words is moot, but a historical materialist analysis might address how the revolutionary tendencies birthed in modernity were suppressed and how that original suppression is re-enacted. Viewed against such potential knowledge, we can see that conceptualising capitalism as merely *one* problem for feminism indicates that capital as the organising force of a social totality is not visible.

ART REVEALING WORKPLACES

In the hegemonic narrative of modernity, we are told that we cannot have personal freedom without a free market, and art as free expression (call it 'autonomy') cannot exist without the art market. Women can only realise their creative freedom in designated markets made for accumulation. Reality says otherwise. In her analysis of feminised labour in the creative industries, McRobbie argued that feminism had failed to 'explore the actual points of tension — the levels of anxiety, the new realms of pain and injury — which accrue from the excessive demands of these multi-tasking careers'.[97] Although no positive answer can be given to McRobbie's question about the 'potential for a new collectivity... at such points of break-down' against an individual's 'exit' becoming 'the only option', feminism in art is alert to the anxiety, pain, and injury and divisions generated by the capitalist workplace.

In 2013, Jenny Richards and Sophie Hope initiated the art research project *Manual Labours* in Britain, using artistic and curatorial methods to explore 'current time-based structures of work (when does work start and end?) and reassert[ing] the significance of the physical (manual) aspect of immaterial, affective and emotional labour'.[98] *Manual Labours* looked at various work environments — art, hospital, bank, call centre — to examine if and how the body 'complained' under kinds of duress rarely perceived as such. In 2017, Richards contributed to a roundtable article on social reproduction and art and discussed the findings of *Manual Labours* as follows:

> We wanted to see if an argument can be made that if we have a passion for work, we are only fit for exploitation under a capitalist organisation of work that thrives on maximising productivity and minimising costs. Or is there something more complex at play in loving work? And if so, how might we problematise and strategise collectivity around these issues?... While we are familiar with freelance roles and precarious contracts in the art field, our research with those working in salaried positions, including staff at a London borough council, shared the same challenging conditions

faced by freelancers.... The common denominator is the breaking down of spaces, both verbal and physical, for collegial relationships and collective workplace complaining. Every colleague is a competitor... and the ideology that bad working conditions are ones you should be able to cope with makes it impossible to discuss challenges at work. Cultures such as 'hotdesking' and 'shift work' also reduce any time you have together with colleagues and the chance for workplace solidarity.[99]

The material conditions of labour in contemporary capitalism's creative and service environments place particular obstacles to collective action. Moreover, a clear boundary between production and social reproduction is indeed hard to maintain, serving not only to isolate workers but also to hide from view the actual conditions of work.

Contemporary artists have addressed this issue by considering the world of labour beyond what capital values as production proper. Marwa Arsanios' film *Amateurs, Stars and Extras, or The Labour of Love* (2018) connects, precisely, the invisibility of the subjects performing domestic labour with the multitude of hidden workers in the economy of creativity, services, and spectacle. *Amateurs, Stars and Extras, or The Labour of Love* opens with a non-famous actress who explains how she tries to be convincing in her television roles as domestic worker. These soap operas are what many women watch as they perform this labour: 'while we clean, we watch other women cleaning', one woman explains. The television screen is the interface of these paradigms of invisibility facing each other: the extras as domestic helpers appear as a fixture of interior spaces that signify the wealth of others and the domestic labourers as viewers who themselves are 'extras' in the families, lives, and neighbourhoods where the need to make a living has placed them. What truly connects the domestic workers and their representation by non-star actors? Answer: neither group of 'extras' revolts. Instead, the socially constructed insignificance of both groups of workers is enhanced through the soap operas' ideological mediation of devalued labour, in which millions of women, across the globe, find consolation. Feminist artworks have addressed the specific effects of the television screen and television culture on women being kept in place since second-wave feminism. Arsanios' work suggests that these effects involve pacifying the working-class woman: her class position softens and fades behind the glamorised consolation that the soap opera offers as a structure of mediation. The invisibility of the maid's labour is concealed by the visibility of a fiction that is nonetheless real labour for the extras that perform it. Can such concealment be undone?

A CONCLUDING QUESTION: FEMINISM AGAINST CAPITALISM OR CAPITALISM AGAINST FEMINISM?

This chapter focuses on a basic opposition between capitalism and feminism in terms of their objectives: although it engenders change, capitalism must maintain its deeper structures that amount to its reproduction; feminism must change these deeper structures so as to disallow the reproduction of women's oppression and exploitation. Capitalism is global, feminism is optional. Feminism's global reach remains at best an aspiration, and at worse a bad idea when seen to originate in an imperialist–colonial modernity. Increasingly, capital must balance its operation of keeping women in place as natural care providers and that of commodifying aspects of social reproduction through the technological compartmentalisation of the body. Capitalism's greatest trick is to turn demands for social change into aids for its own reproduction. In 2009, when Eisenstein was exploring the social consensus on capitalism as 'good for women', Nancy Fraser trod similar ground, wondering about 'the disturbing convergence of some of its [feminism's] ideals with the demands of an emerging new form of capitalism'.[100] Few like to hear this, as it raises the issue of capitalism's impact on feminism's own trajectory.

Like many emancipatory movements, feminism tends to narrate its own history as a series of successes, perhaps in the hope that motivation for further struggle will be generated this way; this is evident in how the feminist art movement has presented itself. An exhibition called *Wack! Art and the Feminist Revolution* at MoCA, Los Angeles (2007) is symptomatic of this approach. There is a Wikipedia entry for this major survey show (which included 120 artists and groups active between 1965 and 1980) where one can click on the phrase 'art and the feminist revolution'. This gets you to an entry called 'Feminist Art Movement', the opening lines of which read: 'The feminist art movement refers to the efforts and accomplishments of feminists internationally to produce art that reflects women's lives and experiences, as well as to change the foundation for the production and reception of contemporary art'.[101] The entry discusses efforts and accomplishments but not failures. And yet, while efforts to realise an 'art reflective of women's lives and experiences' may have been accomplished, efforts to change 'the foundation for the production and reception of contemporary art' did not succeed. Rather, we have artworks converted to assets, including through their *invisibility*, as we saw above.

Moreover, organising art as part of the public sphere, where competition among social actors finds a distinct figuration, cannot be understood without grasping the persistent feminisation of social reproduction under capitalism and its effects: that is, the *gendering of values* (and not just human beings) in a hierarchy essential for capitalism, even if the intensity of this gendering can be 'adjusted' according to capital's contextual needs. Presenting feminism as a success story subscribes to the capitalist logic of hiding — hiding anything that might undermine the self-narration of capitalism as a success story in its own right. In 2013, Tolokonnikova and Žižek disagreed on how capitalism succeeds. That in 2016 Žižek would see 'open-door solidarity with refugees and drawbridge-minded protectionism' as 'two versions of ideological blackmail' facing Europe and in 2023 Tolokonnikova would curate a good-cause auction of women's art at Sotheby's shows that capitalism is a success story for capital, drawing even its critics into affirmation of its cardinal institutions and precepts.[102] In this success story, the 'abode of production' and the abode of reproduction are forgotten or kept apart, so that that the cash-strapped mass of women artists, curators, theorists, and art students can buy their '$12 dress' made by workers in factories that never close and that procure astronomical profits for their owners.[103]

Capitalism and feminism do not share goals, unless feminism is perverted to mean success as represented by women like Ivanka Trump: a born-millionaire, art collector with 'a taste for rebellious "bro art"', as *The Guardian* put it, 'wife, mother, entrepreneur' and author of *Women Who Work: Rewriting the Rules for Success* (2017) but whose female (and some male) workers in Indonesia reportedly complained about 'verbal abuse, impossible targets and "poverty pay"'.[104] In 2019, Jennifer Rubbel's performance, *Ivanka Vacuuming*, presented in Washington DC an Ivanka lookalike endlessly vacuuming (while smiling) the crumbs that visitors would throw on the floor. Widely discussed in the media, the performance offered the public the unlikely image of a woman from the dominant class performing the proverbial 'woman's work' that is never done by that class.[105] What did the artwork suggest? Ivanka Trump read it as follows: 'Women can choose to knock each other down or build each other up. I choose the latter'.[106] Is presenting a successful woman of the capitalist class vacuuming a way of knocking her down? If so, this reveals the values capitalism relies on: who would want to become a working-class cleaner? Ivanka Trump's tweet implies that a woman's success relies on her self-constitution through this system of values that affirms the extant relationship between production (leadership) and social reproduction (servitude). The theories of joyful 'becoming' that dominate feminist philosophy and artmaking at present rarely think about this becoming through class.

A *New Statesman* article asked: 'Is Ivanka Trump the feminist we deserve?'[107] Hopefully not. If second-wave feminism in art entailed practices of disaffirmation, as discussed by art historian Griselda Pollock and artist Mary Kelly in 1989,[108] such practices need to be renewed. What, however, needs to be undermined today is the perception that feminism can achieve its aims by affirming capitalism. Kelly made her landmark *Post-partum Document* in the 1970s: an archive–installation consisting of 135 items that testified, in diverse ways, to the gradual separation of mother and child. Drawing on psychoanalysis, the artwork took years to complete as it charted the passage of Kelly's son into the symbolic order through the acquisition of language. *Post-partum Document* did not explicitly tackle how a mother, through social reproductive labour, ensures the supply of workers and labour-power for capital, but it did address the fact that 'unproductive' work, typified as women's work, is the ground for the reproduction of socialised life. In grappling with the nature/culture divide, *Post-partum Document* considered whether alienation — the separation: the mother's loss of the child as the founding process of the latter's personhood — might also be observed in reproductive labour which includes the transmission of language.

As is well known in feminist art history, the press complained at the time about 'dirty nappies' entering the art institution through Kelly's work: that is, the refuse of the private sphere that should have remained *hidden* had entered the public domain of art. The hidden abode of reproductive labour had entered the artwork as a labour output made for the purposes of display, participation, communication, externalisation, and visibility. Kelly had inserted her reproductive labour into her work as the producer of culture, but this happened within the parameters of the capitalist art field which sees certain artworks as carrying value due to their originality. This was the case for *Post-partum Document*, which, according to the Tate website in 2025, has been shown only twice in its entirety (in 1984 in the US and in 1998 in Austria), as it is divided among collections: the Tate collection, a private collection in California, the Art Gallery of Ontario Collection in Toronto, the Zurich Museum Collection, the Australian National Gallery Collection in Canberra, and the Arts of Great Britain Collection in London.[109] In the course of writing this book, the last exhibition I visited and which included only one part of the artwork was *Arts of Creation: On Art and Motherhood* in Dundee Contemporary Arts in 2025. Kelly's radical artistic gesture in exposing the hidden abode of reproduction is not to be doubted, but what is the meaning of this compartmentalisation? This is more complex. On the one hand, the capitalist art field has managed to undermine the social visibility of Kelly's vision, making the complete artwork invisible to the public, including to women. Fragmenting an artwork seems to be at odds with the interests of feminism. On the other hand, the dissemination of the artwork's parts internationally may allow many publics to connect with this emblematic feminist work. Underneath both options sits the logic of collections, private and public, that acquire valuable art in a global art world underwritten by competition. Competition sustains the art canon as form, even if the content of the canon becomes more diverse.

Thinking about what determines the visibility of and access to artworks of feminist intent draws our attention to structures that, once again, cannot be described as patriarchal. Fragmentation can sustain value. Invisibility, whether partial or total (in the case of freeports), is carefully orchestrated, affecting human beings, objects, and actions, as dictated by capital's regime of exchange. Thus we glimpse the degrees of entrapment in capitalism's success narrative and criteria, where processes of concealment abound. In later chapters, the parameters of this entrapment will become more concrete. Next, however, I consider some of the challenges faced by feminism in the ideological landscapes that shape contemporary sociality.

2

Feminism and Ideology

In 1973, Nicos Hadjinicolaou published in French a groundbreaking study on art and class struggle, examining how 'visual ideology' was transmitted by artworks beyond artistic intentions, translated into English in 1978. In 1981, Rozsika Parker and Griselda Pollock published their equally groundbreaking *Old Mistresses: Women, Art and Ideology*, which argued that to confront women artists' excision from the history of art, we should look at 'the unacknowledged ideology which informs the practice of this discipline'.[1] Both studies made use of the concept of ideology as socially diffused perceptions that operate beyond our awareness, and around and through us, to reproduce, directly or indirectly, the status quo. Thus defined, as these two studies show, ideology finds expression in artworks but also intellectual paradigms and academic disciplines. What is ideology then and what is its function?

In the turbulent late eighteenth century of the French Revolution (1789) and the ascent of the bourgeoisie as the dominant class, the term 'ideology' appeared, referring to a coherent set of rational ideas. In the nineteenth century, Marx gave ideology a different meaning: 'Marx affirms… that the real problems of humanity are not mistaken ideas but real social contradictions and that the former are a consequence of the latter', and so as long as 'these contradictions' are not solved 'in practice', they tend to be projected 'in ideological forms of consciousness, that is to say, in purely mental or discursive solutions which effectively conceal or misrepresent the character of these contradictions. By concealing contradictions the ideological distortion contributes to their reproduction and therefore serves the interests of the ruling class'.[2] Here, ideology performs an important act of concealment for capital in burying the mode of production's contradictions by making certain ways of doing and thinking appear natural: as simply the way things are. So, 'things', whatever they are, go unquestioned.

Societies built on inequality require ideology in order to distort the reality of exploitation in the minds of the exploited. Ideology can perform an inversion of reality: an obvious example, discussed by Marx, is that we attribute *inherent* value to commodities which inverts the reality that value is produced by human labour. In this inversion, the material reality, which is always historical, is concealed. Not only that, however. Attributing inherent values to commodities constructs a particular subjectivity and generates a whole set of values that we take for granted. These permeate society. Think for example of a student who is ideologically constituted as a consumer, and so believes in market choice and sees university education as a (costly) commodity. She/he/they may demand that this product (say, the modules prepared by staff) has particular characteristics (as commodities do) that she/he/they favour/s; or the student may perceive of striking university staff as withholding the commodity.

Ideology as a concept has a varied history in Marxism. Some Marxists maintain that in a future post-revolutionary society of achieved liberation, ideology would disappear as it would serve no purpose. In the early twentieth century, Antonio Gramsci elaborated a philosophy of praxis, and thought about how ideology connects to hegemony by generating social consensus and what passes for 'common sense'. In the 1960s, Louis Althusser, influenced by psychoanalysis's concept of the unconscious, and especially by Jacques Lacan and his emphasis on language, destabilised the expectation that social subjects could have access to reality unmediated by ideology. Some feminist art historians of the second wave and later were influenced by Althusser's conception of ideology, and some adopted Lacanian psychoanalysis, with its emphasis on subjects constituted in and through language, as an analytic method for artworks and visual culture. Although ideology finds expression in language, this perspective did not always pay attention to the material conditions that generated the contradictions in capitalism as a mode of production and reproduction. Ideology is not another word for 'false consciousness' nor can it disappear by and through language: the contradictions ideology serves to conceal are historically material. Ideology is lived through by the subjects it forms, and is certainly not static. How hegemony is articulated in a given period (or context) within capitalism may differ from its articulation in another. This is why the work of identifying how subjects are ideologically constituted is never done once and for all, but needs to consider the period and context of feminist struggle.

Feminist art history that drew on Gramsci's notion of hegemony elucidated, for example, how modern art presented images of women in ways that affirmed and strengthened in the public sphere stereotypical ideas about what a woman was: closer to nature and the animal world, passive (think of all the reclining nudes), existing as an ornament, or as a threatening or irrelevant 'other' to civilisation, and so on. Less attention was paid to how understandings of feminism as such might have been shaped ideologically, especially where feminism lost sight of the mode of production. My starting question is therefore whether ideology constituted as capitalist hegemony exists in conflict with feminist consciousness as a potentiality. I argue that the ideology that sustains capitalism works principally to privilege our understanding of people as individuals or, in postmodernist terms, as processes of fragmentation, delimitation, and particularisation, and that this impacts the formation of feminist consciousness, including in art. This ideology can be understood as hegemonic because it finds multiple functions with minimal resistance.

Hegemonic ideology may implicate us in sustaining the status quo without understanding that we do so. Ideology, that is, may also shape emancipatory and progressive politics — in fact, that 'progress', a notion embedded in capitalist modernity, is seen as welcome and positive, without further qualification or political criteria, indicates the difficulty of coming up with truly transformative ways of thinking. Exposing ideology is not the endgame goal of a Marxist feminist politics, but it can help us grasp what the feminist struggle entails in its contextual historical figuration. This bears particular relevance to art, where the highly ideological notion of art's 'autonomy' is hard to shake, despite the numerous critiques. Before we think about art, however, we need to think about society. This chapter first traces developments in relation to feminism in the 2010s to examine the ideological constitution of the present, introducing themes to be pursued in subsequent chapters.

FEMINISM IN THE 2010s: THE FIRM, THE STRIKE, AND CONCEPTS IN CIRCULATION

Defined by the social slaughterhouse of austerity economics that was capital's response to the 2008 financial crisis, the 2010s witnessed continuous unrest. The decade opened with uprisings that were in large part against economic hardship (Occupy, the *Indignados*, the Arab Spring, and more); continued with what capitalist governments dubbed a 'refugee crisis' in many parts of the world and certainly in Europe (which decided to act as a 'fortress'); witnessed the transnational counter-revolution of a bolstered alt-right, far right, and the fascist tendency, as well as deepening climate destruction; concluded in 2019 with 'protests in every corner of the globe'[3] which were curbed with Covid-19's cataclysmic impact early in 2020.

Neoliberalism did not morph into a 'softer' capitalism in the 2010s, despite the state protection of banks and a heightened protectionism towards national capitals that now marks the 2020s. The grotesque socio-economic divides between the swathes of poor (alongside the 'squeezed' middle classes) and a tiny top percentage of wealthy exploiters continued. The ascent of patriarchy-strikes-back governments, as part of capitalism's deepening authoritarianism and reliance on fascist values, was counteracted by a resurgence of feminist mobilisation: *The Guardian*'s column 'The Week in Patriarchy' launched in 2014; the Ni Una Menos (Not One Less) movement emerged in Latin America in 2015 and focused on the rampant violence against women and the precarisation of lives made vulnerable under capitalism; transnational campaigns sprung up against sexism and sexual harassment such as #MeToo in 2017;[4] international conferences, such as Feminist Emergency in London also in 2017, addressed the rapid reactionary developments by bringing together activists and theorists.[5] Grassroots feminist collectives were activated, some re-animating the strike as protest in relation to unwaged or low-waged women's work, often beyond typical industrial contexts. The strike was already embedded in 1970s feminist mobilisations, some of which had never ceased: connected to the activism and writing of Selma James and extending the Wages for Housework initiative, the Global Women's Strike formed in 1999, campaigning for 'recognition and payment for all caring work, in the home and in the land'.[6]

In the 2010s, the alignment of activism and theoretical analysis was strongly represented by the International Women's Strike (hereafter IWS). IWS was launched in 2017, with initial discussions in November 2016 in the US, upon Donald Trump's first election to office.[7] IWS positioned itself explicitly as a critique of 'lean-in' feminism. Presenting itself as an international 'community', Lean In was launched in 2014 by Facebook COO Sheryl Sandberg, following her 2013 book, *Lean In: Women, Work and the Will to Lead*.[8] Let's look at this formation first.

Lean In's self-representation as a community, a word typically found in grassroots contexts, already suggests that some concepts migrate with ease, appropriated as the jargon of very rich people (Sandberg's net worth was $2.4 billion in 2025, according to *Forbes*). The suppression of Marxism and references to class in the post-modern 1980s (more on this later) made 'community' an appealing concept in the 1990s and since, with art remaining a field where this can be notably observed — often with feminism's involvement. Probably everyone reading this book knows of a 'community' initiative, whether in art or otherwise. In 2025, 'community art' is defined by the Tate as 'artistic activity that is based in a community setting, characterised by interaction or dialogue with the community and often involving a professional artist collaborating with people who may not otherwise engage in the arts'. No entry titled 'art for the class struggle' exists because no such art developed. At a certain moment in art's history, the term 'community' functioned ideologically (that is, beyond artistic intention) to conceal class and even prevent the emergence of art explicitly addressing class. Community implies inclusivity — another key term of contemporary feminist discourse to be addressed in due course. For now, we just need to keep in mind that as community does not necessarily speak of class, it could be appropriated by a discourse coming from above, such as Lean In. It was not the only appropriation with which Lean In was associated.

For Susan Faludi, Lean In appropriated the idea of female and indeed *feminist* leadership to present market-led, divisive, and exploitative capitalist structures as somehow conducive to women's emancipation.[9] The idea of the free worker who freely sells her capacity to labour to the equally free capitalist (discussed in Chapter One) was central to capitalism's representation as a system of opportunities for all, and thus for women too, if they only leaned *in* within the capitalist firm rather than leaning *on* a man. And it is women who should, ultimately, lean in to the system that surrounds them rather than the system being questioned by them. In a nutshell, lean-in feminism, still active as I conclude the book in early 2025, advocates transnationally for women's further participation in capitalism.[10] That very few women can reach the top of the pyramid that capitalism sets up for all is conveniently disregarded, despite the fact that the 'share of women running Global 500 companies' fell 'to just 5.6%' in 2024.[11] Lean-in feminism is a salient expression of individualism as hegemonic ideology crossing with feminism, camouflaged as community. This commitment to individualism is not openly stated by Lean In, the strategy of which has been to appeal to women as a universally meaningful group, its motto (on its website) being 'we help women achieve their ambitions and work to create an equal world'. Against a capitalist reality that creates a top (conceptually and materially), lean-in feminism tells *all* women, irrespective of colour, creed, sexuality, or location that they can 'succeed' if prejudices against them are removed and, especially, if they work hard.

For Lean In, everyone has the right to work hard: in 2024, an illustration on its website presented a group of differently-bodied women, including one in a wheelchair, while we also encounter a feature titled 'Leadership Fundamentals for Black Women', complete with photographs of happy-looking Black women.[12] Lean-in feminism presents itself as inclusive, anti-racist, and anti-ableist, and its use of imagery bolsters this presentation. Lean-in feminism does not talk about class, although it might conceivably find fault with 'classism', nowadays widely used to refer to the exclusion of working-class people from 'opportunities'. Eliding the knowledge that capital *requires* a working class to exploit, 'classism' has been a most useful addition to the inclusion discourse, organised around the right to participate. But participate in what? In the case of Lean In, participation affirms capitalism. In other cases, what participation means is hazy. For example, previous executive editor of Vogue.com and senior features editor at MarieClaire.com Koa Beck wrote *White Feminism: From the Suffragettes to Influencers and Who They Leave Behind* (2021), where 'white feminism' stands for 'privileges' associated with race and class. In an interview about her book, Beck pointed to the hypocrisy of feminist companies in how they treat their workers, but also said: 'We have to redefine what it means to be a feminist workplace, a feminist company and a feminist leader'.[13] How does being positive about the existence of feminist companies not indicate support for *reform* through the lean-in mentality? As seen even in its visual culture, lean-in feminism argues for having an inclusive feminist 'workplace' in an otherwise unchanged capitalist imperialist world. This is the world where in 2025 the UK's Labour government and its female chancellor cut vital benefits to the disabled, arguing that they should work: they have the 'right' and should be 'included'. Like community and leadership, the discourse of rights and inclusivity can thus be used to various ends. It can serve hegemonic ideology, and has since the decline of labour critique and struggle after World War II, as Luc Boltanski and Eve Chiapello argue in *The New Spirit of Capitalism* (1999 in French): with class politics coming under attack, 'new categories have gradually been devised to express social negativity — in particular, exclusion (in contrast to inclusion). It was difficult for the notion of exploitation to find a place in this new manner of expressing indignation at growing poverty'.[14] This allows us to see why 'work', unmoored from class antagonism, could be fashioned as a right rather than what keeps capitalism going.

Already since the 2010s and extending to the 2020s, inclusivity and work appeared prominently in the discourse of what came to be known as 'neoliberal feminism',[15] with Lean In being a notable example. Yet these same concepts and themes of inclusivity and work were also present in the discourse of a feminism that disparaged neoliberalism and Lean In. If we focused on inclusivity and work as mobilising themes in the feminism of 2010s, we might encounter some difficulty in differentiating between Lean In and the IWS, despite the latter having formed precisely to elaborate a feminism 'beyond Lean In'. Proposing a 'new, more expansive feminist movement' in a text signed by veterans of 1970s militancy, including former Black Panthers member Angela Davis, and a younger generation coming of age after 2000, IWS stated:

The kind of feminism we seek is already emerging internationally, in struggles across the globe: from the women's strike in Poland against the abortion ban to the women's strikes and marches in Latin America against male violence; from the massive women's demonstration of the last November in Italy to the protests and the women's strike in defense of reproductive rights in South Korea and

Ireland. What is striking about these mobilizations is that several of them combined struggles against male violence with opposition to the casualization of labor and wage inequality, while also opposing homophobia, transphobia and xenophobic immigration policies. Together, they herald a new international feminist movement with an expanded agenda — at once anti-racist, anti-imperialist, anti-heterosexist, and anti-neoliberal.[16]

Both the cross-generational authorship of the text and its embrace of multiple struggles in an attempted synthesis of a common feminist struggle are important, amounting to a call for feminism to achieve greater confidence in its radical vision and declare this politics for what it *can* be: a transformative force rather than a reformist project. Seen this way, it made sense that the IWS declaration was titled 'Beyond Lean In' rather than 'Against Lean In', thus indicating the *potentiality* of a global anticapitalist feminism rather than taking it for granted.

'Beyond Lean In' was also the title of a 2013 review article of Sandberg's book by Black American feminist cultural critic bell hooks, who insightfully exposed how 'Sandberg uses feminist rhetoric as a front to cover her commitment to western cultural imperialism, to white supremacist capitalist patriarchy'.[17] hook's critique of the global power structure supported by Lean In or corporate feminism also underpinned IWS's outlook. The undermining of lean-in feminism would rely on positing a feminist multitude as a political subject; IWS claimed a feminism 'for the 99%', extending the key Occupy slogan from 2011 'we are the 99%'. Feminism as proposed by IWS was directed to the reinvention of the entire fabric of socio-economic relations, with Cinzia Arruzza highlighting a fundamental connection between social reproduction and the turn to the strike as a feminist tactic of resistance: 'While not all the organizers of and participants in the women's strike had a theoretical commitment to social reproduction feminism, *the women's strike can legitimately be seen as a political translation of social reproduction theory*'.[18]

As Arruzza notes, 'politically relegitimising the term "strike" in the United States' was one of IWS's major achievements, given the extreme decline in unionisation in the country that had sold the ideology of the American Dream domestically and across the globe.[19] But the IWS stood symbolically for more: it claimed for feminism a leading position within a broader terrain of left politics and across the spectrum of its struggles. In this respect, raising the idea of a feminist multitude was important, despite the tension that existed between IWS's emphasis on class and the less clearly defined 99 percent. The 'multitude' was not a term used by the IWS, but it is an apt designation for the subject implied in any 99 percent. The notion of the multitude came to prominence through Michael Hardt and Antonio Negri's *Empire* (2000), as a Marxist or, for some, post-Marxist theorisation of globalisation. Hardt and Negri's study minimised references to the working class, arguing that a new oppositional political subject was emerging through changes in capitalist production, and, especially, informatisation, but also by the migrating masses of the dispossessed generated by global capital. In *Empire*, the multitude assumed the role of a composite counterforce that would generate structures of solidarity and command diverse skills. This counterforce would not necessarily share a consciousness of class belonging.

The figure of the 99 percent adopted by the IWS indicated that only 1 percent of society truly benefited from capitalism. Still, the enormous mass of the 99 percent could not have been free from class conflict, interests, antagonisms. Even if the idea was that different constituencies in this enormous mass could start from their specific concerns and seek the deeper cause of their oppression and/or exploitation, a tension between the actuality of class and the mass of the 99 percent becomes obvious: the constituencies comprising the 99 percent would not just be different but of unequal power and locked into relations of exploitation among themselves. For example, a businesswoman owning a small business with three women employees would find herself in this 99 percent, but it would be in the interests of the businessowner to make her three employees work more for less so that the business remains competitive. The discursively articulated 99 percent as a political subject of feminism, evoking the need for a mass uprising, cannot resolve the material contradictions of class interests. The tension observed in the feminism for the 99 percent (as in Hardt and Negri's multitude) was itself an outcome of the defeat of labour movements by the late twentieth century: that was when the discourse on 'difference' gained momentum.

The theorists associated with IWS were aware of the tension. In a 2018 article, 'From Women's Strike to a New Class Movement: The Third Feminist Wave', Arruzza attempted to resolve it by arguing that the centrality of the strike (carried out by workers to resist capital's interests) in the new feminist struggle meant that 'the feminist movement is increasingly placing itself as *the* international process of class formation of this phase'. The feminist multitude of the 99 percent was thus proposed as a process of 'class subjectivation'.[20] In short, the function of capitalism could not be understood if women's position was sidelined as a supplementary problem — something that had certainly characterised Marxism without feminism in the past. The multitude implicitly claimed by IWS can then be seen as a formation enabling consciousness-raising around obstacles to revolutionary prospects that were entrenched by the 2010s. A declared aim was to overcome the fragmenting effects of identity politics that dominated the turn of the century:

> The problem of the replacement of class struggle with identity-based struggles should therefore be articulated as a political problem arising from the hegemony of the liberal articulation of feminist discourse. This articulation turns feminism into a problem of self-promotion for elite women by erasing the key issue of the structural relation between gender oppression and capitalism.[21]

What about the businesswoman and her three women employees then? If through such consciousness-raising the businesswoman came to an understanding that the social reproductive labour she does at home for free for her family is part of her working day *and* that this social reproductive labour connects her with her three women employees, she might understand that capitalism is not ultimately to her benefit: her life as a woman of the petite bourgeoisie (her work at home is unpaid and unrecognised while her small business is constantly threatened by capital's monopoly tendency) might lead her to rethink her interests. In this imagined example, the three women employees could also be expected to ask why another woman owns the business and see that what separates them from this other woman is not mere 'difference'. Such realisations could only be the outcome of an understanding of labour's historically material actuality.

Tithi Bhattacharya writes about the importance of rethinking the constitution of a 'global working class' in the twenty-first century. She argues against the misleading separation between class politics addressing the waged workplace and struggles not taking the workplace as their focus:

Understanding the complex but unified way in which the production of commodities and reproduction of labor power takes place helps us understand how the concrete allocation of the total labor of society is socially organized in gendered and racialized ways through *lessons learnt by capital from previous historical epochs* and through its struggle against the working class. The process of accumulation, thus, in actuality cannot be indifferent to social categories of race, sexuality or gender, but seeks to organize and shape those categories that in turn act upon the determinate form of surplus labor extraction. The wage labor relation suffuses the spaces of non-waged everyday life.[22]

It is for the reasons presented above that identity politics — tending to imply *recognition* — is not where emancipatory demands can stop. And they don't. As *Transgender Marxism* proposes, 'class politics' cannot be articulated 'as somehow in opposition to any consideration of gender minorities, who are framed as a sideshow to the simplicity and ordinary concerns of workers' and that 'how gender nonconformity can survive in a capitalist context more generally' is an important question.[23] At the same time, there is no doubt that capitalism learns 'lessons' from its history faster than emancipatory movements, including feminism. If *overall* women (trans, cis, of any phenotype) are (unequally) oppressed and (mostly) exploited in capitalism, they are also 50 percent of the human population spread in the pyramid of the capitalist lifeworld. And yet marginalising women as the subject of feminism does occur. 'Do you think women is still a useful category for feminism to center on?', a journalist asks the author of *White Feminism*. 'No', the author replies. Why keep talking about feminism at all then? Why assume that to 'acknowledge a spectrum of marginalised genders', which Beck sees as important and which is a salient struggle of recognition of our times, must stand in conflict with retaining women as feminism's *political* subject?[24] Does this assumption not undermine trans women's place *as women* in feminism and does it not run against Sojourner Truth's question 'Ain't I a woman?' as a definitive lesson around labour for feminism?

Even if feminism for the 99 percent suggested that feminism was of benefit to the 99 percent of society, a political subject would continue to be needed. A most useful clarification made by legal theorist Kimberlé W. Crenshaw, who coined the term 'intersectionality' around 1990, was: 'One version of antiessentialism, embodying what might be called the vulgarized social construction thesis, is that since all categories are socially constructed, there is no such thing as, say, Blacks or women, and thus it makes no sense to continue reproducing those categories by organizing around them'.[25] Feminism posits a potential collectivity challenged not by differences among women but by the fact that capitalism requires that women exploit women through the class relation extending to imperialism. Moreover, in the capitalist organisation of social reproduction and production, women are overall exploited as a *social group*: it is their cumulative social reproductive labour and their ushering into part-time employment that counts for capitalism. Yet it has been easy to lose sight of all this where ideology constantly hides from view the question of labour and women as classed subjects.

Despite the sidelining, and at times vanquishing, of references to women and class, it is impossible to understand feminist demands if we do not think of class as gendered. To give art-related examples: in nineteenth-century Greece, a new nation-state where a modern class structure was forming under the supervision of the then Great (imperialist) Powers, feminists' emphasis on women's access to the profession of artist was a call to expand the incredibly limited pool of 'respectable' jobs and income for educated women.[26] The reason was that the gender norms attached to their sex (as they saw it) made their class position precarious. Women's class position emanated from that of the man they were attached to: absence of a man could mean *déclassement* — loss of their class position — as in the case of widows. In Britain, Emily Osborn's 1857 painting, *Nameless and Friendless. 'The rich man's wealth is his strong city, the destruction of the poor is their poverty' (Proverbs: 10:15)*, exhibited in Tate Britain's *Now You See Us: Women Artists in Britain 1520–1920* (2024), showed a modestly dressed woman artist, accompanied by her young brother, trying to sell her work to a male dealer in his shop. In this realist painting, the woman's expression shows that she expects to fail. The painting's caption noted 'the difficulties faced by women artists' and that 'Osborn shows a young woman offering a painting to a sceptical dealer. With no reputation ["Nameless"] and no connections ["Friendless"], she has little chance of a sale'. But connections were, and are, absolutely determined by class. Does the story end there? No. As the same exhibition showed, that upper social strata women could be seen as 'professionals' rather than 'amateurs' was itself a problem: entering the world of labour appeared as a problem to their husbands, families, and society. Financial independence through remunerated labour might undermine how women were classed (through dependency on men's class position). Financial independence through labour might generate a different conception of labour and women that would be diffused across society, challenging women's subordination to the demands of social reproduction as something that all women should aspire to. After all, many women had paid employment since the working-class man's wage could often not support a family: 'the image of the angel in the house, the domestic Goddess of Victorian domestic ideology, was something that those living in the slums of the East End could only dream of'.[27] Working-class women should keep dreaming that dream as much as possible. If not, they could pose a real threat to the reproduction of the social order: as Arruzza states, 'the first feminist wave — in the last decades of the 19th and early 20th centuries — took place within the process of birth and consolidation of the workers' movement' and 'claimed the full realization of the universalist promise proper to both democratic liberalism and socialism by agitating around the slogan of equality: equality of capabilities and rights'.[28] This is a historical knowledge that contemporary feminism must recover to challenge notions of art's exceptionalism within the capitalist economy: even if artworks are not made so as to generate capital's surplus, they are produced by social beings living through the relationship of remunerated labour and unwaged work. Can we understand how the current art field, feminised in terms of numbers, is exploitative if this relationship is occluded?

In the turbulent 2010s, the rise of the IWS enabled questions such as this as an expression of feminism's return to questions of work; the term social reproduction was accorded central status in the Marxist feminist art theory of the decade. But at the same time, in referring to a feminism for the 99 percent, the IWS could not altogether evade the ideological determinations of its moment in history, even as it attempted to overcome the 'cultural turn' that had dominated the last quarter of the twentieth century — that is, the doxa that what matters are 'identities rather than interests, volition rather than capacities, perception rather than economic facts'.[29] The entwinement of class, racialisation, gender–sex at the emergence of feminism is multi-dimensional, but picking up this thread in relation to feminism in the 2010s must begin from an awareness of ideology's central role in *what* feminist demands are formulated, and *how*. The centrality of work in both corporate and anticapitalist feminism indicates that work is mired in ideology. Lean-in feminism might see nineteenth-century feminists fighting to be able to become professional artists as the epitome of celebrated individuality, possibly even as precursors of corporate feminism's emphasis on individual success. Why nineteenth-century educated women were so attached to their class position would not come in. A rejection of neoliberal feminism must also begin from the latter's reduction of feminism to a short-term project of instant gratification rather than a trans-generational struggle in the course of which feminists might learn from their own history. Instant gratification characterises a modern subjectivity shaped through the proliferation of (material and immaterial) commodities and, consequently, a social hierarchy and sense of self-worth based, one way or another, on spending power, as seen in Chapter One.

If in the late 2010s, the IWS indicated the *possibility* for a global synthesis of feminist demands into a transformative social cause that is necessarily set against individualism as capital's pervasive ideology, we should note that a possibility is precisely *not* an actuality. In the pandemic-defined early 2020s, despite protests taking place on International Women's Day, the IWS seemed to have lost its momentum. Taking a broader look, no transnational women's strike has so far managed to forcefully impact the capitalist system. Does this mean that women do not largely see themselves as a social group exploited through production and reproduction? Some women's ideological alignment with their own oppression is particularly notable. In 2018 'as a response to… the emergence of the #MeToo movement, a group of one hundred women, mostly high-profile professionals from the fields of art and culture, argued in favor of the male "freedom to disturb"… as "indispensable for sexual freedom"'.[30] In this we have a clear example of women who come to uphold their oppression in ways that affirm predatory hetero-masculinity. This is not unconnected to the normalisation of violence against women; 'the *first* systematic review of reviews to synthesize a fragmented evidence base from specific reviews of interventions to prevent and reduce VAWG [violence against women and girls]' was not published until 2014, and focused on the Global North.[31] Although the 'Lessons Learned' section of the World Bank-commissioned study does not mention this, the chief lesson to be learned is that in the twenty-first century an overwhelming amount of violence is needed to keep women subjugated. This is a universal fact, a totality of numerous permutations, which is partly why arguments about women making the choice to 'lean in' — to participate and affirm the social relations that capitalism organises — must be exposed as an outcome of subjectivation through hegemonic ideology. Against a socio-economic system that tends to totalise women's oppression and exploitation, feminism has achieved something less than unity. Once more: why?

FRAGMENTATION I: ON FEMINISM AS PERSONAL CHOICE (WHICH ONE MAY NOT MAKE)

The move from feminism to *feminisms* is now a staple of contemporary feminist politics. In terms of art, the word appears in exhibition titles such as *Global Feminisms* (2007, USA) and book titles such as *Feminisms Is still Our Name: Seven Essays on Historiography and Curatorial Practices* (2010).[32] Whether there can be a plurality of feminisms is complex: on the one hand, such plurality appears democratic but, on the other, it turns feminism into a nebulous cause emptied of political criteria. Whether 'feminisms' represents different understandings of key concepts and posits competing rather than aligned endpoints of liberation is an issue in its own right. Although towards the end of the twentieth century it became fashionable to talk about feminisms (plural), seeing feminism (singular) rather as an ideologically divided field introduces questions about how a social movement or political cause becomes shaped by socio-economic forces.

One such question relates to how this ideologically divided field is related to historically generated material divides among women, meaning there is no straightforward correspondence between adverse material conditions and feminist consciousness. That is, women of the working class do not necessarily display an anticapitalist or socialist feminist consciousness and being lesbian does not necessarily prevent one from endorsing authoritarian, patriotic (of the *pater*), populist conservatism. In 2017, a headline read: 'Germany's far-right AfD picks lesbian leader for election campaign';[33] that was former investment banker Alice Weibel, but the headline disregards this lesbian's class position. Women joined fascism in the interwar period as much as they support it today. If the founder of British Fascisti was Rotha Lintorn-Orman, a restless, apparently 'mannish', upper-middle class woman, not prepared to live a quiet, domestic life, Greece's neo-Nazi party Golden Dawn recruited among ordinary, working-class women, and female workers in retail are big fans of France's far-right party Front National.[34] How what Chandra Talpade Mohanty calls a 'ladder of privilege' plays out in specific contexts,[35] forming political subjects, is rarely transparent. What follows is an example drawn from my personal involvement in the arts.

In September 2008, as the global financial crisis was exploding, I contributed to a participatory performance during *The Privilege Walk/Symposium: Feminist and Intersectional Aspects of Contemporary Art* weekend in Malmö, organised by The Yes! Association art collective, founded in 2005 in Sweden. Participants were all women, so that privilege could show in relation to this gender. We all had to stand next to each other in a line and answer mentally (and honestly) a series of questions asked aloud by the artists. If one answered 'yes' one could take a step forward; a 'no' meant you stood still. In short, we were taking part in a race to the top portrayed as the front. The person who came first was white and identified as a lesbian from Sweden; the second most privileged person was me. I was puzzled: how was it possible that a South European woman from a family with no 'connections' and two low-waged parents, who had to migrate to get a job in her field, stood out as privileged? Yet, by 2008, labour mobility (read: migration) in art-related professions was ingrained in our consciousness. No question asked: 'Did you have to migrate for economic reasons?' or 'Did labour mobility take you to a national economy whose wealth and thus better labour market was the outcome of imperialism?' The questions, that is, were already ideologically constituted by capital's demand for selective labour mobility.

However, other questions asked by the artists did point to my privilege: I had benefited from such things as: tuition-free university, as neoliberalism was less dominant in 1980s Greece; a buoyant feminist movement during my childhood and adolescence and therefore an open-minded milieu; as well as formal changes in family law and secondary education that both feminism and capital's need for more skilled workers had enabled (my 'good' state-run secondary school admitted only boys until 1981). The question that would have revealed my greatest privilege was not asked: above all, my privilege was that my mother had delegated social reproduction tasks to her mother so that our nuclear-yet-expanded family unit could benefit from the double parental wage. My class privilege was based on having my illiterate working-class grandmother (who had raised her own children alone in getting whatever unskilled manual labour she could) provide unwaged care labour well into her old age. Capitalism's promise of upward social mobility is seldom free from the fundamentals of gendered exploitation that familial ideology hides.

Further notes can be made. Although privileges are structural, based on a range of socio-economic relations, the Malmö performance demonstrated that in a race to the top (for us, to the front) they appear as individual rewards. The performance was successful in showing this. Despite the artists' intentions, however, one felt pride rather than shame at having won the race. The race — the principle of competition — was where inequality among women translated into individual achievement or non-achievement, and the race was all that was available to us: there was no outside to the race, in the context of which even feminism became a privilege from which *one* could benefit. This is a general trend. Often today one's relationship to feminism is established as an outcome of self-assessment: do I need feminism, and which one? Which feminism addresses my identity/circumstances best? Is the feminism that I need available, and if not, can I invent one that suits me? Second-wave feminism's rallying cry that 'the personal is political' was not enough to prevent the depoliticisation of feminism into requests for atomised privilege that certain contexts confer while others do not.

The depoliticisation of feminism as personal choice means that one may *not* make the choice. For in this ideological context of individual success or failure, if you accept that you need feminism, you also admit to having been victimised by the circumstances of your life (scripted as choices). Such knowledge is hardly ever desirable. The issue of differences among women, flagged up in the art field, carries substantial value when it helps outline the complexity, variability, and asymmetry of oppression. But if led to feel personally victimised rather than oppressed as part of a collective social subject, the 'differences' approach risks generating an adjustable feminism at best — and, at worst, a refusal to let your own life be used as empirical evidence for someone else's idea of a 'better' society. In an effort to avoid being identified as a victim of sexism, a woman may well choose to collude with sexist or misogynistic values — even to fully embrace them, as seen in the example of women affirming entitled hetero-masculinity in France.

The notion of aesthetic labour as part of beauty politics delivers this disdain for being scripted as victim and an ideological attachment to remaining within the community of capital and its (gendered) values:

> in this moment of ubiquitous photography, social media, and 360-degree surveillance, women are increasingly required to be 'aesthetic entrepreneurs', maintaining a constant state of vigilance about their appearance… this work is not just on the surface of bodies, but requires a transformation of subjectivity itself, characterised by notions of personal choice, risk-taking, self-management, and individual responsibility.[36]

Personal choice, risk-taking, self-management, and individual responsibility are general traits of neoliberalism as hegemonic ideology and thus a deepening of capital's domination, underwriting the idea that one's body can be the site of one's business. Choosing to be a feminist may clash with the business you want to *be* (rather than just *have*). Choosing feminism might victimise you: this is what lean-in feminism addressed and why it gained traction as an articulation of positive thinking. Going against the impetus to draw affirmation through capital as a social relation may require conscious alienation, which is extremely hard to practise. Such alienation is not that which arises from the non-fulfilment of goals; nor is it the alienation that, for Marxists, the worker experiences in seeing the fruits of her labour being appropriated by capital. By 'conscious alienation' I refer to a deliberate process of estrangement from things that reproduce, usually in subtle ways, the consensus of our participation in social norms: giving up such 'things' tends to be experienced negatively, as loss, by the subject in the conditions of strong atomisation that characterise contemporary societies. We need therefore to differentiate between experiences of 'losing' and 'gaining' in relation to feminist struggles, and examine to what extent the perception of losing or gaining is shaped by hegemonic ideology and our socialisation.

Women's access to jobs and financial independence, as much as to the vote in earlier times, was experienced positively — precisely as gaining rather than losing something, and so was widely embraced.

In many cases, struggles associated with gaining concern access to what a dominant social group already has and the inferiorised group does not; this may leave little room for the oppressed/inferiorised group to consider the formulation of a programmatic radical critique of what the dominant group has, or to see this dominant group as already hierarchically differentiated within itself: most male artists are also 'unsuccessful', but feminism has paid less attention to why this is the case. The hardest part of feminist struggle comes when giving up aspects of life and values that are socially prized. Is, however, a transformative feminist politics, in art as much as elsewhere, possible without giving up what extends our consent to the existing order of things — that is, without being prepared to face a degree of painful alienation from what already constitutes us? The challenge for contemporary feminism is how to make acceptable a political demand for *collectively* executed rather than personally enacted alienation, a collective rather than personal giving up, a challenge that the chapter's concluding section addresses.

FRAGMENTATION II: ON FEMINISM AS IDENTITY POLITICS

The pluralisation of feminism into feminisms should not be associated exclusively with the depoliticisation of feminism as personal circumstances and choice; rather, such pluralisation also denoted a political solution at a time when 'difference' and 'diversity' carried hopes for democracy as a flat horizon of co-existence where subjects could learn to respect their antagonistic positions as the best of possible worlds. This was a form of democracy suited especially to economic inequality: democracy without the threat of revolutionary praxis but with enough emphasis on 'participation' and 'representation'. It was the trend of an era: the era that, in art and culture, became associated with postmodernism — a term inevitably present when considering feminism and ideology, and one that will also appear later in the book.

Defining contemporary art and theory, postmodernism became the hegemonic paradigm for over two decades (1970s to mid-1990s) — in the West and sometimes beyond — generating a voluminous body of writing. Pace Fredric Jameson, postmodernism arose as 'the cultural logic of *late* capitalism' — capitalism's advanced stage after World War II. Besides its obvious meaning, Jameson's definition entailed a second one: that social life and subjectivity started being explained in cultural terms, deflecting attention from the economy.[37] Discussion of the economy was jettisoned as 'economic reduction- ism' (another expression of the 'class reductionism' accusation long levelled at Marxism). However, postmodernism was not devoid of political meaning, as some of its detractors believed. Postmodernism's repudiation of large-scale social visions and explanatory frame- works that connected the dots known as 'metanarratives' was itself political enough. More than that, presenting the prospect of universal emancipation as a myth, postmodernism oversaw the strong particu- larisation of social struggles. The desire for universal emancipation was a delusion of a past modernity; the prefix 'post' signalled the abandonment of this supposed delusion.

As such, feminism could not be a metanarrative about women's oppression and exploitation that would explore and seek to undo what divided women. Rather, its epistemologies would be about 'situated knowledges', as Donna Haraway famously put it in 1988.[38] Central to all this was the very real 'problem of speaking for others',[39] high- lighting that oppressed and inferiorised subjects are always concrete and should develop their own political consciousness on the grounds of this concreteness rather than being spoken for. Yet both the actual antagonisms within capitalism and the ideology of particularism led to a debilitating turn, prompting constant splintering and, at times, a sectarian mindset (this was also when the Western communist left was splicing into smaller parties and groupuscules, in the context of the breakdown of labour struggles). It was this mindset that the IWS narrative about a feminism for the 99 percent attempted to overcome in connoting the rise of a feminist multitude, but it proved difficult, to say the least.

Looking at an example from the art context, as greater contact developed between the former Eastern bloc and West European art histories post-1989, the provenance of feminist art historians came to matter much more. Feminist art historians principally represented a geographical location rather than, say, clustering around an adopted epistemological framework. Obtaining a view on gender and art from Eastern Europe required 'embedded' experience and local knowledge that outsiders lacked, as the curatorial project *Gender Check: Femi- ninity and Masculinity in the Art of Eastern Europe* argued in 2010.[40] No doubt this reflected a resistance to the very real cultural imperialism of Western art history, but it was also an externalisation of global capitalism's geopolitical tensions onto a political discourse about knowledge (feminist art history).

The implicit question 'who has the right to speak for whom?' was not new: we encounter it, for example, around the time of the October Revolution in the early twentieth century and the fear that feminism was about 'ladies' uniting with their 'maids' in ways that, as female socialist revolutionaries observed, would maintain the very class system that exploited the 'maids' and allowed 'ladies' to exist.[41] In that case, however, the issue was understood not in terms of difference but interests attached to women in *classed* societies which, for the revolutionaries, could be abolished; the rupture of the revolutionary process would not preclude those transformed through it to rise in solidarity with working-class and peasant women, many of them illiterate. With postmodernism, however, the possibility of standing in solidarity was shaken. In the early 1990s, Linda Alcoff noted:

> In feminist magazines such as *Sojourner*, it is common to find articles and letters in which the author states that *she can only speak for herself*. In her important paper, 'Dyke Methods', Joyce Trebilcot offers a philosophical articulation of this view. She renounces for herself *the practice of speaking for others within a lesbian feminist community*, arguing that she 'will not try to get other wimmin to accept my beliefs in place of their own' on the grounds that to do so would be to practice a kind of discursive coercion and even a violence.[42]

The problem of speaking *for* others elided the possibility of speaking *with* others. And so, as the problem of speaking for others arose within feminism as politics, the response was a particular/ist interpretation of 'the personal is political': my personal is political for me, if I say so, and you should find your own strictly personal political voice that may be impossible to share. In this state of affairs, assumptions of authenticity could easily turn to assumptions about uniqueness, in an affirmation of capitalism's best-selling idea: individual self-realisation.

Indeed, capitalism has long privileged the individual author of one's life with exclusive copyright on the narrative and its meaning. Contrary to the still prevailing view of postmodernism (seemingly against authorial intent), the sectarian impulse of postmodernism ultimately expanded the remit of singularisation. At the same time, the new authorships did not seem to matter much: it did not escape feminists' attention that as marginalised subjects were claiming the right to be authors, Roland Barthes was writing 'The Death of the Author' (1967). A reader mainly fashioned as consumer would be the source of the text's meaning. Postmodernism thus had its own contradictions. For all its rhetoric of 'destabilisation', 'unfixity', 'decentered subjects' — prevalent in feminist art theory and theory in general in the 1980s and early 1990s — postmodernism came very close to merely adding new atomised subjects to the old position available: the I. Postmodern feminism thus became a discourse where the specificity of women's experiences (or perhaps, *a* woman's experience?) was effectively weaponised against both a politics of feminist solidarity *and* efforts to keep the class antagonism in sight. Hence, feminism conveniently, and perhaps politely, fractured into feminisms, in spite of divide-and-conquer being a long-term strategy of governance for any ruling bloc. Significantly, postmodernism celebrated the refusal of unity, essentialising it as necessarily oppressive (all contemporary extensions of postmodernism still do).

The pluralisation of feminism as feminisms was patterned on the bourgeois/liberal interpretation of democracy as mere representation of diversity, which is what identity politics affirmed. Thus, a semblance of social peace, necessary to bourgeois/liberal democracy, would be maintained through the right to express oneself. In this social calm, disconnected processes of contextual and fragile micro-empowerment would supress awareness of class power. Mass action becomes difficult, of course, when feminist constituencies have agreed to just differ rather than enter into careful argumentation around the social truth of each position in a totality that connects them. In the even greater challenges of the 2020s, feminists would not even agree to differ and the route of identity politics would lead to the feminist search of enemies *within* feminism, giving us 'enemy feminisms'.[43] This twist of the plot shows the precariousness of inclusivity that stumbles against the logic of identifying internal enemies. This ideology does not practise dialectical thinking: it would prevent me from seeing a working-class Black woman joining the police as an outcome of socio-economic contradictions that exceed her. I would not see that the policewoman is herself ideologically constituted by hegemonic values and, crucially, that she does not own the means of production (women of the capitalist class don't become police-women). I would see *her* as an enemy rather than the institution of the monopoly of legal violence she enters in service of the capitalist state. I would thus transfer onto her my justified hatred of the police. And in doing so, I would become the carrier of the contradictions that cannot be resolved 'in practice', exactly as Marx argued.

Fragmenting feminism into demands attached to discrete groups without re-introducing them into the counter-public sphere of a shared struggle bears some resemblance to the task of an advertising agency seeking to identify consumer groups. Indeed, postmodernism is very much identified with 'consumer society'.[44] In this consumer society, which rested and rests on the promise of becoming through commodities, a politics of identity could function as a counterforce. Consumer society sold the idea of finding your identity in lifestyle and conspicuous consumption and was 'bad postmodernism'. Identity politics problematised belonging, argued that some identities are visible while others could become so, implying a connection between identity, choice, and the destabilisation of oppressive norms, and functioned as 'good postmodernism'.[45]

Going a bit further, we could look at the shift from feminism to feminisms in relation to the transition from Fordism to post-Fordism — from mass to flexible production — which defined late twentieth-century capitalism: 'This shift brought a change in how feminism was viewed from a consumption standpoint. Rather than being viewed as a mass feminism to be served by mass consumption, women began to be viewed as different groups pursuing different goals that could be better served with small batches of specialized politics'. This is a fictitious quote. The real quote, from Wikipedia in 2017, describes the key changes from Fordism to post-Fordism, but only four words had to be substituted in the fake quote: 'Production' was replaced with 'consumption', 'market' was replaced by 'feminism', 'consumers' by 'women', and 'goods' by 'politics'.[46] The quote I made up serves to show that the edifice of ideas that inform our politics is far from unconnected to capitalism's organisation of production and the concepts that must be naturalised for any change therein to become normative. Marxist art history has already pointed out that such a process is integral to art. In *Working Aesthetics: Labour, Art and Capitalism* (2019), Danielle Child examined shifts in artmaking that corresponded to shifts in capitalist production. Or, as art critic Ben Davis reminds us about a topic salient in the art history of the twentieth and twenty-first centuries, 'locating "bourgeois" values with either authored or unauthored work is futile. Both tendencies exist within capital, which on the one hand transforms everything into equally exchangeable units, but on the other reintroduces distinction in the hunt for the kinds of "monopoly rents" that only unique status symbols can provide'[47] — with art being one such symbol.

The field of social-movement politics can then change in tandem with the organisation of production: the latter is accompanied by specific values and ways of thinking that increase in circulation through their social refraction — becoming ideology. This is what makes it hard to determine whether the fragmentation of feminism into feminisms should, after all, be seen as a consciously adopted political strategy responding to the very real material divides among women or an expression of the zeitgeist, essentially surrendering to capital as a social relation. What is certain is that the tendency to fragmentation, reconceptualised positively as pluralisation, has been an outcome of historical forces that did not only apply to women's struggles but rather encompassed them.

The circumvention of feminism by the logic of consumer culture did not just happen in the late twentieth century. In discussing the perversion of feminism by corporate marketing in Lean In circles, Faludi notes that the appropriation of feminism by capitalism goes back to at least the 1920s. Concluding with a world-shaking capitalist crisis in 1929 (the Great Depression), the 1920s was a decisive decade. It opened with the description of communism by Lenin as Soviet power plus electrification, while on the other side of the Atlantic capitalism was electricity plus consumerism. If the Soviet Union was a revolution against the class system, the American advertising sector appealed to feminism as a revolution for the 'middle classes' to be realised through household technologies. This demeaning parody of the very idea of revolution has been a staple of the light-hearted consumer society. Faludi presents examples: '"Enjoy 'positive agitation' at home", Hoover vacuum ads entreated, "with the new machine's 'revolutionary cleaning principle."' Or: '"Woman suffrage made the American woman the political equal of her man," General Electric cheered.' Faludi concludes:

Women's quest for social and economic freedom had been reenacted as farce. The rising new forces of consumer manipulation — mass media, mass entertainment, national advertising, the fashion and beauty industries, popular psychology — all seized upon women's yearnings for independence and equality and redirected them to the marketplace. Over and over, mass merchandisers promised women an ersatz version of emancipation, the fulfillment of individual, and aspirational, desire. Why mount a collective protest against the exploitations of the workplace when it was so much more gratifying — not to mention easier — to advance yourself (and only yourself) by shopping for 'liberating' products that expressed your 'individuality' and signaled your (seemingly) elevated class status?[48]

This memory did not enter postmodern feminism's eclectic approach to history. The farce that Faludi describes occurred again in the 1980s, when American corporations admitted tiny numbers of qualified women into their upper ranks while masses of women were kept in low-paid clerical labour with no prospects of advancement.[49] In the pre-internet 1980s, as the world's greatest capitalist ideology-dispenser, Hollywood both lied and told the truth about women's corporate lives in easy-going films such as *Working Girl,* released in 1988, the same year as Haraway's idea of 'situated knowledges'. In the film, a low-paid female secretary takes the place of her highly-paid female boss, presented as the ultimate achievement for a woman. In the 1990s, the farce continued with postfeminism in art being associated with young women artists representing 'babe power'.[50] And in the 2020s, the farce goes on, with feminism translated into self-care in cosmetics ads that visualise the ideology of becoming-who-you-really-are, attaching self-determination to spending power.

Regarding the visual economy of neoliberal feminism in particular, the Lean In website set the trend. Diversity, manifest as skin colour and the occasional hijab, is essential. Later, the word allyship also appeared as an add-on to personal empowerment: to succeed, a woman should have allies in the office or in the family ('How to be a feminist dad', an article on the website read in 2023).[51] In 2024, allyship was promoted as a mentoring programme in corporate contexts, advertised as 'rooted in *intersectional* research'.[52] Why not? After all, despite the immense popularity of intersectionality on the left, Crenshaw herself stated in 1991 that intersectionality was 'a provisional concept linking contemporary politics with postmodern theory'.[53] Given Crenshaw's soft critique of identity politics (seen earlier), the intent to link intersectionality with postmodern theory might strike us as strange. Yet it is not; 'intersectionality' came about as a concrete concept long after the suppression of labour movements and when 'class' had become a provisional referent — if not entirely absent. Intersectionality did not cut ties with the identity trope, which is why it could be adopted by the capitalist firm, as indeed it was.

Initially developed to help Black women in the US challenge discrimination in firms and factories owned by capitalists, intersectionality did not advocate a politics of ending private ownership of the means of production. Crenshaw stated in 1989: 'Discrimination, like traffic through an intersection, may flow in one direction, and it may flow in another',[54] meaning towards gender or towards race, and that the intersection is what should matter. The spatial flatness of Crenshaw's metaphor should not be missed. It reveals that intersectionality, at least at the moment of its conceptualisation, was deeply tied to a postmodern way of seeing. Flatness was the signature quality of the postmodern spatial imaginary, widely noted in divergent theoretical expositions of postmodernism: we find it both in Jean Baudrillard's references to the prevalence in postmodernism of the flat map over the complexities of the physical territory and in Fredric Jameson's emphasis on the allure of the flat surface as an effect of the aesthetics of commodities as such. Art history and theory was well aware of all this, legal theory less so.

Lean-in feminism, seeking reform of the capitalist workplace, was the perfect context for embracing intersectionality. But for which workers? What was allyship about? In 2025 we read:

LeanIn.Org's new Allyship at Work program is designed to… empower employees to take meaningful action as allies. 94% of program participants feel more equipped to practice allyship and would recommend the program to a colleague. Find out why organizations like Adidas, Walmart, and WeWork are using the program and how you can bring it to your company.[55]

Adidas, a company reportedly hiring more women than men workers, has been in the spotlight for poverty pay. In 2023, it was the object of one of art group The Yes Men's staged performance-hoax interventions on corporate duplicity. Clean Clothes Campaign noted: 'The Yes Men hoax highlights the hypocrisy of adidas, a brand that portrays itself as invested in women's empowerment, while earning billions in revenue from the ongoing exploitation of women garment workers in production countries that lack adequate social protection systems'.[56]

A new visual culture of intersectionality has emerged. Its politics is confusing or rather shared. Photographs of groups of women signifying diversity (which is scripted as appearance using the familiar signifiers of multi-ethnic women, wheelchairs etc.) feature on the websites of the neoliberal university as proof of its commitment to inclusivity. Similarly 'inclusive' illustrations and photographs appear on left feminist websites, though here the women are joining protest rallies rather than becoming empowered as private capital's employees and student customers. Whether one likes it or not, then, through the visual culture of the internet, feminism as a revolt against the system is drawn into competition with feminism as underwriting the system, reduced to an option that might appeal to some consumers but not others. This is another totalising process that feminism in art must grapple with politically.

In studies of 'feminist visual activism',[57] we encounter analyses focused on embodiment and the body — a reference in feminist art and theory since the 1970s — where activisms, implicating a transnational setting, are connected with struggles extraneous to art. Mapping these activisms is perhaps the most important contribution of feminist art history to social knowledge today. But if 'disaster capitalism' is what necessitates these visual activisms, why are we left with 'multiple differing perspectives, often interlaced with one another, that decentre single narratives and address imbalances of power'?[58] Is the issue to decentre single narratives or *which* single narratives are being decentred? What does 'decentring' mean exactly? Feminist theory and image work has engaged little with the possibility of disrupting the visual cultures that emanate from what Jodi Dean has termed 'communicative capitalism'[59] and which re-affirms capitalism as social totality. Can these visual cultures be disrupted at all in privatised media and social media? Is the fact that Facebook/Meta is on the stock market and had a revenue of $164.5 billion in 2024 not enough to see how anyone's activities on the platform are centred by capital?

Returning to the question of the image in circulation in the environments of communicative capitalism, what is the ideological role of images of equal representation among women — what I would call diversity images — in a social reality of profound inequality among women? Do diversity images script an anti-realism that subdues the need to even grasp the social totality because they indicate that positive change as inclusion is already in progress? Or are they prefigurative images of a revolutionary collectivity of women? Does the meaning of diversity images depend on the context in which we encounter them, which would suggest that they somehow avoid being merely content circulating in communicative capitalism? Or should we think along the lines of feminist art historians who in the 1970s and 1980s argued that images of women in modern art signified not women but male creativity and say that, in the last instance, diversity images signify not women but the dynamism of capitalism?

Questions such as these are hard or even impossible to answer; yet posing them helps us come to terms with the fact that feminism is not exempted from the conditions that capital creates for its successful reproduction. For this reason, feminist art history must in the current moment address how women artists assist and even embody this reproduction, which relies on subtle affirmations of hegemonic ideology. In 2014, Amalia Ulman created a fictional social media persona and performed online for several months, mixing truth and irreality: she would actually diet but only pretended to have breast augmentation. She engaged viewers by displaying 'emotional content'. She 'garnered the support of other women who had endured similar makeovers or procedures', but also criticism for promoting 'retrograde physical ideals'. The performance, in other words, probed themes central to feminism. Titled *Excellences & Perfections*, and 'evok[ing] a consumerist fantasy lifestyle',[60] the performance has been understood as a critique of how women engage with social media. Who was the audience of this critique, if those actually following a woman's online life were led to believe it was real? What the duped public got was interaction with a woman in expensive lingerie and interiors (the mise-en-scène of the performance). The artwork's impact on the women who thought they were sharing experiences with the artist remains largely unknown. The performance simply stated its 'end' one day of September 2014. Who did the work benefit apart from anyone in the orbit of art's attention economy? If the convention of art's autonomy is upheld, Ulman had the choice to make a different artwork but opted to exploit social media's attention economy around femininity. The attention economy of social media entered art's attention economy and vice versa. Radiating through this inter-penetration was an ideological operation: Ulman's feminine persona was affirming the desire to be of a certain class — one which, like in the nineteenth century, still finds in the ornamental feminine on display its ideal realisation. Apparently, diversity images have not managed to displace such affirmation. And all the while, the artwork as carrier of hegemonic ideology that shapes desire *en masse* continues to clash with the autonomy principle (the freedom to say something unique, new, transformative) that makes artmaking so desirable to women.

PERFORMING SUBJECTS: WHO IS A FEMINIST?

The analysis so far suggests that today saying 'I am a feminist', whether in the art field or any other context, does not necessarily indicate a recognisable political engagement. When I say I am a feminist, what do I actually mean? The idea that the world is divided into territories that do or do not need feminism is still prevalent as a legacy of postfeminism: the perception, dominant in the West in the early 1990s, that feminism had achieved 'equality' and was therefore redundant. Already in 1975, Silvia Federici criticised the role of the United Nations in neutralising feminism's 'struggle and subversive potential' by institutionalising the movement as 'global feminism' in ways that make it compatible with neoliberalism at its genesis:[61] this is something we must reflect on 50 years later, if we wish to understand the choices made by the second wave, including feminism's institutional turn within the art field. The idea of 'global feminisms', which has also preoccupied feminists in the art field, can be invested with quite a different meaning to that indicated by the 99 percent claimed by IWS as an anticapitalist formation. In fact, it can mean the very opposite: a leaning into capitalist globalisation.

This state of play can be seen as a world of work, composed of visible and invisible zones. In terms of global capitalism this is a state of war: an economic war in which women also take part. Abuse is endemic in industries that employ women workers and there is a reason why a book titled *Global Woman* is subtitled 'Nannies, Maids, and Sex Workers in the New Economy' rather than 'Financiers, IT

Engineers, and Entrepreneurs'.[62] Could we imagine a Workingwomen's International in the era of the 'globalization of care'?[63] In the early twentieth century, women workers tried to organise internationally. International congresses were held as the first decade of the twentieth century was moving to the second, the tumultuous 1920s. The experiment was short-lived, with historians deeming the International Federation of Women Workers (IFWW) a 'failure'. Among the reasons for this failure we find not only the perceived clash between organising around gender and around class, not to mention disagreement about whether women and especially mothers should be protected in specific jobs or not, but also 'nationalism', with 'women committed to internationalism put[ting] a stronger and deeper loyalty to the land of their birth first'.[64] This is another example of the power of ideology, with nationalism being embedded in capitalist modernity and continuing into twenty-first-century globalisation. Today, nationalism continues to be deeply divisive for feminism, as it informs both national liberation struggles and imperialist aspirations, with the feminist imaginary often unable to proceed beyond arguments about a *transnational* feminism.

Meanwhile, 'feminism' is still a word greatly associated with the private sphere rather than with a critique of the *privatised*. Feminism in the popular press — which co-produces, justifies, makes meaningful the practices of the everyday — often amounts to little more than advice to women to stop being 'perfectionists'. In ideological terms, this advice is just one step above the one saying: stop wanting to have it all, make a choice. In my days on social media, the following quote appeared on my feed, posted by a 40-year old female friend who is a scientist and a mother in a Western high-income economy (having migrated from a Southern economy), and who found it hard to cope with it all:

> Can we draft a joint resolution to drop the crazy-making expectation that we must all be perfect friends and perfect mothers and perfect workers and perfect lovers with perfect bodies who dedicate ourselves to charity and grow our own organic vegetables, at the same time that we run corporations and stand on our heads while playing the guitar with our feet?[65]

The quote typifies how many women associated with the so-called middle class think about their lives: solidarity (friends), love ties (motherhood), waged labour (workers), sex (lovers), image (bodies), social cohesion (charity), ecology (organic vegetables), hope for upward mobility (running corporations), yoga (standing on heads), culture (guitar). All this is presented as a woman's private life: situations to which a woman offers a personal response and achieves personal success or failure. Perhaps the most troubling ideological collusion here is the suggestion to 'draft a joint resolution', as it appropriates collective action to essentially affirm that women consent to their identification as fully private beings.

This appeal to the collective in order to forge and legitimise the private is among the most successful ideological *détournement* tactics in neoliberalism's appropriation and distortion of feminism as 'personal politics'. If the formulation 'personal politics' strikes one as a contradiction in terms, it nonetheless has traction in societies where atomisation is embedded in the anti-totalitarian principle sustaining liberal democracy. This principle has lived beyond the 2010s, and in the 2020s is still being defended as the core of a 'healthy' capitalist civil society undermined by the rise of right-wing populism. We can expect that the political mainstream will continue to advocate a democracy of atomised citizens, and that democracy will be debased to being little more than civil liberties (increasingly jeopardised because of capitalism's authoritarian renaissance) as functions of the private individual.

For women who are the beneficiaries of earlier feminist struggles, the private is not limited to material spaces, such as those explored by feminist art historians in the 1970s and 1980s. The private is now a state of being that a woman carries wherever she is and in whatever she does. Internalised as ideology, the private mediates and organises the experience of social reality. My scientist friend who shared the quote advising women not to be perfectionists was fully qualified to grasp that different categories appear on its list in misleading equivalence, but she did not. In principle, she accepted that not being 'perfect' as a worker carries the same weight as not being 'perfect' when working out. After all, both are tied to atomised performance. Performing to your best, and eliminating what prevents you from doing so, is part of the ideological universe of 'self-management', of great purchase in the art field where freelancers abound, where an artist or curator must balance teaching for income and developing complex, original projects independently, and where youthful energy and creativity are marketed as assets. In the 1990s, when the so-called global art scene was emerging, artists — women included — could be grouped together and marketed precisely as young national subjects practising entrepreneurial self-management and representing a desirable market economy: this is what the formulation 'young British artists' captured.

In the context of socio-economic relations where we find the notorious gender pay gap and weak trade unions, equating the workplace and the gym is instrumental in discouraging women from developing consciousness as labouring subjects. Equating the workplace and the gym fulfils an important ideological requirement: a chain of human activity is subsumed to the logic of being abstractly productive and self-disciplined. The neutralising equivalence of different kinds of 'production' (labour outputs, the ideal body, networks, and so on) permeates contemporary social consciousness, as well as artistic and curatorial projects: the Athens Biennial of 2018, titled ANTI, referred to 'the realms mostly shaping our lives today: from gym to online forum, from church to airport security area, from shopping mall to sex dungeon'.[66] The biennial's critics pointed out that the list betrays the class affinity of art-world liberalism while, increasingly, such equating might also apply to political positions (in 2018, there were fears about platforming the alt-right).[67] We see, then, that what impacts women's lives and may be posited as a specifically feminist issue can emanate from a broader hegemonic ideology. In pursuing a critique of capitalism, should feminism seek then to differentiate between women's lives and women's work? Or should feminism accept that women's lives and work are intertwined into a whole permeated by the ideology of total production in its service to 24/7 accumulation,[68] as art historian Jonathan Crary argued about everyone's time back in 2013? In the twenty-first century, making art is interwoven with the flows of total production: the life of the artist rather than her 'artworks' is where the claim to artistic identity is made. As we will see in the concluding section, feminists of the second wave did raise the question of the distinction and relationship of art and life.

ART AS IDEOLOGY AND THE DIFFICULTY OF EXIT:
BEING A FEMINIST LIKE CARLA LONZI

Carla Lonzi (1931–82) was an Italian feminist who used to be an art critic; she eventually felt that being a feminist was incompatible with being in the art world. For a long time, Lonzi did not feature in the anglophone literature on art and feminism. This has changed as an outcome of recent work in feminist art history, along with art's increased interest in labour, as well as in 'practices of refusal' after the 2008 global financial crisis. Refusal, you may ask, of what? Specifying the object of refusal is often left open to the imagination but, broadly, refusal refers to non-participation in the mechanisms sustaining the status quo.

In 2013, artist duo Claire Fontaine whose work explores the strike. beyond sites of industrial production, and operating with she/her pronouns in defiance of the art world's persistent devaluation of female labour, published a piece in an influential anglophone journal on Lonzi's significance for contemporary articulations of opposi- tional politics.[69] In 2015, an exhibition on Lonzi opened in Lisbon, co-curated by Giovanna Zapperi, whose research has been central to introducing contemporary feminism to the issues raised by Lonzi's defection from the art world.[70] In these reclamations of Lonzi, we already see a dilemma that many feminists face today: to make available an instance of feminist disruptiveness (even of refusal) as feminist knowledge may well require dissemination through the available channels and structures of participation and therefore affir- mation of the art field we have. Claire Fontaine's article on Lonzi as an arts professional who rejected the art field was published in *e-flux journal*, part of a complex enterprise (e-flux) established in 1999 where artmaking, theory, and business communication come together — a configuration or 'an economy of circulation', as co-founder and artist Anton Vidokle put it.[71] If we see that there might be a conflict or tension in the fact of an exhibition by a contemporary feminist art historian about a feminist who chose to leave art for her feminism, this indicates that art-world structures do exist. Contrary to the wide- spread belief that everything is possible in a free capitalist society and thus its art choices tend to be predictable carla restrictive. Observing the limits of feminist acting on and in the social (feminist 'praxis') is not the last but rather the first word on the matter: it is the point of departure for understanding the material basis of ideology as the habitual behaviour that produces us as subjects — including as writers, artists, grassroots activists.

Here, I want to consider the threat that Lonzi might still represent, as well as the limits of this threat, and ask whether certain acts may indeed constitute a legacy that exceeds the parameters of becoming mere content in the circuits of communicative capitalism. Lonzi was not a friend of Marxism, though she was involved with Marxist activism as a student.[72] Possibly she found that the Marxist men she knew were dismissive of feminism. In her fierce 1977 pamphlet, *Let's Spit on Hegel*, she frames what followed Marx and Engels's writings as a distortion of their radical take, especially on the family. The pamphlet represents radical feminism's frustration with a male-dominated left in the 1970s that trivialised women's oppression as a problem that a revolution would automatically solve. To Lonzi, writing during the Cold War, the Soviet Union's fate told otherwise ('the family has remained untouched by the socialization of the means of production'), while the prospect of nuclear annihilation led her to see war as the outcome of an inherent and transhistorical (if worsening) aspect of the male psyche. In the same pamphlet, Lonzi also argues for a feminism unconvinced about the conceptual usefulness of equality and inclusion, averring that 'equality is what is offered as legal rights to colonized people' and asking: 'But do we, after thousands of years, really wish for inclusion, on these terms, in a world planned by others?'[73] Lonzi exercised admirable foresight in perceiving that the status quo would be sustained under the flag of inclusivity and would use on-paper equality to pacify women.

Despite Lonzi not targeting capitalism (at least not exclusively or consistently) in her writings, I see her critique as seeking to eradicate the distinction between life and work in a way that inverts how capitalism currently strives to erode this distinction. If capitalism benefits from the blurring of life and work into a regime of total production from which capital can reap harvest, Lonzi wanted to be a feminist *all the time*. To do this, she had to leave both art (work) and her relationship with a male artist and some friends (life). For Claire Fontaine, Lonzi as 'a woman seeking freedom, and above all a politically creative subjectivity', posed a problem: 'The problem with her oeuvre, which is also a problem with her persona — the two cannot be dissociated — is that it fights a merciless battle against complicity with the existing culture, against the incomprehension that accompanies each social and professional recognition, beginning with Lonzi's own'. Where did this refusal of complicity come from?

Conceivably, Lonzi came to the realisation that the master's house cannot be dismantled with the master's tools, as Black radical feminist poet and theorist Audre Lorde would say in 1979,[74] and that this applies both to work (as legitimate public engagement) and life (as normalised private engagement). There was no third space, no other set of tools, apart from a constant, daily process of feminist disruption to conforming. In 1970, she co-founded Rivolta Femminile (Women's Revolt) in Rome as an all-women group.[75] Claire Fontaine stressed Lonzi's practice of thinking against herself, enacting an alienation from what she had been. Today, in the temporality of total production, such a stance can appear as futile heroism: capitalism is perceived as a prison of 'no outside' as Claire Fontaine's own artworks declare. A notable point made by Claire Fontaine concerns Lonzi's confrontation with the demand for women to perform across work and life:

> The attempt to perform in all of these fields can only lead to schizophrenia and solitude: the dream of being a militant, an intellectual, an accomplished person, a mother, and a spouse appears as pathetic and dangerous. This open secret needs to be told over and over again, because without a radical change of perspective, women won't truly have any other model for subjectivizing themselves — no matter how rebellious and anti-conformist they are, no matter what their sexual preferences are. In the preface to her journal, Lonzi gives her final word on the feminine skill of multitasking: 'For me, doing one thing has a value *because* it prevents me from doing two.'

The 'feminine skill of multitasking' was decried by second-wave feminism (in Greece, we've had pop songs about it since the 1980s), decades before the art field embarked on its critique of post-Fordism as a reorganising of the capitalist economy where precarity and so-called flexibility forced workers, and especially women, into the 'skill' of being constantly available and doing several things at once. In rejecting multitasking, Lonzi was rejecting the sad future of a non-revolutionary feminism where the conflict between women's participation in production and social reproduction would be lived out like Sisyphus' punishment in the underworld: stoicism, resilience, and perseverance marshalled for the arduous perpetuation of the same state of captivity.

Zapperi notes that Lonzi rejected institutionally produced knowledge, even when such knowledge would come to the aid of feminism. She rejected the university, an institution she associated principally with the suppression and containment of a potentially transformative radicalism claimed by women. This opens a chasm between her and the direction taken by most feminist artists and critics in the 1970s. Lonzi's interpretation of feminism not only did not lead her to support living women artists or to excavate the histories of dead ones so as to showcase them in museums and have their work acknowledged for its market value; for her, being an artist was to collude with patriarchy. Lonzi saw in art the corollary of a masculinist principle of division: art was separate from life. She perceived that this separation involved contempt: life was scorned as purposeless, messy, and deprived of a concrete, perfected output (the artwork) which was the result of directed labour. Translating this into contemporary debates, we can say that Lonzi sought to expose that art affirmed creativity as production in principle. Contrary to the Marxist view that sees art as unproductive for capital and thus possibly as unalienated labour (labour not formally subsumed to capitalist production, unlike making cars in a factory), for Lonzi art exemplified a pivotal alienation: from life as such. Etymologically, she was right: *arte* or art means that something is artificial, constructed, as opposed to something that is not. Seeing the binary, she chose art's opposite. In alienating herself from elevated art, Lonzi sought a disalienation from inferiorised life as the real matrix where revolutionary aspirations could take hold.

For Lonzi, art in the historical setup that she encountered and studied was de facto counter-revolutionary. Art was gendered *form* rather than just gendered *content*; the separation art glorified was de facto ideology: it covered the reality of domination and kept one from even perceiving the domination. Art was the will to master (as in 'masterpiece') rendered positive as autonomous creativity. If you were a feminist, the labour of art was the form of labour that subverted you: art forced the feminist to accept male domination and its ideological expression as the object of her desire too, for who becomes an artist because they are forced to? A feminist who desired to be in art was a feminist who has swallowed and learned to love the sword of patriarchy — and pulling out the sword could only be extremely painful, if it could actually happen. Artist Suzanne Santoro notes in 2019:

> In recent years, mostly women art historians… were finally asking questions about feminism and art in Italy. They were particularly interested in Carla Lonzi and why she had become a very radical feminist and stopped being an art critic. How could she do this? Many feminists said she was a traitor to women artists![76]

For Lonzi, being a woman artist was being a traitor to feminism as revolution.

What was wrong with art, according to Lonzi, was what Theodor W. Adorno and many others critical of capitalism saw as art's true radicalism: its *non-identity* with life — that is, a life completely enclosed within the vulgar production–consumption cycle that capital requires and the abstract domination that this installs. Lonzi's problem with art was not the elitism instituted at the moment that art emerged as privileged territory, rescued from the banality of life (from life as banality: full of bans, stoppages, prohibitions), but that art was structurally part of an edifice of pacified subjugation. Any emancipatory radicalism given to art would be wasted. Yet some men were seeing the same problem as Lonzi: the early twentieth-century revolutionary avant-garde's political aspiration to dissolve art into life was taken up in the 1960s by the programmatically anticapitalist Situationists who regarded art as alienation from life and, as Mikkel Bolt Rasmussen tells it, 'refused any contact with the art institution'.[77] In reading that 'few art historians have been able to uphold the Hegelian-Marxist philosophy of history to which… [the Situationists] subscribed',[78] we are left to wonder: how is it possible that Lonzi, who spat on Hegel and rejected Marxism, arrived at the same conclusion about art as a male-dominated group that embraced both Hegel and Marxism? We begin to see here the *necessarily* historical grounding of emancipatory politics: Lonzi and the Situationists, who acted in their European synchronicity, could only shape their radical ideas through their shared historically specific experience of art. Those aspects of the experience of art that radicalised the Situationists and Lonzi have intensified today. As Ben Davis observed in 2022, the politics of social justice in general are persistently managed by being pushed into art.[79] Drawing on Sinead Murphy's *The Art Kettle* (2012), Davis contends that the police strategy of 'kettling' in public demonstrations is transferred into culture, with art used to undermine the real-world momentum of political struggles.

Yet Lonzi's feminism demanded a radicalism that also targeted the private. The negation of art as the site for transformative politics did not justify, for Lonzi, an immersion in life in its recognisable form. Lonzi proceeded to cut the ties of normative intimacy: she rejected the actuality and idea of the 'couple' as a microcosm where the contradictions of the gendered capitalist social world are performed and internalised as inevitable, organising the 'normal' troubles of shared everydayness. Zapperi notes that *Vai Pure* (Now You Can Go, 1980) — the book-form document of Lonzi's dialogues with her male partner, sculptor Pietro Consagra, on their separation, the reasons for which had to be understood by both — suggests that Lonzi was embarking on a translation of the social critique presented in the *Manifesto of Rivolta Femminile* (1970) into private subjectivity and interpersonal relations. She writes: 'the manifesto's call for a rejection of competitive capitalist structures, including efficiency and labour in favour of free sexuality and non-productivity' was to be how 'the personal is political'.[80] In other words, the refusal of art was the negation of the personal/political binary as mediated by the compulsion to work.

Lonzi significantly upped the stakes of what being a feminist might mean, refuting the separation of public from private that allows many of us to engage in anti-conservative politics publicly while carrying on with our private lives in their degrees of conformity. Her rejection of the production of 'culture' would be incomplete without abandoning the consumption of intimacy — intimacy being where one retreats when confronted with the demands of production. She brought into question the notion of intimacy as the locus of rehumanisation and replenishment after work, indeed as the affective–sexual cradle of the renewal of labour-power. For most, this take on social reproduction is off limits, for what Lonzi experimented with was a withdrawal through which she was indeed hurting those she loved, including herself. In rejecting the intimacy of the couple-form, Lonzi was perhaps counting on the possibilities opened up by the surrounding feminist multitude of her times. But she was unable to go all the way, prevented by the material conditions of her own reproduction; it is unclear to what extent she maintained a financial dependency on the husband she left (with whom she had a child), and also perhaps especially on her partner after their feminist separation, and whether her rejection of multitasking drove her not to seek financial independence through paid employment.[81] Here we find another parallel with the Situationists, though inverted in terms of gender: the waged labour of novelist, critic, and Situationist Michelle Bernstein, also the first wife of prominent Situationist Guy Debord, led art historian Frances Stacey to declare Bernstein 'the hidden motor running the SI [the Situational International], its economic secret'.[82]

Instances of political refusal as a breach in hegemonic ideology encounter limits. We find these limits in the privatisation of social reproduction that capitalism enforces, articulated as economic dependency. In a tentative conclusion, it was the material basis of society, the economy, that undermined Lonzi's course to achieving feminist singularity through a feminist multitude and that ultimately enabled an alienating process only for herself, that is, for an individual subject. This does not diminish the contemporary value of Lonzi's extraordinary life as a political act, at the core of which is the questioning of feminism as such: what does it mean to practice feminism beyond compromise? It is hard to overcome conformism in a mode of production that intensely scripts economic subjects. How to undo a social totality that allows little more than (subsidised) dreams of freedom is the problem that persists.

3

Feminism in the Contradictions of the Capitalist Art Field

Research about art has been of marginal relevance to 'real' politics. Political parties do not prioritise art-based research in policy-making nor do trade unions consult such research. Insights from feminist art history and theory are rarely discussed in interdisciplinary contexts of feminist research (unless initiated within or by the art field). Indeed, feminist insights about art are commonly seen to concern the status of 'women artists', a grouping perceived to refer to privileged, educated women. It matters little that these insights are misinterpreted (second-wave feminism regarded 'women artists' as a political category, to begin with), for 'art' is ideologically legible mainly as a leisure or luxury pursuit: few would choose to fund art over funding a hospital, even as many visit art museums or contribute to art activities in their free time, if they have any. This is what allows the capitalist state to deliver art to capital's philanthropy. Art's attachment to autonomy brings it closer to 'the realm of freedom' than the 'realm of necessity'.[1] Art may be what is worth living for, but first one must remain alive. Despite the rise of socially engaged art — a constellation of practices flourishing since the 1990s as interventions in social problems — art is still understood as an ensemble of activities that prioritise aesthetic gratification, seen as removed from more pressing needs (and, for some, the political solutions these require). This perspective on art has had different purchase on the left and right, and this chapter opens with an admittedly schematic examination of these broad positions, as both illuminate what the problems with art are, building on the discussion that opened in the preceding chapter. This will help put into perspective the contradictions that feminism encounters in the art field, and that, I argue, should not be seen as particular to feminism.

POSITIONS ON ART AS DIFFERENT FROM LIFE:
ART AS REWARD, ART AS RESCUED

When it comes to the right (that I am here defining as a political position openly in favour of capitalism and competition), the idea that art is different from life is of evident usefulness: art is a reward of heightened enjoyment for those who can access it. What does 'access' mean here? Obviously, artworks can be accessed as luxury commodity and sound investment.[2] But this access is about something more than trade. The appreciation, and not just material ownership, of artworks was a class prerogative before the consolidation of capitalism, but the rise of the bourgeoisie gave it another spin: since in capitalist society everyone is free to compete in the market and can potentially achieve a better socio-economic status, art as enjoyment would be a reward (potentially equally) for anyone capable of self-improvement. This reward can be attained through upward social mobility, where the possibility of jumping to a higher class through education, hard work, and so on, has been capitalism's most attractive promise to the social body.

Collecting art, for example, became a marker of social distinction, cosmopolitanism, open-mindedness, and worthiness, and in that sense, it would be a mistake to stress the merely economic value of art for wealthy collectors, be they individuals or corporations. The enjoyment of art by those who cannot afford to own artworks is also a marker of distinction: as Pierre Bourdieu and others have shown since the 1960s, visiting an art museum denotes privilege scripted through class.[3] Yet Steve Garlick, in arguing that this classed enjoyment of art was 'distinctly feminine', posed the question of why gender has not received equal sociological attention as class.[4] Class and gender do not, however, exist in competition here. On the contrary, women of the upper classes embody the right to leisure that sustains access to art.

Complementary to the appreciation of art by the 'cultured', access to art spaces and art's enjoyment by 'the people' affirms capitalism as democratic, showing that the capitalist system works for society's overall benefit. This is why governments are keen on the metrics of art-space visitors or contributors. Of course, people visiting art spaces nowadays tend to post images of their visits on social media as 'self-display';[5] the hallmark of capitalist visual culture in the twenty-first century, self-display through technical images is evidence of leisure capability, first, and being cultured, second. This is of no concern to the right that believes democracy and access are a matter of numbers. Capitalism, the argument goes, has generated comfortable lifestyles for more (if not most) people, and it is these people who populate art museums and visit the planet's art biennials as art tourists, while 'outreach' art programmes and art education departments indicate that some people, perceived as 'disadvantaged', may need guidance and encouragement to encounter art. Some art museums have free entry, at least as regards their permanent collections, and a visit to temporary shows, where 'the new' either in curatorial or artistic imagination is tested, while not cheap is affordable and can cost less than a ticket to a football match or music festival.

And so, many can in principle visit art spaces. But not everyone does. Given the free or affordable entry, this implies that only some individuals are able or desire to do so. These individuals know how to behave in art spaces. They will not destroy or loot the artworks like the UK rioters who looted retail shops in 2013, or throw stuff at artworks in prestigious institutions as 'vulgar' environmental activists do in the 2020s to implicitly argue that saving the planet is in the realm of necessity.[6] The general expectation is that the people visiting museums won't touch the artworks or the artist-as-artwork — unless instructed to do so. Yoko Ono and Marina Abramovich are among the best-known creators of such artist-as-artwork performances, seen however to carry 'risk'. Making art publicly available should entail as little risk as possible; risk is reserved for the creative act, not consumption. In a 2022–23 exhibition of celebrated feminist artist Carolee Schneemann's work at the Barbican in London, just leaning towards an artwork would activate a sound barrier alerting visitors that they should step back. This policing-by-sound disrupted any (mis)perception about the feminist artist's work as belonging somehow to the public. Many art displays are guarded, implying that the public is potentially a threat (the institutional argument would be that the public itself needs protection from potential accidents); but in the Schneemann exhibition, the hi-tech sound barrier against anyone trespassing into the designated 'vital' space of the artworks contrasted sharply with the art institution's description of the artist as 'transgressive'.[7]

Those who visit art museums or any other exhibition space are aware of, and adhere to, a *savoire faire* underpinned by the dynamic that posits art as property; everything else about art comes second. The work of feminist artists gets exactly the same treatment by the art institution as befits an environment of property protection. Most importantly, when people leave art spaces, they are not expected to rebel in agitation inspired by the sometimes radical critique they have just been exposed to. Rather, they will return to their day, looking forward to the next challenge and intellectual/moral/aesthetic stimulation art can offer. This is how it works. For the right then, art does not just offer an opportunity for aesthetic enjoyment and a good investment. Besides these obvious benefits, the way art institutions function and appeal to the public separates artistic critique from political action, irrespective of an artwork's engagement with feminist or anticapitalist positions and/or activist efforts.

For the left (a politics questioning or rejecting capitalism unless forced or co-opted into partial, 'pragmatic' acceptance), the impetus to establish art as separate from life is different. The left's approach is defensive: given the banal world of commodities (objects and services sold to generate profit), given capital's instrumentalisation of what clutters the everyday, given the predicament of everything that is 'of use' (to be turned into something that is ultimately 'for exchange' for privatised wealth), it is best that art should state its non-identity with life — at least as we know it: life in and as capitalism. There is a rescue operation at work: what to be rescued, if possible, is art. A 2007 essay by Thierry de Duve looking at the fate of art in globalisation argued exactly that:[8] if we wish to preserve art as the embodiment of a value other than economic, we must not identify it with globalisation as an economic paradigm, but link it to Immanuel Kant's propositions from the eighteenth century about the (assumed/potential) universality of aesthetic judgements as a prefiguration of global peace. It is this universality that Carla Lonzi, with whom Chapter Two closed, specifically rejected as patterned on man's worldmaking. And yet, never before capitalist globalisation, with its internet, airplanes, and art tourism, was it possible for the aesthetic to come close to the universality craved since Kant.

De Duve does not just hold that art should not be identified with capitalist life, but that it should be separated from the workings of the art world, be it global, local, or 'glocal' (the context-dependent articulation of the global and local). This is because such workings (his example is art biennials, but we could compose a long list) are clearly part of the world of commodities, spectacle, circulation, and exchange-value. Art, he avers, should not be reduced to crass economic relations. Before De Duve, there was Theodor W. Adorno, whose widely discussed position was adequately complex: 'art is and is not being-for-itself'. Adorno accepted art's grounding in the social and empirical but placed the truth of the artwork in its form–content dialectic, in its independence as object. This object does not deserve an emotional response (coming from life) but a 'cognitive faculty of judging justly'.[9] In his 2013 clarification and defence of Adorno's position from a Marxist perspective, Jackson Petsche concludes: 'in the consortium of commodity images (and commodity forms) it becomes increasingly necessary to differentiate the work of art from the commodity if art is to have any promise for the future at all'.[10]

Positions that, one way or another, present art as the antithesis of capitalism's vulgarity, or as in need of protection from the latter, tend to be imbued with and instil a romantic voluntarism. Such disavowals allow the left to uphold art as one of the few sites where critical experimental imagination may not get crushed under market pressure. Today, however, the ideology of expanding markets seems to have completely fused with the politics of recognition that had once been termed 'good postmodernism'. In 2000, Nancy Fraser observed that globalisation's progressive discourses were substituting redistribution demands for recognition demands 'despite — or because of — an acceleration of economic globalization, at a time when an aggressively expanding capitalism is radically exacerbating economic inequality'.[11] I would bet on 'because of', given that communicative capitalism's attention economy doubles as a distraction economy. Globalisation's art structures reached into every nook and cranny of the planet in search for 'knowledge exchange' and 'the new', to the extent that there is even an Antarctic Biennale.[12] Broadly, 'the new' is an essential ingredient for expanding the pastures of saleability, and globalisation's art structures came back with, for example, Indigenous art. Who is categorised as Indigenous? This recognition enterprise refers at least partly to art by the survivors of genocidal settler colonialism's massive land grab project, but no one calls non-Indigenous art from those territories Genocidal Settler Art: *this* recognition cannot be made because it would reveal what should remain hidden. In the

2020s, as globalisation is being reconfigured by Trump-modelled conservative nationalisms, the left fears that cultural supremacists' calls for art to abandon recognition politics and return to 'quality' will get louder. The fear is justified. But, at this dismal juncture, what does the market say about Indigenous art? The co-founder of an Australian gallery said in 2025: 'At some stage who knows when it becomes unfashionable… it's like everything in life, it's not going to be forever but we hope we get the best of it while it lasts'.[13] 'The best of it' is frightfully close to 'the most out of it'.

The simplest question to pose here is: if the globalisation of neo-liberalism post-1989 signalled the dominance of economic relations across the board, what exactly warrants the belief that art encountered in these very conditions is an exception that can be rescued from the economy? Is it that artmaking constitutes 'unproductive' labour? If so, other examples of such unproductive labour exist in capitalism — why not rescue them? For an unproductive, non-value-generating form of labour, art is so steeped in economic determinations as to enjoy its very own market (the art market), built around the specificities of artistic labour and its product (the artwork). A blanket argument about artists owning the means of production (computers, brushes etc.) would not stand up to scrutiny at a moment when many artists cannot even afford to rent a studio. The argument could be inverted anyway and become something like: only those who can afford the means of art production can be artists. That, overall, artists do not produce directly for a dealer or collector (though sometimes they do) merely connects artists to the contemporary petite bourgeoisie in its fear of further precarity. Contrary to what has been claimed after the gigantic expansion of precarity in the early twenty-first century, the 'precariat' is not a class, for classes are defined in relation to people's position in the means of production.[14]

It wasn't just precarity that expanded, however; it was also the sheer number of artists, in comparison with the smaller art world of an earlier capitalist modernity. With this expansion, art was drawn more and more into the logic of capital. 'Can artists be entrepreneurs? Absolutely!', said *Forbes* in 2016.[15] 'Only a third of artists' income comes from their art', said *Arts Professional* in relation to the UK in 2019, and this art-practice income was just £6,020 while 70 percent earn less than £5,000 in a feminised field where women earn consistently less than men.[16] Moreover, the global art world has so far worked to siphon creativity to the West or the Global North, in a pattern that economic migration as 'brain drain' for countries in the periphery or semi-periphery exemplifies (this may well change, depending on where production and finance concentrate). The findings of cultural historian Chin Tao Wu from the 2000s were re-affirmed in 2018, when a major metrics-based study, which 'reconstructed the exhibition history of half a million artists', found that not any art institution will do as entry point. Rather, 'early access to prestigious central institutions' as opposed to 'starting at the network periphery' almost guaranteed 'success' and reduced 'drop-out rates': 'The network core was a dense community of major European and North American institutions, underlying their access to a common pool of artistic talents'.[17]

What the left would like art to be in capitalism differs significantly from what art actually is. Capitalist art institutions are now adept at appropriating collaborative paradigms associated with socially engaged art: the name of a shipping tycoon can be given to funded programmes encompassing such art, as we see with Onassis AiR in Greece since 2019. One may be divided on the outcome: artists get funding and so can survive but at the same time the politics of autonomy from below that is claimed for social practice is undermined. Private art foundations find great usefulness in the diversity images discussed in the previous chapter. On the Onassis AiR website, photographs of people of different skin colours and genders hugging, speaking, collaborating indicate the spirit of this 'international artistic research residency program… founded on the principles of learning and doing with others'.[18] In contrast to such authorised, capital-regulated sites of 'doing with others', any actually autonomous attempts to build frameworks of cooperation through art, such as through the occupation of a disused or still-in-use theatre, are attacked. In Athens, home to Onassis AiR, police — the armed guardians of the status quo — have attacked art occupations and, in some cases, arrested artists offering free cultural events to the people.[19]

In general, attempts at autonomous action are mostly ushered into capital-controlled or capitalist-state-sanctioned settings. Feminism is not exempt from such processes of appropriation, policing, or simply agreement to the terms imposed by capitalist property relations — even when such feminism actualises cooperative feminist pedagogy. The women artists (art teachers and art students) who created

Womanhouse in California in the early 1970s as a temporary zone of feminist artistic autonomy had to find a large enough private space and then get a 'special lease agreement' with the owner of the decrepit mansion they found.[20] According to accounts, they had to input many hours of manual labour, in poor conditions (no heating, no plumbing) to transform an uninhabitable site into what they regarded as their *real* workplace: an art exhibition and performance space. This was voluntary labour and many of the women 'had jobs as librarians and waitresses and had to commute the enormous distance from the school to the house and back again, sometimes twice a day'.[21] Such collaborative work may not be enough to undo the ideology that constructs the artist as individual (in the strong sense). Are we not reminded of Carla Lonzi's insistence that art is a web of male-patterned domination when we read that 'building strong egos in the young women took a high priority in the educational program' that would lead to *Womanhouse*, 'because a firm sense of self is indispensable to an artist, the center and source from which personal and therefore original expression flows'?[22] This is indeed the profile of the successful artist in capitalism: it's as if women had to prove that they possessed the generic artist profile's psychological characteristics, as well as exercise the 'feminine skill of multitasking'.[23] *Womanhouse* is merely one among many examples that caution us to refrain from romantic voluntarism in designating art as an exception or somehow rescuable. And although Adorno advised us to encounter the artwork with 'knowledge', an effort of awareness might be better directed at thinking about the contradictions that meet emancipatory desire when it enters art.

WHAT IS 'CONTEXT'? URGENCIES, ARGUMENTS, IMPASSES

Contradictions abound in the contexts that mediate art within capitalist worldmaking, occasionally leading to injurious impasses. The debate that grew around the 11th Istanbul Biennial (2009) is instructive. *What Keeps Humanity Alive?* took its title from a song in German Marxist playwright and poet Bertolt Brecht's famous 1928 *Threepenny Opera*. Curated by the Zagreb-based women's collective of Marxist leanings and feminist consciousness WHW, the socially-minded biennial was heavily critiqued in 2011 by Angela Harutyunyan, Aras Özgün, and Eric Goodfield in the pages of *Rethinking Marxism*:

By looking at the sponsorship, curatorial strategies, and formal aspects of the exhibitions constituting the Biennial, we argue that the contradictions between overt ideological commitments and actually existing economic conditions undermined its ambitious claims to a radical emancipatory politics… the demonstrations that emerged [in Istanbul] to counter the Biennial assumed the ideological stand of the precariat, speaking in its own voice, demarcating the events' actual ideological exclusion of the masses.[24]

In contrast, in a *Historical Materialism* article of 2010, Gail Day, Steve Edwards, and David Mabb praise the same curatorial project, admitting nonetheless that 'if the strategy of the Istanbul Biennial involves bringing in critical curators and artists then the question remains, have they been bought off? As far as outsiders can tell, the answer of the Turkish Left has been "yes"'.[25] Following a careful consideration of criticisms addressed to the biennial, however, along with a warning to Marxists that a lot more work is needed to understand the relationship between art and commodification, these authors conclude that a notable achievement of this curatorial project (besides making explicit art's left turn and a new proximity between Marxism and the avant-garde) was its 'crystallizing the contradictions'.[26]

The contrasting views of the two articles stem from their different response to contradictions. Both groups of authors are aware that contradictions exist for art today, but whereas the authors of the *Rethinking Marxism* article see these contradictions as intractable and leading to conflict between radical curatorial aspirations and the *realpolitik* of art's economic relations, the authors of the *Historical Materialism* article ascribe political value to rendering visible these contradictions for the public and being hopeful about where such a demonstration might lead. However, optimism is hard to uphold in a political context of piling crises: in 2020, Zeyno Pekünlü, a widely known Turkish artist and activist engaged in social practice, observed that her European networks started disintegrating in 2015, with artists locked in their specific political realities, while in Turkey the art field before the pandemic had not managed 'to construct a convincing, concrete and sustainable public discourse and debate, or an agenda for action — apart from what could be called "charitable positions"'.[27]

So far, it seems that contradictions merely reproduce themselves. Eight years after the 11th Istanbul Biennial, documenta 14/d14, headed by Polish curator Adam Szymczyk, faced similar contradictions in exacerbated conditions in Greece, Turkey's neighbor. In the 2010s, when the ramifications of the 2008 global financial crisis reached Greece as a sovereign debt crisis, the country stood as a symbol of the devastation that neocolonial capitalism could bring even to Europe. Titled 'Learning from Athens', documenta 14 made the bold move to locate half of its activities and half of the exhibition in the Greek capital (the other half would remain in Kassel, Germany). Trans activist and theorist Paul Preciado devised a cutting-edge public programme titled 'Parliament of Bodies', prioritising questions about neoliberalism and the 'refugee crisis', queer politics, democracy and post-democracy, autonomous organising, and the activation of political agency. Despite this angle, documenta 14 was met with fierce critique in Athens (and beyond), seen as an appeasing ambassador sent to a Southern European country from which German capital was benefitting. Relatedly, documenta was seen to largely exclude the local art scene while absorbing local art funding. This disadvantaged local women artists too.

In 2017, d14 faced a worse predicament than the 2009 Istanbul Biennial because of the more acute divides and conflicts of its context. It was too late for arguments drawn from institutional critique, feminist or other; rather, arguments related directly to *realpolitik*, including first and foremost the exploitative hierarchy between Western/Northern European capital and Southern Europe. A photography-focused collective poignantly calling itself Depression Era had formed in 2011 in Athens to counter the dominant Western media understanding of the Greek crisis as the outcome of a troubled and incompetent South (parts of the European press would enter full racism mode, arguing that modern Greeks were an undeserving ethno-racial mix as opposed to their glorious ancestors). Depression Era organised the urban campaign *The Tourists* while d14/'Learning from Athens' was taking place, interrogating how 'learning' from a position of power was articulated. *The Tourists* contrasted images of refugees with images of tourists in a visual culture that distinguished between desirable and undesirable 'foreigners' (d14 was a passing visitor that had attracted more cultural passing visitors). The collective would also put their posters up on the outside walls of venues that hosted d14 events. Within d14 as such, things went quite far: a group of refugees that had agreed to collaborate with artist Roger

Bernat on transporting the replica of a sacred ancient stone stole the 'artwork' during the performance in protest against how an institution of privilege (a cultural/art institution) obscured the fate of the multitude of refugees: denigration, persecution, elimination.[28] Symbolically hiding an artwork was intended as a rebellious act, effectively claiming that real politics is elsewhere. Art was found guilty of aestheticising the horrors and dispossession of real life under capitalism.

Depending on one's political affiliation and convictions, d14 was seen as an undesirable neocolonial imposition or a desirable opportunity to put Athens on the art map. In the years of d14 (before the actual show in 2017), Greek banks were under capital control, unemployment was skyrocketing, and the German government (seen by many as essentially being in charge of the Eurozone) pursued predatory policies to recoup the 'Greek debt', to which some locals counterposed what Nazi Germany owed to Greece, of which Germany had paid only a fraction. No amount of art activism introduced by a Kassel-originating art show would have been enough to move beyond already drawn battle positions, and contradictions undermined documenta's nearly every step. To sum it up, everything that documenta 14 did in Athens could be seen to have two sides: a discursive one characterised by a progressive mindset and a structural one found to sustain capital's divisive geopolitics.

Would it have been possible to establish politically meaningful connections between the feminist artists brought by d14 and feminist artists in Greece? The divides of economic violence interfered with the prospects of transnational feminist dialogue. What remains is a spiraling Airbnb-isation of central Athens, and lingering memories of the stenciled wall message and public activist artwork that stated: 'Dear Documenta, I refuse to exoticize myself to increase your cultural capital. Sincerely, oi Ιθageneis.' The signature, which translates as 'the Indigenous', delivered instructive irony — Greenglish marks the linguistic hegemony that orders international communication. The stencil remained anonymous for some time, before it transpired a few years later that 'the Indigenous' behind this urban visual activism included women artists Eirini Efstathiou and Mary Zygouri (the latter would participate in d14 with the *Round-up Project*, rekindling memories of the bloody suppression of communist resistance against the Nazis in Athens). In 2022, Efstathiou explained to visual culture scholar Julia Tulke that the careful strategy developed around the

Indigenous signature intervention (the choice of locations in the city, making use of social media, etc.),[29] summarised documenta 14's contradiction: to present in Athens Indigenous artists drawn from the West's map of colonial horrors while positing crisis-ridden Athens as an object of real-time knowledge extraction (learning from…) enabled through economic and cultural power.

Just a few years before, in 2014, Boris Groys had referred to the 'new phenomenon' of art activism, seeing it as strewn with contradictions: 'Art activists do want to be useful, to change the world, to make the world a better place — but at the same time, they do not want to cease being artists. And this is the point where theoretical, political, and even purely practical problems arise'.[30] Yet art activism was not new. Many feminist artists in the 1970s sought to effect change in the 'real' world *and* be artists. Arguably, in their case, the prospect of being accepted as artists was itself part of changing society. What, on the other hand, was new in feminist art theory in the early 2010s was the idea that being a feminist could mean 'being a fan' of feminism, as Catherine Grant put it. Prompted by 1970s feminism's 'being-fashionable' in the exhibition networks of the first decade of the century, in 2011 Grant explored fandom in art-based feminism as emotional attachment and 'a model through which to explore the psychic and political pull of the past on the present'.[31] This was an informed and attractive argument, permeated by what I read as generational melancholy (which I share) over losing the last traces of the feminist art movement that the second wave had birthed (for example, feminist art magazines closing and becoming archives) while the most intricate of second-wave feminism's trajectories in art remained less known. The emotional attachment structuring fandom is what, however, ties it to commodity fetishism — fandom is a rather developed form of commodity fetishism, boosted by the hyper-circulation of signs in contemporary visual culture: through it celebrities (actors, artists, dead revolutionaries) and material culture (vintage china, vinyl records) become objects of affective consumption, associated with the lightness of recreation rather than the heaviness of living politics.

The urgency that Groys described as animating art activism stands at odds with the slower mediations of feminist fandom in art. Both arguments were made in the years immediately following the 2008 financial crash, pauperising millions and indicating a grim political future. Still, the argument for fandom feminism made no mention of capitalism, even as the latter had momentarily been representable as an explosive crisis. In a feminist imaginary shaped through the experience of contemporary art, was feminism's emotional attachment to its past placing feminism at a political distance from its present? The question is not rhetorical, though of course feminist art activism would fuel art's social practice in the 2010s. For Hilary Robinson, it is women who have tended to lead activisms in the aftermath of the 2008 financial crash.[32] Groys pointed out, however, two problems in activist art that feminist theory at the time was not centring. The first was complaints about the 'aesthetic quality' of activist art (and one recalls similar complaints about feminist art in the 1970s); this could be easily dismissed given that modern art had already met with multiple charges of low quality in relation to its experiments. The second was the aestheticising process as such, from which the spectacle could not be absent. Rather than exiting the contradictions of the art field and engaging directly in politics (not so far from Carla Lonzi's efforts), the art activist, feminist or not, refuses to abandon art and tries instead to make art useful. In doing so, she aestheticises real needs; and if not, its value as 'art' is questioned. This is where we see that art is principally understood as the domain of aesthetics, and that aesthetics is still perceived as a safeguarded exception to the mundane.

What makes contemporary activist art problematic is that it tries to be avant-garde in a non-revolutionary social context. Unlike artists at the time and place of the October Revolution, activist art today is realised in pockets of support and without a vision of large-scale transformation. This is raised both by Groys and Keti Chukhrov who said: 'Dissolution of art within life under the conditions of capitalist production is different from the same process occurring in the frame of a noncapitalist economy'.[33] Drawing a tentative parallel, we can say that feminist art activism at a time of a general feminist uprising, as in the 1970s, is different from feminist art activism when feminism as a social movement is precarious. In the late 2010s, feminism was merely trying to resume as a transnational social movement reacting to a backlash: this is what the IWS, discussed in the previous chapter, and similar initiatives indicated. On 7 November 2017, a manifesto-petition titled 'We Propose: Declaration of Commitment to Feminist Practices in Art — Permanent Assembly of Women Art Workers', authored in Argentina and circulated on social media, ended with the words: 'We call on the global art community to organize the International Women's Strike on March 8, 2018'.[34] The call proved less than a catalyst. No global rapport could be observed between the theoretically astute anticapitalism of the IWS and art-based feminism. No new feminist art movement emerged. The historical conditions of the 2010s differed to those of the 1970s; in the 1970s neoliberalism was taking form, in the 2010s it ruled the globe. The 2010s also witnessed a debilitatingly confusing traffic between political discourses and value systems (women's rights figured in arguments nurturing ethno-nationalisms, for example)[35] as if the methods of the then ascending alt-right (appropriation and distortion) were contaminating political life at large. All this created a very unstable ground for concretising feminist goals across fields of action.

Groys sought to resolve the conflict he detected in activist art by suggesting that such art accepts aestheticisation, but that this aestheticisation serves to demonstrate the impossibility of realising activist art's objectives. In other words, by showing us what it cannot do (rather than what it can), activist art renders visible the suffocating limits of its historical juncture. Following that, however, Groys proceeds to argue: 'total aestheticization does not block political action; it enhances it. Total aestheticization means that *we see the current status quo as already dead, already abolished*'. It is unclear what would authorise such a projection, except if one opts, as Groys indeed suggests, to '*not differentiate between victory and failure*'. The art activists of today are thus found to practise an advanced form of political voluntarism — or, simply, strong wishful thinking — and the issue of contradictions is addressed by proposing not the suspension of aesthetic but political judgement. This goes a step further towards art's political disempowerment: not just accepting art as negativity, not just embracing it as radical failure, but accepting that you fail to even try to distinguish between failing and succeeding in your political objectives as an artist, curator, theorist, and activist.

Insofar as feminism is a politics, operating in the art field as elsewhere in real time (seeing 'the current status quo as already dead, already abolished') would be debilitating. It would not be a way out of contradictions but a licence to become hostage to them, foreclosing a consciousness that sees the struggle as historically determined and, consequently, in need of updating its strategies and tactics. For nothing in the current state of global affairs permits us to imagine an 'ultimate horizon', as Groys puts it, of change as planetary social justice: 'every action directed towards the stabilization of the status quo' is, precisely, *not* proving 'ineffective'. The transnational rise of the fascist tendency, circumscribed in the horizon of what Richard Seymour calls 'disaster nationalism', and where emotional attachment plays a key role, has been very effective.[36] The speedy dismantling of DEI (Diversity, Equity and Inclusion) policies in the US early in 2025 as a redistribution of wealth upwards shows the fragility of contextual gains that mitigate structural inferiorisation. The problem is that even actions not directed to the stabilisation of the status quo can ultimately contribute to its propagation. In the face of all this, political judgement is required.

FEMINISM, ART, AND CONTRADICTIONS

The varying positions taken in relation to the contradictions in which art is mired, that we saw in the previous section, are highly relevant to how we presently practise feminist politics in the art field. The dilemmas faced are not new — some have intensified in the networked artscapes of global geopolitics, others have been sidelined as capitalism's hegemony has consolidated. A key issue remains whether the contradictions faced can be overcome or if some at least should be understood as unsolvable antinomies. Three such conflicts or contradictions are discussed below: autonomy and dependency; reform and revolution; work and non-work.

Contradiction 1: Autonomy and Dependency

Being an artist (also a curator or a writer) means having a professional identity. Professional identities are associated with the remuneration for labour. The neoliberal higher education regime, where education is seen as an investment (irrespective of whether students actually pay fees), has built on the professionalisation of the artist. There is an assumed equivalence of the degrees on offer: you choose to study art, physics, or law according to the career you want to have. The currently popular term 'art workers'[37] indicates the need for artists to sell something in the private or public sector in order to make a living (it is instructive, in this regard, that the term 'worker' is being widely deployed rather than, say, 'civil servant'). Some (few) artists become successful entrepreneurs, implying also the possibility of upward social mobility. More often, artists secure wages in higher education or art institutions or chase whatever irregular income they can by providing various kinds of services in the sector. Andrea Fraser's 'How to provide an artistic service'[38] is perhaps more relevant than in the 1990s when she was writing. Artists (and curators) can also seek employment outside the art field, thus subsidising their creative labour, but the potential of finally making a living through the latter does not disappear. As regards the difficult conditions of art-field labour in post-Fordism, the situation is well known, addressed in myriad conferences and a voluminous literature.[39] As the feminist Danish collective Kuratorisk Aktion said in 2010:

> So far, we have been able to finance our projects through public and private funding without compromising our politics, which has been a privilege! But since the Nordic region still doesn't have funding programs for curatorial research and labour, we have been unable to secure salaries for ourselves. Like so many other cultural producers, we thus support our families by doing odd jobs after Kuratorisk Aktion 'office hours,' but are painstakingly aware that being in our early forties, we may not 'have the muscle' to keep up Kuratorisk Aktion for another ten years while attending to two-three 'day jobs' on the side.[40]

The precarious economic and labour conditions remain the same, the extent of which was apparent when governments had to intervene to save artists from loss of income during the Covid-19 pandemic. Tone Olaf Nielsen, of the Kuratorisk Aktion duo, went on to co-found CAMP in the refugee community centre Trampoline House in Copenhagen in 2013: a non-profit art center focused on migration, 'realised with support from private sponsors' and a long list of state and related institutions.[41] Located in a multicultural neighbourhood where relatively affordable rent permitted setting up such an art space, CAMP organised carefully thought-out exhibition cycles, *Migration Politics*, and then *State of Integration: Artistic Analyses of the Challenges of Coexistence*.[42] Yet CAMP, which addressed an urgent social issue, folded in 2020, the first year of Covid-19, due to lack of funding and, to an extent, the exhaustion of its organisers.[43] Feminist collectives in the art field are dependent on the institutions that control the flow of cash (and even credit) and, through this, also control art workers' mental and physical health, generating burnout as a matter of course.

It is impossible to understand women artists' marked attachment to the art institution without grasping their financial dependency upon it; and it is a mistake to suggest that in the 1970s, empowered by feminism, women sought to enter the art institution exclusively in order to achieve visibility as creative subjects and challenge the male canon. These two political objectives constitute pure idealism if disconnected from the economic imperative that underpins them, unless one were to assume that class privilege uniformly freed women and feminist artists from financial pressures. What feminist would accept to study art and art history while incurring debt, and anxiety, merely in order to advance her political cause by gaining feminist knowledge?

Entering the institution was an objective of 1970s and 1980s feminism in art that has been discussed almost exclusively as a political goal and not in terms of access to income and wages, that is as an economic imperative. Much feminist energy and activism focused on making the art institution, historically hostile to women artists (dead or alive), open its doors to them.[44] As entry to the art institution was not just a matter of rewriting art history through a feminist lens, but also an avenue to remunerated work and a sector of the economy, separatism — a strategy considered by feminists in the 1970s — was doomed to remain marginal.[45] A self-reproducing feminist art commons never emerged as a transformative alternative sustained by a critical (feminist) mass — and in the 2020s we can merely speculate about how a feminist commons might have impacted the capitalist art field. Feminists sought autonomy but opted for dependency: in fact, they perceived (creative and financial) autonomy as the outcome of (institutional) dependency.

In a 1973 essay in the *Feminist Art Journal*, Irene Moss and Lila Katzen rejected separatism both because of the accepted universality of art's aesthetic criteria but also because separatism would exclude women from competition in the art world — thus accepting capital's organisation of labour as an unalterable reality.[46] Yet, that separatism survives in contemporary feminist consciousness in art is indicative of the exacerbation of capitalist relations of art production. In Sweden, the feminist art collective *Malmö* Fria Kvinnouniversitet, or *Malmö* Free University for Women (MFK), defended 'strategic separatism' in terms of claiming space for the open discussion of contradictions faced by the art world's female workforce.[47] Active from 2006 to 2011, MFK argued that 'the importance of feminist spaces is that they provide opportunities for self-definition' while jettisoning a biological definition of femaleness and including 'all persons that now or at some point have identified as women'.[48] Economic dependency would remain. In the case of MFK, separatism became a feasible, limited-time experiment because there were no expectations for it to function as a lasting alternative economic model for its participants. 'Self-definition', a key concept of second-wave feminism and the goal MFK sought to explore through strategic separatism in the twenty-first century, had to be claimed, perhaps inadvertently, as a position in discourse rather than in the material conditions of economic dependency — when it came to that, participants could not, of course, achieve self-definition. To the extent then that contemporary feminism in art re-deploys second-wave concepts, political judgement on these concepts' contextual potential but also, crucially, limits must be regularly renewed.

If in the 1970s there were hopes for this field's large-scale transformation through women's participation, it is hard to entertain such hopes today: what has changed is the artwork's content and form, while the structural elements of the art field remain intact. For many women, being recognised as professional artists (or professional anything) is a hard-won gain achieved through generations of feminist effort to embed women in the public sphere. Women may thus be less prepared to undermine this gain by questioning the feminist goal of access to wages and 'entrepreneurial' income in relation to the competition principle (the implications of the wage relation and how it shapes subjectivity) — less prepared, that is, to theorise and practice refusal. The limits that Carla Lonzi faced in that regard, as we saw in the previous chapter, are a cautionary tale. As a political stance, refusal can only be practiced collectively and with a loud bang. If not, it becomes a conceptual *Drop Out Piece* (begun c. 1970) by an individual artist — Lee Lozano — more likely to be recuperated and neutralised as an 'original artistic vision' by the institution than having an impact on the institution's functioning;[49] or it dissipates into disparate micro-events of women's withdrawal from the art economy without a trace, affirming the myth of female 'weakness' faced with the harsh conditions of the 'jungle' outside the home. The politicisation of women's withdrawal in terms of feminist refusal is therefore indispensable to the analysis of the autonomy–dependency contradiction.

Contradiction 2: Reform and Revolution

The struggles of the 1970s demonstrated that making women artists 'visible' would require lifelong and transgenerational commitment. 'Despite the high number of female university graduates, this year's report shows that 63% of the most senior staff at art and design institutions were male, an almost inverse ratio to students,' Kate McMillan reported about Britain in 2018. 'Progress is not inevitable,' she would write in 2020.[50] But young women persist: the art internship culture is symptomatic of this. And as regards instances of resistance to the culture of 'employability' with which art degrees are forced to comply in Western economies, Silvia Federici has stated that as a feminist she recognises 'many of these tools from past and contemporary practices of consciousness raising'.[51] Yet such instances of resistance (drawing on feminist strategies) remain few and far between. Concerted efforts have been made to present the art institution as a progressive friend rather than a reactionary enemy of feminism. The numerous exhibitions (including blockbuster ones) on feminism since 2000 have served to normalise the presence of the art institution in feminist culture, presupposing feminists' acceptance of its role as the showcase for feminist artworks and a celebrated archive of feminist impact.[52] The discussion has been about inclusivity, not about the terms on which this happens.[53]

In recent years, such acceptance has been reviewed and discussed critically by feminist scholars.[54] In many cases, the art institution is found to perform a dubious ideological trade-off: the exclusion or discrediting of feminist politics and struggles is compensated for by the inclusion of women artists' work. In the 2010s in the UK, the incorporation of socialist feminism (and work concerning working-class women) and of Black women artists (seen as doubly undermined by the art system in terms of gender and race) under the aegis of BP at the Tate constituted cases in point. In 2011–12, the group exhibition *Thin Black Line(s)*, curated by artist Lubaina Himid (winner of the Turner Prize in 2017 and referred to as 'a star at Art Basel' in 2018), took place at Tate Britain as part of the 'BP Art Displays 1500–2011'.[55] Art historian Victoria Horne critically discusses the BP-framed shows of 2014 *Sylvia Pankhurst* and *Women and Work: A Document on the Division of Labour* (a legendary research-based installation by Margaret Harrison, Kay Hunt, and Mary Kelly created in 1975 and acquired by the Tate in 2001).[56] In 2017, the BP ended its sponsorship of the Tate under sustained pressure from climate activists; yet there had been no large-scale protest by the feminist art community against the BP–Tate agreement, despite the company's record of environmental destruction and boycott calls over its role in Apartheid in South Africa and the exploitation of workers.[57]

What these exhibitions, as projects of institutional incorporation, imply is that feminist struggles in the art world may have lost connection with feminist politics in the 'real' world where 'Indigenous and ecological-centered feminists have long affirmed that neoliberalism's founding ideology of endless growth — achieved through the infinite extraction of finite natural resources — is rooted in a historical and contemporary intersection of the domination of women, minorities, and the Earth'.[58] Including a socialist such as Sylvia Pankhurst in a setting funded by a corporation is a poignant way of discrediting feminist critique. In 2017, the exhibition *We Wanted a Revolution: Black Radical Women 1965–1985* at the Elizabeth A. Sackler Center for Feminist Art at the Brooklyn Museum nearly coincided with the explosive headlines about how the Sacklers made their fortunes: through the mass misery generated by Oxycontin addiction. In March 2018, 100 demonstrators, including artist Nan Goldin, gathered at the Metropolitan Museum in New York to protest its acceptance of a $3.4 million donation from the philanthropic Sackler family.[59] Unsurprisingly, the liberal establishment sought to extricate the individual Elizabeth Sackler from the mess of unethical capitalism (implying that another kind is the norm), while admitting that 'implicating Elizabeth via her father jeopardizes both of their legacies, and could make it more difficult for the Elizabeth A. Sackler Center for Feminist Art to continue to bring art, diverse audiences, education, and activism under one roof'.[60] Facts were presented and careful distinctions were drawn between family members. What the liberal establishment cannot touch is the phenomenon of accumulation as such: the exploitation that generates capital's wealth concentrated in a few families, and who this process has prevented from realising their creative potential in their first place.

What is the political meaning of placing radical women, activism, and capital 'under one roof'? If artist Artur Zmijiewski, curator of the 7th Berlin Biennale, could be criticised merely for 'the attempt to frame political movements [Occupy and the Indignados] within an art exhibition', what happens to feminist radicalism when framed within the big-money agendas of self-legitimisation by means of championing social causes?[61] In an age when business executives can sell lean-in feminism, it should be obvious that feminism is not uniformly attached to anti-status quo radicalism. Bringing radical women, activism, and capital under one roof means that the public is educated about something called 'feminist art' in terms of an imaginary unity that conceals schisms and divisions, fails to distinguish between critique of the system and leaning in, and is saturated with the hegemony of capital as a social relation (rather than merely an economic one). When, for all their differences, dead radical women are made to return to contexts that represent the hegemony that they sought to fight, feminism as a critique of actually existing social relations should be hearing the alarm bells. Living feminists are in a position to ask themselves what might constitute practices of 'leaning in' specifically in art — practices that would leave us with an instrumentalised feminism as 'individual choice' that may or may not provide a slice of the pie to the 'deserving' few (this used to be called 'token inclusion'). Such cynical incorporation is the logical outcome of feminism seeking mere reform.

Struggles for reform tend to prioritise participation and representation, and they have a much better chance at 'succeeding', if with a lot of effort. The effort this requires is such that when the objectives are met, with whatever embarrassing and even politically humiliating compromises, there is hardly any energy left for carrying out a political anatomy of the 'achievement' of inclusion — when inclusion of the few in terms set by capital's competition principle presupposes and propagates exclusion of the many. Such an anatomy was nonetheless attempted in a letter authored by the four shortlisted artists for Germany's biggest art prize, Preis der Nationalgalerie, in 2017: Sol Calero, Iman Issa, Jumana Manna, and Agnieszka Polska declared that their institutional recognition placed emphasis on their gender and foreign nationalities rather than their work, perverted diversity as a public relations exercise, generated no artist fee in the apparent assumption that their new visibility would translate to market value, posited them as competitors against the spirit of artistic collaboration, and placed them in an environment plastered with the logo of the industrial sponsor, BMW.[62] The letter showed a heightened awareness of the terms of inclusivity but is hardly representative of a collective feminist stance: we do not have a feminist mass of such critiques, exposures, and rejections.

Overall however, progressive forces in the art field striving for inclusivity seem to uphold a strange view that it is an even field of play despite its articulation in a society of antagonisms and rampant inequality: the 'Open Letter in Response to the Announcement of the Exclusionary Belgian Art Prize Shortlist of Candidates 2019' protesting the shortlist of white men stated: 'As active practitioners, we know that a thriving and complex artistic landscape is only possible when artists of different genders, sexualities, ethnic backgrounds, social classes, generations and so forth, are able to access and participate in it, and enrich it with their sensibilities and world views.'[63] The mention of different social classes presenting their 'world views' to, and within, the art establishment betrays an anthology mentality that buries the question of why social classes exist in the first place, as much as what it means for art to regard social classes as merely 'different'. Likewise, genders, sexualities, and ethnic backgrounds are not merely 'different' but rather constituted through entrenched relations of power — which is why their equal representation in an art world not so different from the real world tends to be denied, unless it serves as a veneer of progressiveness or a showcasing of 'the new'.

The question of reform or radical break underpinned the dilemma of participation versus separatism (and even refusal) discussed above. It echoes an old division. In her discussion of the first half of the nineteenth century, Sheila Rowbotham notes that supporter of women's emancipation William Thompson argued (in 1825) that 'the liberation of women was impossible in a competitive system' and thus advocated 'cooperative feminism':

By offering suggestions for actually effecting a change rather than simply describing and analysing what was wrong, these cooperators [the cooperative movement] and early socialists discovered a new potentiality for feminism. They transformed it [feminism] from aspiration and ideas and integrated the liberation of women to a social movement which could envisage alternatives to the suffering and waste of early capitalism. From this point *the conflict was explicit between the two feminisms, one seeking acceptance from the bourgeois world, the other seeking another world altogether.*[64]

Rowbotham detects a schism between a reformist-liberal and a revolutionary anticapitalist tendency at feminism's emergence. In the early 1980s, Griselda Pollock, working on feminism and art history, wrote 'there are several feminisms', but what followed this statement referred to 'distinct political definitions' of key concepts feminists use (her example is 'patriarchy') and *not* to the delineations of plural feminisms.[65] Pollock, however, concluded her essay (on feminist art histories and Marxism) by admitting that 'the bourgeois revolution was in many ways a historic defeat for women and it created the special configuration of power and domination with which we as women now have to contend'.[66] Why then are not all feminists aligning their politics against this historic defeat? Should we accept, following Rowbotham, that there have been two incompatible feminisms all along, and that feminism in the singular can be an aspiration but has never been a reality? Or, as considered earlier in this book, could it be that a pluralisation of feminism is a concession made to the contradictions that the cause of 'ending women's oppression and exploitation' faced from the start? In other words, could the pluralisation of feminism, previously examined in terms of hegemonic ideology, be preventing us from seeing the implications of a historic bifurcation of feminism from the outset?

If pluralisation would be a concession, it would be motivated by the same spirit (of overcoming an obstacle) as Groys's admonition to stop distinguishing between failure and success in activist art: saying 'there are many feminisms!' would be the easy way out of debate, discussion, argumentation, having to form political judgement, evaluate progress in relation to a common political cause, and assume collective responsibility for any outcomes. If, however, the schism were accepted as inherent and generating two antithetical feminist perspectives on the capitalist status quo since the shaping of modernity, it would mean that modern feminism has proceeded with an internal limit to unity: women cannot ultimately be considered a social group to which a political cause can be attached; maybe two (or more) competing, political causes can, but not one. It would mean, in other words, that the level of racially inflected class divides is so high as to make 'women' a non-subject. And this, in turn, would mean that the very reality (the society of appropriated common wealth extracted through degrees and methods of exploitation) that feminism is attempting to change is itself the limit to feminism's political imaginary.

When Rowbotham was writing in the 1970s, feminists in the Western art field were not always demonstrably placed into opposing ideological camps, although the intense search for the right 'strategy' (unavoidable for a movement at its genesis, by which I mean the feminist art and theory movement) had specific outcomes. One of these was that painting as a feminist, especially if deploying the figure, tended to receive little attention in feminist art history (the implications of which will be further examined in Chapter Six). Looking back over the 1970s, Judith Barry and Sally Flitterman's 1980 essay on categorising and assessing the strategies of feminist artists articulated a clear preference.[67] Barry and Flitterman announced 'deconstruction' as the winner among the feminist strategies they surveyed. They gave good reasons for their choice, echoing the sentiments of those feminist critics who realised that the mechanisms of women's subjugation in capitalism were so sophisticated as to require pioneering methods of address *within* the space of the artwork — Griselda Pollock's essay 'Screening the Seventies' would be a case in point.[68] Yet the real causes of the division and the fragmentation that the movement suffered did not primarily emanate from different opinions about strategies and tactics that concerned the creation of artworks. Rather, such division had to do with the experience of oppression by women who necessarily occupied hierarchically differentiated positions in society and had to negotiate their living-through oppression in specific terms. This fact did not, however, dictate or prompt a perfect alignment between an individual's subject constitution and her political consciousness, discussed as a general characteristic in capitalism's political life in Chapter Two. In short, you can (and do) have women artists associated with a working-class background who can at some point assert that 'Tories are [the] only hope for the arts'.[69] This is hardly surprising, given that the art world is presented as the glamorised epitome of self-realisation, and to what extent feminist advances and reforms were or weren't tied to that horse remains a moot point.

In the first half of the 1970s, the strategies concerning the making of radical artworks had to do with the intended public for feminist art practices. In (political) principle, the very notion of 'strategies' contested the idea of the artwork as the playground of an individual imaginary and self-realisation. The well-known debates in anglophone feminist art history around an 'accessible' and a 'difficult' feminist art need not be reiterated here; yet it is worth stressing that the feminist conflicts echoed Marxist debates on aesthetics and politics over whether artworks should be realist (understood by and connected to the many) or disruptive of art's normative form of gratification (demanding or, worse, elitist). This dilemma (presented with many inaccuracies here) typically arises in relation to artistic practice engaged with emancipatory politics because, in the material divides that sustain capital's rule, access to or exclusion from critical knowledge becomes a biopolitical tool: an instrument, distributed across gatekeeping institutions, for managing populations and social antagonisms. If, in the twenty-first century, this dilemma no longer arises collectively for feminists in art, we need to ask what this means. It may, for example, mean that art practice committed to feminism today is unable to posit with sufficient clarity an addressee for its political imagination. Whose emancipation, then, does such practice seek to facilitate? Is there an expectation that there will be a cumulative (political) effect of individual artistic visions? Or is the feminist curator and her narrative, illustrated by artworks, meant to enable meaning?

The critical analysis of feminist curatorial mediation has been a defining characteristic of feminist scholarship since 2000. In this regard, feminism has been part of a broader and complex trend: the appreciation of curatorship as equivalent to art practice in meaning creation. What makes this trend complex is that, on the one hand, it exists in tandem with the high value that contemporary capital attributes to management, administration, and mediation practices overall, while, on the other, it allows more people to have jobs appreciated as creative, bearable, and of social value (as opposed to the drudgery and anti-social elements of many other sectors that may pay better). An additional issue has been the need to mediate and unify perspectives from very diverse contexts in an art field defined by post-1989 globalisation. Again, we see that a key direction of feminism in the art field has been defined by developments external to feminism, and it is these developments that oversee the transference of political responsibility from artworks to curating, in the art field's historical constitution as a set of practices that closely follow the capitalist (re) organisation of creativity into professionalised slots.

If today the stakes of feminist politics, in the art field and beyond, differ from those of feminism in the 1970s, is this because we (feminists) know how far pushing for reforms can go? As long as these reforms do not challenge core elements of the economic status quo they are potentially realisable with the right amount of pressure and when certain parameters coincide: the system can allow for a few 'successful' women artists so long as they don't shun art fairs. At the same time, however, we need to safeguard (or worse, reclaim) the right to reform, currently under threat by the rise of white male supremacy. Ultra-conservative tendencies are always present in periods of protracted crisis. The issue is whether feminist politics can be simply reformist or whether reforms pursued need to be relentlessly assessed by a revolutionary, transformative consciousness — one that does not foresee, through unfounded projections, the corpse of the status quo as a future *fait accompli* but that engages in a larger-than-life struggle of uncertain outcomes. This would mean renewing political judgement of art at any moment, which can only happen within the context of a feminist *art* movement: the idea of 'politics' implies contestation in the semblances of the 'polis' we have. Reforms realised without this intensity of struggle tend to placate the spirits.

Abandoning reforms is politically unthinkable for feminism, its gains being so far a history of reforms. But what must be acknowledged and accommodated is, first, that reforms are insecure and, second, that reforms do not cumulatively lead to social transformation. When revolution was a prospect, in the early twentieth century, Rosa Luxemburg wrote that 'the struggle for reforms' is 'the means' while 'social revolution' the 'aim'.[70] In saying this, she opposed tendencies within partisan positions that regarded the 'now' of the socialist movement — the struggle — as the exclusive focus and an end in itself, without a clear idea about a long-term goal. This long-term goal would be the criterion for developing strategies and tactics in the here and now. Broadly, we need to ask: what is feminism's long-term goal and can it be achieved within capitalism's class society? If the goal is women's equality with men, which men does feminism mean, as it is unlikely these would be the Black men populating the prisons of

America. In 2013, Jeannine Tang argued for the need to acknowledge 'the multiples axes of transnational and queer feminism today, as such feminist projects intersect issues of war, law, immigration, human rights, antiracist, economic, urban and rural justice projects, propelled towards uncoercive rearrangements of masculinity and femininity beyond the limits of woman, as a project of decolonizing feminism'.[71] This is what the IWS represented beyond the art field, which sought to draw attention to how all this was circumscribed in capitalism. But we are presented with a very limited view of feminism in the 1970s and 1980s if what is implied in the quote is that this earlier feminism — with its internal ideological conflicts, unprecedented intellectual radicalness and militancy — did not address the issues listed, including the problematising of 'woman'. Many second-wave feminists in art saw their uprising as a revolution, as Lynn Hershman Leeson's documentary *!Women Art Revolution* (2010) suggests about the US context — and if it was contained, living in the knowledge that a revolutionary advance was once possible can raise the hope that such a breakthrough can become possible again. Taking Tang's mention of war however, completing this book while Palestinian women — indeed, their entire society — are destroyed in a genocide makes me think of the non sequitur of calls for decolonisation that do not explicitly centre capitalism, its necro-biopolitics, the capitalist state (its structure and objectives recognisable besides electoral outcomes), the military–industrial complex, and the violence of real estate (think of Trump's proposal for the US to 'own' a Gaza emptied of Palestinians early in 2025). Can a feminist consciousness attached to reforms grasp the magnitude of our juncture?

In the art field, there is much need for a feminist debate around whether seeking reforms contradicts feminism as radical break, and a collective elaboration and rethinking of these very terms in their inter-connectedness. In short, we need a feminist dialectic on reformist pragmatism and revolutionary agency. 'We Propose: Declaration of Commitment to Feminist Practices in Art — Permanent Assembly of Women Art Workers', the manifesto–petition mentioned earlier in this chapter, included a spectrum of demands, some of which contradicted each other in essence: the call for more women in positions of power within actually existing, capitalist institutions, reflective of a lean-in agenda, jarred with the call to work towards the anticapitalist International Women's Strike.[72] In the book *Feminism for the 99%: A Manifesto*, the authors state: 'We have no interest in breaking the glass ceiling while leaving the vast majority to clean up the shards. Far from celebrating women CEOs who occupy corner offices, we want to get rid of CEOs and corner offices'.[73] An effort to understand the origins, propagation mechanisms, and political impact of such contradictions is long overdue in the face of a new strongman political culture, not unrelated to the kind of charisma that art honours. Hito Steyerl wrote in 2010: 'The traditional conception of the artist's role corresponds all too well with the self-image of wannabe autocrats, who see government potentially — and dangerously — as an art form. Post-democratic government is very much related to this erratic type of male-genius-artist behavior'.[74] Given that feminism in art was seeking to undermine the male genius doxa back in the 1970s, its recurrent manifestation in the twenty-first century raises questions about the efficacy of reforms aiming at its eradication.

Contradiction 3: Work and Non-work

As seen in previous chapters, Marxist feminists engaging social reproduction theory have thought it 'essential to recognize that workers have an existence beyond the workplace'.[75] At the same time, the twenty-first century has so far been a 'work society', as Kathi Weeks put it in 2011, in which work is far more than an economic practice but connects with (racialised and gendered) practices and imaginaries of freedom.[76] Under the guiding principle of fewer workers but greater productivity, the lengthening of the working day applies at large, while Weeks stresses that work 'is widely understood as an individual moral practice and collective ethical obligation'.[77]

Artists face the additional complication that artmaking is considered desirable, self-fulfilling work. Women artists can then face a double confrontation with expectations to perform labours of love: work done in the home and artworks made for display, in the broadest sense, outside the home. Feminist artists who see their work as politically invested and may undertake political commitments operate on a triple front: home, workplace, political meetings. This troubling triangle is well known. Artist, curator, and educator Marion Von Osten (1963–2020) offered an excellent account of its radicalised iteration (the version that includes emancipatory politics as constitutive of the female subject) in her discussion of Helke Sander's 1978 film *Redupers. Die allseitig reduzierte Persönlichkeit*, or *The All-Round Reduced Personality*. Von Osten notes:

> [The protagonist] is not only photographer, feminist activist, and theorist, that is, cultural producer, but also a product of emancipatory demands and capitalist impositions, a subject who has pulled away from wage labor and its regulatory apparatus in the factory or in the office, as the Autonomia Operaia called for. At the same time, she is a Reduper (an all-around REDUced PERson) — a figure who cannot be located biographically, and instead requires a new form of subjectivity to be realized in the *contradictions* of capitalist socialization.[78]

The triangle organises a subject, but few political biographies of this subject exist. There are many 'contradictions of capitalist socialization' and for women and feminists in art, the relationship between work and non-work remains a central one. The dividing line between public and private corresponded to the one between work and non-work, mapped onto a series of related binaries: 'work' was culture, social recognition and visibility, creativity; 'non-work' was nature, social obscurity and invisibility, (domestic) drudgery. Yet, as oft repeated, art is now a field of engagement where work and non-work are significantly blurred, which is why Steyerl sought to interpret art today as a field favouring 'occupation' over labour.[79] Occupation is fuzzy, a grey zone between wilful attachment to something of personal interest and making oneself potentially useful to the social body. Still it takes time — it's just one is unsure what this time is spent on. Being involved in art politically only intensifies one's inability to distinguish between work and non-work, as Von Osten observes.

The destabilisation of work and non-work as categories does not constitute liberation from the private–public antagonism. The woman 'photographer, feminist activist, and theorist, that is, cultural producer, but also a product of emancipatory demands and capitalist impositions' becomes a decentred subject in a strongly negative sense. Rather than discover that she has always been such a subject and locate in this discovery the potential of re-assembling herself, she realises that, in the inescapable materiality of her life, she is unable to align her internal multiplicity with her political direction towards de-compartmentalising herself. (And is her multiplicity genuinely internal, in the sense of belonging inherently to her psyche since the moment of its emergence? Or is it, in fact, the internalised multiplicity of demands and impositions that have piled up in the course of her life?) In the objective conditions of her life, her sense of fragmentation can be the end of the road, stemming from the depressing realisation that she's all dressed up with nowhere to go. She is permanently locked — locked *individually* in the solitary confinement effected through the division of labour *among women* — in a social complex where her ultimately personal revolt cannot be completed (despite capitalism promising exactly this: individually realised freedom). In the clash between the need to work for a living and taking up an alternative life as (hard) work, the best she can hope for is to find herself (pun intended) in an alternative work environment — a promise the art field makes.

Since the late twentieth century, as artists' mobility became a requirement, perhaps especially in non-studio-dependent practice, travel became gendered work in the art field.[80] Artists are expected to conduct research and fieldwork, to install work, to take up residencies, to give talks, to network internationally, to be kept informed about the work of other artists and developments in the field, or even take up a teaching post wherever in the world to make ends meet (which may be temporary or part-time, in which case you don't, for example, move your dependents but you live in two places, e.g., 'London and Berlin'). The 'itinerant artist' is not a figure of speech, but rather describes the work conditions of many 'successful' artists.[81] Being successful involves having built an international profile — the main aspiration of entry-level artists, which is another way to say that in globalisation, mobility has solidified into an ideology. The mobility requirement embedded in artistic labour at present (including retreats and the ubiquitous 'residency' culture) is in direct conflict with the work of family-focused social reproduction — and where women are single mothers, entire 'components' of the contemporary art-work culture (such as residencies) may become impossible. Not having children means not being homebound, and this can apply more in cases where artistic labour involves weeks or months spent in 'real' social relations encountered outside the home, the studio, one's town, or one's country of residence, all complicated by the artist as taxpayer and by immigration law. Marina Abramovic was certainly right to say that 'children hold back female artists' although putting the matter this way is a covert affirmation of the oppressive social relations that men in art (and all sectors) benefit from as a group.[82]

The 'refusal to procreate' was possibly the most radical break from social norms that feminism ever brought forth: its consequences in advanced economies, as Mariarosa Dalla Costa explains,[83] have been profound and reverberate today, when with the rise of ultra-conservative social values women in childbearing years are increasingly seen as a potential liability to employers. And this gives the refusal to participate in reproductive labour a different meaning: does refusal count as liberation when imposed by the unwritten requirements of productivity of a woman's waged labour or search for income? A woman artist may choose to drop mobility after having children, which is likely to bear most negatively on her career. In 2013, Jennifer Thatcher discussed labour relations in the UK art field where 'news of pregnancies' was 'met with barely concealed irritation. Sometimes it seemed that no one [e.g. artists' assistants] ever came back from maternity leave, or else they left soon after. That they occasionally sued seemed to be treated as a necessary cost of getting rid of them.'[84] Let's say, however, that if an employer in an 'advanced' economy with legislation enshrining anti-discrimination and reproductive health rights tells a pregnant woman to get an abortion otherwise she will lose her job, the woman would be expected to take the case to a court of law. If an arts professional has so internalised the production requirements of her profession as to exclude the possibility of pregnancy, it is seen as the free choice of a liberated woman. Women artists — or any artist with a womb — can believe that they are making such a free choice (practicing the feminist 'refusal to procreate') as liberated subjects. Yet such choice can be pure ideology — indeed, an ideology necessary for submitting to the demands of the labour market as organised in capitalism, even when (as in the case of art) wages may well be absent and the woman is asked to practice self-management towards the promise of procuring income.

Women also believe that they are making a free choice ('I'm doing it for myself, not a man') when they use cosmetics or get cosmetic surgery, but one's self tends also to be constituted through dominant ideology defining 'gender'. Feminist artists since the 1970s, from Europe to Latin America and beyond, have created numerous artworks exploring the social imperative for women to use make-up and beautification instruments and procedures — the Buenos Aires militant feminist art collective Mujeres Publicas (Public Women) displayed many of them in their installation *Museum of Torture* (2004). Yet the beautification imperative is not unconnected to how capitalism wants its workers to be. When beautification becomes a requirement for women to compete in a newly launched capitalist labour market, as happened in certain Eastern European countries during the so-called transition period after 1989, the new imperative is noticed precisely because it has *not yet* congealed into ideology: Estonian artist Mare Tralla has addressed the valorisation of 'looks' in the work ethic introduced in her native post-Soviet Estonia and post-socialist countries at large. On the other hand, a comment such as 'she's in excellent shape for a 39-year-old', made about Andrea Fraser in her *Untitled* (2003) where she appears naked and having sex with a male collector, seems unremarkable: the artwork was made in the US, chief exporter of the valorisation-of-looks work ethic.[85]

The issue, however, of free choice in having children has been contentious for feminism: feminists had to fight very hard and for many generations so that women could access jobs, as well as gain the right to abortion, and the right to choose whether to procreate or not. Childbearing remains a politically contested issue and, in our century, it will only increase in intensity as 'lower fertility rates' are (covertly or not) blamed on women and their choices. What generates panic is the 'serious challenges to the economic growth of a shrinking workforce' and that 'these future trends in fertility rates and livebirths will completely reconfigure the global economy and the international balance of power and will necessitate reorganising societies'.[86] The second wave of feminism was not facing such a situation. At the same time, the feminists who already in the 1970s referred to raising children as providing labour-power to capital have been vindicated. The demographic panic makes sense if we connect it to capitalism's anxiety about limits to growth as the left calls for 'a materialist understanding of why the world is tending toward lower rates of fertility'.[87] A new iteration of consciousness-raising is required: one examining what individuals' 'free choice' means in relation to the reality of the labour market rather than in relation to the potential of self-definition and self-determination that capital has every interest in retaining as a useful myth. This is partly what is at stake in the work/non-work conflict for feminism at large, and specifically in art. There should be no doubt that for now capital is in charge of this conflict.

IN CONCLUSION, THE MOTIVATIONAL QUESTION

The clash between life, work, and our capacity for political subjectivity and agency are affected by the expectations tied to art, as presented at the beginning of this chapter. Contradictions are faced at every step: the writer's/curator's/artist's autonomy is in conflict with the complex dependency that atomised work-labour in the public domain constitutes; the political necessity to engage in reformist rethinking of the specifics that in any given context shape feminists' relationship to institutions continues, as do the divides that prevent a shared view of a transformative horizon; the objectively generated inability to differentiate between work and non-work still compels feminists to decide, day in day out, what activities are to be prioritised so as to achieve the so-called life-work 'balance'. A paradigm of concessions takes hold, one that we are able to endure because of the freedom to discuss it with others. But in the 2020s, the overwhelming rise of censorship and self-censorship undermines even discursive exchanges: among those who have jobs or are blessed with exhibitions, few would risk losing either to confront institutional guidelines or decisions, especially if they have dependents. How, then, can the transition from politically informed theoretical exchange to the praxis of a critical feminist mass be imagined? This can be the motivational question from which to start facing up to the reality of contradictions that both shape involvement with the presentness of feminist struggle and function as limits to such involvement as practised through art. The following two chapters look deeper into this question.

4

The Long Modern I:
Notes on the Contemporary

This is the first of two chapters that consider the following question: as the feminist struggle can only take place in real time, that is, in 'the contemporary', how can we understand this contemporary? The contemporary is constantly revisited in art writing, which now even includes references to a 'post-contemporary' as the old concept of 'future' appears too hopeful against capital's realities of capture. I see the distinction established in many art history curricula between 'modern' and 'contemporary' art as unhelpful for understanding how capitalism shapes the art field; that, instead, capitalist modernity necessarily brings forth a conceptual, institutional, ideological, and subjectivation apparatus recognisable since the nineteenth century[1] — though this apparatus changes in an evolving capitalism, as does resistance. I use the term Long Modern to indicate this trajectory, which brings us to the twenty-first century and which includes reconstitutions of 'the contemporary' as historically specific articulations. Grasping the Long Modern as largely a continuum within a mode of production and reproduction is necessary for formulating the politics of feminism in the *current* contemporary. The chapter is divided into three parts: the first outlines how capitalism underpins the construction of a (prized) artistic masculinity as the fulfilment of modernity's potential versus a (denigrated) femininity that was its very antithesis, essentialised as anti-modern. This helps us understand second-wave feminism's political critique of the modern and modernism, where we also find, for example, context for Lucy Lippard's suggestion in 1980 that 'feminism's greatest contribution to the future of art has probably been precisely its lack of contribution to modernism'.[2] The second part of the chapter examines the specific contemporary in which the feminist art movement was able to be realised in the Long Modern.

The third part considers why the contemporary must be privileged by feminism when theorising art.

WHAT DOES CAPITAL WANT? THE IDEOLOGICAL FUNCTION OF THE ARTIST

Modernity, the story goes, gave us 'modern art', a known category embedded in art history curricula. In the 1970s and 1980s, the first generation of feminist art historians investigated the extent to which the experimental imagination of modern art relied on a sharp division between the 'signifier' (what was visible in the image) and the 'signified' (what the visible element in the image actually referred to), to use the semiotics jargon of the period. The female body, sometimes naked, was found to be a key signifier in modern art, which, despite the latter's questioning of tradition, did not altogether give up the noble category of 'the nude'. But — feminist art historians argued convincingly — what these images of the female body signified was, principally, a particular conception of masculinity. It was this idea of masculinity, embodied in the male artist (and certainly the male painter), that was conveyed to the viewer, contributing therefore to the affirmation of the male sex–gender, in its constructed whiteness, as the apex of society's creative energy and the rightful maker of culture. Irrespective of an artist's intentions and political declarations, modern art as a racialising and gendering system favoured attributes that reflected and made desirable the values that capital deployed in its worldmaking operation, such as exploration, conquering, breaking new ground, innovating. In an article published in *Artforum* in 1973, Carol Duncan discussed virility as a key attribute of the heroic artist of the historical avant-gardes, arguing that the

> vogue for virility in early twentieth century art is but one aspect of a total social, cultural and economic situation that women artists had to overcome. It was a particularly pernicious aspect. As an ethos communicated in a hundred insidious ways, but *never overtly*, it effectively alienated women from the collective, mutually support-ive endeavour that was the avant garde.[3]

Yet the cult of virility, associated with individual independence, freedom–autonomy, and self-determination as prized social values, stood in contrast with the social experience of most men, including those who lived lives of wage-dependency, numbing everyday-ness structured by long working days, and subjugation to capital's needs: the industrial proletariat.[4] In Britain, this existed in a context where 'work' was 'central to masculine identity'.[5] At the same time, bourgeois propriety could also be oppressive for men through the routines it demanded. Norma Broude argued, for instance, that the perceived 'misogyny' of French artist Edgar Degas had to do with his self-conscious distance from the sense of entrapment with which the bourgeois-patterned private sphere was associated.[6] Also, constructed as sites of unspoilt, primitive (read: pre-capitalist) experience, the colonies provided notable routes of escape for white male European artists such as Paul Gauguin: this is curatorially confirmed by exhibitions such as *Paul Gauguin — Why Are You Angry?* (2022), not unlikely to be held in prestigious art institutions of colonial powers (here, Germany).[7] Contemporary research has tried to disentangle Gauguin from the colonial imaginary by arguing that his interest in adolescent girls from the colonies merely matched that of European men for European girls and that 'Polynesians loved him' while 'the French hated him' for trying to expose their oppressive rule;[8] this hardly changes the fact that Tahiti as a destination was enabled by colonialism.

The 'brilliant', exceptional, non-conforming, white individuality of the modern artist, free to pursue and realise his humanity in terms of a personal, creative vision, was the obvious antithesis to the proletarian experience of labour. To an extent, it was also a positive and glamorised rendering of the proliferating wageless men, 'the rascal, swindler, beggar, the unemployed, the starving, wretched and criminal workingman'.[9] On the level of ideology, it was also a useful exception to the morality that the public/private divide imposed, a divide necessary for capitalism to function, as we have already seen. Coded white, the bohemian, eccentric male artist was a broadly operative necessary idea and ideal for capitalist modernity: if the majority of men were condemned to stultifying, identical lives given to alienating labour, and if middle-class status largely dictated enslavement to conformity and (comfortable if precarious) routine, what did modernity have to offer? Creative, bohemian masculinity was thus implicitly defined as aspirational manhood: an exodus to which a man could aspire, and moreover, one that did not need a revolution against capital in order to exist. *This* masculinity was conferred as the cardinal, sought-after privilege in specific historical conditions. The man who claimed time as his own to realise his personal, unique, experimental vision — inspired by visits to brothels where women's sexuality was offered for consumption (Pablo Picasso) or by the feeling of being more liberated in the colonies than at home (Gauguin) — held the promise that life without alienation was, in the last instance, possible within capitalism.

Perhaps even life without labour that was appropriated by capital was possible, as it was unclear whether 'artmaking' was labour at all. If it was, it held a degree of freedom because it did not valorise capital directly, but only entered capitalist circulation if it was bought and sold. In any event, it was obvious that art was more pleasant than useful, serving individual self-realisation. Keeping art apart from the 'usefulness' (valorisation of capital) that capitalism demanded of labour has informed theorisations of art as autonomous/protectable. Something called 'craft', as the other to art, had to be distinguished because it produced usable objects, and especially ones that were potentially reproducible, even if with variations. There exists a socialist lineage of men taking us back to the nineteenth century that tried to subvert the craft–art distinction by practicing what Sven Lütticken calls 'aesthetic utilitarianism',[10] its presence still niche in the narrative of modern art. In 2018, it had to be re-asserted that textiles 'have always suffered as an art medium because of their association with domesticity and femininity', and so Anni Albers' Tate Modern show had to be justified as that of a 'former Bauhaus student' and 'the first weaver to have a significant solo show at the Museum of Modern Art in 1949'.[11] The first generation of feminist art historians had pointed out that the craft–art distinction exemplifies women's devalued work. True as this was, it cannot be understood outside a broader tendency of capitalist modernity to scorn manual labour.

Craft has not been limited to domesticity in the history of capitalism. Silvia Federici notes that already in the fifteenth century, at capitalism's emergence, men craft workers started a war against women craft workers, excluding them 'from their workshops, presumably to protect themselves from the assaults of capitalist merchants who were employing women at cheaper rates'.[12] This more complex history of women's labour at various stages of capitalism must be taken into account if we wish to understand the meaning of the strict imposition of the private/public divide in the nineteenth century, and how women's exclusion from the public world of labour came to be a *class* ideal. To this, we would add David Beech's lucid analysis of the material conditions in which the artist-as-genius 'presents the hyperbolic image of the independent white, propertied male as a universal exemplar of freedom' while being 'simultaneously a *mythic trope of labour*':[13] the artist-as-genius should be free from handicraft. Beech traces the gradual transition from the artisan who performed various kinds of labour to an art world of compartmentalised labour performed by various agents. In 1964, philosopher Arthur Danto referred to the 'artworld' as a highly specific context of specialisms. Andy Warhol's sculptural replication of Brillo soap pad boxes, for example, was incomprehensible as art unless one was clued in with and versed in theory,[14] that is through intellectual labour. However, Brillo pads were not merely an industrially produced commodity used to clean dishes of hard-to-remove food residue; Brillo pads were overtly associated with housewives and their not-so-muscular middle-class husbands trying to clean saucepans, as the product's period adverts aptly demonstrate. Perhaps such ads increased the philosopher's shock over what was admissible as art in the early 1960s.[15]

In Beech's account of the division of labour, handicraft (what was *shed* for the artist to emerge) became denigrated while the 'artist' became a valued exception in more ways than one: 'the artist emerges from the scholarly occupation of the Fine Art into capitalism not by becoming worker but by becoming an *anomaly* to both the old regime and the modern industrial system'.[16] From a Marxist feminist perspective, this is less of an anomaly: the artist's 'uselessness' was a reward reserved mostly for select men — those rescued from the oppressed and exploited productive subjects (coded male) and reproductive subjects (coded female). Feminist opposition to capitalist social reproduction arrangements was intolerable: '"feminist aspirations" —particularly those relating to higher education and entry to the professions' were set 'against Britain's imperialistic ambition' by depriving the nation of 'virility'.[17] This polarity cannot be comprehended if class is sidelined, for not all women ushered to the private sphere were 'useless'. Maids were very useful: they freed others' time rather than merely supporting these comfortable lifestyles.

There is an interesting relationship between the 'uselessness' of bourgeois women, as observed by Sheila Rowbotham, and the 'uselessness' of the male artist's work — his artmaking — which did not fit squarely within normative production. Whereas the presumed uselessness of art became identified with freedom, non-alienation, and novelty, the uselessness of the bourgeois woman became identified with an anti-modernity within modernity: passivity, docility, a parasitical existence. When a woman's existence was not 'parasitical', it was nevertheless framed within this ideology of femininity: factory owners expressed 'a decided preference to married females [as employees], especially those who have families at home dependent on them for support; they are attentive, docile... compelled to use their utmost exertions to produce the necessaries of life'.[18] The conscious refusal of the bohemian male artist to capitulate to the demands of capitalist production (the dull, exhausting, and generally oppressive working day) was the very antithesis of the bourgeois woman's guarded removal from labour. And as already discussed, because of her class position, the 'useless' bourgeois woman inevitably embodied an ideal that impacted women overall. In this class-defined script — despite some women's revolutionary politics — womanhood, as such, stood as the opposite of self-determination or revolt. If we add to this that women in revolt would spell the loss of very material benefits for men, the operative misogyny of modernity seems to be enmeshed in contradiction. And yet, it was very real. When Surrealism in the interwar period sought to admire and value femininity, the women that the male Surrealist vanguard chose for worship were the polar opposite of tamed bourgeois femininity: 'mad' women, violent women, poor women, 'prostitutes', and women generally 'lost' in the labyrinth of the capitalist metropolis.

So tainted has 'femininity' been in the history of modernity and its art that anything implying an association with it, *including feminism*, had to be repudiated even by many women artists. As Jo Applin put it, 'for many women artists in the 1960s their primary aim was precisely to avoid being categorised, and so marginalised, solely as "women" artists'.[19] Applin quotes artist Bridget Riley who said in 1973 that 'artists who happen to be women need this particular form of hysteria like they need a hole in the head' — women's liberation being characterised by this successful woman artist as 'hysteria' (a 'disorder' etymologically connected to the womb). Is hegemonic ideology, examined in Chapter Two, perhaps relevant here? The reluctance of many women artists to be associated with a 'mass' (a social movement about them) is grounded in the myth of exceptional women — claiming access to expressive individuality as social status — which complements the male genius myth.

Despite a longer history of feminism, both material constraints and ideology combined to disallow the emergence of a feminist *art* movement up to the late 1960s and 1970s in the West, the territories that were the base of capital's gradually expanding global hegemony. Women's exclusion from art education, as well as from regular education arguably required to bring forth a feminist counter-public (in Britain 'even for a girl born in 1950, there was... no equal access to education'),[20] alongside the hegemony of an ideal of femininity that mirrored bourgeois propriety — and therefore retreat from the public sphere — were strong components of this reality. The pervasive ideology of meritocracy, whereby a worthy individual could escape the general experience of gender/race/class, was another factor, combined with art's perceived autonomy and operation on the plane of high culture, aesthetic detachment, and 'uselessness'. Reading Julia Bryan Wilson's *Art Workers* (2009), a study of the development of left tendencies in the American art field in the late 1960s and 1970s, we see that the contestation of art's uselessness — what the idea of the 'art worker' opposed — was crucial for shaping the feminist subject in American art.

Yet the history of the emergence of feminism as a large-scale, cross-border, collective endeavour specifically in the art field in the late 1960s and 1970s requires further examination, despite partial, and still extremely important, records, such as Rozsika Parker and Griselda Pollock's *Framing Feminism: Art and the Women's Movement 1970–1985* (1987) or, more recently, Amy Tobin's *Women Artists Together* (2023). Why at a certain point in the Long Modern did many women artists and art historians enact feminist critique and generate an art movement in dialogue with feminism as a social movement? Given that there is no clear answer to this crucial question in sight, we can consider some aspects of 'the contemporary' in which the feminist art movement emerged.

IN WHICH CONTEMPORARY DID THE FEMINIST ART MOVEMENT EMERGE? NOTES ON POSTMODERNISM AND THE COLD WAR

The seven-week popular uprising in France known as May 1968 is a symbolic date–event and is the date most associated with the rise of 'contemporary art'. Historical and philosophical accounts reiterate the transnational relevance of this student–worker-led uprising, for which, it is often said, imagination was a political weapon against the dreariness of capitalist life: May 1968 started in Nanterre, a modern-style university campus where 'thirteen thousand students, many of them from the privileged western districts of Paris, [had] dropped onto this isolated site, with no life or attractions, in the midst of the overcrowded zone inhabited by Algerian laborers'.[21] Literary theorist Kristin Ross stresses that May 1968 was a large-scale anticapitalist insurgency, opposing American imperialism and Gaullist nationalism, but, crucially, that later narratives successfully cleansed it of its concrete revolutionary takes,[22] defanging public memory of 1968 as the youthful letting off of steam.

As an insurgent *political* moment, May 1968 was defeated. Some see contemporary art as shaped by this defeat. In 2009, Grant Kester painted a complex picture of the impact of May 1968 as a political defeat for the left, which he summarised with some irony as follows: 'We cannot yet be trusted with the freedom that would result from a total revolution. Instead we must practise this freedom in the virtual space of the text or artwork, supervised by the poet or artist'.[23] The May 1968 defeat would indeed signal the extreme marginalisation of the revolutionary left in the socio-political field, and the partial rechannelling of its energy (or, perhaps, frustration) into art or, less strictly, 'culture' where imagination could be as separate from life as it wished. In *The New Spirit of Capitalism*, Luc Boltanski and Eve Chiapello mark May 1968 as having far wider repercussions: already in the 1970s capital was making the most of May 1968's rejection of hierarchy and factory-like discipline by reforming the workplace as less rigid and more creative, responding to 'differences' and 'lived experience'. A defeat for labour can inspire capitalist strategy.

This assessment constructs quite a complicated context for understanding the emergence of the feminist art movement in the capitalist West — including in France where Swiss feminist filmmaker Carole Roussopoulos (1945–2009), from an upper-class background, would, after being laid off from *Vogue*, proceed to buy a Sony Portapak. She would document the women's liberation movement as public presence in the streets but also expand to works such as the 26-minute-long *SCUM Manifesto* (1976), with Delphine Seyrig performing a reading of Valerie Solanas's inflammatory words from 1967 against a TV set showing the imperialist atrocities of a male-dominated world. Roussopoulos and her partner, Paul, a Greek communist exile and intellectual, became involved in radical left cultural activism within a far broader circle, including Jean Genet. The co-founder of important video collectives in the 1970s, and not least feminist ones such as Les Insoumuses (The Disobedient Muses) which claimed video as non-art, Roussopoulos and her milieu far from disregarded women in labour and production. They couldn't have: what is widely considered the first feminist video in France, which Roussopoulos was asked to edit, was about a women-led strike during massive lay-offs of women workers.[24] Her work addressed women in production, social reproduction, and their representation in the media. It would be very hard for a Marxist feminist art history to see the work of Roussopoulos, or anyone like her, as tied to labour's political defeat. Roussopoulos would later collaborate with Greek performance, film, and media artist Leda Papakonstantinou in works that shed light on the conditions of working-class women in Greece during the twentieth century.[25] It is important to acknowledge the trajectories of such collaborations among feminists, especially where class and women workers re-appear in their artworks — and especially as these trajectories move beyond the Western core, so favoured in art histories (feminist or not) that are only nominally international.

That said, second-wave feminism as a social movement gained momentum in the streets and through collective action mainly after May 1968. One important reason was that feminists on the left began questioning their marginalisation within the left. In the US, where the Vietnam War and oppression of African Americans met with resistance, the Combahee River Collective's Black lesbian socialist feminists wrote in the 1970s: 'We realize that the liberation of all oppressed peoples necessitates the destruction of the political-economic systems of capitalism and imperialism as well as patriarchy'.[26] Contra Kester's assertion that there was suspicion towards political organising post-May 1968, feminists *did* organise both in society and the art field — exhibitions such as *Women in Revolt!* at Tate Britain in London (2023–24) indicate the imbrication of the search for political agency and artistic agency. It is therefore doubtful whether the eruption of feminism in the 1970s should be seen as the outcome of the left's blanket political defeat. The ideological formation of the second wave was complex, though Boltanski and Chiapello's insightful assessment that May 1968 was a lesson for capital and its managerial functionaries cannot be ignored: the elements that we encounter in an 'inclusive', better-governed capitalist workplace, and eventually social whole, were set in motion then. That in the 1970s, leftist feminist artists initially turned to the documentation of women workers' lives but later abandoned it,[27] in fear they would be speaking for others, unfolded in the context of such broader shifts: these 'others' (working-class women) were as a group 'excluded' from the making of culture. That attendance to class and economic relations waned within the feminist art movement had a lot to do with the intellectual climate that formed following the containment of the revolutionary left. Arguably, this containment played a role in the dilemmas faced by feminists generally, including in art.

Often seen as the endpoint of modern art proper, the 1960s closed at an ambivalent moment for women — a moment that should form a distinct, collective research project for feminist art scholarship today. In 1969, Canadian social theorist Margaret Benston published 'The Political Economy of Women's Liberation' starting, as political scientist Heather Brown notes, 'the domestic-labour debate and discussions of the reproductive sphere' while in the fall of that year, art historian Linda Nochlin, whose thought had also been shaped through Marxism (to the shock of her milieu), taught Vassar College's *Art 364b*, a course on women in art, seeing a notable gap in art history.[28] In the art context of late 1960s America, women did some strange things: as already seen, Mierle Laderman Ukeles wrote *Manifesto for Maintenance Art 1969!* that highlighted the opposition between 'The Death Instinct: separation; individuality; Avant-Garde par excellence' and 'The Life Instinct: unification; the eternal return; the perpetuation and MAINTENANCE of the species; survival systems and operations; equilibrium'. Lee Lozano, 'a quixotic, confounding rebel' according to *The New York Times*,[29] experimented with going on strike as an individual artist *and* ceasing her contact with other women — 'boycotting women' — as a life-long art project. Playwright Valerie Solanas' outright rejection of 'Great Art' features in her 1967 self-published *SCUM Manifesto*,[30] which inverted modernity's social script that placed women and ideal femininity as the opposite of the modern artist by stating it was men who could not be artists: '"the male artist" is a contradiction in terms' since, for Solanas, men depended on women and could not be autonomous subjects and actually 'living'. In her militant parody full of purposeful inversions (against entrenched essentialising misogyny, her *SCUM Manifesto* essentialises and hates men),[31] it is precisely the fact that art must draw on life that makes it impossible for men to be artists. Yet one gets the sense that the outspoken Solanas of a fierce intellect — a survivor of sexual molestation by her father in her troubled working-class childhood and suffering from mental illness later in life — was mostly an embarrassment for arts-based feminism, possibly because she shot Andy Warhol in 1968, seeing him as the embodiment of the neglect and insignificance she faced as a woman. In 1969 in Italy, Carla Lonzi published *Self-portrait*, her 'farewell' to art criticism, seeing art as the antithesis of life. As the feminist art movement was forming, we can observe all these dispersed moves of agitation: pointing to the violence of actually existing misogyny through what we might call gender role reversal (Solanas); rejecting the art world, declaring it antithetical to a feminist life (Lonzi); questioning and subverting the gender division of labour that had defined modern art and the avant-garde (Ukeles); over-identifying with modern art's contempt for women *and* with the avant-garde's wish to be sublated into life (Lozano). All these acts announced the damaging conflict that women as creative subjects were facing in contexts that projected onto art the highest-order realisation of freedom.

Situated between the existential and the political, women artists' restlessness was observed in the non-Western geographies of Eastern Europe and Latin America. In 1967 in Poland, which did not belong to the capitalist West, documentary filmmaker Krystyna Gryczelowska made *24 Hours from the Life of Jadwiga L.*, highlighting the production/social reproduction cycle in the life of a female factory worker.[32] That women in state-socialist countries worked impossibly long working days imposed by productivity requirements suggests that capital's values were pulling the strings in a global context of competition — history never really witnessed capitalism confined to one country or region. In the non-aligned, yet socialist, Yugoslavia, Sanja Iveković started juxtaposing photographs of herself and other women taken between the 1950s and 1970s with photographs of women from lifestyle magazines; titled *Double Life* (1976), the pairs of photographic images highlighted the absurd expectations attached to women in a visual culture ultimately shaped by capital as an economy that constructed desire beyond the confines of the West. For some women artists, imperialist interests generated contexts of particular oppression. Anna Maria Maiolino, who grew up in Italy's Calabria amidst the deprivation of World War II, made the woodcut *Anna* in Brazil, where she had settled, in 1967 during the country's military dictatorship (1964–85): two figures none of whose facial features remain except for black mouths screaming her name: 'Anna'. Cecilia Vicuña started her precarious objects, meant not to last, in 1966; in exile to escape Pinochet's dictatorship in Chile (1973–90), the 'indigenous mestiza', as she called herself, eventually addressed through multiple deployments of precariousness those who perished under the extremely violent regime, as well as the vulnerability of '"despised peasant ideas" that secretly fuelled centuries of resistance against colonialism'.[33] Anyone who would today call for a transnational feminist art movement should remember the complexity of the late 1960s and early 1970s for women and feminism. Stemming from profound discontent, these artists' decisions on how to narrate women's position/s in their juncture are interconnected. Modernity was seen as a problem and was questioned, and postmodernism emerged as a convincing concept for such a questioning.

Often associated with the Situationist International in Europe and Pop Art in the US, in their radically different take on the capitalist everyday, the 1960s saw the publication of two books whose impact would be long-lived: Marshall McLuhan's *Understanding Media: The Extensions of Man* (1964) and Guy Debord's *Society of the Spectacle* (1967). The phenomena these texts described — the signs-based circulation of capital as a social relation (Debord) and the technological mediation of social values and the self (McLuhan) where 'the medium is the message' — would underwrite postmodernism as the emerging hegemony. The feminist art movement, including feminist art history, took form and acted in this context. As regards art, 'postmodernism' is normally used to describe developments roughly from the 1970s until the early 1990s, the period defined by the technologically mediated spectacle, also marked by the struggles and gains of feminism in the arts. The avant-gardes of modernity were subjected to rigorous and melancholy-driven critique — both by those who regarded them as failed and irretrievably co-opted and by feminists who critiqued the avant-gardes' masculinism and, often, misogyny. Feminists' powerful critique of the historical avant-gardes played a role in allowing feminism's association with a postmodern vision, despite Griselda Pollock arguing in 1987 that 'the role of feminism is not to be incorporated as a new-ism to add richness to the pluralism popularly labelled Post-modernism'.[34]

What was the postmodern vision about? Largely, it was about the prioritisation of an immaterial register: signs, texts, codes. The materiality of class relations, production, labour, and so on, receded to total or relative obscurity. When considering the way that women artists in Britain gradually dropped the class enquiry, we must remember that they made choices in the context of a dominant postmodernism. Since postmodernism was broadly understood as the cultural milieu of a consumer society premised on the technology–spectacle nexus, feminist analysis shifted to the consumption of femininity across the immaterial sites of representation from Hollywood film to art, literature, and visual culture at large, with the adoption of psychoanalysis as a methodological tool. Psychoanalysis was a great aid to the project of deconstructing representation circulating across the many technologically connected sites of the spectacle. Despite its patriarchal bias, psychoanalysis — which had discovered 'the unconscious', and paid attention to the construction of the psyche and subjectivity, or, as per Jacques Lacan, addressed the subject through language — was helpful in averting reliance on crass biologism as the source of women's oppression. Still, psychoanalysis as a method in art theory was compatible with hegemonic postmodernism, for it primarily enabled the reading of signs and the relationship of individuals, marked by 'sexual difference', to a social context that appeared dominated by exchange on the immaterial plane.

One may object: what about 'the body'? The body was a keyword for that generation's feminism, but it was often caught in a debate structured between the poles of 'essentialism' and 'social constructionism', with the latter often limiting the social to language and code. This essentialism versus social constructionism polarity was itself already expressive of a postmodern way of seeing that sidelined the mode of production as a mode of reproduction. Feminist art history and theory was far from a unified field because the decentred subject privileged by postmodernism stood in conflict with feminism as a discourse rooted in an earlier moment of the Long Modern, where the author/artist was the locus of valid self-expression. This was a real contradiction for feminism in art, and led to an internal culture war occasionally translated into geographical terms: a more icono-clastic, theoretically sophisticated, yet eclectic, approach in Britain and a more woman-centred approach in the US. This schema is inac-curate and simplifying, and upholding it would only conceal a deeper conflict related to feminism and postmodernism. In 1995, Mary D. Garrard offered a witty account of this intellectual history in Western art's postmodern moment, concluding that:

> By the 1980s, the orthodox position for postmodern feminism rested on three incredibly negative tenets: (1) the notion of Woman is not real; woman exists only as a cipher of male dominance; (2) no possibility exists within a patriarchal social structure of a positive or empowered image of woman in art; and (3) the only possible move for women artists is to resist visual pleasure and expose the patriarchal system through deconstruction.[35]

Although Garrard did not attend to capitalism as the historical ground that may favour specific epistemologies, she pointed out that in the 'poststructuralist view, the category "woman" is a fiction, and fem-inism's task is to attempt to dismantle the whole system of thought that has imposed the tyranny of the binaries', wondering 'why should the category "Man" not come under similar microscopic scrutiny?'[36] Garrard's questioning of the epistemologies on which postmodern-ism relied was an important intervention. In 1997, Carol A. Stabile would take issue with the same epistemologies in 'Feminism and the Ends of Postmodernism'. Turning her attention to these episte-mologies' geographies of origin, and observing American academia's adoption of Michel Foucault's theory of abstract power as strongly 'anti-Marxist', she rhetorically posed the question regarding why 'at a time when the division of wealth is deepening, intellectuals discover that identity is actually fluid and discursive, that the economy is really discursively constructed, and that class position no longer matters'.[37] Debates around feminist aesthetics were very much caught in the essentialism–constructionism binary, but these debates were already expressive of a conflict between the dominant intellectual paradigm of postmodernism and the retention of women as an emancipatory subject enabled at an earlier moment of the Long Modern — as UK-based Pollock would stress, writing in 2021, that in around 1970 'women' were the collective subject addressed in the emancipatory struggle that she joined.[38] But the aforementioned conflict mediated this struggle and a degree of confusion reigned. Even an interwar period Marxist playwright such as Bertolt Brecht could be seen as postmodern, with Garrard writing: 'Feminist artists of the 1980s embraced other postmodern strategies, such as Brecht's idea of "distanciation": that the postmodern spectator should not experience an artwork naively, simply enjoying it aesthetically or accepting its message, but should instead be self-consciously aware of experiencing it as a text'.[39] Brecht was not a postmodernist but rather believed that the mode of production is the basis of historically formed, dominant forms of seductive spectatorship and that revolutionary art should challenge them, which is why Pollock used Brecht in her feminist critique. This critique however was eclectic and would combine Marxism with deconstruction, semiotics, poststructuralism (the very negation of structures in favour of fluid processes), and psychoanalysis in a context that prioritised language or anything like language over materiality. Eventually, the body would be viewed mostly through the lens of phenomenology (hence, references to 'embodiment' and 'lived experience') and, generally, through perspectives that would bring it close to the anti-historical materialism of the theoretical framework known today as new materialism/s.[40] Hiding the mode of production from view was what postmodernism achieved generally, and specifically for feminism.

If, as Stabile noted, feminism's direction in academia during postmodernism's heyday was co-extensive with the prevailing intellectual climate in the US, this climate was diligently cultivated, and indeed generously funded, by capitalist philanthropy. In 2018, Susan Watkins examined the funding sources of American academic programmes where 'the wealth of the philanthropic [capitalist] foundations played a crucial role… in the humanities, and above all the literature departments, where new generations of gender activists were generally schooled' and where 'the predominant influence remained Foucault'.[41] To date, much feminist thought continues to draw on Foucault. Nonetheless in the 2020s, Mitchell Dean and

Daniel Zamora argued that Foucault himself embraced neoliberalism in post-May 68 France, and that he advocated for neoliberalism seeing it effectively as a post- or anti-Marxist '*left* governmentality'.[42] This implied capitalism as the unmovable horizon, generating for many the melancholy of so-called post-politics. The implosion of the left today is not unconnected to these developments. Feminism in the 1970s and 1980s could not have foreseen this, yet the adoption of theoretical frameworks that marginalised or suppressed labour and class must be taken into account when considering the trajectory of the feminist art movement. Watkins notes the impact of benefactors and foundations, and specifically the Ford Foundation:

> In 1975 the [Ford] Foundation organized the launch of *Signs* as an interdisciplinary feminist journal, and in 1977 helped found the National Women's Studies Association and the National Centre for Research on Women, led by former Ford official Mariam Chamberlain. In the 1980s the Foundation switched to 'mainstreaming' feminism, as a component of the undergraduate core curriculum... by the early 90s, its priority was integrating research on minority women; its officials initiated a series of conferences that would prepare the ground for the take-up of intersectional theory. A consultant's report could justly note that Ford's project for the field of gender studies had 'actively influenced the direction it would take'.[43]

American capital paid to get the feminism it found suitable for its needs — an issue not raised in any feminist art history conference I have attended. Given America's cultural imperialism as an enhancement of its geopolitical imperialism, this suitable feminism became intellectually dominant well beyond the US, giving us the conceptual toolkit we broadly recognise as feminism today. This feminism made up a big chunk of the 'cultural turn' that postmodernism was about, where culture became the site where recognition would be sought. Dominated by the spectacle, the part of the Long Modern known as postmodernism was all about visibility. Feminism in art history paid much attention to women artists' exclusion from the circuits of dissemination that could guarantee visibility. Well into the 1990s and even after 2000, the emphasis continued being on art as the terrain where recognition and visibility would be achieved. What edited volumes nearly 20 years apart such as *Generations and Geographies in the Visual Arts* (1996) and *Women, the Arts and Globalisation* (2013) have in common with an exhibition catalogue such as *Global Feminisms* (USA 2007) was a desire to render visible the transnational spread of feminism in art and its diverse expressions.[44] The work on reproduction that Italian Marxist feminists were doing in the 1970s (Silvia Federici, Maria Rosa Dalla Costa, Leopoldina Fortunati, and others) was either not taken up by, or was not known to, the first wave of anglophone feminist art historians and artists. Griselda Pollock, for example, says that she was introduced to Silvia Federici's work in 2012 by the younger art historian Jaleh Mansoor,[45] who works on Marxist feminism. Today, we can only speculate whether Marxist feminism connected to Operaismo (Workerism) would have gained traction in a transnationally hegemonic Anglo-American paradigm which moved from the postmodern emphasis on the sign to the sign-like performativity of the (gender) code. This movement seems almost imperceptible in the history of ideas, as it retains the perceived immateriality of the language-form at the antipode of which awaits the primacy of matter as such (new materialism/s), and one wonders how long the age-old mind/body binary, opposed by feminist art history and theory, will persist in the Long Modern. This raises the question regarding what entered the internationalism of the feminist art movement in its important and necessary theory work. What have we received as the general idea of feminism?

A most important but also underexamined aspect of the contemporary in which the feminist art movement emerged involves postmodernism's connection with the Cold War. Postmodernism emerged in the West in the context of the Cold War: the polarised, militarised (but not armed) conflict between the US and the Soviet Union after World War II and lasting until the end of the 1980s. Postmodernism's attachment to semiotic instability, its embrace of 'anything goes' (endless fluidity), its undermining of history (delivered through the eclecticism of 'pastiche' and eclecticism overall), and its rejection of so-called 'grand narratives' denoted cultural freedom and experimentation as distinctly Western. This geographical belonging of postmodernism had political repercussions, as the West was identified with capitalism as an object of desire in its own right — to which postmodernism's affiliation to a libertarian, libido-driven consumer culture attested, even if some Western theorists would be critical of postmodernism. Postmodernism was symbolic of an 'open culture', and its Western matrix was where people (in the abstract) consumed.

Practicing the Good (2020), Keti Chukhrov's philosophical investigation of desire and sexuality, in the frugal and needs-based Soviet context and in Western capitalism as a culture of surplus and excess, offers an engaging account of how capitalism was made appealing.[46] Critiques along these lines were largely unavailable in the Western contexts where second-wave feminism, its art projects, and art history formed. The radicalism of feminist demands obscured the geopolitical reality in which these demands were shaped, and why they were supported by 'progressive' capitalist foundations. Feminism's alliances at the time drew it into a conflict between two worldviews and economic systems of asymmetrical power, in which feminism came to signify a Western/capitalist privilege that others lacked, irrespective of the very real social conditions that necessitated feminism.[47] Postmodernism was also desired: regions convinced that they were 'peripheries' would strive to show that they had postmodern art first. As, however, the readers of *International Affairs* were reminded in 1995:

> By 1970 'post-modernism' was being associated with another significant neo-philosophical and critical tendency: deconstruction, much concerned with the instability of all discourses, the slippage of all meanings and the fading of the grand narratives… the philosophy was generated in Paris, but mostly disseminated in the United States… 'America is deconstruction', Derrida enthusiastically said, while, explained a literary critic, Alan Wilde, 'postmodernism is essentially an American affair'.[48]

The feminist art movement was shaped by epistemologies, such as deconstruction and poststructuralism, that served postmodernism as a cultural project of freedom from a distinctly American angle. It is unclear to what extent this was seen by the majority of Western feminist art historians of the first generation, many of whom embraced these epistemologies, occasionally blending them with elements of Marxism they found compatible with the language turn. In his famous 1983 essay 'The Discourse of Others: Feminists and Postmodernism', which argued for the affinity of postmodernism and feminism, art critic Craig Owens (1950–90) disparaged Marxism, reflecting the spirit of the times. The suppression of Marxism — a key demand of the capitalist West during the Cold War — was overt, even if stated with slight concern:

> To claim that the division of the sexes is irreducible to the division of labor is to risk polarising feminism and Marxism; this danger is real, given the latter's patriarchal bias. Marxism privileges the characteristically masculine activity of production as the *definitively* human activity…; women, historically consigned to the spheres of non-productive or reproductive labor are thereby situated outside the society of male producers, in a state of nature… What is at issue, however, is not simply the oppressiveness of Marxist discourse, but its totalizing ambitions, its claim to account for every form of social experience.[49]

Marxism was thus charged with being both too reductive (focus on production) and too general (accounting for all social experience). Besides this, in the above passage we witness a typical transposition: the elements that actually characterise capitalism — the gender–sex division of labour, the prioritisation of production and the devaluation of reproduction, the need to proceed as a totality since more and more areas of life must be taken over by capital for accumulation to occur — are described as elements of an analytical framework (Marxism) that tries to explain and critique capitalism. The passage is indicative of what the dismissal of 'oppressive' grand narratives actually targeted: an analytical framework that addressed the structured interconnection of social relations brought forth by capital. The anti-totality principle of postmodernism haunts recent approaches to intersectionality that try to work out a relationship with Marxism: here, we find a confusing oscillation between conceiving of capitalism as one among many systems of oppression and capitalism as the predominant or structuring system of oppression.[50] The discrediting of a critical perspective that joined the dots in a totality was absolutely crucial for capital's intellectual hegemony in the 1980s when Margaret Thatcher and Ronald Reagan, in the UK and US respectively, were implementing the deregulation of markets known as neoliberalism. For the most part, feminism in art aligned with the perspective represented by Owens, despite feminist voices protesting the engulfing of feminism by postmodernism, which would eventually also give us postfeminism.[51]

Postmodernism was an updated 'cultural freedom' project of capital in the Cold War context — as far as we know, the first was the political instrumentalisation and export of Abstract Expressionism in the 1950s, apparently funded by the CIA, and according to filmmaker Johan Grimonprez the CIA also played a role in exporting distinct traditions of music.[52] In the case of postmodernism, there was no need for such exigency. Postmodernism was articulated as a cultural moment rather than a more narrow art movement. Unlike Abstract Expressionism, which could appear 'difficult', elitist, and circumscribed in male-dominated high art, postmodernism was far more multifaceted and diverse, ticking all the boxes. First, in generating a mostly accessible culture as it recycled the familiar tropes of consumerism, postmodernism signalled Western art's democratic expansion: its crucial pull to the discourse of identity would be presented as the democracy of equal representation through a transposition of politics into an anthologising diversity and pluralism. Second, postmodernism was the galvanising context of intellectual currents of anti- or post-Marxism, with the CIA being very much interested in them. A 'sanitised' (as the stamp on it says) declassified CIA document from 1985, released in 2011, uses the term 'post-Marxism' the same year that Ernesto Laclau and Chantal Mouffe's *Hegemony and Socialist Strategy* came out — seen as the cornerstone of the post-Marxist left. Stabile provides an insightful critique of this book in her 1997 essay, noting that the impact of 'postmodern social theory' on feminism's conception of democracy, was underpinned by the belief that 'social relations... are discursively constructed'.[53] Available on the agency's site, the 22-page-long CIA report, even in its 'sanitised' version, mentions the positive role of American popular culture for American geopolitical interests. It also discusses the role of new French theory, including the work of Foucault, in having created a new intellectual scene, which could be of service to American capitalism and imperialism: 'There is a new climate of intellectual opinion in France — a spirit of anti-Marxism and anti-Sovietism that will make it difficult for anyone to mobilize significant intellectual opposition to US policies in Central America'. Discussing how these interests were served even by diluted uses of Marxism (such as that of the Annales school of history in France, included, I note, in my high-school material in

Greece by the country's reformist social democratic government), the report discloses the agency's assessment that the 'centre-Left' will be all that remains of the left, that the 'unity of the left' is 'defunct', that the student movement is dead (even in May 1968's Nanterre campus). The report is an enviably astute analysis of how the core philosophical ground of postmodernism served American capitalist interests in the Cold War context. To this we could add recent research that reveals the cultivated anti-communism of American labour, its use by the CIA, and the impact on labour movements elsewhere.[54]

The CIA's efforts to create a postwar culture where freedom (and art) would be instrumentalised against communism takes us back to the 1950s. In June 1950, the US had already set up the Congress for Cultural Freedom in western Europe; its purpose was to support anti-communism, deploying the idea of freedom to do so. As the CIA says, the 'Congress for Cultural Freedom is widely considered one of the CIA's more daring and effective Cold War covert operations' and 'somehow this organization of scholars and artists, egotistical, free-thinking, and even anti-American in their politics managed to reach out from its Paris headquarters to demonstrate that Communism, despite its blandishments, was a deadly foe of art and thought'.[55] For those in the art field who at some point became concerned with this forgotten cultural engineering, the Cold War did not remain contained in its moment in history: in 2018, the exhibition *Parapolitics: Cultural Freedom and the Cold War* in Berlin sought to examine 'the ideological foundations of the conflict lines of today's global contemporary art'.[56] In 2017, Gabriel Rockhill had noted:

> The theoretical practices of figures who turned their back on what Cornelius Castoriadis called the tradition of radical critique — meaning anti-capitalist and anti-imperialist resistance — surely contributed to the ideological drift away from transformative politics. According to the spy agency itself [the CIA], post-Marxist French theory directly contributed to the CIA's cultural program of coaxing the left toward the right, while discrediting anti-imperialism and anti-capitalism, thereby creating an intellectual environment in which their [the US's] imperial projects could be pursued unhindered by serious critical scrutiny from the intelligentsia.[57]

What the 1985 CIA report describes occurred within a broader context of the agency's interventions, where we even find feminism was implicated: the scandal that erupted in the 1970s around the possibility that Gloria Steinem, a figurehead of the American feminist movement, had collaborated with the CIA in the late 1960s is a case in point.[58] As the US-based Redstockings left-radical feminist group lucidly put it in 1975, 'Women need a revolution and the CIA's job is to prevent revolutions'.[59] This succinct conclusion is not merely true; it also connects that historical moment with ours, as the first quarter of the twenty-first century closes with the apparentness of imperialism (complicated by Trump's second election to office in the US which entails the possible reconfiguration of American foreign policy, though still of course serving a project of hegemony, based on autocratic alliances, land grabbing, and various 'interventions'). The question of how to best serve capital — through liberalism or illiberalism — is now a structural component of the transnational fascist tendency, but capital will be served whatever the strategic choice made. For Marxist feminism in art history, it is imperative to excavate the intellectual and ideological formation of feminism in the political context of the 1970s and 1980s under the reign of postmodernism and the capitalist–imperialist strategy of the Cold War period.

Among the critical voices of the 1980s we find American art historian Hal Foster, who attempted a differentiation between a 'good' (pro-emancipation) and a 'bad' (conservative) postmodernism in 1985. He was ambivalent, however, about the accuracy of this distinction. His ambivalence concerned poststructuralism as the epistemology and philosophical current privileged by postmodernism, which destabilised 'truth'. Roland Barthes, Jacques Lacan, Julia Kristeva, Gilles Deleuze, and Michel Foucault are among those associated with this current, which exerted much influence on art-based feminism. Concerned with how '(poststructuralist) textuality differ[s] from (neoconservative) pastiche as a form of representation,' Foster wrote:

Do these opposed practices of textuality and pastiche differ in any deep *epistemic* way? Whatever else is claimed for them, is not the subject decentred, representation disentrenched, and the sense of history, of the referent, eroded in both?… If this is the case, then the neoconservative 'return' to the subject, to representation, to history may be revealed — historically, dialectically — to be one with the poststructuralist 'critique' of the same. In short, pastiche and textuality may be symptoms of the same 'schizophrenic' collapse of the subject and of historical narrativity — as signs of the same process of reification and fragmentation under late capitalism. And if these two models of postmodernism, so opposed in style and politics, are indeed historically one, then we need to consider more deeply what (post)modernism might be.[60]

Foster's observations are of heightened resonance today, as postmodernism — a term no longer in wide use in theorisations of contemporary art — has given way to the milieu of post-truth politics, irony-infused memes, and supremacy narratives, all staples of a newer world order in which fascism thrives.[61] This is the twenty-first-century contemporary. To return to the intellectual context of the feminist art movement, the belief that relations of power could be subverted discursively, through analysis of and changes in language, constituted the period's hegemonic idealism, which we now see was not a historical accident in more ways than one. Kester's observation that May 1968 prioritised freedom under the poet or artist's supervision meets Stabile's observation that postmodernism, which eschewed class in favour of 'articulation and articulatory practices', ultimately privileged 'those trained in the nuances of discourse and discursivity: namely, intellectuals'.[62]

But at what moment in capitalism's economic history was all this happening? Projects of cultural imperialism are only part of the story. Postmodernism's dominance coincided with a general pull to immateriality as Western capitalism was leading a data-driven society and a service economy through de-industrialisation and financialisation, where, through speculation, money is presumed to make money. In a brilliant book-length exposition, *Speculation as a Mode of Production* (2018), Marina Vishmidt highlights that 'what is at stake is the establishment of a historical, not to say epochal, symmetry between what might at first seem like, and what once perhaps really were, two distinct registers or domains of significance: financial speculation and speculative or *aesthetic* judgement'.[63] Vishmidt, who considers feminism in her analysis, finds in the 1960s and 1970s the enactment of 'a new concept of socially necessary activity for the artist… as both a producer of speculative value and reproducer of social norms of individualism, progress and democracy under the sign of *radical indeterminacy* — a position which the artist continues to occupy today'.[64]

Many cultural paradigms that marked that era, including Conceptual Art which inspired much of feminist art, signal the pull to the immaterial. The 'immaterial' was tied, in a whole new vocabulary, to 'floating', 'fluidity', 'flexibility', 'contingency', 'risk'. Where did this now familiar vocabulary come from? We may choose to see as a coincidence that the dissolution of the Bretton Woods Agreement of 1944 occurred between 1971 and 1976, which meant that the US dollar, as the dominant global currency, would no longer be tied to something as material as gold.[65] Globalisation as we know it today was established then. By the 1980s, as the incredibly detailed Wikipedia entry informs us, 'all industrialised nations were using *floating* currencies'.[66] This economy propped up the lexicon of fluidity, unfixity, dematerialisation, and indeed this is when 'floating' signifiers gain traction in cultural criticism and art theory. Philosopher Catherine Malabou opens a 2024 article on the 'floating signifier' as follows:

> In the 1980s there was a transition in poststructuralist and post-Marxist discourse from economic unity to symbolic unity. Such a transition caused a paradigm shift in critical theory and coincided with a strategy of resistance against essentialism. Essentialism, for many thinkers, Ernesto Laclau and Chantal Mouffe in particular, is bound up in the notion of class, particularly to the idea of an objective unity of the proletariat. More generally, the fight against essentialism aims at dismantling the categories of ground, substantiality, and universality.[67]

In the second paragraph of this article, Malabou proceeds to an implicit association of Marxism (which remains unnamed) and thinking about class with 'economic determinism', 'political essentialism', general 'determinism', 'dogmatism', while she traces the 'symbolic organization of the real… to both Claude Lévi-Strauss and Jacques Lacan'.[68] Those of us of the generation who entered feminist art history around the millennium need to pause here, for it seems that second-wave feminist art history and theory fits perfectly with the period's dominant intellectual trends. This compels a rethinking of the conditions of intellectual hegemony in which the feminist art movement formed.

Overall, a politics of signs (including the body being the sign of identity) continues to dominate, tied to numerous modalities of situated conviction and, occasionally, revivals of spiritualism. In the context that gradually developed in the 1970s and 1980s, materiality became tied to 'embodiment' in strands of the philosophical current known as phenomenology, thus aligning with a politics of appearance. Speculation and indeterminacy were compatible with appearance, especially as performativity and performance. As Vishmidt argues:

> Although Conceptual Art was initially impelled by anti-commodity principles (the famed, and famously misleading, 'de-materialisation' thesis), it actually reflected and anticipated a transition in capitalism from an economy centred on the industrial production of commodities to an economy centred on the control of intellectual property, trade in speculative assets, and the financialisation of older productive forms such as industry, while post-object art forms such as performance forecast a shift to (self-)'performance' as the evaluative prism for all labour.[69]

This observation enables a rethinking of art practices favoured by a feminism influenced by postmodernism, and calls on us to ask to what extent performance marked a transition from the inanimate object (say, a painting) to the human body as figuring reification — or, simply, objectification. This was especially useful in conflating (human) labour and 'human capital', as Vishmidt observes throughout *Speculation as a Mode of Production*. If certain practices were thought of as liberating and foregrounding the real-time presence of the artist as precisely a barrier to objectification, could they have only been perceived as such in ideological conditions that enabled an expansion of commodity fetishism? The aesthetics of post-2000 biopolitical art inflected by feminism, which moved from a consideration of the artist's body to the artist's life, as I have examined elsewhere in relation to Tanja Ostojić's and Andrea Fraser's work, formed within an expanded capture of subjectivity by capital. In literally advertising her naked self and entering the marriage contract to actualise the mobility requirement of artistic labour (Ostojić) and in performing contractual sex and relaxed intimacy with a male art-world agent as part of artistic labour (Fraser), both artists acted within and exposed the circuit that conflates human capital and human labour.[70] Entailing considerable risk, such practices exemplified and perhaps pursued the logical limits of the historically specific figuration of freedom that the open system of postmodernism originally provided within the Long Modern — that is, the principle of artistic autonomy that underpinned the postmodern 'anything goes'.

As regards the Cold War 'contemporary' where the feminist art movement arose, then, it is hard to describe it confidently in a positive light, should our criterion be its emancipatory capacities. The perhaps unavoidable ideological entanglement of emancipation with postmodernism demands critical revisiting because 'much of the intellectual and cultural debate around post-modernism was itself created from the Cold War climate — was born of Cold War issues, and fed by Cold War philosophies'.[71] To flag up the affiliation of postmodernism to capitalism in the exigencies of the Cold War and finance indicates the need to problematise the history of the feminist art movement's emergence in the West, by revisiting the movement's alliances and/or (sometimes) forced choices so as to situate them, in a more nuanced way, in the Long Modern. The very concept of postmodernism arose in this Long Modern to oversee the severing of modernity from its revolutionary prospects against the totality of capitalism. Postmodernism bagged together all 'metanarratives' as an unmitigated evil, producing historically false equivalences: the so-called post-political centrism that dominated formal politics for decades, hiding from view that capitalism goes unquestioned as the ground of these equivalences, owes a lot to postmodernism. On the other hand, postmodernism remained very modern in retaining artistic autonomy and authorship, and in its enchantment by technologies of connectivity and the spectacle where signs appeared to circulate freely. Postmodernism thus generated an inattention to what would shape capitalist globalisation after the US's victory in the Cold War. Feminism in art shared this inattention.

THE CONTEMPORARY: CLARIFICATORY NOTES

In the socio-economic reality of globalisation consolidated in the 1990s, but becoming legible later with the normalisation of precarity, we note a partial shift on the part of artists, curators, and theorists to an engagement with the logic and practices of production and labour.[72] Feminism played a relatively modest role in this shift, if compared with the explosion of feminist thinking and practice in the 1970s and 1980s addressing modernism and coalescing with post-modernism. Some of the assumed new features of postmodernism, such as the technologically mediated spectacle and, overall, an accelerated dominance of the digital, are still with us. Despite voices now arguing for 'digital degrowth',[73] these markers of postmodernism continue to define the terrain, through the fusion of entertainment, work, data, and information flows. If social media allowed feminist anti-fascists in London to know what their counterparts were doing in Rio, this applied also to the proliferating fanatics of authoritarian capitalism. The distance between postmodernism relativising truth as positional and social media abandoning fact-checking proved short;[74] the 'anything goes' of postmodernism has become society: ours is a contemporary where big tech-capital enters government openly ('We will coup whoever we want. Deal with it',[75] Elon Musk declared in the lithium wars of the early 2020s). Capital could never abandon 'interventionist' imperialism, even as we observe in-fighting among capitals that are presented as 'national' to voters.

The financial crisis of 2008 demonstrated once again that capitalism thrives on crises, treating them as opportunities to crush oppositional movements. But, also, by having its political functionaries and technocrats speak about an abstract 'economy' and an abstract 'system' that must be saved, it uses crises to further control labour. This has been the case with the post-2008 contemporary. As the surveillance apparatus extends from streets to laptops and smartphones and our data are sold to private companies by other private companies (or used by the invincible necro-biopolitical capitalist state), we must think about how a gendered reality forms part of this picture, including Anne Boyer's insight that 'the work of care and the work of data exist in a kind of paradoxical simultaneity: what both hold in common is that they are done so often by women... it is work that can look invisible'.[76] As asked in the pages of *African Argument* in 2023: 'Is it surprising that the unequal global division of labour that built Western capitalism is being reproduced on the world wide web?'[77] No, it is not. Invisibility of, and hiding the truth about, labour continue to define the contemporary.

As regards the polity — democracy — that presumably tolerates oppositional discourses and in which the feminist art movement emerged, its unravelling has been widely noted. Astra Taylor's documentary *What Is Democracy?* (2018) implied an uncertain 'contemporary' for emancipatory politics. Actually existing democracy has its own methods of invisibilisation. Taylor, who enters in dialogue with political theorist Wendy Brown and Silvia Federici in the documentary, sees the very discussion of democracy as 'methodologically feminist'. For Taylor, this is reflected in the documentary's focus on those that democracy punishes, from refugees stranded in prison camps to the racialised poor of the US. Taylor interviews an ex-convict casting light on 'the ghastly and oversized US prison–industrial complex [that in 2018] sees the country hold 5 percent of the world's population, but 25 percent of the world's prison population — and [where] a staggering 60 percent of that prison population are people of colour'.[78] While the destruction and expropriation of land continues on a global scale, women often find themselves at the forefront of struggles, with Federici in the film attending specifically to women's social reproduction movements in Africa and Latin America. Works such as *What Is Democracy?* argue, however, that invisibility is an outcome of socio-economic forces, connected to broader projects of brutal control and domination — and such invisibility can certainly not be addressed through attention to language, signs, and the symbolic. A second question here is whether visibility comes from an earlier moment of feminist politics premised on the belief that visibility would mean at least the betterment of these subjects' condition (if not the abolition of their condition). In other words, the belief in the bourgeois iteration of democracy as representation is not really questioned. Visibility is too confusing a term for a multitude formed through the formal and informal economy of capital: in our juncture, the passages of migrant and refugee populations, to give one example, cannot enter the field of visibility. Given this, we may ask if visibility presupposes a degree of proximity to power.

The debates around the contemporary signal a political desire to identify, explicate, and even resist the configuration of forces that deliver this 'contemporary'. But this raises a certain threat: that of closing down the past, making its potentialities irrelevant to the potentialities of the present. In 2014, Pollock lamented the 'mad dash' of:

> the wholesale shift in doctoral studies, curating, and art writing to 'the contemporary' and curatorial studies/practice. What is art

history if it is becoming the companion of the endlessly and pro-liferatingly synchronous? How is the past of art becoming merely an archive of referents against which the constantly novel and emerging might be legitimated? What kinds of art and historical consciousness does the liquid modernity of this 'new' new Art History promise, or perhaps evacuate? Of what are the globalizing and the contemporary symptoms?[79]

Yet the globalising is entangled with postmodernism. Postmodernism was a necessary ideology for globalisation's acceptance. As I complete this book, postmodernism is no longer discussed in art history, which prevents us from observing how it informs globalisation. That globalisation is seen by some to have ended in 2008 (financial crisis), 2020 (Covid-19 crisis), or 2025 (crisis of American democracy and crisis as more war) — information that global Google permits me to find — is symptomatic of what the globalising is about. The questions posed by Pollock have thus gained relevance, prompting us to think about why the contemporary demands attention and why it is something more than fashion as a modality of capital's need and push for obsolescence, or what Lars Bang Larsen identified as the art world's voracious appetite for 'turns': 'Forget what you have read and nix what you know because from this very minute that is all oblite-rated by a new Turn!'[80] I end the chapter with tentative responses to Pollock's questions.

(a) The shift to 'the contemporary' since 2000 in art history and curatorial work has been determined by the economy. This is true in at least two ways: both because knowledge of contemporary (rather than, say, medieval) art offers employment opportunities in a wider range of institutions in the arts sector, and because capitalist economy is in the process of changing the moment we live in so aggressively and speedily that getting to know the contemporary via vectors of critique (art history being one) is perceived as a form of resistance. To begin with, this wish to know also involves the conditions in which researchers and students exist as labouring subjects, conditions so problematic as to often lead to giving up: Francesca Coin's article 'On Quitting: The Labour of Academia' (2017) is an incisive critique of the devastating impact of precarious labour[81] — made precarious through related financial and political decisions — on the subjectivity and lives of many involved in the production of knowledge, especially in the humanities, including art history, gender studies, and related disciplines, where women tend to outnumber men. In the 2020s, the threat posed by AI (or more precisely, large language models) to the humanities includes the learning process itself: students' ability to summarise texts critically is undermined by such summaries provided by AI tools embedded in library provision. The consequences are unforeseeable, but are led by capital investment of $110 billion in 2024,[82] in turn led by US-based firms. Can the humanities today sustain and transmit the criticality that made feminist art history possible in the 1970s? Attending to these challenges is part of attending to the contemporary in terms of political engagement, as opposed to apathy and resignation before what capitalism presents as inevitable. The term 'post-internet art', available since the mid-2000s, already seems inadequate for capturing art's mediation by digitality as a global real that goes beyond simply structuring spectatorship, to also generate the fiction of art as produced by digital rather than human actors and labour.

(b) The concept of 'history' (from the Greek verb *ιστορείν/historein*) refers to a way of gaining knowledge of a certain period and piecing together a narrative, which does not exclude the possibility of this narrative being obtained from within a political discourse. 'History' does not necessarily mean 'the past' but can encompass the now. As for art history, it is not the 'companion' to whatever is synchronous to it, but a site for the conjuncture's critical analysis: not only because of how the contemporary can be articulated through the imagination that gives us artworks in terms of content and form, but also because of how we can observe the imbrication of a field (art), discussed in terms of autonomy and exceptionalism in connection with capital, as a social relation. Moreover, this 'synchronous' is not 'endlessly proliferating'. On the contrary, it has specific contours, which may or may not be immediately obvious, but which is the job of (feminist) art history to contextualise and, hopefully, interpret politically — that is, through reference to the power relations permeating the historically shaped social body and its cultural expressions, always and necessarily enabled by specific relations of production and reproduction.

(c) The past is not becoming a mere archive of references for the legitimation of 'the constantly novel and the emerging'. For instance, trying to script an anti-fascist feminist art history would require a political activation of the archive so as to attend to the intricate history of feminism and historical fascism (opposition to fascism was certainly not the position of all feminists), as well as of women's creativity in relation to the brutality of, and the desire for, power. Indeed, the histories of women's anti-fascist struggles, often tied to the hope for a communist future, as in Greece, Spain, and former Yugoslavia (to stay just in Europe), were not addressed by feminist art and photography histories in the formation of the feminist art movement. The reason for this formative oversight — concerning, in reality, women and revolution — was both that these histories did not form part of Anglo-American history, on which the idea of what feminism in art is about is based, and that they did not fit with the intellectual trajectories described earlier in this chapter. Sanja Iveković's activation of the archive in search for women anti-fascists has been perhaps the most noted. In 2019, State of Concept in Athens presented both visual and participatory works by Iveković on women and anti-fascism under the exhibition title *Red Star Fear Not*. The narrative performance *Whether We Were Brave* was a form of affective anti-historicisation for those of us present, in sensing that anti-fascism would be more rather than less relevant in the coming decade. How to make anti-fascism a practice that does not deflect attention from capitalism as fascism's matrix has been an open question.

Another example: Martha Rosler already noted in 1979 that artists tend to function as 'the Research & Development arm' of capital's technologies.[83] Women artists embraced technology. Was it because of a fear that they would be left behind? Understanding how contemporary technologies implicate sex and gender requires an exploration of capital's development of forces of production (technology and labour-power). Moreover, proposing UBI as a tentative, if problematic, solution to populations made redundant (useless as economic agents), finds its parallel in art, as seen earlier in this book. Artists today are mindful of the ongoing crisis of social reproduction under capitalism but also of the possible obsolescence of art as such, at least as encountered in the Long Modern. These concerns are justified now, but were less pronounced in the 1970s and 1980s. Attending to our contemporary means making known the causes and origins of these concerns.

And yet another example: the social movement defending the rights of trans people is already impacting art history and the critical interpretation of images — not just images made now but also those that the first generation of feminist art historians used to draw connections between the hyper-visibility of the female nude and the marginalisation of women artists. In 'How to Teach Manet's *Olympia* after Transgender Studies' (2022), published in *Art History*, David J. Getsy argues that Édouard Manet's *Olympia* (1863), of salient importance to feminist art history's critical analysis of women's gendered and racialised bodies as signs, should instead be read through 'gender's multiplicity and transformability'.[84] The (legitimate and ethically honourable) anxiety of how not to exclude trans students in a pedagogical context of modern art history permeates the text — an anxiety for historical reasons not evident in feminist art history classes of the 1980s, 1990s, and even 2000s. Getsy's reading makes use of Carol Armstrong's 'compelling arguments about how Manet looked across a gender binary' to suggest that her arguments 'can also be seen as the basis for questioning the absoluteness of that binary itself — and for challenging the belief in the body as a natural (rather than conventional) sign for gender'.[85] Yet Getsy reprimands Armstrong for relying 'on a conviction that bodies must be seen as either (and unquestionably) female or male: despite her attention to Manet's complication of the ways that gender is assumed and mobilized through contingent signs such as clothing, she nevertheless avowed that the body obscured beneath that clothing is necessarily and self-evidently sexed'.[86] He further contends:

> An account of transgender history allows us to see the workings of misogyny and sexism in a new light. For instance, the vicious language used by critics to attack *Olympia* shows how much a narrow view of femininity and women was at issue, with deviations from those norms being derided as monstrous, animal, or inhuman. Any response to these attacks necessarily involves resistance both to their imperious adjudications of proper gender and to their patriarchal attempts to control others' genders and bodies.[87]

This is true: an account from a transgender studies perspective may well allow us to 'see the workings of misogyny and sexism' — but not 'in a new light', as Getsy contends, for this was exactly the light that feminist readings sought to shine on *Olympia*: that nineteenth-century ideology led to Olympia-the-sign being derided as 'masculine' because Olympia-the-sign's stare disaligned the feminine from passivity. It was the restricted criteria of what femininity ought to look like and consist of that permitted certain depictions of the naked body-sign to be thought of as unfeminine. Neither did feminists argue that because Olympia-the-sign has breasts, her femininity should be undoubted because only those with breasts are women. For feminist art history, the question can start from the other end especially when practicing historical materialism: what is historically *lost* if a nineteenth-century painted sign of a naked body with breasts — before medical science could provide breasts to a range of bodies — is *not* seen as that of a woman? Would this prevent us from acknowledging the socio-economic conditions in which women became courtesans, and what about their clothed maids? This is what *two* painted signs in *Olympia* point to — the reclining naked Olympia and a Black clothed maid — offending bourgeois propriety but upholding its apparatus of racialisation in presenting female whiteness as sexually desirable (the breasts) and female blackness as, at best, 'standing next to it'?[88] Engaging the archive, Getsy notes: 'I am not proposing that we read the figure of Olympia as trans or non-binary' but that a 'transgender capacity is proposed through Manet's interrogation of the nude's status as sign.'[89] A transgender capacity can be seen to be present in many archives, while all signs of the body can be found to entail indeterminacy. The exception might possibly be if the artist has explicitly described the sex or gender of the sign included in a given representation, preventing other readings and fixing meaning, but locating meaning in the artist's stated intentions, and thus disregarding the complex ideological currents and material conditions in which works become legible, would render void a significant part of the feminist art history corpus. On the other hand, we certainly have artists who have presented painted signs of trans or intersex bodies through the nude convention or pursued the indeterminacy of sex and gender in a range of visual contexts.[90] Moreover, should assertions of gender instability and 'transformability' necessarily be associated with people who have made an effort to express and exist as social beings in the gender they *know* they firmly inhabit — an effort that perhaps does not burden cisgender people of whatever sexual orientation? What connects and what separates feminist and trans art histories centred on the destabilisation of signs? This is a strongly contemporary question.

These revisitations of the past, such as those described above, put much pressure on rethinking the ascription of the 'female nude' (or the male nude, for that matter) in feminist studies such as Lynda Nead's *The Female Nude: Art, Obscenity and Sexuality* (1992), as well as on numerous works of art re/presenting genitals from a feminist perspective, as in the 'central core imagery' that feminist artists developed since the 1960s. The undated entry 'Central Core Imagery' of the Elizabeth A. Sackler Center for Feminist Art reads:

> [Judy] Chicago began experimenting with 'central core' imagery in the late 1960s, along with other artists, including Hannah Wilke, Carolee Schneemann, and Miriam Schapiro. Each of these artists, in her own way, sought to give women's bodies back to them, to assert a positive female sexuality by claiming her sex.[91]

In the 2020s, readings of such artworks informed by trans politics might differ to those of feminist art history of the second wave (note: they might also not). Such questions were not necessarily anticipated by the first generation of feminist art historians. They are here now, and must be addressed as politically 'new'. Indeed, as both feminist and trans politics constitute the target of a reactionary agenda, exploring these questions has particular urgency.

Historians are typically confronted with 'novel and emerging' elements, but they can critically place such elements in a broader context where instructive continuities can be established. Whichever way one looks at the matter, art history on the left, let alone a Marxist feminist art history, cannot afford not to draw a distinction between the cult of novelty in capitalism's Long Modern and the new in terms of political contestations. Pollock refers to feminist interventions in art rather than feminist art,[92] in realising that readings are contextual and that feminism does not inhere in artwork determined simply by an artist's intentions. However, the artist's political intentions are central to what kind of artworks we get, though less so when examining the contexts from which these artworks are drawn. For example, 1970s 'feminist art' enters collections because of its prized newness and can be claimed as an avant-garde,[93] despite feminism's repeated questioning of the avant-garde. The newness of feminist art puts pressure on artists committed to feminism today; they also must be 'new' rather than 'derivative': they should stop rehashing the themes of the 1970s avant-garde, such as 'the body', they are told by exhibition reviewers. In 2007, Roberta Smith of *The New York Times* dismissed women's work in *Global Feminisms* as 'essentialist, body-oriented and familiar to the point of being old-fashioned'.[94] As I hope to have shown, such criticisms can be challenged precisely because political contestations around the body are themselves ongoing.

(d) Pollock's question concerning the promise or evacuation of a 'historical consciousness' by a '"new" new Art History' is harder to answer, because she wishes to know 'what kinds' of consciousness this promised or evacuated consciousness might consist of. Instead of a '"new" new Art History', perhaps we could refer to a historical reality in which entrenched and emergent elements co-exist dialectically. The art history examining this reality draws on disciplines that range from political science, philosophy, geography, sociology, and more, and attends to such things as the environment, algorithms, data, speculation, migration, dispossession, post-democracy, protest, the art pyramid, collectivism, the commons, social reproduction, the relationship of the modern and contemporary, to mention but a few. Although there is no one kind of historical consciousness that emerges out of the interdisciplinary underpinnings and preoccupations of the art history of the contemporary, there is an emphatic attendance to difficult social issues. Art history has not retreated to the study of a past safely distanced from capitalism's present contradictions. Some of these are carried from the past, others are new. The history of art as a discipline is burdened by them. In 2021, Pollock wrote: 'I disown the label *feminist art historian* because in that phrase *feminist* is reduced to an adjectival qualifier of Art History, placing me and my work safely in a sub-category of the unchallenged disciplinary formation'.[95] I think this disciplinary formation is today challenged much like art as living human labour. It is challenged by capitalism's efforts to prevent part of human faculties from functioning rather than by feminism. The issue thus may be whether keeping feminism in this challenged paradigm would operate as merely yet another iteration of 'all that is solid melts into air'.

(e) Finally, the globalising and the contemporary are not 'symptoms'. The globalising has been a totalising process of profit-hunting, supported by a polymorphous institutional reality, and generating conflicts between an infrastructural approach (China) and one enacted through military bases (US) — a reality in which artists, writer, curators, dealers, collectors, and publics also participate. It is highly possible that capitalist globalisation, as understood until the

2010s, has eroded. International law certainly has. In October 2023, Israel's attack on the Palestinian people in Gaza, livestreamed for the most part, rekindled questions on the use of the technical image in genocidal settler colonialism and the history of imperialism, without which the capitalist modernity we know would not come into existence. In 2024, the Tricontinental Institute for Social Research published the study *Hyper-Imperialism: A Dangerous Decadent New* in an effort to provide an understanding, from a Global South perspective, of the forces shaping the twenty-first century, while Ali Kadri's *The Accumulation of Waste* (2024) not only connects waste with surplus value (of relevance to all bodies and subjects labouring in capitalism), but also questions Western Marxism's ability to fully illuminate the ravages of the 'cannibalising' Western capitalist class.[96] Carina Brand's article 'A Materialist Reading of Abject Art: Performance, Social Reproduction and Capitalism' (2021) pressed a new Marxist feminist lens on histories of waste and the abject since the interwar period, from Japan to the US, connecting them to capitalism's social reproduction crises. Brand argues that 'abject art is not only a single response by artists in the 1990s, but a century-long project of artistic engagement, with the tensions that capital places on the gendered, sexed, racialised and classed body'.[97] Having shed postmodernism's emphasis on consuming the immateriality of signs, Marxist feminism is already scripting the globalising tendency of capital in the Long Modern. Will these efforts continue? What intellectual paradigms will prevail and what struggles will these be connected to? The discussion of postmodernism in this chapter indicated that capitalist strategy is not indifferent to this question. Neither should feminism be.

5

The Long Modern II: Feminist Art Theory, the Contemporary, and the Disaffirmation of Capitalism

This chapter works towards the possibility of a feminist art theory for our contemporary that prioritises the disaffirmation of capitalism — by 'possibility' I mean to denote that such a theory would be a collective rather than individual labour of theoretical praxis. My efforts below focus on merely pairing some of the concepts encountered in contemporary art-based critique and exploring their dialectical tension. As feminism in art no longer constitutes an art movement but still strives for change, how concepts meet each other and relate to a historically material reality perhaps becomes more complex, and more pressing.

Let me give an example. In the previous chapter, I considered Griselda Pollock's valid concerns about the emphasis on the contemporary in 'Whither Art History?' In this article, Pollock follows literary theorist Gayatri Chakravorty Spivak who in opposing capitalist globalisation suggested in 2003 that 'planetary' be adopted as a 'counterconcept to the global' positing that: 'The planet is a species of alterity, belonging to another system: yet we inhabit it, on loan.'[1] Despite Spivak's proximity to Marxism and feminism, thinking in terms of loans presupposes property, while alterity speaks the language of ontology in terms of immutability and so may obscure how capital engages labour historically with the planet.

The issue is therefore how to historicise the concepts we deploy in considering their ideological service. To think of history does not condemn us to empiricism and anti-theory. The dissonance between Marxism and feminism has sometimes been presented in this distorting light, with Marxism being about theoretical schemas, feminism being about lived experience, in a polarisation that does justice to neither. The different entry points to the question of how feminism, art, and capitalism are connected, making up the previous chapters, necessitate a theoretical realism as offered by the apparatus and modality of seeing of a Marxist feminist critique that persists with art.

POINTS OF TENSION AND CONTENTION: WHAT IS TO BE UN/DONE?

Feminism in art exists in dual form: as an internal history of the feminist art movement and its legacy and as a presence within a composite critique of capitalist modernity. After 2008, this composite critique underpinned a direction in some women artists' work whereby feminism informs perspectives on class formation within the capitalist nation-state, exposes the ruses of the 'creative' workplace, addresses the networked production landscapes of globalisation, visualises the future of capitalism as one where resistance is dispersed and easily manipulated. What we find in such works, I argued in 2022, is an 'engagement with class politics' that 'makes manifest an *anxiety* about how women, values associated with femininity, and feminism have been connected with an expansion of capital as a social relation — which, in turn, bespeaks of a reflective attitude with regard to how to take forward the feminist struggle'.[2] In considering the dual form of feminism in the art field, we see a potential feminist art theory of our contemporary as maintaining a reflective attitude that prioritises points of tension and contention — that is, a theory that starts from the conflicts that take hold in art but that are imbricated with social antagonisms. The points I prioritise here are (a) emancipation and limits, (b) identity and economy, (c) political aesthetics from representation to prefiguration, and are intended to pick up threads and concerns that traverse this study as a whole in its effort to elucidate the connections between feminism, art, and capitalism.

Emancipation and Limits

Feminism in art has regarded its internal history in terms of a gradual overcoming of obstacles, but as discussed in Chapter Three, this has also been a history of dependency. Any claim to an autonomy of feminism — the struggle for recognition that feminism had to practice in art — has been circumscribed within a web of limits. Referring to limits rather than obstacles indicates the weight that these conditions carry and can help us grasp why feminism has been more reformist than revolutionary. Hegemonic ideology has been such a limit, while in the late 1990s Luc Boltanski and Eve Chiapello referred to 'the new spirit of capitalism' to capture determinations that attend to how ideology changes along with capitalism. Feminism, as we have seen, has also been affected by the new spirit of capitalism.

In the early 1980s, a group of women in Britain set up the Greenham Common Peace Camp, protesting against the Western powers' decision to place guided nuclear missiles at the Greenham Common Air Base. Their action, sustained over the years (1981–2000), was a rejection of military technologies of annihilation. It was carried out to protect human beings and life at large, and 'many women faced court cases, fines and sometimes imprisonment for their actions'.[3] Thousands took part in this years-long women's claim to a protest commons and so there is a rich archive of visual and oral history of material. Yet this feminist act of civil disobedience has had little impact on feminist theory and the trajectory of feminism as such, although it has been thoroughly examined recently in Alexandra Kokoli's art historical research.[4] The spirit of the times did not favour this action's humanist orientation. On the contrary, feminist theory was greatly impacted by a text that attributed liberatory potential to a military technology — the cyborg as the foundation of contemporary feminist posthumanism.

In the mid-1980s, at the peak of postmodernism, Donna Haraway set out to write a socialist, anti-essentialist feminist critique of gender relations: her 'A Manifesto for Cyborgs' was published in *Socialist Review*. Haraway's notion of 'socialist feminism' was in tune with the spirit of the times, championing the progressivist belief that techno-science was the inevitable path and solution to the contradictions that capital generated for feminism. 'A Manifesto for Cyborgs' professed that women might be free only in overcoming their humanness and becoming hybridised as part-machines — that is, women as human beings should have no hope for liberation. In 1967, when playwright and essayist Valerie Solanas, in the US like Haraway, had emphasised the importance of automation for women's liberation, she had not found many willing ears; nor did Shulamith Firestone's *Dialectic of Sex*, making a similar proposition and published in 1970, become a feminist art bible in the 1970s. In the mid-1980s, things were different. Haraway's proposition might have been ironic, but irony was already a key feature of the diffused postmodern mentality and embedded in the intellectual climate dominating high-income societies and certainly the US. When Haraway was writing in California, the US was already exercising its global hegemony through technology; it would be there where 'a mix of cybernetics, free market economics, and counter-culture libertarianism' would take hold and be described as 'Californian ideology' in 1995.[5] The authors of the eponymous essay stated: 'cutting-edge artists and academics have been championing the "post-human" philosophy developed by the West Coast's Extropian cult. With no obvious opponents, the global dominance of the Californian ideology appears to be complete'. Particular attention should be paid to how the authors implicated the 1960s counter-culture of (environmentally conscious) anarcho-'hippies' in Californian ideology as many of them became eventually tech-preneurs. Fernando Pessoa's novella *The Anarchist Banker* (1922) comes to mind here as a cautionary tale of the Long Modern.

Today, it is hard to keep disaffiliating 'A Manifesto for Cyborgs' — so influential to feminism in art — from its origins in technophilic capitalism. Even within new materialism, the essay is seen as exemplary of the 'specific political and technoscientific constellation that materialized at the height of the Cold War'.[6] Haraway has denied being a 'social constructionist' but has also admitted: 'We invited those misreadings in a range of ways. We could have been more careful about listening and engaging more slowly'.[7] Yet the issue with deploying cybernetics as a proposition for liberation is not social constructionism per se, but that the struggle of liberation becomes hostage to the military–industrial complex's dream of the full subjugation of humanity. Irony and metaphor both die at this point. This intellectual history and its impact cannot be undone. It facilitated a collusion of feminism with capitalist technologies, generating a limit to feminism's oppositional imaginary, irrespective of Haraway's intentions.

In the 2020s, the cut-throat competitive reality of research funding compels feminist researchers, artists, designers, and scholars to partake in affirming such technologies and exploring how they can be put to 'good' use. Such use is certainly good for the private tech giants that organise our lives, as the push for datafication makes obvious. The Greenham Common Women's Peace Camp is not merely rendered irrelevant under today's hi-tech domination and militarised reality. The camp's feminist humanism set against capital's extinction drive is properly defeated by Google's plans to set up nuclear reactors so as to obtain the huge amounts of energy required for running its AI centres. Why did feminism abandon an anti-extinction peace camp and embrace the cyborg as the figuration of anti-life? Was it because Haraway concluded her famous essay by setting up an outrageously false binary, choosing to be a 'cyborg' rather than a 'goddess'? When Judy Chicago had mixed historical women and prehistoric goddesses in *The Dinner Party* in the 1970s, feminists had complained. But in the fully neoliberal America of the 1980s, providing feminism with a choice between goddess and cyborg was convincing as an ideologically fashioned limit to human agency. The first page of Haraway's essay describes 'the relationship of organism and machine' as 'a border war' and her essay as 'an argument for *pleasure* in the confusion of boundaries and for *responsibility* in their construction'.[8] From what position in capitalist society does historical humanity become an abstract organism and the historical materiality of borders enter a project of responsible pleasure? Border wars are lethal and no feminist can take pleasure in them while capitalist nation-states and arms-and-surveillance private capital are sadistically responsible for them — which indeed entails pleasure.

In the social world of borders, the global artworld tends to receive a geographic interpretation cleansed of conflict. However, this global artworld of uneven 'development' is primarily a sector of the global economy, formal and informal. We hardly have any new concepts to grasp the role feminism's contextual articulations play within this global artworld — note that 'transnationalism' presupposes the existence of national spaces, often obliterating from view the intricate relations of feminism *within* any such national space or *across* borders, as well as the hierarchy of vastly unequal national spaces in the global economy and imperialism and, consequently, in the production of culture.[9] Europe is an example: is it a transnational space made up of national art scenes where feminism operates according to some national identity or even in relation to national issues? I would argue not. Marxist feminists from Europe can be far more dependent on Marxist feminists from Latin America (and vice versa) for developing their arguments than on corporate feminists in their own countries.[10] Yet all of them exist and work constrained by the limits of the nation-state and its relationship to transnational structures and institutions. For those with the right passports, finances, social reproduction infrastructure, art-based feminism has been a culture of mobility, which at the present juncture of hard borders cannot be taken for granted. Feminist artists who have incorporated in their critique the biopolitics of borders know this: Tanja Ostojić, from the 'disappeared' Yugoslavian state, realised a series of performative pieces on the possibility and illegality of crossing borders.[11] Although Ostojić's real-time and real-space action-based works such as *Illegal Border Crossing* (2000) examined the border as a mediator of the class–gender–ethnicity relationship of post-socialist Eastern Europe to Western Europe as the territory of capitalist privilege, her work entailed foresight as regards the ubiquity of the border as a limit to feminism 25 years later. As a multi-layered limit to feminism, the border is an indispensable reference in a feminist theory of contemporary art investigating its own conditions of existence, when the cosmopolitan feminist subject has been shown to be untenable in contemporary geopolitical landscapes.

Feminism in art also depends on a range of art and cultural institutions for funding and hosting which may be private or state-sponsored. What limits do they constitute for feminism? Since the 1970s, the balance has clearly tipped towards feminism deepening rather than withdrawing its participation in art institutions, but it is unclear if feminists can say 'we are the institution', following artist Andrea Fraser in 2005.[12] Fraser said that the issue is what kind of institution 'we' are, but can 'we' as a tentative feminist collectivity be *any* kind of institution of capitalist logic? From a labour perspective, there is certainly a 'we' in a kunsthalle, an art biennial, and a museum, but such a 'we' is about ensuring the collaborative yet hierarchical realisation of productivity with the lowest possible cost to the institution.

In discursive democracies, where citizens can complain but are prevented from acting, the art institution is repeatedly exposed as enmeshed in insidious ways with economic power that translates into social and political oppression — also, very much in relation to borders. In December 2018, the activist group Decolonise This Place protested at the Whitney Museum in New York 'against Warren B. Kanders', vice chairperson on the museum's Board of Directors and 'owner of Safariland, a tear gas manufacturer whose products were used on immigrant families approaching the US–Mexico border, seeking asylum in the United States';[13] in July 2019, only four artists had opted to leave the Whitney Biennial in protest at the museum's failure to address the issue while the biennial itself addressed 'race, gender, and equity; and explorations of the vulnerability of the body'.[14] At the same time, art history was exposing the broader collusion of art philanthropists in the US with the facilitation of the alt-right and neo-fascism.[15] A conflict thus arises in the art institution's double function: on the one hand, the institution as the repository and circulation site of feminist art practice and ideas and, on the other, the institution as the validation of a damaging economy that connects the art world with society.

This mention of feminists' dependency on and imbrication with art institutions and borders is only indicative of the range of limits faced by art as an emancipatory way of being. Mapping the dependencies of feminism in relation to its emancipatory promise appears to be an exercise of pragmatism through a gauging of limitations, but it is proposed here as a necessary empirical guidance on the realisations of feminism in a global context: the Kurdish women's movement, as described by Dilar Dirik,[16] has been facing different limits than most of the feminists who will be reading this book and certainly the one writing it. How different limits — as points that force self-reflection — impact the purview of feminist agency can help expand our remit and narratives of emancipation beyond what cultural imperialism permits.

Sometimes it is hard to distinguish between dependencies and limits. The wage is a dependency but also a limit: the wage is what numerous precarised art workers are made to desire. A possible distinction between wage (normally corresponding to hourly pay and lower ranks of employees) and salary (paid monthly or annually and connected to the more fortunate) is connected to class. This is rarely raised in art debates — Siegfried Kracauer's classic *The Salaried Masses: Duty and Distraction in Weimar Germany* (1930) is largely forgotten. Those who have secured this dependency — the generic wage — do not necessarily examine how it impacts subjectivity, and what limits it sets to a radical imaginary disaffirming capitalism. What a radical imaginary is, in a state of financial emergency, is hardly clear. Persisting with revolutionary theory, the Endnotes collective cited Marx in 2010: 'The result of the capitalist process of production is not just commodities and surplus value; it is the reproduction of this relation *itself*... Capital and wage labour only express two factors of the same relation'. But the wage can never be available to all. As the 2008 crisis was generating unemployment and job poverty, Endnotes observed that as 'that part of the global population diminishes whose reproduction is mediated through the exchange of productive labour for the wage, the wage form as the key mediation in social reproduction may appear increasingly tenuous'.[17] Here is the catch: the tenuousness of the wage form makes it all the more desirable for social subjects circumscribed in the capitalist horizon.

This contradiction that inheres in the class relation informs art too. Activist organisation W.A.G.E./Working Artists for the Greater Economy (USA, founded 17 September 2008) describes itself as follows:

> [in] the context of contemporary art, where the unpaid labor of artists supports a more than $60 billion industry, W.A.G.E.'s mission is to establish sustainable economic relationships between artists and the institutions that contract our labor, and to introduce mechanisms for self-regulation into the art field that collectively bring about a more equitable distribution of its economy.[18]

Obviously, this is necessary, though paying for labour would introduce 'sustainable economic relations' for artists and curators rather than for art institutions which, abandoned by the state that could fund them through a redistribution of tax income, sustain themselves precisely by not paying for labour as much as possible.

The W.A.G.E Womanifesto states that 'we, as visual and performance artists and independent curators, provide a workforce', calling 'for the remuneration of cultural value in capital value'.[19] Given art's association with privileged uselessness and autonomy in the Long Modern, (and as artistic labour is not immediately subsumed to capitalist production norms), given also capital's structural reliance on wagelessness, it is radical to present artists and curators as a 'workforce'. But what would it mean for 'cultural value' to be remunerated 'in capital value'? Would this mean that if this demand were to be realised, no segment of cultural value could escape the subjugation to capital? Second, how can these radical demands issued by precarised subjects be differentiated from arguments about the creative industries' contribution to the reproduction of capitalism? Our century opened with such arguments, and in 2005, the US's

National Endowment for the Arts stated that 'artists are workers' before concluding: 'From global exports to local investments, the new American economy depends on imagination, innovation, and creativity, and those are the skills that artists develop, nurture, and promote'.[20]

To state the obvious, innovation is a structural feature of capitalism, accompanied by the devastations of planned obsolescence. Innovation is not, however, typically tied to the repetition of tasks required from the waged labourer. Rather, innovation is attached to market enterprise and beating competitors through competitive advantage. Would some artists prefer to be entrepreneurs of free creativity versus others who would prefer to receive wages and thereby be protected from the market and the need to sell works? The critical analysis of the wage relation and the conflict between artmaking as enterprise and as potentially waged work did not inform the feminist art theory of the second wave, but now enters an emergent Marxist feminist approach to art, which asks how affect connects unwaged social reproduction and unwaged art.[21] An equally revelatory enquiry would concern how waged labour in *non*-art sectors has enabled the voluntary labour that produces feminist art — such labour appears to have made the emblematic *Womanhouse* possible, as we saw in Chapter Three. The wage relation must then be seen as a material and ideological limit for feminist praxis.

To be fair, the art sector's precarity makes taking up entrepreneurialism almost inevitable, and someone can move from socially engaged art support worker and/or a waged curatorial post to building a consultancy for artists, on the very premise that 'the life of an artist is not a typical one'.[22] Successful women artists are often seen to have risen beyond wage dependency to become entrepreneurs — the same as successful male artists rising from the ocean of artistic obscurity. The shift from the ideal of the artist-as-genius, addressed by feminism in the 1970s, to the ideal of the artist-as-entrepreneur today is in dire need of feminist analysis. In 2013, Marina Vishmidt stressed the importance of:

> think[ing] about the dispositions, subjectivities, and sensibilities — in other words, the aesthetics — that are produced in the encounter of art with the 'disruptive influence' of business. The cell-form of art is the entrepreneurial artist who reproduces the institution

simply by reproducing herself as an artist. She is thus mimetic of the 'automatic subject' of value, which is self-reproducing as a social form once the presuppositions (for capital, private property and wage labor; for art, the institution of art) are in place.[23]

The relevance of this to feminist interventionist practice is apparent. One question here is whether in capitalism it is at all possible to practice social engagement (including by feminists) without relying on business logic and models. Capitalist institutions persistently undermine non-capitalist instituent practice. In how many countries today would a socially engaged artist working towards the regeneration of urban housing for classed and racialised people not have to use a bank and/or a private foundation, and how would this artist avoid becoming a project manager? Supported by a long list of benefactors, including the Ford Foundation mentioned earlier in this book in relation to its role in shaping American feminism as postmodernism, the ongoing and famous non-profit Project Row Houses in the US includes a 'Business Incubations' section: 'the incubation program afforded creative entrepreneurs the opportunity of operating within a close-knit community of artists and activists'.[24] The revolutionary 'monstrous' institutions that Michael Hardt and Antonio Negri called for in *Commonwealth* (2009), the institutions committed to abolishing class, race, and gender, are confined to imagination.[25] Instead, recent art historical research, examining through case studies the intersection of feminism, labour, and socially engaged art, emphasises the formation of a contemporary 'organising subject' unable to escape bureaucratisation and without a coherent vision concerning what this subject is organising about.[26] When does contemporary art's dependency on the logic and schemas of capital become feminism's material and conceptual limit? This is not a rhetorical question.

An earlier feminist art theory involved a hopeful institutional critique (largely enabled by its inattention to the limits of democracy under capitalism), yet the theory produced by the women's art movement was silent on the violent, life-destructive anti-communism of the 1950s, known as McCarthyism, and its impact on feminism.[27] As both the myth and experience of capitalist democracy are unravelling today, however, a feminist art theory of the contemporary must reflect on the rules of engagement underpinning institutional dependency. Such rules are not harmless, which is why in 2023 Western 'art institutions' were mentioned in the Index on Censorship for silencing Palestinian voices and those standing in solidarity against genocidal violence. Among the cases listed was Candice Breitz, a 'Jewish filmmaker and artist who had her exhibition on sex work activists' cancelled in Germany 'after commenting on the conflict'.[28] This is an example of the rules of engagement that Western art institutions both represent and force in serving broader imperialist and arms industries' interests as well as their nation-states' narratives about foreign policy (here, Nazi Germany's perpetration of the Holocaust is used to justify post-Nazi Germany's commitments to Israel and present state censorship of Palestinian solidarity as a moral act). That the presumed liberal façade of the art institution can disappear for reasons unrelated to the artworks exhibited, but rather based on the technological surveillance of artists' public speech is defining of our contemporary. The liberal façade can reappear at a more convenient, less fraught geopolitical moment; and it can disappear again. The switching on and off of the censorship tap is a more than plausible future for the art institution where feminists place their emancipatory aesthetics.

Identity and Economy

Since the last quarter of the twentieth century, feminism — including in art — has been associated with identity politics. According to a basic dictionary definition, 'identity' is the set of facts that make up what one is. The whiff of ontological essentialism is unmissable here. Then capitalist law comes in: always favouring property, it tells us that identity is owned and can thus be stolen, as exemplified in the criminal offenses of 'identity theft' and 'identity fraud'. Identity now enters capitalist biopolitics: capital needs to know who you really are so that it can work out the taxonomies of control and fortify its enormous bureaucratic apparatus. Currently, streams of data making up individual identity and group identity enter the capitalist market, in the interdependency of capital and governance. This capitalist reality makes it all the more curious that in the late twentieth century, emancipatory discourses, including feminism, wilfully came under the tent of identity politics. At that point, a culture of pride arose around identity: subjects wished to be recognised publicly and formally on the basis of their distinct identities, seeking equal status. It was as if

Joan Robinson's famous quip 'the misery of being exploited by capitalists is nothing compared to the misery of not being exploited at all'[29] was rebranded as: 'the misery of being recognised by capitalists is nothing compared to the misery of not being recognised at all'.

Equal status across the board cannot be achieved under capitalism as a mode of production and reproduction that both presupposes and generates the class relation. This is why we find a distinction between status and class in feminist thought that engages Marxism. This distinction has been helpful in examining why capitalism could at certain times confer status to some social groups while maintaining the class relation. In the words of Nancy Fraser:

> Misrecognition is an institutionalized relation, not a psychological one… In capitalist societies… where the institutionalization of specialized economic relations permits the relative uncoupling of economic distribution from structures of prestige, and where status and class can therefore diverge, misrecognition and maldistribution are not fully mutually convertible.[30]

This raises the question: what does status mean in relation to identity? It means access of an inferiorised group to what a group higher up in the social hierarchy enjoys, thought of as 'privilege'. As discussed in earlier chapters, for the illusion of equal status to take hold in emancipatory politics, the unsettling question of class had to recede — as it did in postmodernism.

However, Marxist art historian Nizan Shaked has been critical about Marxist thought that does not draw identity into the dialectical relation, highlighting how Kimberlé Crenshaw's intersectionality can be mobilised to reveal social stratification.

> If, for example, we place the focus on the plight of the black woman worker, any resolution for her will necessarily mean a resolution for those who are already better positioned on the scale of social hierarchy. If we understand how identity-based oppression serves the ends of capitalist exploitation we conclude that we should work from the bottom up, not from the middle and down.[31]

Shaked signals the necessity of thinking from the bottom up as an occasionally sidelined commitment of Marxism, which, however, is what Marxist feminists were doing, especially in the 1970s, in finding a hidden abode of reproduction under Marx's 'hidden abode of production'. This commitment was disrupted, as seen earlier, when identity became embedded in the ideology of choice serving the diffusion of post-Fordist values as general social logic. In art, this also found expression in the exhibition-form, where identities find their recognition.

In 2000, when a global art world was promoted as conferring anthologised visibility, Rasheed Araeen, founder of the postcolonial art journal *Third Text*, published in its pages an astute critique of how identity politics is practised in 'institutional structures' of 'neoliberal agendas' — structures being an almost forgotten concept at the time. 'The issue', Araeen wrote, is 'not about the exclusion of others from the contemporary art scene and their recognition. Although there have been deliberate exclusions, the real issue is the way others are accepted and accommodated by the dominant culture'.[32] Under pressure from globalisation as capital's totalisation, questions about the pull of recognition as the sister-concept of identity politics arose in feminists' dialogue with Marxism, yet mostly outside the art field: identity was being appropriated in ethnic cleansing projects while also leading to the 'reification' of groups,[33] generating pressure to conform to the general/dominant tendency within an identifiable group. The structures mentioned by Araeen proved hard to keep in sight. Meanwhile, Marxist thinkers, such as John Roberts, were pointing out that 'the exponential increase in under-employed and unemployed artistic activity exists in the gap between the relative decline of industrial labour and the rise of a new global proletariat comprising all those excluded from wage-labor'.[34] Yet this and related assessments can hardly be unpacked outside the framework provided by social-reproduction feminism: 'those excluded from wage labor' are mostly women on the global scale, while the usual outnumbering of men by women in today's art schools and art history classes indicates the need to look at the gender composition of the 'under-employed and unemployed activity' which gives us the nebulous lower strata of the art world pyramid. Moreover, thinking dialectically about subject formation and capital as a social relation is integral to overcoming the staples of postmodernism, which survives as pervasive ideology despite the term's near-eclipse from the conceptual apparatus of contemporary art theory after the mid-1990s.

Identity politics built on the specificity of experience, especially in art where 'marginalised' subjects carried the burden of a struggle that always appeared as 'particular', exactly as Araeen argued: not only artworks, but also the bodies of artists, curators, historians, and theorists came to represent an experience that was immediately transmissible and expected to tie them to specific politics. A hegemonic feminism was always lurking, and, depending on the context, hegemony could assume various guises. It is not unusual to attend conferences where a highly visible art-biennial Black artist from America would address invisible and sometimes destitute white waiter-artists as carriers of white privilege — in crisis-ridden Greece in the 2010s, with migrants of any racialisation present, this appeared absurd, as if the private art institutions inviting the famous artists were committed to proving Araeen's point about postcolonial theory celebrities affirming such institutions. Does a white feminist woman artist in Bucharest or Athens doing minimum-pay care labour four days a week embody hegemonic feminism as a wealthy white woman art collector inclined to feminist work, whatever their sexuality, embodies hegemonic feminism? Speaking of collectors, of whatever gender, the practice has been so problematic that a multilingual 'code' about the 'ethics of collecting' had to be drafted, instructing collectors to treat artists (called art workers) fairly.[35] This plea forgets that capitalist markets, including art collecting, are not organised around fairness but around assets. Should we perhaps see hegemonic feminism as a shifting category that never quite materialises in full but that highlights feminists' participation in maintaining the pyramid of hierarchy and exploitation that constitute art in the Long Modern? When in 2018 a report aptly named *Panic!* and subtitled 'Social Class, Taste and Inequalities in the Creative Industries' highlighted 'the significant exclusions of those from working class origins, women and those from Black, Asian and Minority Ethnic (BAME) backgrounds across the cultural and creative industries', it was the first of its kind in the UK[36]— which, it should be emphasised, is not a peripheral art scene. The issue the *Panic!* report brought up keeps being re-affirmed, but it was hardly accidental that the report subtitle prioritised social class, meaning one's proximity or distance from capital. Yet it is not at all clear how the art field relates to class. In what conditions does the art field become the site of upwards or downwards classing? And should 'being working-class' be seen as an identity to be excluded from or included in a 'diverse' art world?[37]

In an ideological framework where authenticity is scripted as identity, a 'successful' working-class artist is one who has actually moved upwards class-wise and has done so by bringing forth for art consumption their own working-class origins. Such artists can and do become role models for entry-level artists whose mothers worked 'two jobs' while raising the kids and whose fathers worked 'irregular shift patterns in a factory', and the reasoning is:

> More often than not, our house did resemble [Tracey] Emin's Turner Prize shortlisted installation [My Bed, 1998]. But the fact Emin *did* do it and created a piece so vulnerable, so raw, and — let's face it — working-class was groundbreaking. As the art world is often elitist and dominated by the upper classes, for me, Emin represented the existence of a world beyond class, and how we can break through into those elitist circles without losing sight of our humble beginnings.[38]

Here, upward class mobility in capitalism, possible only on individual terms, is conflated with the prospect of a classless society ('a world beyond class'). Eclipsed here is the social truth that most working-class people will be prevented from upward class mobility because, in that case, capital accumulation would cease. The truth is concealed by the imperative to see class as an identity, and thus as a matter of *status*. Misconstrued as status, working-class-ness is reified: it becomes a thing which may or may not find recognition in the art field. Working-class artists/historians/curators are thus found to be 'underrepresented' in a framework where class analysis is replaced by a concern about elitism. Elitism can be challenged by deploying a glass-ceiling perception of the art world — the very same that sustains the politics of recognition and visibility. As Vishmidt observes,

> emblems of structural violence such as housing privatization, unemployment, and racialized domination turn into resources for a cultural project that exposes them to the light, only to push them into the background as irrelevant in the face of the real, positive change partially bankrolled by the market and non-profit entities responsible for those very same ills.[39]

In 2014, Larne Abse Gogarty noted that 'gentrification is a helpful metaphor to describe the current state of social practice'.[40] In 2017, the conflict in Boyle Heights in eastern Los Angeles between socially engaged art and dispossession through art-led gentrification entailed an anti-gallery campaign, despite the fact that such galleries might be collaborating with underrepresented artists.[41] Magally Miranda and Kyle Lane-McKinley highlight that 'the members of BHAAD [Boyle Heights Alliance Against Artwashing and Displacement] coalition who prominently feature the women of Union de Vecinos have posed the ultimate provocation for social practice — they want to see childcare centers and laundromats in the place of art galleries'.[42] Bringing the diversity-focused, well-meaning art institution to working-class neighbourhoods thus stands in contrast to well-documented feminist art practices of the 1970s that sought to use such everyday working-class spaces as exhibition sites in a process of consciousness-raising, with the Hackney Flashers feminist collective in London being a salient example. Today, however, when identity politics can be used for an expansion of gentrification through the progressive art institution, how does feminist theory see art that finds itself enclosed within an economic reality that places it against the very subjects it addresses?

The intricate relationship between identity and economy is not, however, exhausted in institutional mediation. Treating the working class as an identity appears to also place class within a more diffused ideological project that enhances the appeal of hegemonic values in the field of social reproduction itself, whereby social reproduction extends beyond the domestic to the community/social body level. Replenishment techniques abound in contemporary capitalism, being integral to addressing the worker as an ultimately sustainable unit. This sustainable unit is crucial for the general availability of labour-power, but also serves to pacify the social body by making capitalism appear to be maintaining and even increasing levels of wellness. Heavily promoted by the press, platform capitalism, and social media, wellness is a strongly ideological industry, essential for a high productivity economy. Wellness thrives in the often-gendered politics of self-care ('downtime', 'time for myself') but addresses a collective body in its composite labouring capacity. The history of wellness and wellbeing, however, is more expansive as a culture and cult of the worthy body, which is what connects it to historical Nazism and fascism, as well as the 'politics of white nationalism' today, where it promotes 'parallel economies' connected to social reproduction 'through traditional female domains' such as 'healthy cooking and home remedies'.[43] The emphasis on creating an autonomous space away from the state embeds the project of an alternative/parallel economy in identitarian communities that see themselves as anti-systemic. This history and its contemporary articulations are troubling but not widely known, despite press mentions of wellness hubs as promoting conspiracy theories.[44]

An important aspect of wellness culture is that its replenishment techniques have mostly been directed at the work force that practices cognitive and service labour (the office body), presumed to be able to afford healthy food, exercise, and meditation, which indicates a class element in wellness culture. Wellness can thus appear as class privilege that should trickle down to all, becoming democratised. Such democratisation of wellness can be undertaken by socially engaged art. The Community Wellbeing Collective in Edinburgh is 'a diverse, intergenerational, intercultural, working-class organisa-tion imagining, practising and creating space for collective wellbeing towards change', and believes in the democratisation of wellness. An initiative of artists Jeanne van Heeswijk and Bobby Sayers and orig-inally a commission of Edinburgh Arts Festival, the Community Wellbeing Collective is a 'living art-work' where 'local members host the space and deliver political events and wellbeing activities which suspend the suffocation of intersecting oppressions, creating space to breathe and the possibility to dream together', combining pursuits that are conducive to 'looking after our bodies' with events on 'employability and workers' rights.'[45]

From a Marxist feminist perspective, the Community Wellbeing Collective's durational project epitomises the dilemmas faced by working-class artists sensitive to 'intersectional oppressions'. Being working-class intersects with other oppressions in the identity spectrum. Wellness, we might say, is here repurposed as a generally available, rather than class-exclusionary, care culture. The collective's publications refer to an ethics of 'healing' community research, 'emotional safety', and 'words of kindness' as a workplace exercise: people are asked to write down kind words in their actual work meetings so as to have a nicer working day. In many ways, the project appears to be a solid example of relational-aesthetic 'microtopias' (temporary, small-scale, convivial get-togethers as a refuge from a brutalising normality), critiqued by Claire Bishop over 20 years ago as hiding from view the real world of antagonisms where social subjects function.[46] Yet for the 'marginalised' working class, daily reality has worsened considerably in the past two decades. Is the charge of art performing a temporary suspension of capitalist reality still relevant against the urgency of survival among today's working class? Arguably, artistic intentions here prioritised survival, but they did not overcome ideological circumscription in seeking to make the intolerable tolerable. Wellbeing culture central to subduing the middle-class employee, as seen in earlier iterations of the Google office, now reaches the working class, in its diversity, as a shared gift economy actualised as everyday life and dispensed by art activism. And insofar as wellness, wellbeing, and care are principally attached to a female/feminine subject (which is one reason why feminist scholarship takes up this line of enquiry), we observe here that gendered values are mobilised against the insufferability of the class condition.

A more complex issue arises in relation to anti-racism politics and the art field, highlighting the field's connection to capital: in 2017, Dana Schutz's painting *Open Casket*, based on a truly horrific social document, a '1955 photograph of 14-year-old Emmett Till's lynched body', generated calls to have the painting removed from the Whitney Museum, while artist and writer Hannah Black argued in her open protest letter that 'it is not acceptable for a white person to transmute Black suffering into profit and fun'.[47] In 2018, the London curatorial collective BBZ protested the inclusion of Luke Willis Thomson's *Autoportrait* in the Turner Prize, 'a silent film portrait of Diamond Reynolds, the black woman who live-streamed on Facebook the fatal police shooting of her partner, Philando Castile, in July 2016'; whereas the protesters appeared at Tate Britain in shirts that said 'Black Pain Is Not For Profit', their statement was more specific, arguing 'against the utilisation of black death and black pain by *non-black artists* and arts institutions for cultural and financial gain'.[48] That overwhelmingly white institutions profit from the spectacularised portrayal of Black pain is undeniable; but both Black's and BBZ's statements are less clear about whether Black artists can use Black pain for profit if they gain access to these very same institutions. It can certainly be argued that the artworks which, thanks to feminism, entered these very same institutions made available women's pain to the mechanisms of 'profit and fun'. This is one side of the problem that arises in seeing the divides that characterise capitalist societies in terms of identity, as identity is never too far from ownership.

In the early to mid-1990s, postfeminism was taking hold, along with the young British artists' (yBas) rescripting of a past feminist critique along the lines of a personal confessionary mode, as Rosemary Betterton argued in 2000.[49] Entrepreneurial femininity and 'funny' sexual innuendo informed this paradigm, contributing to its media appeal and popularity. The yBas had spotted the successful appropriation of working-class lives by the media that packaged them as a curiosity spectacle, sold back to screen-glued masses through reality television. The spectacle of real lives arose as a historically specific form of mass entertainment where class and status merged seductively — in favour of status. Identity became more lifestyle and less politics. Ellen Meiksins Wood, who placed emphasis on the historical understanding of class, observed:

> the politics of identity reveals its limitations, both theoretical and political, the moment we try to situate *class* differences within its democratic vision. Is it possible to imagine class differences without exploitation and domination? The 'difference' that constitutes class as an identity *is*, by definition, a relationship of inequality and power, in a way that sexual or cultural 'difference' need not be. A truly democratic society can celebrate diversities of lifestyles, culture or sexual preference; but in what sense would it be 'democratic' to celebrate *class* differences? If a conception of freedom or equality adapted to sexual or cultural differences is intended to extend the reach of human liberation, can the same be said of a conception of freedom that accommodates *class* differences?... In particular, the abolition of class inequality would by definition mean the end of capitalism.[50]

Meiksins Wood's critique boils down to the idea that capitalism is itself the articulation of socio-economic classes, while it can promise the end of gender and racial discrimination in celebrating diversity. Historically, however, we have never had a capitalist society that did not rely on gender and racial 'difference' in order to achieve the required levels and kinds of exploitation for its reproduction. Contemporary critiques of imperialism and the North/South divide demonstrate this on a global scale. Still, few are prepared to admit that capitalist strategy relies on the selective accommodation of emancipatory demands as identity and that the global competition between capitals can find expression in domestic politics. Dominated by two capitalist parties, the American political scene has long afforded a clear view of capitalist strategy by offering a liberal (Democrats) and a conservative (Republicans) version of the same economy. The rise of Donald Trump in 2016–17 took the conservative party along a neo-fascist path. In 2017, a roundtable on 'Art History in the Age of Global Trump Politics' was organised at Edinburgh University in acknowledgement of the pressure on what used to be New Art History in the 1980s to rethink its conceptual apparatus and theoretical propositions.[51] A new level of authoritarianism would soon be sweeping the Global North, undermining the gains made in civil liberties through anti-racist, queer, and feminist struggles. There was no agreement among the panelists on if and how the immensely threatening political configuration was connected with the 'business as usual' of an art field structured through capital as a social relation. What does 'business as usual' mean? That year, artist filmmaker Morgan Quaintance provided examples:

> At the institutional level, consider how the anti-racist sentiment in curators Mark Godfrey and Zoe Whiteley's much trumpeted celebration of art in the age of Black Power 'Soul of a Nation' is profoundly undermined by the funds Tate received from Leonard Blavatnik towards the eponymous gallery extension opened in 2016. The Ukrainian billionaire also gave $1 million to Donald Trump's inaugural committee, a president favoured by the Ku Klux Klan, Neo-Nazis, and White Nationalists.[52]

Quaintance offered a fact-and-name-packed analysis of the 'structural right-wingness of the art world' and the reproduction, both ideologically and in actual institutional and curatorial practice, of business as usual. The web of relations connecting the art world's offshores, public institutions, and the good intentions of showing feminist social practice at Frieze London or the Tate is extremely dense, and is the context which has made inevitable the rise of neo-fascism as 'capitalism without a filter'.[53] In analysing Trump's second victory that has consolidated filter-less capitalism, Vivek Chibber considered the role of identity politics. He argued that identity politics

> loom largest for the elite sections of the population, because they've already achieved an appreciable standard of living. What they want to get is the full value of their class position. Whereas for the lower rungs, for the working class, they're not trying to get the full value of their class position. Their problem is the class position itself.[54]

This may be so, but it does not explain why at least some working-class votes went to a clique of billionaires. This outcome already required an ideological mobilisation of class as identity, but this was a nationalist, anti-immigrant identity set against the prospect of working-class unity and consciousness. Instead, it is worth thinking about the role that a gendered economy played in the Democrats losing. Given the visibility of care politics in art for years now, it is interesting to note that Kamala Harris's 'plans to develop a new "care economy"' were largely ignored; instead, many working-class votes were cast to the promise of waged employment and the production economy, as the Covid-19 'care economy' that many women counted on was removed post-pandemic.[55]

What the above tells contemporary feminism — especially Marxist feminism — is that identity is a weak and unstable ground of politics because of the economic reductionism that capitalism itself performs in everyday life. Economic reductionism forces urgent choices on those who live and die in 'capitalist social reproduction', to use Martha E. Gimenez's term, who calls for *more* feminist class analysis rather than the measured and proportionate mention of class (typically encouraged in post-1989 progressive feminism).[56] These forced urgent choices can range from opposing the gentrification brought on by diversity-focused art galleries to voting for a billionaire who promises paid employment. How could it be otherwise in a society where self-worth and social worth are predicated on the compulsion of work and on being acknowledged as 'productive'? Art workers' struggle for wages, examined earlier, is but an expression of this. Despite intellectual currents opposing it, the compulsion remains as it is generated from the real 'bottom' of any 'up': the economic determination or *oikonomia*, the large *oikos* (home) that capital encloses and where *nemein* or distributing takes place, bringing with it the nomos/law and even *naming* as in conferring identity.

What then finds expression as identity through the economy, as well as how social reproduction meets the labour that capital is willing to pay for, are difficult yet central questions for a feminist theory of the contemporary in art. If they are not explored, the art field's recent turn to social reproduction is at risk of registering as yet another expression of art's familiar middle-class stamp: a neglect of the anxieties of actual society.

Political Aesthetics: Representation and Prefiguration

You are a curator/artist/art writer. You sometimes conceptualise projects alone, sometimes with a small team. You do interventionist projects addressing gender inequality. You work freelance and sometimes receive wages or a salary: you have secured a two-year post at an art college, but before it's over you need to start looking for the next one, which would require you to relocate or commute. Is this feasible? Obtaining funding for a project continues being a drag. You constantly need to compete for funding (or jobs) with people you don't want to compete with, including fellow feminists. You have to draft funding application after funding application, presenting each project as original, though you are aware that it is impossible and unnecessary to invent a new form or new content for each — after all, you tackle ongoing social problems, but you must promise funders originality, visibility, impact. You need to report. You are stressed all the time about various aspects of a project: its realisation, its appeal, the possibility of failure. Your funders often evaluate your work on the basis of numbers visiting or participating. There exist questionnaires that you have to push on 'participants'. There exists immense paperwork. There exists the management of others, of time, of yourself. You are in a rat race but also love what you are doing: you try to convince yourself that you take pleasure in experiencing the conflict, living it out, embodying the contradiction. Isn't this what life is about? No one has it easy. Perhaps you could migrate to a country more generous towards the arts — but you hear it's getting bad everywhere. And children hate moving — you don't have children, but you still need a patron. Isn't this self-defeating? You were once part of a feminist collective but 'life' took you in different directions: one retrained as a social worker; another sells her hand-made objects in flea markets and travels up and down the country, you hardly ever see her; you heard that the third threw one of her sculptures out in the street and was hospitalised with mental health issues. You knew she couldn't afford storage and renting a studio. Neither could you. You adapted your creativity to work in a corner of your bedroom. You feel lucky, but also exhausted. You need to re-invent yourself. Not all of it, just parts. The part about leadership. After 40 (or was it 50?), opportunities shrink. You can't quit. You know you can be socially useful. Leaving *work* after so many years of effort would mean your *life* has been wasted.

You can add to, subtract from, and modify the above, but this is the general schema of the life–work–fantasy nexus of many feminists in the contemporary art field. In the above paragraph I combined phrases from friends, drawn from several countries and different age groups to suggest a recognisable pattern — a collective political biography. I have been unable to find in contemporary feminism a representation of such a collective political biography that centres the conflict that a capitalist society instils in feminist subjects. This I attribute to the divide that has characterised contemporary art between representation and performativity. In incipient form, this divide is encountered in the 1970s and 1980s as the politics of performance and the politics of representation: performance deployed the active body's presentism in its truth as process; representation offered finished works that invited reflection on an already thought-out position. In the feminist art movement, this incipient divide registered more as a complication in feminism's political aesthetics. As an art movement, feminism had to grapple with the question of strategy but also with urgency, which dictated use of tools and know-how already at hand — notwithstanding debates on this strategy, with some of their ramifications to be addressed in the next chapter.

The divide presented itself as such after the folding of the feminist art movement (by the early 1990s), when cultural producers engaging feminism came to operate more concretely within the broader trends of art. Already in the 1990s, Suzanne Lacy, a veteran of the feminist art movement's participatory and performative aesthetic, coined the term 'new genre public art'[57] to describe these practices which were to become dominant in the coming decades and concretise as socially engaged art. Many others — curators, theorists, artists, producers, communicators, educators — contributed and elaborated distinct positions and phrasings, with relational aesthetics, dialogical aesthetics, and art as a response to biopolitics perhaps being the best-known. In 2002, Boris Groys observed how 'art in the age of biopolitics' was 'hidden' away from institutional reach: performed within actual social relations, it would enter the art institution as art documentation, practising a contempt for spectatorship. Greg Sholette would later argue that 'the construction of a counter-public sphere will necessitate that we move away from the long-standing preoccupation with representation and toward an articulation of the invisible'.[58] In 2011, Nato Thompson would list a departure from representation as a defining feature of socially engaged art.[59] A repudiation of representation was declared as an identificatory attribute of the paradigm especially around the 2008 global financial crisis that brought millions of protesters onto streets and squares. This real-time public presence of bodies itself appeared as a political argument and informed feminist work. The 'politics of representation' that feminism had previously engaged with so strongly receded in the crucial decade of the 2010s, at least as a prominent theme in feminist art theory.

Against this background, and before I turn to the complications of the prefigurative, participatory, and commons-orientated current connected with socially engaged art, I want to address what has been lost through the repudiation of representation practiced by the contemporary vanguard. To do so, I return to the late 1970s and Helke Sander's film *Redupers: The All-Round Reduced Personality*, presented briefly in Chapter Three as a reflection on the contradictions that arise out of the multiple demands placed on the feminist subject. As members of a feminist photography collective, the film's women grapple continuously with the politics of representation, while also offering a view on the pleasures and difficulties of collectivism. Despite being made in West Berlin during the Cold War, the film's women are fully recognisable half a century later as creative subjects of modest means (or working-class) and politicised within the feminist left. They strive for political agency in deploying an outward-looking lens that records their surroundings and contests the privatisation of their lives. Their lives craft a predicament but are also the time–space of resistance, fitting the composite life narrative with which I opened this section. The women's efforts depend on competitive funding, on which both their publicly articulated creativity and survival from one day to the next depends. This oppressive economy is scrutinised in the film both in its guise as public/governmental funding and as liberal–leftist private employers (sympathetic as these are, they run a business which drives their decisions). The women photographers dislike the capitalist funding framework but must abide to it as no other avenues are available. Their daily reality is a division of labour, it is where everything becomes work: taking photographs, looking after their own or each other's children, going to an art show, getting connected.

The main character, Edda (played by Sander), lists numbers: how much everything costs, the bills, when she had her last holiday, and how much 'sick pay' she had: 'none'. Glimpses of the women photographers' personal stories place them within the social majority of heterosexual women, while some are also single mothers of small children. The film's reference to this majoritarian category is central to how interlaced impasses appear and resonate. For Edda, her child and her lover are both joy and burden. This, in many ways, is where the women's recognisability starts, despite the film's investment in black and white as an allusion to its constructedness, an allusion perceptible already in the role of photographs in the film. Photography mirrors the constant multitasking of the women, split between recording, interpreting, imaging, and imagining. Photographs, the women's labour output that hovers between recognition and dejection, make frequent appearances in the film, examined among the group about what they show (or don't show) and distributed in the urban setting as ciphers of a feminist 'right to the city', a concept that Marxist philosopher and sociologist Henri Lefevbre introduced in 1968 in his *Le droit à la ville* [The Right to the City]. Wall-divided Berlin is the open-air theatre where the women place their photographic vision, ultimately rejected by the gatekeepers, to ask: where is 'the constructed' actually located? Perhaps, we hear in the film, the answer lies in the way that they have been conditioned to view their capitalist reality as freedom. The women wonder if, despite being in capitalist West Berlin, they are in fact the ones who are trapped, but they do not really believe that in East Berlin women have escaped the known division of labour. The women photographers often seem disappointed, anxious, on the verge, as if they live in a theatre set that is a trap, that keeps them in place.

The collective manages to get a commission to photograph their free city (West Berlin), but only because for the funders the women's creative labour is cheaper, and the women are aware of this. As noted by many commentators, *Redupers* articulates a complex realism within the parameters of feminist counter-hegemonic cinema. One notes, for example, that 'the images in *Redupers* are nearly always framed or mediated through another medium or level of discourse — radio broadcasts, conversations and debates, or the film's voice-over narration'.[60] This was, however, typical for much of the rebellious and now often inaccessible counter-cinema of the period, which elaborated visual techniques against the spectator's easy and presumed passive identification with a film's characters. Such identification or seduction was what Laura Mulvey's detection of a 'male gaze' sought to undermine in the early 1970s. Yet that *Redupers* involved feminist protagonists shaped through their contemporary queried the premise of seduction: identification might be neither politically detrimental nor passive, but rather enact dialogical reflexivity.

Beyond a film-theory-based reading of *Redupers* (plenty exist), I see the work's feminist value in its demolishing the myth of self-determination under capitalism. The film achieves this as a *representational* effort that calls for, or at least permits, a difficult identification with feminist lives on their material, ideological, and psychological registers. Represented here is the very possibility of narrating feminist lives in the unfinished process of their entwinement and in the actual conditions of blockage that constitute these lives' 'contemporary'. There is no glorification: these lives are not a success story. The work's closure-dependent narrative effort — the film has a beginning and end — brings on a confrontation with feminist lives' slow failures but also with the meaning of not giving up. The feminist realism of *Redupers* relies on condensing the feminist time it performs and the acceptance of linearity: feminist lives are finite, just as other lives, and organised as working days, which brings them into conflict with an existential register. 'Only constant effort gives meaning to the units of time in which we live', Edda says in bed, reading the East German writer Christa Wolf. Through its representation mechanisms, *Redupers* delivers with devastating precision the somatised effects of the effort to live the contradiction: the desire to represent the world through a feminist lens; to understand the trap of participation while refusing to abstain from either life or political struggle;

to proceed through the accumulation of micro-destructions and the limits of feminist solidarity and friendship in a social field that persistently abandons the subject in the 'intimate' and the private.

Redupers takes no prisoners, one might say, yet it does not invest in tragedy: no one dies by suicide, no one abandons the feminist territory of art/life/agency, but, in one of the last and most remarkable scenes of the film, Edda suddenly vomits, after a meeting with a man that seemed to be going well until she has to push him away. Edda vomiting discreetly in the dark, on the sidewalk, comes as a shock: this is a spontaneous, involuntary, unstoppable act that summarises the blunt terror that grasps this feminist subject at the prospect of starting another cycle of the same, be it love or work. And yet she does. Edda has a moment alone to recover in a bar, and the next day her life then continues as before, impossible to exit. And so, Edda the feminist photographer becomes the all-round reduced personality — as Mary Hennessy puts it:

> an ironic reworking of the East German idea of the 'all-around developed (socialist) personality', or the opportunity to lead a fully realised life under socialism. In *Redupers*, 'reduced' becomes a gendered category that refers not only to women's marginal position in patriarchal society but also to the difficulties of life under Western capitalism.[61]

Half a century later, capitalism is no longer exclusively Western, and the all-round reduced personality is a general anti-privilege, yet still particularly available to feminist lives. In its anti-representational turn, the contemporary feminist imaginary affords few such instances of summarising, and thus making legible, the non-radical decentring of the feminist subject that capitalist life imposes. Second-wave feminism figured such a political aesthetic by exploring realism against the taboo that deconstruction had placed on it *tout court*, and I see in a feminist art theory of the contemporary the potential of seeking out this lost thread against the doxa of endless becoming that masks our human finitude and that of our creative actions and political agency.

Given the protracted trans-generational effort of women to exist in the art field, we can ask: is this constantly reproduced all-round yet reduced life what the feminist struggle has been about? Integrating this question into a feminist art theory of the contemporary would allow us to acknowledge that though the Long Modern's vertical account is populated with examples of collective practices, it ultimately valorises exceptional cases of self-realisation — it is the latter that constitute an alternative art canon of women's achievements. Having an alternative canon (that may well overlap with a hegemonic canon) means replicating the processes that propagate antagonistic relations as the foundation of art in the Long Modern. A salient issue in relation to our synchronicity is how to minimise antagonisms within arts-based feminism and reproduce political hope against the structures of competition, which can morph into social hatred. I think this is what philosopher Ewa Majewska's conceptualisation of 'weak resistance' partly delivers in her discussion of the common.[62] Although, as observed earlier in the book, a feminist art common was not the outcome of the feminist art movement, in the past few decades much attention has been paid to strengthening commoning practices in art generally, in part situated against the oppression of competition. Commoning practices involve individuals collaborating towards the generation of contexts that destabilise private property but also question the capitalist state's will to provide public ownership. Commoning practices are often seen as 'prefigurative': that is, they give contours to what cannot exist within the totalising worldmaking of capital but must be imagined as a plausible liberated future.

The prefigurative aspiration is tentative. The formation of a global capitalist economy has this meaning: no space or time of human activity is beyond the jurisdiction that sustains the reproduction of capitalism, and 'autonomous zones' can refer both to special territories of capitalist production *and* tolerated small-scale occupations of areas stuck in perpetual vulnerability. Therefore, for Vishmidt, 'the commons strategy would need to find a way of using the law to contest the law also on this unspoken and unspeakable basis — the historical and ongoing, ever-renewed and shifting process of dispossession, commodification and violence which produces subjectivities unable to envision a "good life" (Berlant) without those conditions.'[63] Vishmidt refers to literary and cultural critic Lauren Berlant's exposure of the 'good life' as a popular, purposefully sustained fantasy under capitalism. In 2008 Berlant wrote:

> A public is intimate when it foregrounds affective and emotional attachments located in fantasies of the common, the everyday, and a sense of ordinariness, and where challenging and banal conditions of life take place in proximity to the attentions of power but also squarely in the radar of a recognition that can be provided by other humans.[64]

The question that arises for a feminist theory of the contemporary that remains critical of capitalism is whether art's commoning practices, absorbing the energies of many feminists, break with the fantasy of a good life in capitalism or underwrite it.

In contemporary art, as in political theory, references to the common, the commons, and commoning proliferate but are rarely thought through the prism of Marxist feminist critique. In the 2010s, debates on commoning existed across sites of contemporary art, from biennials (such as the Athens Biennial 'Concordia' of 2015–17) to projects on art and life initiated by alternative institutions (such as CASCO's Grand Domestic Revolution in 2012 in the Netherlands) to conferences (such as Culture, Commons, and Institutional Innovation, in Zagreb, Croatia in 2014 and Conversations across Commons at the Jog Ja National Museum in Yogyakarta, Indonesia in 2015) to hybrid transnational art-and-research platforms (such as the Institute of Radical Imagination, set up in 2017 and focused on commoning in Mediterranean nation-states). These references are picked from an ocean of examples, and art theory on the left has endeavoured to negotiate this turn to commoning, perhaps especially in the crisis-defined decade of the 2010s. Sven Lütticken asked in 2016: 'As labour and value spiral into ever deeper crisis, practices of "commoning" come to embody the aesthetic as well as political promise of immanent exceptions. Is it any wonder that art, seeing its exceptionalism eroding, latches on to commonist theory and practice?'[65] What is eroding art's exceptionalism is, partly, the capitalist economy's intensification of the expulsion from labour and thus wagelessness, alongside a confusion between what is and is not labour, work, usership: the distinction is challenged when many (and not just a few) type their views on a social media platform in the name of democracy, irrespective of whether they produce what Marxists debate as constituting 'value'.

The art economy is a model of this confusion. Commoning practices may arise as opposition to capitalist competition, but, unless subsidised (for example, by an art grant that offers income in exchange for obligations), they constitute freely taken activities. In that, they match the illusions of freely chosen artistic activities at large. On the premise of autonomy, these freely chosen artistic activities may take the form of engendering pockets of alternative economies, beginning from a prioritisation or acknowledgement of social reproduction needs. David Beech sees a problem in that 'it is not always the case that campaigns for the commons target value production specifically,'[66] but this happens precisely because commoning practices begin with social reproduction needs, and social reproduction is the substratum of capital's valorisation. It took a lot of Marxist feminist work to show that capitalism as totalising worldmaking is not reducible to the production of value, despite value being the beating heart and objective of capitalism. Marxist feminism, however, has been just as marginalised as Marxism in the art theory and practice of our contemporary. Instead, Foucauldian perspectives have dominated, which see 'power' as being everywhere and in its diffusion informing a general, libertarian opposition to it. Whether commoning might be able to extricate itself from this ideological legacy is an open question.

'Feminist economics' is a term now embedded in the art field and underpinning commoning art that develops collaboratively in 'real' social relations but features in curatorial projects that enter the art institution as a record and theorisation of such practices. Participants may or may not be remunerated for their time, but often the projects generate in-kind returns or networks of solidarity and care. The neglect of care in neoliberal economies is noted, for example, by artists Ruth Beale and Amy Feneck who initiated a collaborative Alternative School of Economics in 2012, partly in response to the 2008 financial crisis.[67] More recently, Beale and Feneck point to the devastating impact of Covid-19 on families and care arrangements, noting also the broader alienation they felt as artists and mothers as a reason for starting the school.[68] What they describe comes frightfully close to the experience relayed in Sander's film *Redupers*, but in the 2010s creating a supportive circle of mutual pedagogy on the economy already functioned as a political aesthetic towards an urgently sought alternative, capable of including other projects such as the 'Speaking to the City' billboard — the city appears here too.

Beale and Feneck refer to J.K. Gibson-Graham's feminist economics and the famous iceberg metaphor:

where the 'official' economy is above the waterline — wages, corporations, taxation — and everything below is outside of it. This emphasises how the economy is actually made up of a plurality of economies — most of which keep the 'official' economy running: care, gifts and favours, volunteering, cash in hand, and the things we do for friends and family.

They then mention that the iceberg 'includes "reproductive labour", a term used by writer and activist Silvia Federici, and others, which describes work that is neither productive or unproductive, but instead cares or sustains'. The fallacy of commoning in the real conditions set by capitalism in art is perhaps exemplified in the clash between feminist economics, which at present postulates that multiple non-capitalist economies exist alongside capitalism but remain invisible, and the Marxist feminism that emerged from Italian Autonomia, exemplified in Federici's thought. The clash often goes undetected.

As Federici puts it, a 'different Marx was discovered in the 1970s by feminists who turned to his work searching for a theory capable of explaining the roots of women's oppression from a *class* viewpoint'.[69] In suggesting that non-capitalist economies exist alongside capitalism but are buried in the part of the iceberg that is underwater, Gibson-Graham conflate capitalism with the formal economy, while class loses relevance as it does not inform these other economies. If the class relation and its reproduction disappear from view, changing the visible economy becomes a matter of scale: a progressive revealing of more and more of the iceberg underwater. The iceberg metaphor becomes particularly confusing at this point, because bringing to the surface the hidden parts might just mean their entry into the formal economy. Marxist feminists do not think that capitalism is just one among many economies. Rather they refer to reproductive labour in terms of a necessary basis to accumulation. While Gibson-Graham's work does consider labour, the project is conceptualised as a kind of 'post-modern form of action research'. A duo adopting the collaborative 'I', Gibson-Graham writes: 'Following Foucault, I would see post-modern feminist politics starting from the assumption that power is everywhere inscribed'.[70] Is it this seeing of abstract power everywhere that permits one to see non-capitalist economies somewhere? Feminist economics has a more complex and heterogeneous history, however: first used by Barbara Bergman in 1983,[71] the term never overcame tensions and the diverseness of the economic thought that informs it, meaning it could never come to function as a coherent alternative to capitalism. In the multiple instances it is connected with commoning in art, feminist economics oscillates between prefiguration and a corrective approach to capital's exacerbated aggressions.

In the real-world conditions where commoning has been practised, the risk of the commons serving capitalism has been noted. Massimo De Angelis referred to the 'commons fix' needed in capitalist society, arguing that

> capital needs the commons, or at least specific, domesticated versions of them. It needs a commons fix, especially in order to deal with the devastation of the social fabric as a result of the current crisis of reproduction. Since neoliberalism is not about to give up its management of the world, it will likely have to ask the commons to help manage the devastation it creates. And if the commons are not there, capital will have to promote them somehow.[72]

The art field provides many opportunities to observe the latter. Overall, the activist impulse and the commitment to social engagement of contemporary art are permeated by a split between intentions and outcomes: the pragmatic need to step in, in protest (against what capital wants), is simultaneously a transfer of responsibility onto the shoulders of the artist–citizens (which is what capital wants). Elke Krasny's analysis of the expectations of the public body that commissioned VALIE EXPORT's public artwork in Vienna, *Transparent Space*, is a case in point.[73] Active since the 1960s, EXPORT has often embedded her work or her body in the publicness of urban space. *Transparent Space*, as Krasny relays, known also as *Cube EXPORT* and *Women's Bridge*, is a large transparent-glass room where Minimalism's aesthetics of power (the cube-obstruction) becomes perhaps more challenging through the added value of open views and surveillance. Krasny discusses the work's double function as singular authored artwork and a space for displaying other women's artistic labour publicly (yet in a glass case), but notes that this second function relied on the *non-artistic* maintenance labour of the female, and often feminist, art workers as a result of a weakened, underfunded public infrastructure. If the artwork were to fulfil its role as an exercise in claiming visibility for women's artistic labour outputs (artworks), the women art workers should engage their capacities as a care labour commons.

This is perhaps one of the most challenging feminist commoning cases in art, precisely because of its evident distinction between artistic and non-artistic labour. Krasny discusses a number of differences between *Transparent Space* and Mierle Laderman Ukeles's ground-breaking art performances centred on the maintenance of exhibition sites in the 1970s. I would suggest, however, that *Transparent Space* undoes and reverses the unity of labour of Ukeles's performances, realised as that of a single artist. *Transparent Space* rather reveals what is often excluded from artistic labour even within art collectives, and queries the persistent division of labour that underpins the art field. As binaries receive much negative attention in today's art, we might as well be reminded that for art to exist, non-art must also be asserted. It is a contradiction we have already encountered. In its conditions of actualisation, commoning in art functions in a twofold way: first, as a repository of labour that capital expels from its proper production needs. Art reconfigures this precarity as social — here, feminist — solidarity. Second, commoning is labour that creates what capital's reproduction requires as ideological and sometimes material affirmation: the semi-autonomy of infrastructural provision required for the apprehension of art itself.

Would the binary be abolished if the women art workers entering the space of the feminist artwork rebelled against its instituent property relations and appropriated it explicitly as a site for commoning? The women art workers would thereby declare void the singular artist's authorship, state authorisation, and the law — the eviction rate of occupied cultural spaces in Europe lowers expectations, however. Before this imaginary transference of rights to the feminist commons can be actualised, all cooperative labour feeding into the maintenance or activation of any context such as *Transparent Space* is an affirmation of the 'element of separation' by which 'the modern world is structurally characterised' for Marx.[74] That is, the division of labour would persist. Women art workers working together do not necessarily constitute a common/s: so-called team work is what capitalist production also relies on. The glaring question is whether the designation 'public art' is but the occupation of a potentially commoning space by the aestheticisation effect of private property relations. When art is in a private gallery, aestheticisation is taken for granted: possibly drawing on Marx who in 1867 wrote that 'capital comes dripping from head to foot, from every pore, with blood and dirt', Hito Steyerl presented contemporary art in commercial sites as another name for capital: 'Contemporary art is everywhere. And when it is finally dragged into Gagosian dripping from head to toe with blood and dirt, it triggers off rounds and rounds of rapturous applause'.[75] If art sees itself as a democratising exercise when placed in public space, commoning can, in principle, reveal the relations that organise actually existing public space under capital. For feminism, the effort towards commoning can nuance the ever renewed public/private divide as one in which neither pole is aligned with the prospect of emancipation.

The prefigurative political aesthetic of commoning became entrenched under neoliberalism and its crisis, figured as austerity economics. Commoning became a seemingly logical response to the new brutal enclosures, but sidelined the fact that defining the common good had, in neoliberalism, become pure speculation: not even nature as habitable environment could arise as a 'common good'. If commoning in terms of prefiguration acknowledges the impossibility of defining the common good in capitalist society, we must remember that society has for years now been perceived as stuck between a decaying old and a deferred new. Zygmunt Bauman described this condition as an 'interregnum'.[76] But how long is this interregnum to last, as it was already observed by Antonio Gramsci a century ago? Gramsci was a communist and saw communism as the deferred resolution of the interregnum. What the appropriation of the interregnum serves in non-communist thought is less clear. When social reality becomes incomprehensible because of the speed of changes that accumulation requires, perceptions arise about the end of an era. McKenzie Wark argued in 2017:

> This civilization, such as it was, is over. And everybody knows it, really. The hysterical nature of denial, and the amount of money pumped into sustaining it, is a sign of its weakness. The thing that is hard to introduce into the existing structure of feeling is this awareness that these are already ruins.[77]

Somewhere between the interregnum and the ruins, we are left with capitalism at full steam — so much so that its critics who appreciate its momentous techno-financialised recalibration make a point of calling it techno-feudalism,[78] thus mixing the present with a pre-modern past. Getting from a fascination with technology in so-called postmodernity to theorising technology as pre-modernity in the span of 50 years places some strain on the meaning of commoning as a prefigurative aesthetic.

As the Cold War's anti-communism succeeded in delegitimising the left's propositional politics, a series of surrogate concepts appeared as consolation politics: anticapitalism and postcapitalism — words often present in discussions of the commons — became the nebulous remains of the borderless anti-communist ideological operation. Invoking feminist commoning from a Marxist feminist standpoint is intended as a question on what is missing in terms of propositional politics beyond the anti- or post-. A surprising affinity can be observed between the feminist economics of Gibson-Graham and formulations of postcapitalism. Beech writes that 'the stage at which the forces of production outstripped capitalism was evident in the middle of the nineteenth century', quoting Marx in support:

> At a certain stage of development, the material productive forces of society come into conflict with the existing relations of production or… with the property relations within the framework of which they have operated hitherto. From forms of development of the productive forces these relations turn into their fetters. Then begins an era of social revolution.[79]

But if capitalism was always postcapitalism, the latter loses any emancipatory currency. If the politics of lived experience has any traction beyond its entrapment in and separations of identity, it is to remove us from the domain of naming and point to a social reality where the social revolution is indeed not happening.

On the contrary, subjugation continues and commoning is often defeated by the privately lived burnout of those who strive for long-term collectivism. Should we then start by asking whether the 'material productive forces of society' tend to 'come into conflict' with the 'existing relations' of *reproduction*? How has capitalism handled this conflict so far? Capitalism has paid much attention to relations of reproduction in the Long Modern, contextually balancing the accommodation of some feminist demands and the suppression of others. The issue is what kinds of commoning capitalism permits and benefits from versus articulations of commoning that pose a threat to it. Commoning is meaningless unless it prefigures a communist organisation of society against large-scale property. Feminist commoning is radical when pressing in a political direction where social reproduction is prefigured strategically as ahead of production organised by and for capital. This would be a first step in reclaiming the right to a future that totalises liberation for a change. Attending to how processes of feminist art commoning are enacted, become appropriated as a 'commons fix', or, rarely, overcome the procession of limits that capital stacks against them, would enable a feminist art theory of the contemporary that stands in opposition to accepting art as a field defined by competition and the antagonisms capital installs.

A SHORT RECAP, WITH A DISJUNCTION

This and the previous chapter focused on a selective presentation of feminism in its dialogue with art in the Long Modern. I started by acknowledging a continuity of forces since the nineteenth century, proceeded to explain and defend art history's focus on 'the contemporary', considered the ideological mediation of concepts and the difficulty of acting against the totalising operation of capital. I then suggested that a feminist theory of the contemporary in art is essential for learning politically — that is, exposing the illusions implicated in capital's reproduction as our own reproduction — from feminism's trajectory within this Long Modern.

The presentation has been partial and incomplete. 'Limit' in the discussion of the points of tension and contention that I prioritised in this chapter was mostly used in the negative. Instead I might have asked: do the limits generate positive articulations of dependency as feminist interdependency? The political aesthetics of representation and prefiguration presented suggest that different paths can be taken in answering this question. The realist representational path might appear melancholic but offers a sobering reflexivity against the current of prefiguration that stops short of envisioning the endpoint of commoning efforts. I chose a representational example from half a century ago, not least because it prefigures intensifying antagonisms for the performative feminist subject of collaborative and sometimes commoning labour. I suggested that favouring the performative over the representational, as is the case with socially engaged art at large, does not lead to art that overcomes either the material or the ideological sustenance of capital.

The art field is a complex site for feminism because it is so many things at once, presented as unproductive and wage-claiming, as exceptional within the capitalist economy and as leading or mirroring changes in this economy, as the site for agency against capital and for business, as time safeguarded for thinking through social justice, but also as the glamorisation of collusion. Claimed by protesters and investors alike, art is where hegemonic ideology is affirmed and pierced by counter-hegemonic consciousness. Feminism cannot extricate itself from these cascading antinomies but can develop what Marxist feminist education theorists Sara Carpenter and Shahrzad Mojab call 'revolutionary learning' through 'a consciousness that is active but also inherited from the past',[80] so as to consider: how do we get from here to tomorrow? The disjunction between, and move from, the spatial to the temporal plane perhaps helps confront what is needed for reaching into the potentiality of praxis.

6

The Technology Question: Feminism, Art, and the Future of Subsumption

In the postmodern 1980s, technology became akin to a force of nature — naturalised, arguably, as the sublime of the information age. In 1985, Jean-François Lyotard's philosophically inflected exhibition *Les Immatériaux* (The Immaterials) put on display the awe before the '"post-industrial" techno-scientific condition', this condition's inevitability, and the 'unease' it imbued.[1] Postwar technologies generated a strong impression of immateriality, and immateriality is configured as the awe-inspiring qualities of the divine and extra-human; the ideology of the soul and spirit would not leave capitalist modernity. Technology was announced as the new awesome and/or the new awful (the sublime represents both) as part of a longer trajectory: technology had been overtaking nature as the new sublime since the Industrial Revolution as much of modern art allows us to see. The formidable military technology's enabling of unprecedented world wars in the twentieth century was when this sublime would show its true dimensions and scope: technology would not just be the main force of production in capitalism but also the guarantee of capitalist security, and any entity that might wish to challenge capitalist security would have to follow its logic, its economic principles, its scale. That is only part of the story, but capital's core of mass violence organised through technology is the spectral condition of the techno-scientific drive that is presented as merely benevolent to global society's pockets of uneasy peace. Social peace requires regular technological updates of surveillance and force against bodies, and, in the 2020s, we see a costly arms race, focused on the reconfiguration of capital's geopolitics of lethal rivalry and absorbing social wealth that could ease the crisis of social reproduction.

Against this background, there has been no effective global movement opposing the military–industrial complex. Humanity continues marking progress through techno-scientific advances of transversal import across social registers. Esther Leslie's *Synthetic Worlds* (2005) shows how discoveries in chemistry in the nineteenth century were felt in industry and art, and also why chemistry advanced so much in that period. The quest for magical transmutations of matter in the alchemy experiments of previous centuries would not die off but be scripted into the technological realm's philosophical apparatus. Leslie notes 'the confusion of human progress with technological progress' and that for the great critic of capital's mantra of progress, Walter Benjamin, on whose work she draws, progress was a 'nineteenth-century phantasm' that informed 'social democratic reformism'.[2] Capitalist modernity appears to have fewer ruptures than one might like to think: techno-scientific progress still informs social democratic reformism, thus organising technology as hegemonic ideology not only for centre-left governments and the remains of Third Way leftism imagining growth through AI, but also for a spectrum of post-Marxist theoretical positions and the postmodern left.

It was World War II's cybernetics and the elaboration of code-dependent technology that opened the way for the 'digital revolution', which was in/famously announced in 1988 by neoliberal American President Ronald Reagan in a demoralised Moscow as a 'bloodless' revolution that would overcome and overshadow modernity's early twentieth-century revolution for workers' liberation. Chemistry was not addressed in that speech, but in the 2020s, cybernetic capitalism is found to entail 'an extremely complex assortment of chemicals, including various rare earth minerals…, heavy metals…, complex plastics…, and synthetic substances' that need to be 'mined from the earth, refined, recombined and heavily processed, producing various toxic byproducts — to say nothing of the effect on the health of the workers across these supply lines' and the phenomenal amounts of electricity required. Given that 2020 was when 'human-made mass' exceeded 'the entirety of global biomass',[3] capitalist technology arises as a force against life, organising a binary that must be concealed or at least invalidated at all costs.

The 'digital revolution', essential for neoliberalism's global drive and the booming of finance, would be a revolt of techno-capital against human agency itself. The problem with human agency was it could turn into labour agency, which was intolerable: neoliberalism had to produce an appropriate subjectivity through both imposition and ideology. Those of us whose youth was marked by the digital transition of the 1990s saw that the vast majority of people, including our working parents, were not asked whether they approved of digitality or not. Workers from offices to factories to farms retrained, and those who did not were pushed into obsolescence as a distinct facet of deindustrialisation. Based on the privatised 'general intelligence' of generations, the digital revolution was more like a soft coup on the part of the capitalist class that not only transformed all labour environments, but also challenged the distinction between work and non-work, and between production and consumption. Capitalist strategy diversified: the 1990s digital chatrooms offered pleasant anonymity or the right to be whoever you wanted to be online, making identity fun. Digital cameras went commercial on a large scale, promising simplified access to both fantasy and indexicality.

The digital transition was capital's most successful ideological battle of the late twentieth century, won after earlier battles on progress and its discontents had paved the way. If we take art's history in the Long Modern as an example, we note that what has been seen as the artist's deskilling evolved as more and more skills passed from workers to the technological apparatus:[4] the ready-made in Marcel Duchamp's artworks of the 1910s accepted the machine privileged in industrial capitalism, long after the early nineteenth-century workers in England known as Luddites had lost the battle against machines; the language turn and dematerialisation efforts in conceptual art occurred during the West's deindustrialisation, which began in the 1950s and accelerated in the 1970s. The digital turn, crucial for finance which saw itself as money making money without the need for labour, required a philosophical script and an artistic vision where the agency of labour would be undermined by displacing the human through its equation with both nature and machine/algorithms. The history of modern art is a history of modern labour — a history of successive losses. These losses of labour — and gains for capital — appeared first in the West as the territory most developed by capital, which is what also explains the Western bias in the history of modern art. That is, we can start by looking at the *material* conditions capital created in the advanced West rather than racism as an ideology engendered by these conditions: racism was essential for primitive accumulation, for deindustrialisation which required cheap factory labour in the non-West, and later for mining vulnerable Global South land for lithium and for recruiting African labour for AI.

This is the broader context of the technology question that this chapter revisits. The chapter asks how the feminist imaginary that crosses through art negotiated the 'becoming' promised by capital's literal and metaphorical investment in technology, or put differently, how the material conditions of history are encountered as ideology that engages the desire of emancipation.

WOMEN, TECHNOLOGY, AND ART SINCE THE SECOND WAVE: FROM REPURPOSING THE 'MASTER'S TOOLS' TO BEING REMASTERED

Modern art and film provide a gallery of encounters with women and machines — that is, of women as signs in the pictorial and filmic space and machines that would often claim anthropomorphism as automata. Importantly, however, the machine is not one thing, but has transformed within the capitalist project of accumulation, centralisation, and control, and therefore theorisations that observe no difference between the bicycle wheel, the internal combustion engine, and the Turing machine are less useful for unpacking either technological determinism or woman's complex proximity to the automaton and corporeal technologies.[5] Women were largely prevented from being scientists and thus shaping technology from a position of highly specialised knowledge and labour, integral to innovation; or they were made invisible, like the six women behind ENIAC, the 'world's first modern computer'.[6] Besides this, as the early twentieth-century fascist-leaning Futurists put it in their manifestoes, women (and feminism) should be despised as the relics of a pathetic subjectivity that could not appreciate speed, technology's masculine energy, and certainly war. If in 2025 the billionaire owner of tech-giant Meta, Mark Zuckerberg, could argue that corporations need more 'masculine energy',[7] tech-misogyny has a longer history. Women were drawn, painted, photographed, filmed as the aestheticisation of machines in a double guise: to assert the machine's otherness such that it needed to be tamed but also to bring forth the machine's seductive powers. With few exceptions, the use of the sign woman in the proximity of machines proceeded along entrenched stereotypes in the avant-garde imaginary.

The 'female robot' of Fritz Lang's German science fiction film *Metropolis* (1927), in a script written by his then wife (and later Nazi party member), author Thea von Harbou, is set in 2026, our contemporary. *Metropolis* offers a startling narrativisation of the imagined condition of woman in the future (now, present) of techno-capitalism.[8] Opening with a scene of pounding industrial machines that overwhelm human scale, the silent film with intertitles presents a society where a class of workers confined underground sustains an overground society of skyscrapers, automobiles, trains, airplanes, and nightclubs ruled by a male arch-capitalist often addressed as 'father' by his son who is portrayed as confused in this machinic world. At the end of the film, the confused son, whose mother died giving birth to him, is the one who cements a deal of affect (mediated by the 'heart') between society's 'head' (his father) and the workers (referred to as 'hands'), thus thwarting the workers' insurgency and keeping them subjugated — for the good of the city. Nazism, then in ascent, surely wanted such a pact of affect with the workers, but which capital does not?

Woman plays an intricate role in all this: the woman as mother is spectral (she appears as an oversized sculpture of her face); some workers are female but the workers are reprimanded repeatedly as 'parents' when neglecting their children for work or the insurgency; early in the film, the ruler's son dismisses the over-decorated women of his class to fall in love with a woman who cares for the workers' impoverished children flocking to her much like a teacher at school. This is Maria, the film's protagonist. Maria is a creature of affective bonds and ecstasy-prone Christian goodness. This is why she goes to the underground factory to address the workers, promising them a 'mediator'. Literally affected, the workers come close to revolt, saying they won't wait much longer. Maria finds this mediator in the ruler's son with whom she has fallen in love. Do the workers understand that Maria's religiosity and craving for harmony mean that this mediator will not be a liberator but will only mitigate their suffering (like social democracy or socialist fascism/Nazism) so that they continue to produce for the upper class? Whatever the case, it is a woman who is cast in this caring role as the ground for harmony that benefits the dominant class.

It is this Maria that the male scientist-inventor fuses into the robot of mechanical breasts and hips to animate it/her as a dangerously seductive, hyper-sexualised cyborg that arouses men, literally and metaphorically. After her fusion with the machine, this post-woman is deployed as part of the dominant class's plot to suppress the workers' potential rebellion. The post-woman will eventually be burned at the stake as a witch — a fate, we observe, meted to women in the days of primitive accumulation. Finally, the human Maria, who somehow survives all this and lives in fear of being confused with her robotic double, will take her rightful place next to the male mediator and inheritor of his father's dominion. This dominion is sustained by the good intentions that find their ultimate expression in the blend of care, technology, and labour overseen by capital. Maria infuses saintly female goodness to class dystopia that appears as the utopia that capital seeks.

In the late 1960s and 1970s, when women as a group were claiming the right to be artists but also when new and old technologies of the image and the spectacle were competing for attention, the camera as the mediator of modernity's gaze became a critical machine. Despite being the master's tool, as Allan Sekula and later on Ariella Aisha Azoulay would detail (about photography),[9] the camera could be repurposed, recording, questioning, deconstructing, and reconstructing figurations of sociality and women's roles. Women artists, whether openly feminist or not, embraced video (new) and used photography (old) to introduce angles, subjects, and narratives that exposed a gendered everydayness, along with instances of resistance, and questioned key concepts of modern art. In their hands, photography became performative and revelatory of the ideology that defined the classed female body (Jo Spence), a medium for critical appropriation (Sherrie Levine), a map of feminine encodings in technologised popular and high culture (Cindy Sherman), a documentary device for charting women's labour across borders (Franki Raffles), and a lot more. As for the video camera, women used it in vastly different ways, including as a recording medium for private and public performances, and to document the social energy of the era. Video eventually became 'video art', but in the 1990s it would confront the processes of globalisation as 'video essay',[10] building on the long tradition of the essay-film, including in its anti-colonial use, as in the 1980s work of Trinh T. Min-ha. In the late 1970s, interactive spectatorship was introduced in art by Lynn Hershman Leeson in *Lorna* (1979–84), where a viewer could decide the life course of the work's homonymous fictional character in a plot where media surveillance met techno-domesticity through the TV screen.

Open archives, such as AWARE, list women as 'pioneers of video art', indicating unwittingly that originality and authorship were only symbolically challenged in feminism's critique of male-dominated modernism — it could not have been otherwise: both authorship (property) and originality (innovation) matter to capitalism and its art world. Debates arose, for example, on the distinction of film and video: viewers of moving-image works could make a major *faux pas* if they conflated a video work with film and vice versa (artists' film persisted), as medium specificity was politically meaningful for the feminist art movement (which also, however, practiced inter- or post-mediality). What is important for the present analysis is that early in the feminist art movement a political aesthetic took hold where the technological apparatus was separate from the female subject who used it to uncover, demonstrate, narrate, disrupt, and decry; these women could drop the camera or pick it up.

A complication arose with performance. French artist ORLAN exemplifies this complication. In 1966, she 'created a performance that involved selling cropped photographs' of her 'body parts in black and white glued to wood. They were displayed on a cart in a vegetable market like a food product next to stalls of carrots, leeks, and potatoes'.[11] Overidentification (here, of woman with consumable goods) is often presented as an artistic strategy for those who cannot speak as a result of oppression. Yet in merely replicating an association, this strategy entails interpretative ambivalence, which was also a compromising aspect of Meret Oppenheim's *Cannibal Feast*: presented at the International Surrealist Exposition of 1959, *Cannibal Feast* had procured for consumption a female model surrounded by foodstuff on a ceremonial table. Later, in her 1977 performance *The Artist's Kiss*, ORLAN placed a photograph of her naked torso on her real-time performing body, walked among attendees of an art fair and offered anyone a kiss for five francs, as the phrase superimposed on the photographed female torso promised: participants would put the money in a slot between the breasts and the money would slide down and accumulate in a small box under the pubic region. The photograph (representation) was superimposed on the artist (presence) with the curious effect of making her look like an automaton/robot that offered sexual pleasure or at least sexual experimentation as part of an exchange economy: this was the art economy and not the typical sex trade (the sexualisation of exchange would be further explored by mostly women artists in the coming decades). It is unclear if *The Artist's Kiss* was intended as a comment on women artists' precarity or merely on the connection of femaleness, sex, and trade enhanced by technologies of spectatorship, but today social media subscription platforms such as OnlyFans thrive on the combination. Whatever the intention, it was articulated through a hybrid: a (young) woman's living flesh and subjectivity and a technological medium (photography).

This reading unsettles feminist and leftist narratives of the 1970s and 1980s about performance as anti-commodity, when painting was then rejected because of its obvious commodity status. Although the anti-commodification motivation was genuine, *The Artist's Kiss* demonstrates that commodification was moving from the inanimate object to the human subject in the delimited yet expanding domain of art, and that technology mediated this transition, or perhaps broadening of art-based commodity fetishism, enabled by the historical association of woman and exchangeability. Performance came to be widely adopted at the historical moment when the self-objectified subject of neoliberal governance and post-Fordism took off. The actual authorship and fantasised autonomy that structures the modern art act constitute the crucial mediator in the substitution of the object with the human being. History took its course. If in 1989 feminism could still say 'Your body is a battleground', as in Barbara Kruger's renowned poster confronting anti-abortion laws, in 2023 ORLAN would state: 'The body is a playground'.[12] This was also when the slogan 'my body, my business' would combine the discourse of autonomy with that of the capitalist market and appear in art's auction houses in sales tied to progressive causes.[13] In the neoliberal market, women performing gendered labour already think of themselves, or misconstrue themselves, as human capital. Drawing on Marina Vishmidt, Stefano Harney and Fred Moten observe that:

> the automatic subject of capital that human capital seeks to emulate, is a hollow subject, and *a subject dedicated to hollowing itself* precisely by expelling the negativity of labor, by exiling the

one who, in being less and more than one, are his figure, his other, his double, the bearers of a generativity without reserve. Now, human capital is the automatic subject's substitute, carrying out its engagement with the skills of daily financialisation and logistics.[14]

The dedication of the subject to hollowing itself/herself out was to be literalised under the star of artistic freedom where anything, including the self, could be re-made as part of post-conceptual critique addressing some aspect of the consumer universe. It is now commonplace to say so: in the 2024 queer film *Leyla*, for example, a gay man who works for a corporation is introduced by Leyla to their non-normative social milieu as a performance artist so that he would make a good impression. The man duly elaborates: 'it's critiquing consumption'.

An even more complicated history of the female performative body emerges if we think of the trajectory of feminist art and theory. As technology would advance its capability of compartmentalising the body as part of neoliberalism's recrafting of the subject, the performative body followed strange routes in feminism. There, the aforementioned rejection of painting as commodity combined with a fierce critique of how the sign woman had been used in modern art (and the longer history of painting) to objectify and essentialise women through persistent sexualisation. This put much pressure on women artists who would be accused of sexualising their own naked bodies when deploying them in static mode even beyond painting. Helen Chadwick was a case in point, active since the 1970s in Britain where the feminist critique of the naked female body on display was prominent. In 2024, Tamara Trodd discussed Chadwick's major composite 1986 installation *On Mutability*, which involved the technology of photocopying as an aesthetic solution against the charge of essentialism: 'In *Of Mutability*, the *photocopied* redoubled [naked] female is not intended to reconfirm a single female "essence" but rather to multiply and "derealise" it in an effort to… embrace metamorphosis and change: from animal to vegetable to human, from living to dead'.[15] Donna Haraway had opted to be a cyborg rather than a goddess just the year before in her 'A Manifesto for Cyborgs', but Trodd argues that Chadwick's 'version of "goddess" imagery' involved 'change' rather than primordial essence.[16] Change was the political demand, and perhaps even goddess spirituality could represent it if technologically mediated. Here, we get a glimpse of the extremely complex context in which feminism's attachment to the vitalism of new materialism and posthumanism would arise at the expense of historical materialism.

The feminist critique of the display of the female body's exteriority required solutions that would give rise to a feminist aesthetic of the body's interior. Feminist critique is not to blame here, of course. What I am pointing to is the need to situate this critique in relation to historical forces beyond its control. Just a few years after *Of Mutability* in Britain, ORLAN in France would explore and put on display her interior body. She would do so as medical science was facilitating corporeal compartmentalisation that made the most of women's socially constructed compulsion to remain youthful or correct 'defections' of 'nature' through so-called cosmetic surgery. ORLAN proceeded to use such surgery in performances that would further invest in hybridity — a concept previously celebrated in postcolonial theory's encounter with postmodernism. In the early 1990s, *The Reincarnation of Saint ORLAN* performances generated still and moving technical images in which the woman artist's face would be seen under the surgical knife, in an experiment with and against stereotypes, sometimes drawn from male-dominated art history. This female saint's 'carnal art' was possible because of medical technology, including the science of local anaesthetic and pain control. Blood, muscle, and tissue would be revealed while surgical tools lifted the skin of ORLAN's face, with her eyes open, her lips sometimes smiling or speaking in 'choreographed' operating theatres where high fashion and high theory also had a place.

Had *Metropolis* not been made, this act of having the face lifted might have registered in terms of Joan Riviere's 1929 psychoanalytic essay 'Womanliness as a Masquerade' taken to its technological extreme. Just two years before that essay, however, *Metropolis* had presented that woman was not a performing mask but human. She had to be offered by science for the posthuman cyborg to live: in an unforgettable scene, the terrified human Maria is hounded by the male scientist–inventor who tells her: 'Come! It's time to give the man-machine your face!' This strikes a chord in relation to the documentary images of ORLAN's surgeries. The 1927 filmic scene comes from a moment in modernity when resistance marked the separation of human and technology. Following a scene that evokes the violence of rape, human Maria is overpowered by the male scientist–inventor who steals her face (and life power). The successful fusion of woman and machine is later announced to the capitalist father–ruler: 'She is the most perfect and the most obedient tool that a man has ever possessed!' Why the hybrid robot had to be constructed by absorbing a woman thus becomes apparent. This is where *Metropolis* and Riviere's psychoanalytic exploration of womanliness as a masquerade that locks woman into pleasing the man converge: either by force and capture (the non-mask face of *Metropolis*) or compulsive consent (Riviere's mask), obedience is the outcome. The counter-revolutionary function of the female cyborg in *Metropolis* indicates that conformity can be the endpoint of pioneering science and of the impulse of transformation that capital's dynamism proffers.

The thread of this suspicion towards technological transformation found in the 1920s would be lost in the expanding maze of techno-logical subsumption. By the end of the twentieth century, the resistive distance that kept machines separate from humans had diminished considerably. ORLAN, who often emphasises that her surgeries were not a personal affair but rather concerned women as a social group, was herself remastered by mobilising various fusions of technol-ogy and flesh. That 'the idea of turning surgical interventions into performance art occurred to her when she was operated on for an extra-uterine pregnancy under a local anesthetic' and that she had to develop a complex funding model to support the operations, including 'vials containing samples of her liquefied flesh and blood drained off during the "body-sculpting" part of the operations... intended to be marketed'[17] to fund further performances situates femaleness at the crossroads of technology and exchange value. The surgery-based performances of the early 1990s extend and update the presence–representation hybridity explored in the 1970s in ORLAN's *The Artist's Kiss*. The distinction of presentness and representation fades.

In the early 1990s, medical technology's increased capability to enter a body that was by then seen as porous found new currency in women artists' work: Mona Hatoum created *Foreign Body* in 1992, where an endoscopy camera entered every orifice of her body, gen-erating a dizzying flow of entries, exits, and re-entries, and affording views of her material interiority in ways that straddled the geo-graphic, medical, and pornographic. Both *Foreign Body* and *The*

Reincarnation of Saint ORLAN invoke and make use of alienation at their confrontation with body-transformative technology, but the latter work would invest this confrontation explicitly with spiritualism, sainthood, and joyful transcendence: ORLAN would insist that her art was the opposite of affirming pain, in the way that so much body art does. *Metropolis'* Maria was also saintly; she cared for others and wanted to help them out of their condition of oppression, yet in a way that affirmed rather than destroyed the social order. This is what underwrites her cyborgian usefulness, setting an engaging precedent. In capitalist modernity, the blend of technology, ethical missions, and spiritualism have had an existential edge that exceeded questions of labour and machine. Sainthood appeals to disciplinary commitment and immortality. It is thus perhaps unsurprising that later in life ORLAN would publish a petition against death declaring 'I don't want to die!', and that wealthy tech entrepreneurs also strive to defy their mortality through bodily technologies.[18] This existential promise is what the fusion of flesh and machine ultimately dangles before capitalist modernity's mesmerised subject whatever the gender. In this promise, wealth and class inflected by self-care play a very material role.

The immortality promise is woven into technophilia, implicitly justifying the destruction that technologies of this magnitude require for their realisation, beginning with the massive environmental impact of plastic surgery. The cannibalising of subtly or explicitly dehumanised human bodies that makes waste a necessary element of production (and not merely consumption) is justified because of this telos. Premised on endless growth, capital is tied to the eternal and infinite, which allows it and possibly requires it to accommodate and enact various orders of the spiritual, religious, and mystical. There is no conflict between the rational and the irrational threads of capitalist modernity; both underpin the production and dissemination of technology that co-constitute it. Danielle Child observes the quest for immortality at the heart of high-tech, data-capturing art in her discussion of etoy's *Mission Eternity* (2005–). The group formed in 1994 and has been 'in hibernation' since 2013, but not before a successful trajectory of exhibiting, performing, selling, getting awards, and imbricating technology and a casual, rather than philosophical, notion of metaphysics in an art enterprise. On the project's website, *Mission Eternity* is presented as 'hybrid art' that is too complex 'to explain' and indeed the description deploys the typical postmodern vocabulary of pseudo-scientific obscurantism and open-endedness.[19] Nonetheless, *Mission Eternity* investigates 'afterlife, the most virtual of all worlds' and builds a 'community of the living and the dead that reconfigures the way information society deals with memory (conservation/loss), time (future/present/ past) and death. Under the protection of thousands of M¥ ANGELS (the living), the M¥ (the dead) travel space and time forever'.[20] Seeing that the project was 'developing its own technologies in the form of code and software (e.g., killertoy.html or the ANGEL-APPLICATION)', Child finds that 'etoy avoids the pitfalls of capitalist technology' and posits that *Mission Eternity* may be 'the ultimate hack', existing 'as a process of ongoing revolution to come in which new modes of existence in a digitized world are predicated on the axes of art, technology and human emotion'.[21] Contrary to this, however, the vocabulary of 'angels', 'sarcophagus' (meaning flesh-eater in Greek), and 'eternity', and mixing the afterlife doxa with data collection for the achievement of technologically assisted immortality, suggest yet another manipulation of humanity's existential anxiety. *Mission Eternity* reiterates and affirms the pervasive idealism structured on the matter/mind (or soul) binary that underpins technological attachment through affect. The 'human emotion' that Child refers to is certainly present, but is now the site of consensus extraction: the tech dream of living forever develops in parallel with technological extermination afforded to those made vulnerable — Palestinians killed by automated drones, migrants pushed to the Mediterranean Sea floor by border technology, those who die in mining tech minerals, or die by livestreamed suicide, while 12,400 known nuclear warheads (and counting) promise capitalist technology's 'final solution' for all.

As art became a field of experimentation with subjectivity, matter, and transcendence, it provided a unique site for the glamorised affirmation of capital's spell linked to the fantasy of technological self-determination. The fantasy was unmoored from concerns about non-human life, unless these became art's articulated subject matter. This created a tension between the materials needed for the production of the posthuman subject and President Reagan's invocation of the 'spirit' that 'unwittingly referring to the horizon that had been delineated by cybernetics in the 1940s: reconceptualized as information systems, humans, machines and nature were rendered semiotically transparent to one another'.[22] The spirit of the times could not let go of spirits, which also inhabit the spectrum of techno-fusions and transpositions. ORLAN's bringing together of the materiality of the body and the immateriality of sainthood updated the old idealism and binary of matter/mind (or soul) that would also animate *Mission Eternity* and its angels over a decade later. Mediated by a technological apparatus geared to satisfying a projection of the ideal self (cosmetic surgery) and transform the body by dividing it into parts, ORLAN formalised a new biopolitical aesthetic for feminism that would find broader application. This biopolitical aesthetic mixed the design of bodies and subjects, as well as emancipation and salvation, and was underwritten by narratives of progress that must be forever renewed under capitalism.

LIBERATIONS: 'TALES FOR AN ACCELERATED CULTURE'

In the history of ideas, a telling example of the ubiquity of the belief in technological progress would be the philosophical current known as accelerationism. Entailing neo-reactionary fantasies of capital overcoming its boundary of human labour to conquer the universe, but also leftist fantasies of a humanity free from labour through automation, accelerationism welcomes catalytic technological change in terms of social change. That said, 'left' and 'right' are frequently dismissed as obsolete under the hold of techno-universalism. In tracing the origins and trajectory of accelerationism, in 2014 Benjamin Noys went beyond the typical social geographies of the West, pointing both to the pressures the early Soviet Union faced to keep up with Western productivity, and to the twenty-first century technological competition between China and the US. This followed his *The Persistence of the Negative*, a critique of continental theory, which in art history has been strongly associated with postmodernism and, partly, post-Marxism.[23] Roger Zelazny referred to accelerationists in his sci-fi novel *Lord of Light* in 1967, the same year that Guy Debord would poetically discuss the technology-fashioned spectacle, where relationships between signs would substitute those between human beings. Zelazny's incorporation of 'Hindu mythology and cosmic dialogue' and the desire of a vanguard wishing to 'take their society "to a higher level" by suddenly transforming its attitude to technology'[24] shows that the trend of liberationist techno-spiritualism now dominant in art (to which feminism also contributed) originally occurred when a spectacular semiotic capitalism was taking hold. Debord could see this, but his *The Society of the Spectacle* did not address how such technologies would deepen the 'metabolic rift' capitalism generated between culture and nature.[25]

Accelerationism garnered attention in the 2010s, when digitality was widespread and the AI transition imminent, with its promise to expel huge amounts of labour and workers from production and the wage. In 1991, however, Douglas Coupland had subtitled his cult novel *Generation X* 'Tales for an accelerated culture': there, a group of young people in a high-income society opt out of the drudgery of low-income jobs, with those in the fast food industry standing out. In 1993, Irvine Welsh's *Trainspotting* also featured youth 'not choosing life' as a dead-end blend of consumerist techno-domesticity and wage ennui. Caught in the implosion of the American Dream and as the Soviet counter-paradigm's collapse was becoming a disavowed generational cultural trauma, this youth preferred the DJ transcendence and human warmth of ecstasy-fuelled clubbing.[26] Some of these people never exited the 1990s drug culture, while some went on to collude with the reproduction of capitalism, and some sought to set up the DIY cultural fringes that drive the critique of institutions but without a horizon of political transformation other than nebulous postcapitalism. This is the generation that adopted postfeminism and the California ideology, the generation of Elon Musk and of the Cybernetic Culture Research Laboratory (CCRL) in Warwick, England (which wasn't exactly New York, I should say, living nearby at the time). Set up in 1995, CCRL incubated both Nick Land's idea of future capitalist monarchy and Mark Fisher's counter-project of refuting 'capitalist realism'. Experimental mysticism was far from absent in CCRL's elaborations that originated in postmodernism's assertion that capitalism was 'natural' and had 'no alternative', as pointed out by Andy Beckett:

> With the internet becoming part of everyday life for the first time, and capitalism seemingly triumphant after the collapse of communism in 1989, a belief that the future would be almost entirely shaped by computers and globalisation — the accelerated 'movement of the market' that Deleuze and Guattari had called for two decades earlier — spread across British and American

academia and politics during the 90s. The Warwick accelerationists were in the vanguard.[27]

By 1999, the Wachowskis' film *The Matrix* would bring in quotes from Jean Baudrillard to visualise an imminent techno-futurity where stressful knowledge of reality or blissful life simulation in virtuality was enacted by pharmacology, and specifically red and blue pills: reality was revealed to be hibernating humans used as organic batteries for sustaining the simulation. Since then, red and blue pills have entered the alt-right imaginary of internet-propped conspiracies, incels, and the manosphere, generating further literary critiques.[28] By the end of the 2010s, Silicon Valley's new phantasmagoria of all the above had congealed into a symbolically rich way of ruling and profiting to the point of becoming a subject for anti-fascist research in art. Addressing the dizzying 'dance of signs' that comprised visual culture, Ana Teixeira Pinto explained the allure in 2019:

> Willing to surrender political power to populists and demagogues of the far right in order to protect its economic interests, the affluent or relatively affluent Western middle classes also have an ambivalent relation to capitalism, typically theorised as an aleatory and chaotic force — by those for whom labour is something to be commanded with a click of the keyboard, not something to be suffered — able to unleash 'powerful utopian energies', the alienating effects of which can be experienced as liberating. The intensity, intoxicating vitality, and almost ecstatic mode of experience that the left is said to lack is what the alt-right has to offer. For fields like contemporary art, whose narrative identity is predicated on doing something that is not of the norm, this offer proved enticing.[29]

As Teixeira Pinto says, numerous curatorial projects engaged technology-sustained transhumanism in celebratory fashion. Posthumanism would at times be seen as a more ambivalent, even benevolent, expression of technological optimism. The cultural hangover of postmodernism would be a crucial component: irony and ambivalence, mixing the historical and mythical, advocating the embrace of alienation via hybridism. Eventually, new materialisms' imagined equivalence of machine–algorithm–animal–stone–plant–human found traction through the ideological thriving of vitalism (infused with minor occultism). Agency would be a property of matter in this magical thinking. Art's propensity to see industrial objects, formerly known as commodities, as possessing agency sounds like a terminal form of commodity fetishism.

Nonetheless, the ideology of agential matter would often appear in curatorial eclecticism — an eclecticism already encountered in *Les Immateriaux* of 1985. In 2012, besides the typical posthuman works drawing on Donna Haraway, Documenta 13 turned to quantum physics, and also wanted to transport a 4,000-year-old meteorite from Indigenous land in Argentina to Kassel. The extraterrestrial stone was desired because of its cosmic agency, but Indigenous people opposed the plan precisely on the grounds of the object's sacredness. Documenta 13 incorporated with ease works of ecological critique, the devastations of the 2008 financial crisis, the mystique of mutations, nature's energy. The artwork's uniqueness and autonomy as the fetish of labour rescued from industrial logic was, and is, the ideal carrier of the new materialism–posthumanism complex. The industrial object, the extracted natural object (bones, tissue, teeth, blood, flesh, trees, etc.), and nominally liberated work (artmaking) all meet in the curatorial synthesis as the search for equivalence and the flow of metamorphosis. This is a search for holism against crucial distinctions and antagonisms, as Andreas Malm has pointed out.[30] In such holism, labour and capital, emancipation and subsumption become indistinguishable.

This all created an overwhelming reality for women artists' practice, especially for those who had an active frustration about women's fate in modernity. Chiara Fumai's art was emblematic of this spirit of the times and, perhaps, of the isolation of the feminist artist in her context. Born in 1978, Fumai, who was previously a DJ, experienced the tail-end of the 1990s club culture and its joyful transcendence and sampling. In her artistic work, the question of the medium and its historicity that informed second-wave feminism — the medium as tool — acquired an altogether different meaning as she herself adopted the guise of the medium that connected her with dead women. Death — like the 'cult of the dead' that etoy practiced after 2000 — became the territory of Fumai's active excavation and invocation of radically different political frameworks and the women who had acted within them. Fumai deployed performance — her performing self — along with photography and video as the media of a new feminist hauntology. Photography's widely discussed role as a liaison to the dead and video's magnetic disruptions pointed to the possibility of performative hauntology. Fumai placed these technological media within the logic, or illogic, of the séance. In her performative re-animations, Valerie Solanas, Carla Lonzi, the nineteenth-century medium Eusapia Palladino, 'freak-show performers Zalumma Agra and Annie Jones',[31] Rosa Luxemburg, and Ulrike Meinhoff (a journalist and militant of the anticapitalist armed struggle in 1970s Europe and co-founder of the Red Army Faction) meet as the parade of the marginalised — marginalised women, as Fumai would relay in interviews. Of Fumai's practice, Kari Conte writes:

> By merging existing historical facts — which she viewed from a metaphysical perspective — with her own fiction, Fumai filled in the gaps in history, thereby giving relevance and reverence to these women and reconceiving their lives in light of female oppression and identity… [encouraging us] to look beyond the binary of fiction and non-fiction.[32]

This hybridising work reflected Fumai's eclectic interests, ranging from 'dance music to terrorist propaganda, radical feminism to occultism, and Italian Autonomist Marxism to nineteenth-century freak shows'.[33] Fumai's intentions were declaratively political: she revisited the longest possible modern to speak again the words of women who had refused to occupy a woman's place. But these intentions were mediated by both hegemony and melancholy. Although it is true that many others have blended fiction and history to shape cultural narratives that reveal what formal documents leave out, filling 'the gaps of history' in this case occluded from view the dead women's distinct and often antithetical political projects (or even their lack of defined politics) — this is one aspect of the hegemony structuring this practice. Another is the unintended violence done to the dead women in casting them as marginalised when some of them were major political figures of their times. Like all the dead, these dead women could not object to this artistic liberty and mediation.

Fumai's suicide in 2017 haunted the feminist art world. On the one hand, she is described as troubled by the political climate in New York following Trump's first election (a political climate, to note, afforded also by irrational conspiracies and their technological-mystical visual cultures) which led Fumai to leave an artist's residency and return to Italy, where she killed herself six months later (in a gallery). On the other hand, Fumai was called 'poor Chiara' and her 'will to die' was spoken about as 'a necessary step in a process of her own, secular, canonization. What is canonization if not a way to create a form of immortality through a mythologized death?'[34] Fumai can neither agree with nor object to any of these readings of her death. It can only be hoped that her political specificity as a feminist who experienced *this* disorientating contemporary will not be compromised in further iterations of techno-mysticism. She is a feminist casualty of a zeitgeist that seeks clairvoyance rather than clarity, and robs many of the possibility to connect their circumstances to historical forces where nothing supernatural exists except as consolation. If the assumed unity of matter makes consolation tentative and mourning optional, feminism's duty to its historical human losses as the outcome of socially constructed vulnerability is to leave the fantasy of equivalence and reinstate women's agency as properly human.

It is important to acknowledge here that the dominance of new materialisms and posthumanism in curatorial and artistic work is in dialogue with feminist theory, encountered in analytical and manifesto form. Valerie Solanas' belief that automation would liberate women (1967) is developed in Shulamith Firestone's *Dialectic of Sex* (1970), which then finds a stronger articulation in Donna Haraway's 'A Manifesto for Cyborgs' (1985), following which Rosi Braidotti's *Transpositions* (2006) blends nomadism with the prospects of repurposing technology, which leads to feminist accelerationism in Laboria Cuboniks' *Xenofeminist Manifesto* (2015) where it is said: 'if nature is unjust, change nature!' The contradictions that feminism faced in the universalism fashioned in capitalist modernity, addressed in the first chapter of this book, shaped a current within feminism where the specific alienation that befell women as culture's 'other' ultimately congealed in the proposal to embrace alienation as what posthumanism had to offer. This project was attached to an ethics that required various iterations of anthropomorphism: it is 'nature' that is 'unjust' rather than the material conditions generated by modes of production and reproduction. This is a notable transposition, indeed. But it is not nature that proposes this transposition, but rather human beings shaped in a concrete historical juncture, where capitalism is found to have no outside. Feminist proposals to repurpose technology are implicitly or explicitly responsive to this. Their leftist eclecticism is an expression of the contradiction that the current 'no outside' thesis raises for emancipatory projects birthed in the nineteenth century of revolutionary possibility, when technologically supported globalisation is pre-emptively counter-revolutionary.

In this current, we also observe a hardening of positions. There is a difference between Braidotti's thought in 2006 and in 2021 when she published *Posthuman Feminism*. Her 2006 book *Transpositions* opens by addressing the neoliberal project after 1989 and its 'one way political model' where 'all programmes of change have exhausted their political function, especially Marxism, communism, socialism and feminism'.[35] The expositions that follow lead to a political melancholy obliged to repurpose itself as joyfulness:

> What is at stake in the ethics of sustainable nomadic subjects, ultimately, is an acceleration that would allow us to jump over the high fence of metaphysics. Not in a utopian mode, but in a very embodied and embedded way; actualised in the here and now. The swift exhilaration that emanates from texts that are clearly indexed on the potential of life, and not on its diminishment or negation — has to put wings on our feet and infuse joyfulness.[36]

This strand of feminism finds consolation in the ethics of becoming and living 'just a life'. In a 2019 interview, Braidotti described the revolution 'now' as 'fascism' and belonging to the far right. In repeatedly deploying the blurry 'we' of discursive democracy, she embraced the 'possibilities' of technology, saying that 'contrary to the Marxist–Leninist idea of a global revolution, the changes that we can achieve are collective, but step by step, by distancing ourselves'.[37] Can 'we' distance ourselves as workers from the jobs offered (or not) by the class that owns the means of production and determines social reproduction? Class antagonism does not enter this step-by-step 'affirmative' perspective (feminism, anti-racism, and anti-fascism are liberated from the oppression of thinking class) which, unsurprisingly, starts and ends with consumption and finance rather than production, with Braidotti arguing that we are not in the capitalism that Marx described: 'Capitalism today does not need to produce anything to earn money, it can make a profit from nothing'. In thinking about feminism against capitalism, the closures through which feminism enables and participates in its counter-revolutionary times should be noted.

In *Posthuman Feminism* (2021), Braidotti caricatures socialist feminism as that feminism which thinks that 'the inferior social conditions of *women and other minorities* will be automatically adjusted once the new socialist system is in place'.[38] Contrary to posthuman feminism's willful or circumstantial ignorance of socialist and Marxist feminism, its arguments and debates, one would not know where to start with scholarship against this claim. Recently, in 2024, Marnie Holborow provided a challenging view on the relationship between social reproduction, production, class, race, and gender (including gender non-conformity) that went beyond neoliberalism to review capitalism's trajectory.[39] Besides this, women have not been a minority in socialist feminist thought while one would struggle to think who this subject's comparable 'other minorities' might be in a way that makes conceptual sense. It is also unclear how many actually existing human beings would concur that 'the human body is now an obsolete piece of machinery by comparison with the speed and liveliness of the new technologies'.[40] This is perhaps 'situated knowledge', to recall Donna Haraway from 1988. It is situated too far from all those who must defend their bodies as human. One wonders who can then claim agency if not 'bodies' — an appellation that curiously invokes the mind/body divide as the cornerstone of western philosophical idealism that historical materialism has worked to displace. *Posthuman Feminism*'s publication during a devastating pandemic and experimental lockdowns, when the ravages of capitalism became apparent in class terms in so many different ways, including gender violence, is instructively ironic. Braidotti is right, however, in arguing that 'the posthuman is not postpolitical' and that 'the posthuman condition' marks a 'recasting' of political agency 'in the direction of relational ontology'.[41] Leaving aside a possible tension between ontology and becoming, the issue is which relations are made visible and invisible by the posthuman perspective.

All this will continue being ignored by those who believe Silicon Valley's tale of 'money making money' without the need for labour. Posthuman feminism's ideological entrapment in technological determinism and its accelerationist impulse exemplifies what Marina Vishmidt called 'visible finance' versus 'invisible labour'.[42] In the antagonism between the visible and the invisible lurks a crisis of representation that imagines the distribution of agency to matter, the imperative of infinite becoming that replicates capital's commitment to its own infinity, the sameness of humanity in its social divides, meteorites, automata, and algorithms. When no distance is said to exist, what should 'we', step by step, distance ourselves from?

THE PERSISTENCE OF LABOUR

In 1991, as women artists were experimenting with medical technology and Generation X was inhabiting accelerated culture, Judith Wajcman's *Feminism Confronts Technology* referred to feminist research since the 1970s that identified 'men's monopoly of technology as an important source of their power', efforts to challenge this monopoly, as well as 'women's efforts to control their own fertility... [that] extended from abortion and contraception to mobilizing around the new reproductive technologies. With dramatic advances in biotechnology and the prospect of genetic engineering, women's bodies have in some respects become increasingly vulnerable to exploitation'.[43] Women artists found these new technologies fascinating, yet not without scepticism. Patricia Piccinini's *The Human Mutant Project* (1994–) proved a work of critical insight. Starting shortly after the launch of the Human Genome Project in 1990 that would last 13 years, Piccinini's digital photography imagines mutant beings but also 'satisfied customers' through the lens of bioethics that accompanies genetic engineering and concomitant anxieties:

> according to the fictitious flyer that accompanies the image [of a smiling female customer holding a cute mutant and a pacifier]: '... highly trained technicians [can] work with you to design, conceive and incubate the child you desire with all the features it needs [including] a variety of useful chemicals for enhanced living'.[44]

In 1996, just before her untimely death, Helen Chadwick would realise *Nebula*, which follows the technology of in vitro fertilisation (IVF). Observing as artist-in-residence at King's hospital in London that pre-embryos would undergo selection prior to being implanted in a woman's uterus, Chadwick photographed discarded pre-embryos and encased these representations in sculpture that invoked

Victorian mourning rings, saying: 'To observe the pre-embryo down the eyepiece of the microscope at the time of fixing feels like a Victorian's view of an early photograph, except here it is life itself that is being fixed, not time'.[45] This is a striking observation on the labour of seeing which crosses through art but originates elsewhere while today 'embryo adoption', based on the surplus from IVF, is a lucrative business tied to Christian beliefs about children waiting to be born.

In their 2023 chapter 'Feminism Confronts AI', Wajcman and Erin Young argued that artificial intelligence 'technologies are gendered by association and by design, where "association" refers to the gendering of work environments and to technology stereotypes'.[46] Most importantly, they identified yet another large pool of invisible human labour supporting 'so-called intelligent machines', concluding that these '"ghost workers", often women in the Global South, are underpaid, undervalued, and lacking labour laws'.[47] This invisible labour, which includes men, is now daily news: *Al Jazeera* reported, for example, 'dozens of Kenyan workers were paid less than $2 per hour to process an endless amount of violent and hateful content in order to make a system primarily marketed to Western users safer'.[48] What drives this input is what Marx identified in the nineteenth century as capital's reliance on a reserve army of labour. One contemporary AI worker says: 'I do not care if the AI companies in the West grow rich because of our work. As long as we are paid. It may not seem like much, but it goes a long way in Kenya'.[49] This is how the social totality of technologically driven capitalist globalisation works: the abhorrently exploitative material conditions of the Global South's working class translate into the consensus on the 'trickle-down' capitalist economy, and thus the reproduction of capitalism.

Left accelerationism is not preoccupied by this reality. Nick Srnicek and Alex Williams's *Inventing the Future: Postcapitalism and a World without Work* (2016) is an influential manifesto-like analysis that imagines in hopeful and positive terms life beyond capitalism. Aaron Bastani's *Fully Automated Luxury Communism: A Manifesto* (2019) imagines a society that has solved all current problems and that begins its history as communism. Helen Hester and Srnicek's *After Work: A History of the Home and the Fight for Free Time* (2023) addresses the impact of technologies on housework and considers historical examples of alternative social organisation, calling for a future of communal living and care where the days of racialised social reproduction infrastructures and 'women's work' would be but a memory. To reach this future, technology should be loved in the present. What the present shows, however, is that housework's technologies have been crucial to maintaining the gender gap both at home and in waged work while, in parallel, capital tries to seize the womb, which might indeed allow it in the future to organise the gestation of the labour-power it actually needs. Projections of acute labour shortages in the near future because of the drop in fertility make the current push for intelligent machines easier to grasp. Yet the social shock of digitality and informatisation is already inscribed in Michael Hardt and Antonio Negri's work, where the cooperative labour essential for cognitive capitalism was expected to sufficiently transform the forces of production for the passage from capitalism to a newly figured possible and plausible communism. This perspective has been criticised for failing to attend either to the vast class, gender, and racial divides comprising the workscapes of what was once perceived as 'immaterial labour' (a problematic term, acceding to the fiction of immateriality), or to the vastly unequal access to technology and the actual labour conditions in the environments where technology is produced.

Such environments will continue to be seen as merely technologically determined until workers act on their collective capacity to refuse work — a prospect that would require building revolutionary trade unions, convincing the police and the army that they are workers, radicalising social reproduction key workers, boosting left parties free from large donations, and, not least, upholding a critical separation of machine and human. The reason that only humans — and not machines, including robots and AI — can produce value for capital is not merely that machines conceal dead labour (labour *already realised* as value within them) and/or transfer the value they already have in them (from the human labour that made them, including all the 'knowledge' and 'skills' they carry) to whatever it is they help produce or achieve, but that, so far, machines cannot refuse to perform. All the way down to the tiniest microchip, machines constitute *realised value* and 'machine learning can be considered as the technical proof of gradual integration of labour automation with social governance'.[50] It is hard to see how this predicament would be undone without the material destruction of the vast data centres that capitalism is building. Practicing 'deconnectionism', as Matteo

Pasquinelli momentarily suggests, encounters the obstacle that digitality is a matter of paid work and thus workers' reproduction in actually existing capitalism. And so, Pasquinelli rightly concludes that there is no shortcut to withdrawal because opposition starts with politics and not with technology, that is with '*abolishing as a whole…* the organisation of labour and social relations on which complex technical systems, industrial robots, and social algorithms are based — specifically their inbuilt wage system, property rights, and identity politics'.[51] Until then, as Naomi Klein has observed, AI will continue to constitute

> the largest and most consequential theft in human history. Because what we are witnessing is the wealthiest companies in history (Microsoft, Apple, Google, Meta, Amazon…) unilaterally seizing the sum total of human knowledge that exists in digital, scrapable form and walling it off inside proprietary products, many of which will take direct aim at the humans whose lifetime of labor trained the machines without giving permission or consent.[52]

CAN CAPITAL'S TECHNOLOGY BE REPURPOSED? ART IMAGINING THE FUTURE OF SUBSUMPTION

The questions that feminists bring to technology concern whether the technologies that belong to capital and serve its reproduction can somehow help emancipation or not. Yet technology is not neutral but necessarily belongs to capital today: there is no alternative paradigm of production that generates different, non-capitalist technologies, even if China thinks it can quickly cross through capitalism to exit, teleologically, into socialism, situating technology at the core of what its government called in March 2024 'new quality productive forces'.[53] Having seen in earlier chapters the actually existing interdependence of production and social reproduction (as understood by Marxist feminists), but also capital's drive to eliminate the distinction between them, I will now turn to how these complexities enter the feminist imaginary as critique in art. A narrative representational work, Melanie Gilligan's sci-fi video installation *The Common Sense* (2015) raises a number of questions and will therefore be used to anchor the analysis. I argue that *The Common Sense* offered, already a decade ago, a stunningly lucid interpretation of a key tendency in contemporary capitalism: the fusion of production and social reproduction, discussed in Chapter One. Social reproduction is a complex term in its own right, encountered as both the reproduction of life and the reproduction of capital. As Vishmidt argued in 2017, the relationship between the two reproductions remains underexamined in art theory — and I would suggest that the scarcity of Marxist feminist analysis in art history is symptomatic of this inattention.

The reflections that follow stem from the hypothesis that technology is where these two iterations of social reproduction increasingly converge — not least because both iterations engage on some level with the problem of labour. The designation 'problem' indicates not just divergent views on theorisations of labour even within Marxist feminism (for example, as regards the contextual interconnections of productive, reproductive, unproductive labour) but also the instability of the category 'labour' under the weight of the development of what Marxism understands as *forces of production* in capitalism. The problem of labour arises in conjunction with the historicity of technologies that implicate corporeality — never abstract — and its inscription as generator of the most precious commodity: labour-power. Of interest here are the degrees of proximity between technology and human beings that the forces of production allow for. This is not a smooth or linear process. As Marxists relay, the realisation of full automation encounters obstacles within actually existing capitalism: 'the contradictions of capitalist accumulation' clash with 'the practicality' or not of 'actual investment'.[54] And contra to feminist accelerationism, Silvia Federici observes no 'necessary connection between scientific/technological and moral/intellectual development, which is an underlying premise of Marx's conception of social wealth'.[55]

Despite (or because of?) all this, capital must diversify its tactics of capture. Biopolitical manipulation is part of this. To speak about biopolitics is, of course, to speak about many bodies as well as the relationship of the one and the many. A thematisation of conflicts proliferates — human needs versus other species' needs; abolition of gender or multiplication of genders; techno-liberation versus a problematic more concerned about waste and de-acceleration. This is what made the commons so important in discussions during the 2010s, when both ecological catastrophe and dispossession via austerity economics raised the spectre of an unlivable life even for those enjoying 'Western' privileges. Some feminists in the field of technology theory begged to differ, arguing that:

> On the left, there are the accelerationists, whose paeon to think tank inspired Universal Basic Income (UBI) as a new form of populist utilitarianism often has all the appeal of a middle management Powerpoint, and who seem to think all that is required is a form of post-agonistic common sense, and some efficient leaders who can ensure the 'most advanced' technology is put into full and most beneficial use. This is as far from a new 'commons', by the way, as it is possible to get.[56]

In *The Common Sense*, Gilligan asks how this 'common sense' is generated. Although my focus is the future-focused narrative of *The Common Sense*, encountering the artwork as a spatial installation through 15 screens balanced on black-coated scaffolding enhances the narrative density and irresolution of 'what happens'. The work is exploratory but also practices a realism founded in Gilligan's sustained study of capital as a social relation in the twenty-first century.[57] Despite granting the viewer (also a listener) a degree of interpretive license courtesy of its narrative convolution, *The Common Sense* refrains from affirming open-endedness and the viewer's interactive choice as staples of postmodern aesthetics. Leading viewers to the diversity of equivalent choices would entail the risk of affirming the illusion that individuals are in control of outcomes through personal techno-mediated 'action'. This was perhaps impossible to see in the 1970s but it is what Jodi Dean's theory of communicative capitalism would come to articulate, when post-2000 social media would magnify the determinations of technological interactivity.

Made when global capital's extraordinary enclosures and extractive mechanisms forced attention on capital's totalising drive, *The Common Sense* is also a child of its times. In the mid-2010s, the *unrepresentability* of capitalism as a dynamic totality, especially in its present global hegemony, was a preoccupation of Marxist cultural theory, with Alberto Toscano and Jeff Kinkle wondering how a 'cartography of the absolute' might be possible at all.[58] Gilligan addresses this unrepresentable absolute in her work overall. Her earlier moving-image works which portray a plausible imminent future, sometimes prophetically — *Crisis in the Credit System* (2008),

Self-Capital (2009), *Popular Unrest* (2010) — all approach capitalism as a totalising procedure, only aspects of which can become representable as effects on social relations. This totalising procedure included one's relationship to oneself — evident in *Self-Capital*, with the same actress, and thus the same 'body', playing the roles of patient and therapist, and customer and cashier. In *Popular Unrest*, the identity of capital and an extra-human, mystified power known as 'the Spirit' is delivered through the metaphor of a knife falling from the sky on random people, alluding to capital's license to expel labour and crush the bearers of unwanted labour-power. This is not an imagined future nonetheless: 'how to extract from the global economy the means to stay alive' was described in 2007 by Malcolm Bull as 'the primary problem' for humanity in extant capitalism.[59]

The Common Sense grapples with the precise figuration of techno-capitalism as totality — how far does it go? Gilligan draws the human senses into it: as Marx had argued in his *Economic and Philosophical Manuscripts* of 1844, the senses have a history. In an elementary summary, the plot focuses on a high-income, liberal society where access to technological innovation is taken for granted (as in most Global North societies). A technological innovation known as 'the Patch', a prosthesis attached to the top of the mouth, permits its human carrier to access other people's emotions and sensations. The senses of the multitude (to recall Hardt and Negri) are here connected in a technologically realised common sense, or the senses as a common. The advanced version of this remarkable technology, the two-way Patch, achieves full sensorial interaction among humans who have instant access to each other's interior engagement with reality. Through the lives and interactions of specific individuals, we watch this future society organised through highly recognisable structures: education, work, debt, entrepreneurialism, science, family relations, and so on. The history of this future society is narrated through a split in the plot: the narrative is composed of Phase 1 and Phase 2, with Phase 2 being divided into two parallel narratives: Phase 2A and Phase 2B. These two parallel narratives (which lose the effect of being parallel when followed on the many monitors embedded in the scaffolding of the video installation) are two explorations of the *same* future, as it transpires, shaped by the invention of the Patch as a corporeal technology.

The Patch is an entrainment technology — that is, a technology enabling a form of synchronisation between specific organisms or entities. 'Entrainment' is a scientific term for how a process or thing finds and shares rhythm with another process or thing. In biology, the Cambridge Dictionary says, it 'is the process of making something have the same pattern or rhythm as something else'. Entrainment is also meaningful when thinking about how data-based technologies of control, labour, and entertainment become intermingled promising more and more access to 'real life' which is then fed back into the 'artificial environments' of these technologies. Previously mentioned Marxist debates on what should be considered labour in the history of techno-capitalism concern this entanglement. The blurring of work and leisure and the merging of control and entertainment for the purposes of 'continuous functioning' is central to how the Patch operates in *The Common Sense* as an enabling technology. The generation of common sense happens when human beings and capital's drive merge.

The Common Sense opens, in Phase 1, with a group of students waiting in a corridor to enter the classroom where their tutor will deliver a lesson on the history of the Patch (technological obsolescence is built into that future society too). The tutor screens a film that presents this history: first, there was the one-way model Patch that did not permit instantaneous exchange of emotions and sensations; then came the two-way model that did. The students know this all too well as, through the two-way communication enabled by the Patch with which they are equipped, they work non-stop to pay their tuition fees, including in the classroom where they are taught the history of their own technologically enhanced sensorial apparatus. Viewers can infer that when capital generates a new(er) technology, we are essentially forced to embrace it, because not doing so would prevent us from making a living: staying alive. This dimension of coercion connects technological obsolescence to selective human obsolescence, and from this perspective, posthumanism's techno-philia is the embracing of coercion for the sake of survival. The main lesson for the students of *The Common Sense* is that the hopes originally offered by the Patch about social transformation proved futile — and the bifurcation of the film plot into two intersecting narratives serves to explore why this was the case.

Following this bifurcation, Phase 2A shows instances of rebellion connected with the Patch technology. Phase 2B presents mostly scientists' experiments exploring the technology's potential, but through an ambivalent relation with predatory entrepreneurialism. However, as poet and cultural critic Jasper Bernes comments, 'the split between storylines in the time of the frame tale juxtaposes and links together in uncomfortable ways the activities of the politicised students and workers with those of a team of patch researchers trying to make sense of and exploit changes in subjectivity and neuroanatomy'. Capital's entry to the body is found to produce changes that can be seen as immaterial but are very material. In this future capitalism, humans remain hopeful in relation to this unknown, against the evidence piling up in their actual lives. As the double plot proceeds, 'the direct "entrainment" of mind-to-mind in line with the imperatives of capital… shadows the entrainment of storylines, linking the experiments of the protesters to the R&D [Research and Development] of techno-capital'.[60] We already inhabit this 'embodied capitalism', as argued in 2006.[61] *The Common Sense* provides a manifestation of a corporeally distributed capitalist totality in which the tenet of 'no outside' describing the scope of global capitalism acquires a terminal meaning in be/coming 'inside'. How did this all come to be? For this consensus to arise, connectivity and access had to be presented as fundamental, legitimate desires, linked to a sociality that understands itself as 'human nature'. The totality of a positive experience that Damien Hirst once wished for himself by claiming, as per the title of his artist's book, *I want to Spend the Rest of My Life Everywhere, with Everyone, One to One, Always, Forever, Now* (1997) is delivered, in *The Common Sense*, as the prison of the experience that arises out of the constructed yet naturalised desire for total connectivity. Connectivity fashioned as ultimate freedom predates the concept of communicative capitalism: it underpinned Marshall McLuhan's 'global village' of the early 1960s and the Cold War politics pitching 'free' West/capitalism against the 'Iron Curtain' societies. The polarisation sustaining the Cold War confrontation played a role in the legitimisation of connectivity and access, fuelling communicative capitalism as an apparent deepening of democracy achieved through communication technologies.

The Common Sense follows to its logical conclusion the Western prerogative of freedom that is tied up with capital's will to access, and gives another spin to Roland Barthes's words from 1977: 'Language is neither reactionary nor progressive; it is simply fascist, for fascism does not prevent speech (*dire*), it compels speech'.[62] This comes long before communicative capitalism enabled scores of internet warriors to call each other 'fascist' at the speed of their smartphones. Barthes's statement was coeval with the overall attention to language and the text, found to be both the problem and solution by late 1970s poststructuralism. *The Common Sense* society has therefore done away with language. The students in *The Common Sense* can hardly believe that once upon a time literature and visual art — as variations of language — were held as adequate channels of human communication. Language, for them as Patch users, was limited, representation-bound, unfree. Mediation and the precariousness of representation (the doubt of interpretation) are a pre-Patch social reality, replaced in this future society with direct reach into sensorial truth. This society sees such direct reach as unmediated exchange — a further step to eliminating the 'middleman' of money (a representation of value), as hoped for by an entrepreneur in the film in his discussion with a (female) scientist. For the scientist, who appears shocked by the entrepreneurial imaginary of relentless profit-hunting, the Patch-enabled sensorial commons is the culmination of human history: a long-sought perfection of communication brought forth by pure science to satisfy natural human needs.

The conflation of human history with the history of a mode of production (capitalism) by science is the hegemonic ideology explored in *The Common Sense* — an ideology that inverts, or perhaps extends, the maxim 'it's easier to imagine the end of the world than the end of capitalism'[63] into an interiority that has lost sight of its formation through prefigurative capitalism (rather than prefigurative communism). This ideology is evident in Jean-François Lyotard's *Libidinal Economy* (1974) reporting on the naturalness of capitalism:

> We must grasp that currency (more generally every object in the system of capital, since they are commodities and therefore currency), actual or potential, is not merely a convertible value in a universal process of production but *indiscernibly* (and not oppositionally, dialectically) a charge of libidinal intensity. We must grasp the fact that the system of capital is not an occultation of an alleged

use-value which would be anterior to it… but primarily that this is in a sense more than capital, more ancient, more extended.[64]

This libidinal intensity is located in the realm of the senses: the frontier that the Patch allows capital to conquer. As expected, prospects of a non-work society are here eclipsed. In the enormous service sector of the high-income society in *The Common Sense*, employees know instantly that they are fired: if a customer *experiences*, not utters, negativity towards a worker, the latter is fired on the spot. Whatever distinction remained between formal and real subsumption is challenged. Formal and real subsumption are terms that originate in Marx and continue to preoccupy discussions of technology and production. In an oversimplified schema: formal subsumption is when a capitalist hires a worker to labour with what is already available; real subsumption is when the capitalist transforms the process of labour itself through the use of science and technologies specific to how he wants to organise production for profit, in which case the worker enters a world of labour already made by capital. Formal subsumption is typically identified with earlier stages in capitalism, while real subsumption with more advanced stages. *The Common Sense* imagines a stage of production where the distinction is superseded in capital's radical act of locating the means of production within the technologically enhanced human subject. What this achieves for capital is truly major: Maria, the cyborg of *Metropolis*. Capital thus retains the human for the production of value but in fusing the human with technology makes resistance impossible.

The Common Sense does away with barriers to capital as we have known them. The burden of the constant spectacularisation of experience as an effect of distance (the condition of the spectacle despite interactivity) plaguing our current social-media age evaporates. And so, the lifeworld of *The Common Sense* is not one where we observe 'the decline of symbolic efficiency [as] a convergence of the imaginary and the real',[65] but one that has eliminated the convergence through sensorial commoning. This is an apt example of how capital realises the commons as a condition for mining and capture. In the capitalist history of the senses that *The Common Sense* examines and projects, the loss of distance between worker and machine (the cyborgian existence of the worker-Patch) means that the antagonism between worker and machine is annulled. For this to be successfully realised, the Patch must not appear as a production/extraction/accumulation technology but as social technology, available to all, desired by all, necessary for all, dictating what it means to be socially functional. It is then that the impossibility of the worker to smash the machine or to stop production (strike) arises. This is the cyborg's counter-revolution, which comes before the revolution can even become conceivable.

PRECARIOUS WORKERS, STRESSED MANAGERS, WOMB BLISS

How indeed do these future social subjects cope with the levels of stress that the achievement of capitalist commoning induces? The answer — predictable in its origins but less so in its realisation through the mobilisation of gestational labour — is what makes *The Common Sense* so engaging in relation to social reproduction imaginaries. The society of the two-way Patch, complete with its entrepreneurs, scientists, counsellors, waitresses (sic), and insurgent yet confused and co-opted multitudes, is closer to accelerationist feminism than the feminism of more or less tech-enraptured lineages. The oppositional impulses that we witness in *The Common Sense* centre exclusively on the possibility of repurposing the technology of the Patch.

The possibility of repurposing arises through mutational 'accidents': hopeful enthusiasm follows the scientific realisation that bodies whose physiology rejects the Patch (sending them convulsing and writhing) are developing a new organ which changes their brains. The future and repercussions of the brain mutation remain unknown in Gilligan's narrative, but the point is that it is seen by these social subjects as de facto positive simply because it is unknown — did anyone say ideology? What appears as hyperbole in a sci-fi script is what contemporary posthumanism advocates. The unknown/mutation is of value in the future Patch society for the same reason that it is in ours: because the social order appears seamless, capital is in everything, and social reality is organised through three interconnected principles: (a) the expansion of human capital (this society appears to have achieved gender and sexuality equality); (b) class hierarchy (a structure encompassing managerial command and any kind of 'other'/subordinate labour); (c) impact (a demand for immediate results, be they the results of scientific experiments or oppositional social action). All three principles provide 'a clue as to how the new continues to appear in the absence of any utopian orientation of the future'.[66] In the Patch society, the extraordinary demise of mediation and representation in favour of immediacy and directness (the direct exchange of inner sensorial experience) staves off the development of a plan to bring forth a non-exploitative re-organisation of the economy because the interiorisation of the economy makes such re-organisation unintelligible. What social actors experience instead is an organisation of labour–life that relies on interactive surveillance, which leaves everyone in panic and in search of temporary relief from the immense anxiety generated. This is where *The Common Sense* recovers, and returns to, the predictably 'natural': the gestation of human embryos in the uterus.

In a startling scene, a highly stressed female high-income employee reads in her transparent monitor: 'Congratulations! Your pre-birth neural entrainment session is ready! Log in to feel the rejuvenating waves of life before birth…' The stressed employee is not pregnant herself but has purchased a relaxation package through which she can experience another woman's pregnancy. The other woman's pregnancy can induce in the high-income employee the necessary calmness and sense of wellbeing so that she can continue being productive. The pregnant woman is a service-industry worker and does various kinds of work to survive: Patch-mediated sex work, Patch-mediated menial labour, and, during her pregnancy, she also sells her 'womb experience' to a company making relaxation packages. The womb experience features as nature's remedy for the anxiety generated by high-intensity, technology-based work. Obviously, even if the proletarian woman were a proletarian non-binary person or a proletarian trans man, nothing would change: the important thing here, besides the exchange, is the assumed experience of pregnancy. It is the affirmation of the womb as the natural, lost state and site of bliss and harmony that constructs the need and desire for the womb's sensory social sharing against the tyranny of productivity. The happy womb features as the inalienable reality of human reproduction put in the service of endless, total production.

Although this is not pursued in *The Common Sense*, there is no good reason why pregnancy might not be collectivised in terms of surrogacy beyond the sex-divide barrier.[67] This would be irrelevant to the politics of exchange explored in *The Common Sense* where the automation of the womb experience as the new 'natural resource' pursued by capital is flagged. The gender–sex of the pregnant body is overridden by the commonsensical, transhistorical 'knowledge' that the pregnant person–foetus bond is imbued with positivity absent in any other inter-corporeal relation. We know, of course, that this mythical construction of the happy womb has historically played a key role in keeping women, and 'woman', consensually tied to the demands of reproduction, even in societies that have experienced a clash between women being active in the formal economy and doing reproductive work as non-work. *The Common Sense* imagines a social context where this conflict ceases to exist, given that reproductive non-work becomes paid labour in the service of capital accumulation. It's better than selling a kidney. But resolving this conflict within a capitalist society does not liberate the pregnant worker, while the pregnant person–foetus bond is signified as the last-instance remainder of biological essentialism, potentially available to anyone as part of the wellness market.

Notably, feminism stands divided with regard to pregnancy and the womb experience. In *The Dialectic of Sex* (1970), Shulamith Firestone argued that pregnancy is bad for women. When science questioned the positivity of the woman–foetus bond, as in the early 1990s when Harvard-based evolutionary biologist David Haig talked about a 'tug-of-war' between the pregnant woman and the foetus, this was seen as patriarchy-biased science in some feminist quarters.[68] Such science might disrupt the normative doxas about the blissful womb experience afforded by the Patch and is therefore ignored in the scientific outlook of *The Common Sense* which invests in capital's principle of 'profit and pleasure' that Rosemary Hennessy has detailed with regard to the commodification of sexuality.[69] Thus, although the high-income society that *The Common Sense* takes as its focus has achieved gender and sexuality equality, deep-seated values and attributes (the harmony of the maternal-pregnant body) must register as transhistorical truths that communicative capitalism can deploy as residual 'human nature' surviving in the sensorial commons.

The Common Sense chooses a different way to question the happy womb. In Episode 2 of Phase 2B, the proletarian pregnant woman who sells her womb experience seeks help because she is sensorially receiving 'the other woman, the one the baby is connected to'. Although this reception is 'unbearable', the pregnant woman cannot violate her contract, or she will be arrested. A third woman offers her help, a female counsellor who has recently lost her job 'on the spot', having received the negative feelings of a dissatisfied customer. The fired counsellor and the pregnant woman meddle with the technology. Yet, this does not have the anticipated results: the foetus now receives the high-income employee's negative feelings — extreme stress — which it then transmits to the already stressed proletarian pregnant woman. And so, in one of *The Common Sense*'s final scenes, the technologically entrained women convulse in pain, stranded between connection and separation.

According to one reading, what remains is 'a portrait of the entrainment technology as self-undermining, destabilising "positive feedback", capable of leading to a moment of breakdown, because (rather than despite) of the self-interested activity of all the actors'.[70] But the issue is that not all the actors are self-interested: rather, it is the solidarity of the female counsellor who messes with the technology that leads to the breakdown. This solidarity is articulated as a personal relationship between two women — a point underlined by the fact that they become a couple, and that when they do, they deal privately with the financial hardship of their same-sex nuclear family. The technology breakdown does not benefit the pregnant female womb worker and means nothing to the high-income female employee apart from the fact that she experienced a faulty commodity. The loop that the sensorial commons realise as contracted intersubjectivity remains unchallenged in the absence of an alternative politics that might help the involved women question the entanglement of work and life, production and reproduction, under capital.

FORCES AND RELATIONS OF PRODUCTION IN THE AGE OF CAPITAL'S INTERIORISATION

The complication that *The Common Sense* puts forward for feminist emancipatory politics is that it imagines a future where, as a result of technological advancements, the distinction between forces and relations of production ceases to be operative. Gilligan has imagined a future in which dynamic change in the forces of production (technology and labour-power) does not necessarily at some point undo extant social and economic relations, as imagined by Marx — a hope that perhaps curiously survives in posthuman technophilia. This future is far from implausible. In prioritising the forces of production, with informatisation leading to their integration (the body–technology), capital may eventually place the salient referent of these forces (technology) right inside the corporeal core of the subject while connecting it with other socialised human organisms, thus immediately appropriating relations of reproduction — as in *The Common Sense*. Rather than being confined to the replenishment of labour-power, such social reproduction enlists gestational capability in a double bind: as labour-power in its own right and as an output of labour. This is a conceivable 'restructuring of reproduction' and yet one that remains hostage to the demand for production. It is the future of subsumption.

In *The Common Sense*, Federici's observation that there is no 'necessary connection' between techno-scientific and moral-intellectual development is tested and found to stand. Gilligan's exploration of a plausible future instructs that social justice is less about moral-intellectual development and more about which political horizons permit the alignment of 'human community' to the 'community of capital' and what this renders visible, as Bernes argues. The alignment of the two communities in *The Common Sense* makes it impossible to conceive of a political idea that exceeds capital: hacking becomes merely the oppositional micro-politics of everyday life. The very idea of nature has moved from the limitations of human biology (perhaps exhaustion in the working day) to making capitalism the inevitable advance of some primordial human impulse. The society of the common sensorial subject is unaware of the possibility of 'common wealth' as a political choice. The 'common sense' of *The Common Sense* is that both forces and relations of re/production are the property of a ruling abstraction that remains unnamed. It can only be inferred from the actions of the managerial elite, while the woman I have referred to as proletarian does not see herself as a classed subject. Consciousness of the class relation is eclipsed before the expansion of the sensorial realm. Capital is hidden. The demise of representation in this future society appears to have eradicated the human ability to think in terms of theoretical frameworks that might explain the conditions of humanity's historical entrapment.

These conditions are quite concrete. The Patch illustrates the fact that, as capital must always subsume reproduction under the imperative of greater productivity, it must identify new frontiers to do so. Anything can be a frontier: the soil, domestic space, the flesh, the womb, the galaxy. *The Common Sense* offers a case study whereby processes of identifying resources can enhance the desire for sex–gender experience (here, anchored in the womb) as a 'good' that enters the circuit of exchange for profit. *The Common Sense* is not concerned with the 'unproductive' home, the 'productive' workplace, or automation. Instead, it envisages phenomenology's embodiment as a multitude of exploitable social beings who are, in their fusion with technology, the locus and temporality of capital valorisation. The interiorisation of technology imagined would create an articulation of forces of production that would deliver bodies that might malfunction but would be unable to revolt. In such a future the distinction between the forces of production and the relations of production might be hard to uphold.

We can imagine that Gilligan faced a dilemma in deciding the gender of the high-income employee who buys the womb experience of the proletarian queer woman: should the high-income employee be a cis-man so that this gender is not spared the pain unleashed by the transmission circuit when 'the entrainment technology' becomes 'self-undermining', thus 'leading to a moment of breakdown'? Or, should the high-income employee be a cis-woman, so that capital's ability to also organise the exploitation of woman by woman is highlighted as the majority norm? Gilligan opted for the second. If the choice was intended to afford an exploration of the ideological constitution of a subject that wishes to reconnect, even if momentarily, with an 'experience' she has given up so as to not jeopardise her labour performance we cannot know (does the senior male manager push her in this direction, precisely because she *is* a woman?). What *The Common Sense* transmits is that a corporeally enacted commonised subject as a technological solution to human individuation — the solution proposed by communicative capitalism today — holds no liberation. If the implication to be drawn is that 'the common is not necessarily the ground of our emancipation' but 'can function as enchainment, entrainment, as ideology become life itself', in Bernes's words, social reproduction imaginaries are called on to address under what conditions a feminist common might arise without falling prey to capital's sharing economy. Such conditions might be found in concretely re-uniting the common with ending the mode of production we know, rather than affirm (as per posthumanist voluntarism) the nebulous becoming that this mode of production requires for its own reproduction.

Postscript: Notes on Feminism and (Art) History in the Making

Twenty-five years into the century, one can feel uncertain about whether history has accelerated or is in stasis. Events abound, but their meaning in and for the mode of production can be elusive. Is it us or is it the century? The horrific event known as 9/11 that for many kickstarted the twenty-first century is now the stuff of conspiracy theories. Back in 2001, the second meaning of 9/11 seemed clear to anticapitalist activism: the sight of airplanes crashing into the World Trade Centre towers in New York would be used in a new anti-terrorist discourse and statecraft to squash the alter-globalisation movement and would usher forth a capitalist future as an enormous surveillance complex. State oppression would be a given in the world of 'free markets'. Protest would be more authorised than televised. A phenomenal bureaucracy around 'health and safety' would ensure the limits of left activism, and eventually of speech, effecting political conformism on a mass scale.

The reproduction of capitalism, against which this book has argued, thus already achieved a new meaning at the turn of the century. Anything and everything, and above all immigration law, would be weaponised in the capitalist politics of surveillance, suspicion, securitisation — including in universities where feminism and art are on the curriculum. Feeling insecure in the hands of the capitalist state is normalised as everyday life, with a paradigmatic state of vulnerability forced on migrants. What is this globally available 'soft' state terror about? If twentieth-century fascism was unleashed against the once real prospect of workers' revolution and movement towards communism, the twenty-first century fascist tendency is pre-emptive: the revolutionary prospect should not cross the minds of the oppressed — and overall art did not challenge this, having already been asked in the late twentieth century, and especially in the 1990s, to be about contextual or 'open-ended' interventions. Discrediting the revolution from *within* the left, including by dominant discourses of the feminist left, has merely been an added bonus to capitalism as a securitised regime sustained by persuasion (ideology) and force (law, police, army). Among those who did not accept that history ended in 1989, many would come to accept that working towards just small improvements to capitalism would justify the expenditure of political effort given capitalism's perseverance. In what's left of the left, the preference has been for theories of capitalism's uncomplicated or inevitable transition to a 'better' future.

Arguments in this book have started from the premise that no such hopeful telos of capitalism is in sight and that feminism should actively oppose capitalism rather than think of it as a dispenser of incremental liberation from the assumed remains of transhistorical patriarchy. In combining active imagination and critique, feminism in art can reconsider what participation in the reproduction of capital as a social relation means, how it is achieved, and what it enables. In thinking across the book's themes, I want therefore to close with some thoughts on capitalist worldmaking at present, and the challenges that such worldmaking presents to feminism crossing through art.

PERMANENT CRISIS

Over a decade ago, when I completed *Gender, ArtWork and the Global Imperative* (2013), I was keen to map changes in relation to feminism, art, and labour as impacted by the shaping of global space. The 2008 financial crash, also mentioned in this book, was a consequential generational event, and we were instructed to see it as a crisis that would pass. Global space would return to business as usual. Leaving aside why feminists might want a return to normal, the return did not happen, and today we are told that we are locked into a 'poly-crisis'. So far, the poly-crisis, an unevenly unfolding and distributed social event, receives technocratic responses from above — possibly not unrelated to the fact that the 2008 financial crisis was only temporarily visible as an attack on the working class. In the 2010s, the 'economy' appeared after decades of keeping a low profile in the art world, but it did not remain in focus for long. For a few years, demands strategically built around the primacy of social reproduction (our right to obtain from the mode of production the means to exist without the threat of dispossession) inspired social movements where feminism was a key force. But sustaining these social movements has not been easy. At present, this fragile politics about the distribution of the wealth we make as waged and unwaged workers is carried through awkwardly, while new rounds of identity disputes have managed to take the floor sowing endless divisions. Who gains from this? Capitalist strategy excels at deflecting attention from how labour becomes capital and thus from why capitalism will never be free of its so-called crises. The question is whether a new politics towards militant unity can break the impulse to help capitalism mitigate whatever it presents as a new crisis. This is a challenge that arises acutely for the art world's care politics and instances of commoning where much feminist energy is expended.

The many crises of capitalism are experienced as the specificity of everyday life. In the 1970s, the falling rate of profit gave us the class war from above called neoliberalism and the post-Bretton Woods global economy of perceived immateriality that drew art's attention away from production. In the mid-2020s, should feminists be paying attention to the markets' renewed interest in gold? Possibly. In the meantime, feminism should certainly be concerned with understanding why capital sees art as an excellent investment, which artworks fulfil the investment promise, and *how*, for investment creates a crisis of meaning for all artworks of emancipatory intent. How, when, and why capital accepts more labour or dispels labour, always gendered and racialised, is also central to making sense of our contemporary. The art field is held up by labour that is instructed to not see itself as such. Capital encouraged women's mass entry to the labour force in the West, and thus exit from the home, when the so-called family wage paid to one breadwinner lost its value. We hardly need to think of how 'freedom', also discussed in this book, is ideologically manipulated by capital's engineering of consent to see how the demands of second-wave feminism were also of interest to capital. This is part of feminist art history, but is its least discussed part.

The more labour is subjugated by capital, directly or indirectly, the more consent will be generated. Promising jobs in industries that are catastrophic for nature wins elections where women also vote: the climate crisis is built on consent. The unprecedented energy requirements of AI is a new challenge on this front, while art has been the site where the glamorisation of such technological 'opportunity' takes place: art students are asked to train for a Big Tech-controlled labour market, that is, to affirm yet another higher productivity technology in the name of 'the new', with adequate feminist enthusiasm. Much can be said about the blind spots of such feminist cooperation. Is there a politics of feminist care towards workers who screen images of rape and abuse so as to train AI? Is there a feminist strategy against the imminent crisis of labour that AI will bring to the feminised lower layers of the art pyramid and to society at large, as we know that each crisis of labour is also a crisis of social reproduction? Peeling off the façade of glamour covering advanced technology's human and environmental costs can take place in art because this is where such glamour is instituted. Feminism in art has enough social knowledge, now drawn globally, to reveal capitalism as permanent crisis for most women and to see that if capitalism were able to resolve its perpetual social reproduction crisis, it would no longer be capitalism.

LEAVING (SOCIAL) POSTMODERNISM

If the global capitalist order was consolidated after 1989, some of its key tendencies were already in place: a finance-configured neoliberalism tied to an enticing techno-solutionism. These two tendencies underpinned postmodernism as a hegemonic cultural narrative in the period of second-wave feminism, examined at length and yet not enough in this book. Although today postmodernism rarely appears in the art theory of the contemporary, we are immersed in social postmodernism that still misconstrues the freedom of capital as social freedom — atomised self-fulfilment, obtained mostly through consumption of some sort. A great variety of 'anti' micro-politics and contextual micro-empowerment have inevitably been available, stopping short of delivering large-scale propositional politics on how to end exploitation. I argued that what organises this contemporary needs to be critically revisited by feminism today, not least for elucidating the trajectory of feminism in art.

Although postmodernism opposed the notion of social totality and, in its anti-Marxism, reduced the economy to merely one aspect of social life, today art and art history students, of whatever gender, are offered 'career days' and transferrable skills for the labour market — meaning for whatever jobs may come up. It is, then, not altogether possible to avoid the economy. Starting with such a realisation, the book has argued that understanding *from below* what makes up the economy is essential for exposing the capitalist art field as a site of cumulative blockages. Contrary to persisting with seeing art as a space–time apart from the organising forces of 'real' life, I argued that art's assumed difference is sustained by contradictions. The very term 'postmodernism', suggesting that modernity had come to an end, was misleading: it led to forgetting the contradictions that capitalist modernity entails for the emancipatory desires it generates.

From a Marxist feminist perspective, some of these contradictions can be understood as antinomies — that is, they are unresolvable in modernity under capital. The book has observed revealing slippages in how art is talked about and what expectations arise in relation to art, not least by feminism. Who has the right to sell whose pain by selling an artwork? What happens when artworks made with feminist intent are institutionally treated as enclosed property, as we are told to forget about the property imperative? Can feminism in art avoid concepts that normalise the lexicon of finance, debt, and labour 'performance'? As many of those who enter the art field do so because they are genuinely interested in social justice, including those who study to obtain relevant qualifications as arts professionals, feminism increasingly has a political obligation to inform them of the salient contradictions this desire encounters in the actually existing art world and that the dominant feminist theory of the late 1980s, the decade of high postmodernism, rendered invisible. It was hardly an accident that such feminist theory came from quarters of American academia where postmodernism was positively taken up as post-class politics. I hope the book enables a questioning of the conceptual apparatus made available to a presumably global feminism through postmodernism as an ideological force. Can feminism today use 'border wars' as a metaphor that does not hurt those living and dying in the actual proliferating border wars? How to decolonise feminism from the legacy of postmodernism is far from simple. It will involve painful alienation from familiar intellectual paradigms. Then again, the building of counter-hegemony has never been easy.

GEOPOLITICS AND FEMINIST KNOWLEDGE PRODUCTION

The totality of capitalism can rarely be glimpsed, and the concept of globalisation proved useful only for a while. Feminism contributed to discussing globalisation in art, but the positions advanced were not always critical. 'Global feminism' was mostly seen as feminism's expansion beyond the Western core: an exercise in welcome diversity where anything goes, as if feminist inclusivity could operate beyond the imperialist reality. And yet the already classed women of the Global South and those of the Global North meet in imperialism as the ground of feminist knowledge production.

The imperialist relation, which is the class relation transported in global space, has been significantly underplayed in the histories of art-based feminism, and it is perhaps time to ask if the feminist art canon generated through the visible geographies of the imperialist Global North core has been articulated as the suppression of feminist art scenes elsewhere. Example: that the CIA was implicated in the military junta in Greece between 1968 and 1974 so that the Greek left would be defeated led not just to the torture of women (and men) but also to *not* having a feminist art movement in that 'periphery' in the early 1970s. How many non-realisations of feminism in art are the outcome of similar geopolitical interventions? Understanding the breadth of imperialism, and its function through culture, is an open research project for feminism today. It is not a matter of reparation, for history is not cyclical and what was done cannot be undone. It is a matter of moving forward together but with accountability: feminist art internationalism as solidarity in this century can be built only through a writing of history that concerns suppressions and not just encounters. Encounters in the geopolitics of capitalism never take place on even ground.

As capitalist globalisation seems to enter an era of heightened competition among (unequal yet connected) national capitals, feminist communication gets more difficult. The world is becoming multipolar, we are told. Yet this geopolitical process is not on the side of feminist internationalism, for the multipolar world has only one economic paradigm to offer: exploitation. The art field core can move to Beijing or Abu Dhabi, but, as the Gulf Labor Artist Coalition showed in the past decade, this does not change the fundamentals. Migrant workers with even fewer rights than 'native' workers build art museums. There is a village known as 'the one kidney village' (its impoverished inhabitants sell one kidney to survive) in Bangladesh, next to India's 'fast growing' economy. Locating the labour relation in the compartmentalised bodies of the subaltern is now habitual — the womb is one such organ of the subaltern body in pieces. This, it needs to be said, is often welcomed by feminism as the path to a subject's financial self-determination. But self-determination thus defined merely deepens the logic of exchange that breeds consent for the socio-economic order. This is the social subject that neoliberalism made: sell what you are, become human capital.

So far, tentative multipolarity is a quest for power in the same global economic paradigm. The art field is where this quest often translates into diversity for the wealthy, including a diverse body of collectors and curators from the upper social strata, often with Western education. How does feminism in the international art field address the subaltern beyond the diversity of the wealthy? What kind of feminist learning is enabled, and for whom, in art's international structures that feminism often joins in advocating a free and joyous 'becoming' available to all who are willing to lean in? Does this iteration of feminism absorb so-called 'other' knowledges to affirm rather than disaffirm the capitalist art structures and their antipathy towards human agency as labour in revolt? Where does the feminist critique of intensified, for-profit extractivism stop, and where is the line that separates inclusivity in knowledge production from a 'learning from' that authorises the imperialist geopolitical logic of capital?

FEMINISM AGAINST CAPITAL'S WAR ECONOMY

In the 2010s, people attempted to practice direct democracy in the squares, in the belief that they could question their polity and the role of oligarchies and finance in controlling their lives. Although the mask of democracy fell, the momentum was not sustained. The laws brought forth against public protest, strikes, and freedom of speech continued, exacerbating the capitalist state oppression witnessed since the turn of the century. Today, however, the epidemic of the suppression of free speech and proliferation of hostile environments finally appear to serve a purpose: they script the social discipline required as the world enters what its leadership calls a 'war economy'. NATO-controlled Europe is not alone in boosting militarisation and the new war mentality: over 100 countries increased their military spending in 2024, when our capitalist planet witnessed an 'unprecedented rise of global military expenditure', standing at $2,718 billion, according to the Stockholm International Peace Research Institute.[1] The figure is nearly impossible to comprehend, but this is the money of the demos feeding the highly profitable war machine rather than being returned to the demos.

For this to be accepted, a broader web of fear, censorship, and self-censorship must become — has become — the very ground of political life. In the course of writing this book, this web has grown exponentially while capitalist states always have a moral tale to tell about why a war economy is necessary. The social fragmentation experienced includes distress but also complicity: watching the lives-treamed genocide of the Palestinian people where AI drones target children and then still being able to sleep at night is a new universal, despite pockets of vocal solidarity at considerable risk. When heroic solidarity is shown by damaging the weapons factories, protesters are treated as terrorists, and when they invoke love as the ground of their actions, the law remains unmoved and incarcerates them. Heroism and love have figured differently in feminist (art) theory under postmodernism's lingering hegemony: the first was caricatured as undesired machismo, the second was embraced in the epistemological 'affective turn'. But is it possible to address the perils and injuries of capital's noxious war economy without love as heroism? A 'war economy' is not two words in a sentence, but a profit-led subjugation of labour dedicated to terrorising, burning, starving, dismembering human beings that are deemed an obstacle to imperialism, settler colonialism, and universal obedience to the perpetuation of capitalism. The question of how this historical reality can be addressed, and how it is encountered by feminist intent in art, is not rhetorical but rather reiterates the need for rethinking what theoretical practice feminism builds in, and for, our contemporary.

Will feminism in art effect an anti-war togetherness and prioritise the critique and repudiation of censorship and anti-protest laws? How can self-censorship cease when institutional dependency thrives? What, at the same time, is the ideological service of autonomy for art — the cherished autonomy that feminism wished to be part of — in a capitalist economy that is openly anti-life? In the social discipline that our historically specific war economy demands, a general hostility takes root. We have many instances to observe this as social movements drop argumentation and strategy, turning instead to a search for internal enemies and traitors of liberation. This logic of hostility — driven from above, but becoming lived experience below — exceeds the legacy of postmodern fragmentation and there is good reason to think that feminism may not survive it, except in authorised form. What can feminism mobilise against the regime of hostility as social discipline? The warmongering of capitalist leaders is not an empty threat against our reproduction, but rather scripts a lethal contemporary that subjugated labour co-produces. Where a war economy becomes convincing, a strong and, crucially, revolutionary rather than reformist labour movement tends to be absent. This is why, above all, the new feminist art movement that must be imagined cannot but start as a movement for the liberation of labour. Starting from reclaiming the rights of workers across the spectrum of visibility and invisibility, such a movement could aim very far, possibly even at reinventing history-making from below.

Notes

INTRODUCTION

1. See *ArtReview* Power100, 2024.
2. On poverty, see OXFAM 2025; on art, see Bull 2025.
3. Duncan 1993, p. 178.
4. Pollock 2015, p. 28.
5. Jameson 1998, p. 88.

CHAPTER ONE

1. Entry 'Sor Juana Inés de la Cruz', *Britannica*; see also Bergman and Schlau 2017.
2. See Grogan 1992.
3. On Flora Tristan, see Arruzza 2013, p. 23; on Sojourner Truth, see 'A'n't I a Woman?' Sojourner Truth, 1851' in Marable and Mullings, eds. 2003 [2000], p. 68.
4. Marks 2016; see the chapter 'Cries of Pain: The Word Capitalism', p. 3–20.
5. Marx 1973, p. 503.
6. Thier 2020a, p. 11.
7. See Marx 1996, p. 705–06. For a discussion on the term's recent translation, see Brown 2024.
8. For an influential analysis of the emergence of capitalism, see Meiksins Wood 2002 [1999], who considered how commerce and urbanisation had not necessarily led to the emergence of capitalism. She looked instead at the specific conditions of late medieval and early modern England, including the enclosures of common land. The large-scale destruction of subsistence in agrarian economies was key to her argument.
9. Federici 2004, p. 11. Federici's collaborative research on the subject had started in Italian; see Federici and Fortunati 1984.
10. See Habermas 1991 [1962].
11. Foster and Clark 2018.
12. See Zaretsky 1976.
13. Federici 2004, p. 12.
14. Mies 1986, p. x. Emphasis in the original.
15. Fraser in Nancy Fraser and Rahel Jaeggi 2023 [2018], p. 67.
16. Anderson 2023.
17. Anderson 1984, p. 98. Emphasis in the original.
18. Simpson 2016, p. 440.

19. 'It is proved in the pamphlet that the war of 1914–18 was imperialist (that is, an annexationist, predatory, war of plunder) on the part of both sides; it was a war for the division of the world, for the partition and repartition of colonies and spheres of influence of finance capital, etc.', we read in Vladimir Ilyich Lenin, *Imperialism, or the Highest Stage of Capitalism: A Popular Outline*, pamphlet, Petrograd 1917, Lenin Internet Archive 2005.

20. The Enlightenment, or the Age of Reason, refers both to a period and a set of philosophical ideas that developed in this period. Horkheimer and Adorno 2002 [1947] remains a classic study.

21. For an accessible reading, see Miéville 2022.

22. Women In Informal Employment: Globalizing and Organizing (Wiego) 2022.

23. Quoted in Steinhauer 2017.

24. Ribalta 2015, p. ii. Emphasis added.

25. See Myers 2025 where the analysis concerns Europe and fault is found with the political parties representing the working class rather than de-industrialisation.

26. First use of 'human resource' is in Commons, 1893. Notably, Commons was a progressive labour historian and economist.

27. Nilsen 2020.

28. Brass, 2022 [2021], p. 6.

29. See Visser 2024 and Baccaro and Howell 2017.

30. Hewison 2021.

31. Magdoff and Magdoff 2004.

32. Bruegel 1979, p. 12.

33. On internships in art, see Kompatsiaris 2015.

34. Day 2022.

35. Sholette 2010.

36. Steyerl 2010.

37. OXFAM International 2023 and 2024.

38. See Sweezey and Magdoff, 1987.

39. Vishmidt 2018, p. x.

40. Shaked 2022.

41. Neveling 2020.

42. Zarobell 2020, p. 2. Emphasis added.

43. Heidenreich 2016.

44. Renauld 2021.

45. Gompertz 2016.

46. Steyerl 2022.

47. Portella and Busk 2024, p. 377.

48. See Walsh 2022.

49. Žižek and Tolokonnikova and Žižek 2013, p. 49.

50. Tolokonnikova in ibid., p. 53–4.

51. Steel 2013.

52. Sunkara 2024. Emphasis added.

53. See Chibber 2023.

54. See Baravalle, Braga, and Riccio, eds. 2022.
55. See Kozłowski, Sowa, and Szreder, eds. 2014.
56. d' Alancaisez 2022.
57. Cope 2019, p. 4. See also Hickel, Sullivan, and Zoomkawala 2021.
58. See the evidence-based analysis of Coote and Yazici 2019.
59. Thier 2020b.
60. See https://www.ilo.org/infostories/en-GB/Stories/Employment/barriers-women, Introduction.
61. See American Association of University Women 2017, where it is mentioned that the pay gap exists across the board but is worse for mothers and Black women. See also McIntyre 2019.
62. ActionAid 2024.
63. See Kain 1993.
64. Bhattacharya in Bhattacharya, ed. 2017, p. 1.
65. Toupin 2018.
66. See Caffentzis 2002 and Hester and Srnicek 2023.
67. See Čakardić 2017.
68. See United Nations Women 2024.
69. See Davis et al. 2020.
70. See Hall 2016.
71. See Ahmed 2024.
72. See McMunn, Bird, Webb, and Sacker 2020, p. 168.
73. Mann 2012.
74. Carter 2025.
75. See Hu 2023.
76. Federici 1975, p. 5.
77. Vishmidt in Vishmidt and Gray 2011. Emphasis added.
78. See European Business Magazine 2024.
79. Cammack 2020, p. 101.
80. Citing the Office of National Statistics, the article also states: 'Easily the fastest growing part of the household economy was childcare. Informal childcare by stay-at-home parents or relatives was worth £321bn in 2014, up from £304bn in 2013 and just £183bn in 2005.' See Collinson 2016.
81. Oxfam International 2020.
82. World Bank 2023.
83. Quote from ArtReview Power 100, 2024; see also 'In Profile: Hoor Al-Quasimi', *Frieze*, 30 March 2016.
84. See Graeber 2011.
85. Eisenstein 2009.
86. Rowbotham 2014 [1974], p. 27.
87. McRobbie 2010, p. 68. Emphasis added.
88. Trudell 2017.
89. Lind 2018.
90. Quoted from Lenin's letter to Inessa Armand, 24 January 1915, Lenin Internet Archive.
91. Portella and Busk 2024, p. 357.

92. Betts 2012, p. 29.
93. Lugones 2010, p. 743.
94. Jameson 2002.
95. Bruce Gilley's 'The Case for Colonialism' was published in *Third World Quarterly* in August 2017 and has since been withdrawn (on the grounds of flawed peer review process) but not before it sparked outrage and a debate on 'academic freedom'. See https://www.independent.co.uk/news/world/americas/colonialism-academic-article-bruce-gilley-threats-violence-published-withdrawn-third-world-quarterly-a7996371.html; see 'Open Letter: A Response from the "100" French Scholars.'
96. Purdon 2024.
97. McRobbie 2010, p. 75.
98. Manual Labours website.
99. See Child, Reckitt, and Richards 2017, p. 151–3.
100. See Fraser 2009, p. 97–8.
101. See entry 'Feminist Art Movement', Wikipedia 2025.
102. See the blurb and video 'Against the Double Blackmail: refugees, terror and other troubles with the neighbours', LSE Player, 2 April 2016, https://www.lse.ac.uk/lse-player?id=7047564e-f755-4486-8b40-6dd73d040c6a and Cox 2023.
103. Bicker 2025.
104. See Varagur 2017. On Ivanka Trump's art collection, which she has with her husband, see Sayej 2017.
105. The performance was at the Flashpoint Gallery, Washington DC, 1–17 February 2019. The press release is at https://www.culturaldc.org/ivanka-vacuuming-by-jennifer-rubell-press-release
106. Ivanka Trump tweet, 4 February 2019, https://x.com/ivankatrump/status/1092803194428801024
107. Glosswitch 2017.
108. Kelly and Pollock 1989 in Robinson, ed. 2001.
109. See Tate, 'Post-partum Document'.

CHAPTER TWO

1. See Hadjinicolaou 1978; Parker and Pollock 1981, p. 49.
2. 'Ideology' in Bottomore ed. 1991, p. 248–9.
3. See Wright 2019.
4. Popularised in the 2010s, 'me too' was coined as a phrase in relation to sexual violence by working-class, Black American activist Tanara Burke, a sexual assault survivor, in 2006. See Burke 2021.
5. See Medina 2023; Kumdu 2024. The Feminist Emergency – International Conference took place at Birkbeck, University of London, 22–24 June 2017. The 'Week in Patriarchy' column, written by Arwa Mahdawi, continues into 2025.
6. See Global Women's Strike https://globalwomenstrike.net/history/.

7.   Information on the initial discussions leading to IWS mobilisations was provided by co-organiser Tithi Bhattacharya at the Marxist Feminist Stream Roundtable (9 November 2017), Fourteenth Historical Materialism London Conference, SOAS, 9–12 November 2017. Sara Farris, Sara Salem, Tithi Bhattacharya, and myself (members of the Marxist Feminist Stream Sub-committee) presented at the roundtable chaired by Svenja Bromberg.

8.   See Sandberg 2013. TV series producer and writer Nell Scovell is credited in the book's Acknowledgements as co-author.

9.   Faludi 2013.

10.   See Lean In https://leanin.org/.

11.   Hichliffe and Ajemian 2024.

12.   See Lean In, Women at Work Collection. The website is regularly updated.

13.   Beck quoted in Solis 2021.

14.   Boltanski and Chiapello 2005, p. 346.

15.   See Rottenberg 2018.

16.   Davis, Ransby, Arruzza, Taylor, Alcoff, Fraser, Odeh, and Bhattacharya 2017.

17.   hooks 2013.

18.   Arruzza 2017, p. 195. Emphasis added.

19.   Ibid.

20.   Arruzza 2018.

21.   Arruzza 2017, p. 195.

22.   Bhattacharya 2015.

23.   Gleeson and O'Rourke, eds. 2021, p. 2–3.

24.   Beck in Solis 2021.

25.   Crenshaw 1991, p. 1296.

26.   See Dimitrakaki 1996–7.

27.   Higg and Wilkinson 2016, p. 28.

28.   Arruzza 2018.

29.   Chibber 2023, p. 9.

30.   Lebovici and Zapperi 2018.

31.   Arango et al. 2014, p. 37. Emphasis added.

32.   See Hedlin Hayden and Skrubbe, eds. 2010; Nochlin and Reilly, eds. 2007.

33.   Duffy 2017.

34.   About Lintorn-Orman, see White 2016; about the Front National in France, see Chrysafis 2018.

35.   Mohanty 2003, p. 231.

36.   Elias, Gill, and Scharff, eds. 2017. The quote is from the Overview at https://link.springer.com/book/10.1057/978-1-137-47765-1#about-this-book.

37.   See Jameson 1991.

38.   See Haraway 1988.

39.   Alcoff 1991–2.

40.   See Pejic et al., eds. 2010.

41.   Cox 2017, p. 32.

42.   Alcoff 1991–2, p. 6. Emphasis added.

43.   See Lewis 2025.

44. See Jameson 1983.
45. On this distinction, see Foster 1985.
46. The original sentence reads: 'This shift brought a change in how the market was viewed from a production standpoint. Rather than being viewed as a mass market to be served by mass production, the consumers began to be viewed as different groups pursuing different goals who could be better served with small batches of specialized goods.' See the section 'Changes from Fordism to Post-Fordism' in the Wikipedia entry 'Post-Fordism' https://en.wikipedia.org/wiki/Post-Fordism (accessed 30 June 2025).
47. Davis 2022, p. 24.
48. Faludi 2013.
49. See Elias 2022.
50. See Pollack 2000.
51. https://leanin.org/circles (accessed 5 April 2020).
52. https://leanin.org/allyship-at-work (accessed 29 March 2025).
53. Crenshaw 1991, p. 1244, footnote 9.
54. Crenshaw 1989, p. 149.
55. See section 'Additional Resources for Companies' in Lean In, 'Women in the Workplace 2021'.
56. Clean Clothes Campaign, 2023.
57. Sliwinska, ed. 2020.
58. Swilinska, 'Introduction', in ibid., p. 7–8. 'Disaster capitalism' (Naomi Klein's concept) is mentioned in the book abstract opening the volume.
59. Dean 2005.
60. Quote from New Museum, 'Amalia Ulman: Excellences & Perfections', undated.
61. 'Since 1975, starting with the UN conference on women in Mexico City, the United Nations has tried to delegitimise all feminism that is not compatible with the needs of international capital, in the same way as it tried to dominate the anti-colonial movement in the 1960s, by ensuring that decolonisation was compatible with the needs of ex-colonial powers and the United States'. Federici in Toupin 2018, p. 246.
62. See Varia 2016 and Ehreinreich and Russell Hochschild, eds. 2004.
63. Dalla Costa 2010.
64. Leila J. Rupp quoted in Van Goethem 2006, p. 1047.
65. Elizabeth Gilbert, 'The Best Thing You Can Do for Yourself and All the Women around You', *HuffPost*, 11 February 2015, http://www.huffingtonpost.com/2015/02/11/elizabeth-gilbert-on-failure_n_6608164.html?ir=India. The page no longer exists and the article now appears as 'The Key to a Well-Lived Life: Lighten Up', OPRAH.COM, undated.
66. Athens Biennale, AB6: ANTI.
67. See SDLD50 2018; see also Batycka 2018.
68. Crary 2013.
69. Claire Fontaine 2013.
70. *Suite Rivolta – Carla Lonzi's Feminism and the Art of Revolt* was a group exhibition at Museu de Electricidade (October 2015 – January 2016),

contextualising Lonzi's work and curated by Anna Daneri and Giovanna Zapperi. See Zapperi 2017b.

71. Vidokle quoted in Lloyd 2012, p. 532.
72. See Corna 2024.
73. Lonzi 1977. See also Lonzi 2012 and Corna and Mascat 2023.
74. Lorde 2007.
75. The Rivolta Femminile Manifesto (July 1970) is included in Weiss, ed. 2018.
76. Santoro 2019.
77. Rasmussen 2025, p. 110.
78. Ibid., p. 111.
79. Davis 2022, p. 31–2.
80. Zapperi 2017a, p. 121.
81. Author's email correspondence with Giovanna Zapperi (22 July 2017). Zapperi wrote in full: 'Lonzi was supported by her partner, Pietro Consagra, that's how she lived. Probably also from her husband, with whom she had only lived a few years in the late 1950s [1960s], but who was the father of her son (there was no divorce in Italy before 1973, and, in any case, they didn't divorce officially, as far as I know). She speaks about money in her diary, and not without contradictions. Around 1975, Consagra would sell two sculptures in order to buy her a house in Tuscany, where she spent a lot of time. She writes about this and about her dependence from him, which sometimes is experienced as a problem, sometimes as a privilege. For example, because of the advantages of not having to work. At one point she writes something like: "thankfully I am a woman, so I can survive without the slavery of labour. If I were a man, I couldn't escape work". Of course, reproductive labour was also something she eventually escaped from… So there is this unaddressed issue of class within Rivolta Femminile, which was clearly composed by women from the middle-upper class. Carla Accardi made a living as a painter, she was more of an independent woman, which was also part of the conflict with Lonzi. Very complicated… I think this issue has to be framed within the specificity of class and gender relations in 1960s–1970s Italy. It would probably have been different for a younger generation.' I discussed this information with Giovanna Zapperi in person in Geneva on 27–28 February 2025, remaining grateful for it.
82. See 'The Situation of Women' in Stacey 2014, p. 114.

CHAPTER THREE

1. The distinction applies to capitalist society as observed by Marx. For a discussion see Klagge 1986.
2. For contemporary art's excellent performance see Sulley 2022; in 2023 artworks were 'the most profitable passion asset', see Belinchon 2023.
3. Bourdieu and Darbel with Schnapper 1991 [1966].
4. Garlick 2004.
5. Stallabrass 2022.

6. Kinyon, Dolšak, and Prakash 2023.

7. I am referring to the exhibition *Carolee Schneemann: Body Politics* (8 September 2022 – 8 January 2023), described by the Barbican as 'the first survey in the UK of the work of American artist Carolee Schneemann (1939-2019) and the first major exhibition since her death in 2019. Tracing Schneemann's diverse, transgressive and interdisciplinary work over six decades, the show celebrates a radical and pioneering artist who remains a feminist icon and point of reference for many contemporary artists and thinkers'. See https://www.barbican.org.uk/our-story/press-room/carolee-schneemann-body-politics (accessed 6 April 2023).

8. De Duve 2007.

9. Adorno 2002.

10. Petsche 2012–13 p. 155.

11. Fraser 2000, p. 107.

12. The Antarctic Biennale was launched in the early 2010s. See Biennial Foundation, 'Antarctic Biennale'.

13. Diane Tanzer of This Is No Fantasy gallery, Australia, quoted in Bakare 2025.

14. See Standing 2011.

15. Connor 2016.

16. See Arts Council, *Livelihoods of Visual Artists Reports* 2018, Romer 2019, and Delagrange 2023, the latter focusing on the US and explaining the difficulty of defining who is an 'artist'.

17. See Wu 2003 and Wu 2009; Fraiberger et al. 2018.

18. See Onassis AiR, www.onassis.org/initiatives/onassis-air, accessed 1 December 2024.

19. The 6 April 2023 police storming of the occupied Olympia Theatre in Athens led to the artists' arrest. The artists called on the public for solidarity stating 'the fight continues'.

20. See Harper 1985, p. 766.

21. Schapiro 1972, p. 268.

22. Harper 1985, p. 763.

23. Claire Fontaine 2013.

24. Harutyunyan, Özgün, Goodfield 2011, p. 479.

25. Day, Edwards, Mabb, 2010, p. 152.

26. Ibid., p. 168.

27. Zeyno in Dimitrakaki 2020.

28. See Voon 2017.

29. See Tulke 2022.

30. Groys 2014.

31. Grant 2011, p. 285.

32. Robinson 2019. See also Deepwell 2020.

33. Chukhrov 2014.

34. See Permanent Assembly of Art Workers, http://nosotrasproponemos.org/we-propose/.

35. See Farris 2017.

36.   Seymour 2024.

37.   Bryan Wilson 2009; Krikortz, Triisberg and Henriksson, eds. 2015; Kunst 2015.

38.   Fraser 1994.

39.   See, for example, the special issue of *Open*, A Precarious Existence (2009); Aranda, Wood and Vidokle, eds. 2011; Kozlowski, Sowa and Szreder, eds. 2014.

40.   Kuratorisk Aktion quoted in Dimitrakaki 2010.

41.   See CAMP website.

42.   CAMP & El Qadim 2020.

43.   See CAMP, 'About Camp', undated. http://campcph.org/about-camp

44.   Some of the issues are addressed by Lucy R. Lippard in her essay 'The Anatomy of an Annual' in *Hayward Annual '78, Exhibition Catalogue*, Arts Council of Great Britain, London 1978. The essay was reprinted in Dimitrakaki and Perry 2013.

45.   I addressed separatism in 'What Is It that Feminism Is up against? Preliminary Notes on Separatism', panel with Catherine Elwes, Margaret Harrison, Johanna Gustavsson, at *Women Working Collectively, What Is Your Value?* organised by The Temporary Separatists at ICA London, 9 July 2015. Access: https://www.academia.edu/23425509/What_is_it_that_ feminism_is_up_against_Preliminary_notes_on_separatism

46.   Moss and Katzen 1973. See also Krumholz and Lauter 1990 where the assumed universality of aesthetics is raised as an argument against separatism.

47.   See MFK 2011. MFK was founded by Johanna Gustavsson and Lisa Nyberg. The collective's inspiring practice and the issues it faced are discussed in their manual *Do the Right Thing!* I am grateful to MFK for providing me with a hard copy.

48.   Ibid., p. 42.

49.   It was striking to see a Hauser & Wirth London ad of a show (30 March–5 May 2007) of Lee Lozano (1930–99), a female artist noted for her critical withdrawal from the art world, in the first few pages of *Frieze* 105 (March 2007), the magazine's issue dedicated to feminism.

50.   McMillan 2018, p. 4. McMillan 2020, p. 8.

51.   Federici 2017, p. 3.

52.   A database of feminist exhibitions is provided by *n.paradoxa: international feminist journal*.

53.   See Dimitrakaki and Shaked 2021.

54.   See *n.paradoxa: international feminist journal* 18 (July 2006), curatorial strategies special issue; Kokoli 2008); Hedlin Haydn and Sjohol Skrubbe 2010; Dimitrakaki and Perry, eds. 2013.

55.   See the *Thin Black Line(s)* exhibition catalogue at http://clok.uclan. ac.uk/5106/22/thinblacklinesbook.pdf. See also Halperin 2018, where Himid is noted as the first black woman and the oldest artist to win the Turner Prize but also as an artist who 'did not have consisent commercial representation until 2013'. Himid has been a pioneering artist and curator

of Black and Asian women artists in Britain since the 1980s; she organised the landmark show *The Thin Black Line* at ICA London in 1985.
56. See Horne 2017.
57. See South African History Archive (SAHA) and cultureunstained.org.
58. Gorecki 2015.
59. Walters 2018.
60. See Frank 2018.
61. Lange 2012.
62. Brown 2017.
63. See Response to the Belgian Art Prize Exclusionary Shortlist 2019, 12 May 2018, at change.org.
64. Rowbotham 2014, p. 50. Emphasis added.
65. Pollock 1988, p. 34.
66. Ibid., p. 49.
67. Barry and Flitterman 1980.
68. See Pollock 1988.
69. Brown 2011.
70. The articles comprising Luxemburg's Reform or Revolution were first published together in 1900 and in revised edition in 1908. Here I have used the 1900 version available at the Rosa Luxemburg Internet Archive. See also Scott 2008.
71. See Tang 2013, p. 253.
72. The declaration–petition started on 7 November 2017 at change.org. The full text can now be accessed at the We Propose site, http://nosotrasproponemos.org/we-propose/. I consulted the English translation (by Jane Brodie) of 38 propositions, divided into five sections: Concerning the Structure of the Art World, Concerning Behaviors in the Art World, Concerning the Artistic Career and Creativity, Concerning Artistic Feminism and Feminist Art History, Concerning the Inclusive Nature of This Statement.
73. Arruzza, Bhattacharya, Fraser 2019, p. 13.
74. Steyerl 2010.
75. Bhattacharya 2015.
76. See in particular 'Introduction: The Problem with Work' in Weeks 2011.
77. Ibid., p. 7.
78. von Osten 2009. Emphasis added.
79. See Steyerl 2011.
80. See the chapter 'Travel as (Gendered) Work: Global Space, Mobility and the "Woman Artist"' in Dimitrakaki 2013.
81. See Kwon 2004.
82. Neuendorf 2016.
83. Dalla Costa 2010.
84. Thatcher 2013, p. 5.
85. Saltz 2004.
86. See The Lancet, 2024.
87. Wray 2025.

CHAPTER FOUR

1. See Perry 2017, for a discussion of how women's association with the domestic facilitated the viewing of art in nineteenth-century London.
2. Lippard, 2017b.
3. Duncan (1973) in Broude and Garrard eds. 1982, p. 301. Emphasis added.
4. Notably, the industrial proletariat was associated eventually with honourable labour whereas other areas of work, such as sex work, where women were the majority, were devalued. See Rodríguez García, van Nederveen Meerkerk, and Heerma van Voss in Rodríguez García, van Nederveen Meerkerk, and Heerma van Voss eds. 2017, p. 3.
5. Toss 2005, p. 333.
6. See Broude in Broude and Garrard eds. 1982.
7. The show tool place at Alte Nationalgalerie in Berlin, Germany from 25 March to 10 July 2022.
8. See Prideaux 2025.
9. Marx quoted in Denning 2010, p. 79.
10. Lütticken 2016, p. 112.
11. Hannah Lamb quoted in Butschart 2018.
12. Federici 2004, p. 95.
13. Beech 2019a, p. 161. Emphasis added.
14. See Danto 1964.
15. TV Advertisements of Brillo Pads in the 1950s indicated that heterosexual couples with a social life would save time on household chores if they used the product. See HantleyFilmArchives, 'Advert For Brillo, 1950s — Film 99774'.
16. Beech 2019a, p. 21. Emphasis added.
17. See Digby 1992, p. 197.
18. Marx quoting Lord Ashley (15 March 1844) in Capital Vol I, Chapter Fifteen 'Machinery and Modern Industry', p. 405–06, note 2.
19. Applin 2014, p. 96.
20. Murray 2011.
21. McDonough 2008.
22. See Ross 2002.
23. Kester 2009, p. 412.
24. See Jeanjean 2019 and Murray 2016.
25. See Dimitrakaki 2024.
26. Combahee River Collective 1977.
27. See McLellan 2020.
28. On Benston, see Heather Brown 2013, p. 68. Nochlin said in an interview about working during the McCarthyist purges of communists in the US: 'It really was a very oppressive period for people in intellectual and artistic pursuits. Even if they didn't come and get you, that was always a threat lying over [you]. I remember I began my Frick talk with a long quotation from Karl Marx. People were dumbfounded. I remember my teacher said,

"Linda, you're so brazen." It was scary times.' Nochlin quoted in O'Hanian 2017.

29. See Smith 1999.
30. Solanas 2004, p. 61. SCUM stood for the 'Society for Cutting Up Men' and was first published in 1967.
31. Author Chavisa Woods (2019) notes about SCUM: 'Much of it is actually a point-by-point re-write of multiple of Freud's writings. It is a parody'.
32. The film was included in the exhibition *All Men Become Sisters*, 23 October 2015–17 January 2016, Muzeum Sztuki in Lodz. See Sokolowska ed. 2018, p. 19.
33. Lippard 2017a, p. 35.
34. Pollock in Parker and Pollock eds. 1987, p. 81.
35. Garrard 1995, p. 473.
36. Ibid., pp. 471–2.
37. Stabile 1997, p. 396.
38. Pollock in Ventrella and Zapperi eds. 2021, p. 251.
39. Garrard 1995, p. 473.
40. See Coole and Frost eds. 2010.
41. Watkins 2018, p. 26–7.
42. Dean and Zamora 2021. Emphasis added. See also Zamora and Behrent 2015.
43. Watkins 2018, p. 25.
44. See Pollock ed. 1996; Meskimmon and Price eds. 2013; Nochlin and Reilly eds. 2007.
45. Pollock 2014, p.10.
46. See Chukhrov 2020.
47. See Dimitrakaki 2004.
48. Bradbury 1995, p. 768.
49. Owens 1983 in Foster ed. 1983, p. 65. Emphasis in the original.
50. See Dimitrakaki 2023.
51. See Jones in Schor and Bee eds. 2000.
52. See Marshall 2023. See also Johan Grimonprez's film *Soundtrack to a Coup d'Etat* (2024).
53. Ernesto Laclau and Chantal Mouffe quoted in Stabile 1997, p. 398.
54. Schuhrke 2024.
55. Warner, undated.
56. See HKW, *Parapolitics: Cultural Freedom and the Cold War*, 2018. The exhibition took place at HKW, Berlin, from 3 November 2017 to 8 January 2018.
57. Rockhill 2017.
58. The literature on the scandal is voluminous, though not discussed in feminist art histories. See Redstockings 1975.
59. Redstockings 1975, 9. Item 27, the *Feminist Revolution* issue (1975) of Redstockings, on sale for $100 in a catalogue of sold items says: 'The anthology included Barbara Leon's article, "Gloria Steinem and the CIA," which exposed Steinem's association with the CIA-funded Independent

Research Service. Due to Steinem's threat of litigation, the article was not included in the Random House reprint published in 1979'. See Fugitive Materials. Fugitive Materials was founded in 2020 in New York and is 'committed to the preservation of radical, lesser-known, and alternative histories, and to the disruption of informational privilege through archiving, publishing, and bookselling'.

60. Foster 1985, p. 129 and p. 132.
61. See Dimitrakaki and Weeks 2019.
62. Stabile 1997, p. 398.
63. Vishmidt 2018, p. 1.
64. Ibid, p. 25. Emphasis added.
65. Britain left the gold standard in 1931, after the major global crisis of 1929, indicating a longer process towards the immaterial within capitalism. See Mazur 1931 and Morrison 2016. Vishmidt briefly notes Bretton-Woods in referring to speculation as functioning in 'a circuit which trades and capitalises on risk, be it its abrogation or maximisation, in the world of unstable currencies and debt arbitrage which typify the post-Bretton Woods, post-Glass-Steagall, post-crisis era'. See Vishmidt 2018, p. 28.
66. Wikipedia, 'Bretton Woods system'. Emphasis added.
67. Malabou 2024, p. 305.
68. Ibid., p. 305.
69. Vishmidt 2018, p. 10.
70. See Dimitrakaki in Dimitrakaki and Lloyd eds. 2015.
71. Bradbury 1995, p. 774.
72. See Dimitrakaki and Lloyd eds. 2015.
73. On digital degrowth, see Dyer-Witheford and Mularoni 2025.
74. See McMahon, Kleinman, and Subramanian 2025.
75. Rushkoff 2023.
76. Boyer 2015.
77. Sefeni 2023.
78. Hancox 2018.
79. Pollock 2014, p. 14.
80. See Bang Larsen 2012.
81. See Coin 2017.
82. Bandhakavi 2025.
83. See Rosler 1979.
84. Getsy 2022, p. 343.
85. Ibid., p. 356.
86. Ibid., p. 357.
87. Ibid., p. 360.
88. Delistraty 2019. See also Grigsby 2015 and O'Grady 1992.
89. Getsy 2022 p. 363.
90. For an early account, see Halberstam 2000.
91. See Brooklyn Museum, 'Collection / Components of The Dinner Party: Curatorial Overview'.
92. See Pollock 1988.

93. See Schor 2025. This is the expanded edition of the well-known volume.
94. Smith 2007.
95. Pollock 2021, p. 267. Emphasis in the original.
96. Tricontinental 2023; Kadri 2024.
97. Brand 2021, p. 18.

CHAPTER FIVE

1. Spivak quoted in Pollock 2014, p. 14. See also Spivak 2003.
2. Dimitrakaki 2022b, p. 286. Emphasis in the original.
3. See Imperial War Museum, 'The Women Who Took On the British Government's Nuclear Programme'.
4. Alexandra Kokoli's recent art historical research on Greenham Common is an exception. See Kokoli 2021 and Kokoli 2023.
5. Barbrook and Cameron 1995.
6. Barla 2017.
7. Haraway quoted in Weigel 2019.
8. Haraway 1991, p. 65.
9. See Meskimmon 2020 and Meskimmon 2022.
10. See Duarte 2022.
11. See Grzinic and Ostojić eds. 2008.
12. Fraser 2005, p. 282.
13. Novick 2018
14. See 'A Letter from Artists in the Whitney Biennial', 2019; see Whitney Biennial Curatorial Statement 2019 written by Jane Panetta and Ruzeko Hockley.
15. See Shaked 2019a.
16. See Dirik 2022.
17. Endnotes 2010.
18. See the 'About' section of the W.A.G.E. website, undated.
19. See Womanifesto 2008.
20. See Florida 2002 and National Endowment for the Arts 2005.
21. See the chapter 'A Feminist Approach to the Disavowed Economy of Art' in Praznik 2021.
22. Quote from Dreaming In Public.
23. Vishmidt 2013.
24. See Project Row Houses. Supporting institutions are listed at https://projectrowhouses.org/about/.
25. Hardt and Negri 2009, p. 332–4.
26. See Fiocco 2025.
27. See Weigand 2001.
28. Ruddock 2023.
29. Robinson 1964, p. 46.
30. Fraser 1997, p. 280.
31. Shaked 2019b, p. 216.
32. Araeen 2000, p. 6.

33. See Fraser 2000, p. 110 and Fraser and Honneth 2003.
34. John Roberts quoted in Charnley 2017, p. 13. See also Roberts 2015.
35. See the multilingual Ethics of Collecting.
36. Brook, O'Brien, and Taylor 2018.
37. See Bakare, Boyd, Khomani, and Vinter 2025.
38. Ind 2023.
39. Vishmidt 2013.
40. Abse Gogarty 2014.
41. See Passoti 2020.
42. Magally Miranda and Kyle Lane-McKinley, 'Artwashing, or between Social Practice and Social Reproduction', *A Blade of Grass*, 1 February 2017, unpaginated. The article is no longer available on the site. In May 2025, it is available on Miranda's profile on Academia.edu.
43. Hay 2025; see also Home 2025.
44. See Wiseman 2021 and Tebaldi 2024.
45. See Community Wellbeing Space.
46. See Bishop 2004.
47. For the first quote see D'Souza 2017; for the second quote, see Greenberger 2017.
48. Cascone 2018. Emphasis added.
49. See Betterton 2000.
50. Meiksins Wood 2016, p. 258–9. Emphasis in the original.
51. Attended by 200 people in a packed lecture hall given the panic generated in the arts by Trump's ascendance, the roundtable at the University of Edinburgh on 30 November 2017 included papers by Amelia Jones, Tamara Trodd, and Angela Dimitrakaki.
52. Quaintance 2017.
53. See Stella-Sawicka 2018; Marina Vishmidt's quote 'capitalism without a filter' is in Abse Gogarty, Dimitrakaki, and Vishmidt 2019, p. 453.
54. Chibber in Nascheck 2025.
55. See Walsh 2025.
56. Gimemez 2019.
57. Lacy ed. 1995.
58. Sholette 2017, p. 201
59. Thompson ed. 2011. See also Groys 2002.
60. Hennessy 2018, p. 59.
61. Ibid., p.56
62. See Majewska 2021 and Majewska 2017.
63. Vishmidt 2015.
64. Berlant 2008, p. 10. See also Helms, Vishmidt, and Berlant 2010.
65. Lütticken 2016, p. 134.
66. Beech 2019b, p. 103.
67. See The Alternative School of Economics.
68. Beale and Feneck 2022.
69. Federici 2018, p. 468. Emphasis added.
70. Gibson-Graham 1994.

71. See Orozco Espinel and Gomez Betancourt 2022.
72. De Angelis 2013, p. 605–6. See also De Angelis 2017.
73. Krasny 2017.
74. Basso, 2016, p. 108.
75. Marx, Capital Volume 1, Chapter 31, p. 748; Steyerl 2010.
76. See Bauman 2012.
77. Wark 2017.
78. See Varoufakis 2024 and Dean 2025.
79. Beech 2019b, p. 102–3.
80. Carpenter and Mojab 2017, p. 3.

CHAPTER SIX

1. Racjhman 2009.
2. Esther Leslie quoted in Pal and Souvlis 2018.
3. See Strom 2025.
4. See Roberts 2007.
5. For a more nuanced approach see 'Part Two: Machines' in Caffentzis 2013.
6. See Kleiman 2022.
7. See Mahdawi 2025.
8. For this discussion, I use the version of the film available since 2010 and held at the British Film Institute.
9. See Sekula 1986 and Azoulay 2021.
10. See Dimitrakaki 2007.
11. ORLAN quoted in De Filippi 2023.
12. Ibid. The full sentence reads: 'The body is a playground that deserves to be explored and questioned'.
13. I refer to this in Chapter One: in 2023, an auction of women's work was held at Sotheby's using this slogan. See https://www.sothebys.com/en/digital-catalogues/my-body-my-business
14. Hartney and Morton 2013, p. 90. Emphasis added.
15. Trodd 2024, p. 34.
16. Ibid., p. 31.
17. See Rose 1993.
18. See ORLAN, 'Petition against Death' and Alter 2023.
19. See etoy.CORPORATION, Disclaimer, 2007
20. See etoy.CORPORATION, Mission Eternity.
21. Child 2019, p. 164–5.
22. Franke and Teixeira Pinto 2016, p. 1.
23. Noys 2014 and Noys 2010.
24. Beckett 2017.
25. The idea of the metabolic rift originates in Marx. See John Bellamy Foster 1999.
26. Dimitrakaki 2019b.
27. Beckett 2017.

28. Harry Kunzro, celebrated literary author of such critiques engaging red and blue pills, was an MA student at Warwick University at the time of the CCRL. See also his novel *Blue Pill* (2020).
29. Teixeira Pinto 2019, p. 326 and p. 328.
30. Malm 2019.
31. Conte 2019, p. 16.
32. Ibid., p. 14.
33. Ibid., p. 13.
34. Gringeras 2017.
35. Braidotti 2006, p. 1.
36. Ibid., p. 253.
37. See Braidotti in Andrés 2019, with video. Braidotti says that revolution 'now' belongs to the far right, but it still includes the rejection of the 'global revolution' while referring to unspecified 'collective' action. The video excerpt where Braidotti says 'revolution now is fascism', on the grounds that the far right is carrying out a revolution, is at CCCB post on X, 6 April 2019, https://twitter.com/cececebe/status/1114430101930823682?lang=en-GB .
38. Braidotti 2020, p. 43. Emphasis added.
39. See Holborow 2024.
40. Ibid., p. 49.
41. Braidotti 2016, p. 690.
42. See title chapters in the section 'Topologies of Speculation: the Tenses of Art, Labour and Finance' in Vishmidt 2018.
43. Wajcman 1991, p. iii.
44. See the work's description at the National Gallery of Victoria (NGV) in Australia, https://www.ngv.vic.gov.au/explore/collection/work/57615/ (accessed 20 March 2025).
45. Chadwick quoted in Buck 1997, unpaginated. The quote is on the third page of Buck's essay, connected to footnote 12, where the date of the quote (conversation with Buck) is given as 8 January 1996.
46. Wajcman and Young 2023, p. 47–8.
47. Ibid., p. 50.
48. Nyabola 2023. See also Nyabola 2018, especially the first chapter.
49. Kidmose 2024.
50. See Pasquinelli 2023, p. 248.
51. Ibid. Emphasis added.
52. Klein 2023.
53. State Council's Information Office, the People's Republic of China 2024.
54. Moody 2018, p. 5.
55. See 'Marxism, Feminism, and the Commons' (2014) in Federici 2019, p. 167.
56. Bassett, Kember, O'Riordan 2020, p. 44.
57. See Dimitrakaki and Lloyd, '(Re)making the World: An Interview with Melanie Gilligan on Capitalist Exchange, Subject Formation and "Social Synthesis"', in Dimitrakaki and Lloyd eds. 2015.
58. Toscano and Kinkle 2014.

59. Bull 2007, p. 1.
60. Bernes 2015.
61. Tsianos and Papadopoulos 2015, p. 123. This is an updated version of the essay first published at *transversal* in 2006.
62. Barthes and Howard 1979, p. 34.
63. Jameson 2003, p. 76
64. Lyotard 1993, p. 81–2. Emphasis in the original.
65. Wark 2015.
66. Berry 2018, p. 34.
67. See Lewis 2021. Lewis is positive on the prospect of surrogacy as formal labour, connecting it to the abolition of the family finding the latter uniformly oppressive.
68. See Wade 2010. See also the letters/responses under the heading 'What's behind the Odd Idea of War in the Womb', *The New York Times*, 7 August 1993, p. 20 (of print edition).
69. Hennessy 2000.
70. Bernes 2015.

POSTSCRIPT

1. SIPRI 2025.

Bibliography

NB: All online sources were last accessed between January and June 2025.

Abse Gogarty, Larne. 2014. 'Art & Gentrification'. *Art Monthly* 373, February. www.artmonthly.co.uk/magazine/site/article/art-and-gentrification-by-larne-abse-gogarty-february-2014

Abse Gogarty, Larne, Angela Dimitrakaki, Marina Vishmidt. 2019. 'Anti-fascist Art Theory: A Roundtable Discussion'. *Third Text* 33(3): 449–65.

Achcar, Gilbert. 2025. 'The Age of Neofascism and Its Distinctive Features'. *Historical Materialism Blog*, 24 February, www.historicalmaterialism.org/the-age-of-neofascism-and-its-distinctive-features/

Adorno, Theodore W. 2002. *Aesthetic Theory*. Trans. Robert Hullot-Kentor. London: Continuum.

Ahmed, Shoaib. 2024. 'Wage Theft, Secrecy and Derealisation of "Ideal Workers" in the Bangladesh Garment Industry'. *Organization Studies* 45(6): 881–901.

Alcoff, Linda. 1991–2. 'The Problem of Speaking for Others'. *Cultural Critique* 20, Winter: 5–32.

Allen, Theodore W. 2012. *The Making of the White Race*, two volumes. London: Verso.

Alter, Charlotte. 2023. 'The Man Who Thinks He Can Live Forever'. *TIME*, 20 September, https://time.com/6315607/bryan-johnsons-quest-for-immortality/

Anderson, Perry. 2023. 'The Standard of Civilization'. *New Left Review* 143 (September–October): 5–29.

Anderson, Perry. 1984. 'Modernity and Revolution'. *New Left Review* 1/144 (March–April): 96–113.

Andrés, Iu. 2019. 'Rosi Braidotti: "What is necessary is a radical transformation following the bases of feminism, anti-racism and anti-fascism"'. CCCBLAB, 2 April, www.cccb.org/en/multimedia/videos/rosi-braidotti-what-is-necessary-is-a-radical-transformation-following-the-bases-of-feminism-anti-racism-and-anti-fascism/231793

Applin, Jo. 2014. 'Mobile Subjects: Abstraction, the Body and Science in the Work of Bridget Riley and Liliane Lijn'. *Konsthistorisk tidskrift/Journal of Art History* 83(2): 96–109.

Aranda, Julieta, Anton Vidokle, Brian Kuan Wood, eds. 2011. *Are You Working Too Much? Post-Fordism, Precarity, and the Labour of Art*. Berlin: Sternberg Press.

Araeen, Rasheed. 2000. 'A New Beginning: Beyond Postcolonial Theory and Identity Politics'. *Third Text* 14(50): 3–20.

Arango, Diana J. et al. 2014. *Interventions to Prevent or Reduce Violence against Women and Girls: A Systematic Review of Reviews*. The World Bank.

Arruzza, Cinzia. 2018. 'From Women's Strikes to a New Class Movement: The Third Feminist Wave'. *Viewpoint Magazine*, 3 December, https://viewpointmag.com/2018/12/03/from-womens-strikes-to-a-new-class-movement-the-third-feminist-wave/

Arruzza, Cinzia. 2017. 'From Social Reproduction Feminism to the Women's Strike'. In Tithi Bhattacharya, ed., *Social Reproduction Theory: Remapping Class, Recentering Oppression*. London: Pluto Press.

Arruzza, Cinzia. 2013. *Dangerous Liaisons: The Marriages and Divorces of Marxism and Feminism*. London: Merlin Press.

Arruzza, Ciniza, Tithi Bhattacharya, Nancy Fraser. 2019. *Feminism for the 99%: A Manifesto*. London: Verso.

Azoulay, Ariella Aisha. 2021. 'Toward the Abolition of Photography's Imperial Rights'. In Kevin Coleman and Daniel James, eds., *Capitalism and the Camera: Essays on Photography and Extraction*, London: Verso.

Azoulay, Ariella Aisha. 2019. *Potential History: Unlearning Imperialism*. London: Verso.

Baccaro, Lucio and Chris Howell. 2017. *Trajectories of Neoliberal Transformation: European Industrial Relations since the 1970s*. Cambridge: Cambridge University Press.

Bakare, Larne. 2025. 'It's not a bubble: Indigenous art comes to London after Venice backlash'. *The Guardian*, 16 February, www.theguardian.com/artanddesign/2025/feb/16/embrace-of-indigenous-artists-reaches-london-thanks-to-influence-of-venice-biennale

Bakare, Larne, Raphael Boyd, Nadia Khomani, and Robyn Vinter. 2025. 'Working-class creatives don't stand a chance in UK today, leading artists warn'. *The Guardian*, 21 February, www.theguardian.com/culture/2025/feb/21/working-class-creatives-dont-stand-a-chance-in-uk-today-leading-artists-warn

Bandhakavi, Swagath. 2025. 'Global AI venture capital reaches $110bn in 2024, driven by foundational models'. *Tech Monitor*, February 12, https://www.techmonitor.ai/digital-economy/ai-and-automation/global-ai-venture-capital-110bn-2024-driven-foundational-models

Bang Larsen, Lars. 2012. 'Turn ! Turn! Turn!'. *Mousse Magazine*, 1 October, www.moussemagazine.it/magazine/lars-bang-larsen-turn-turn-turn-2012/

Baravalle, Marco, Emanuele Braga, Gabriella Riccio (Institute of Radical Imagination), eds. 2022. *Art for UBI (Manifesto)*. Venice: Bruno.

Barbrook, Richard and Andy Cameron. 1995. 'The Californian Ideology'. *Mute*, 1 September, www.metamute.org/editorial/articles/californian-ideology

Barla, Josef. 2017. 'Cyborg', *New Materialism: How Matter Comes to Matter, Almanac*, 4 July, https://newmaterialism.eu/almanac/c/cyborg.html

Barry, Judith and Sandy Flitterman. 1980. 'Textual Strategies: The Politics of Art-Making'. *SCREEN* 21: 35–48.

Barthes, Roland and Richard Howard. 1979. 'Lecture: In Inauguration of the Chair of Literary Semiology, Collège de France, January 7, 1977', *Oxford Literary Review* 4(1): 31–44.

Barthes, Roland. 1977. 'The Death of the Author' (1967). In *Image-Music-Text*. Trans. Stephen Heath. London: Fontana Press.

Bassett, Caroline, Sarah Kember, Kate O'Riordan. 2020. *Furious: Technological Feminisms and Digital Futures*. London: Pluto Press.

Basso, Luca. 2016. *Marx and the Common*. Trans. David Broder. Chicago: Haymarket Books.

Bastani, Aaron. 2019. *Fully Automated Luxury Communism: A Manifesto*. London: Verso.

Batycka, Dorian. 2018. 'The Athens Biennial Negligently Satirizes the Aesthetics of the Alt-Right'. *Hyperallergic*, 6 December, https://hyperallergic.com/471032/the-athens-biennale-negligently-satirizes-the-aesthetics-of-the-alt-right/

Bauman, Zygmunt. 2012. 'Times of Interregnum'. *Ethics & Global Politics* 5(1): 49–56.

Beale, Ruth and Amy Feneck. 2022. 'Why the Artworld Needs Feminist Economics'. *ArtReview*, 23 May, https://artreview.com/why-the-artworld-needs-feminist-economics/

Beck, Koa. 2021. *White Feminism: From the Suffragettes to Influencers and Who They Leave Behind*. New York: Simon & Schuster.

Beckett, Andy. 2017. 'Accelerationism: How a Fringe Philosophy Predicted the Future We Live in'. *The Guardian*, 11 May, www.theguardian.com/world/2017/may/11/accelerationism-how-a-fringe-philosophy-predicted-the-future-we-live-in

Beech, David. 2019a. 'Art and the Politics of Eliminating Handicraft'. *Historical Materialism* 27(1): 155–81.

Beech, David. 2019b. *Art and Postcapitalism: Aesthetic Labour, Automation and Value Production*. London: Pluto.

Beech, David. 2015. *Art and Value: Art's Economic Exceptionalism in Classical, Neoclassical and Marxist Economics*. Leyden: Brill.

Belinchon, Fernando. 2023. 'Investing in Art: A Profitable Activity for the Select Few?' *El Pais*, 12 November, https://english.elpais.com/economy-and-business/2023-11-12/investing-in-art-a-profitable-activity-just-for-a-select-few.html#

Bergman, Emily L. and Stacey Schlau. 2017. *The Routledge Research Companion to the Works of Sor Juana Inés de la Cruz*. London and New York: Routledge.

Berlant, Lauren. 2008. *The Female Complaint: The Unfinished Business of Sentimentality in American Culture*. Durham NC: Duke University Press.

Bernes, Jasper. 2015. 'Capital and Community: On Melanie Gilligan's Trilogy'. *Metamute*, 23 June, www.metamute.org/editorial/articles/capital-and-community-melanie-gilligan%E2%80%99s-trilogy

Berry, Josephine. 2018. *Art and (Bare) Life: A Biopolitical Inquiry*. London and Berlin: Sternberg Press.

Betterton, Rosemary. 2000. 'Undutiful Daughters: Avant-gardism and Gendered Consumption in Recent British Art'. *Visual Culture in Britain* 1(1): 13–30.

Betts, Raymond F. 2012. 'Decolonization: A Brief History of the Word'. In Els Bogaerts and Remco Raben, eds. *Beyond Empire and Nation: The Decolonization of African and Asian Societies, 1930s–1970s*. Leiden: KITLV Press: 23–37.

Bicker, Laura. 2025. 'The Truth behind your $12 Dress: Inside the Chinese Factories Fuelling Shein's Success'. *BBC News*, 12 January, www.bbc.co.uk/news/articles/cdrylgvr77jo

Bishop, Claire. 2004. 'Antagonism and Relational Aesthetics'. *October* 110 (Fall): 51–79.

Bhattacharya, Tithi, ed. 2017. *Social Reproduction Theory: Remapping Class, Recentering Oppression*. London: Pluto Press.

Bhattacharya, Tithi. 2015. 'How Not to Skip Class: Social Reproduction of Labor and the Global Working Class'. *Viewpoint Magazine*, 31 October, www.viewpointmag.com/2015/10/31/how-not-to-skip-class-social-reproduction-of-labor-and-the-global-working-class/

Bohrer, Ashley. 2018. 'Intersectionality and Marxism: A Critical Historiography'. *Historical Materialism* 26(2): 46–74.

Bolt Rasmussen, Mikkel. 2025. 'Guy Debord and Marxist Art History'. In Tijen Tunali and Brian Winkenwender, eds., *The Routledge Companion to Marxisms in Art History*. New York and London: Routledge.

Boltanski, Luc and Eve Chiapello. 2005. *The New Spirit of Capitalism*. Trans. Gregory Elliott. London: Verso.

Bottomore, Tom, ed. 1991. *A Dictionary of Marxist Thought, Second Edition*. Oxford: Blackwell.

Boyer, Anne. 2015. 'Data's Work Is Never Done'. *Guernica: A Magazine of Global Arts and Politics*, 13 March, www.guernicamag.com/anne-boyer-datas-work-is-never-done/

Bourdieu, Pierre and Alain Darbel with Dominique Schnapper. 1991 [1966]. *The Love of Art: European Art Museums and Their Public*. Trans. Caroline Beattie and Nick Merimann. Cambridge: Polity Press.

Braidotti, Rosi. 2020. *Posthuman Feminism*. Cambridge: Polity Press.

Braidotti, Rosi. 2016. 'Posthuman Feminist Theory'. In Linda Disch and Mary Hawkesworth, eds. *The Oxford Handbook of Feminist Theory*. Oxford: Oxford University Press.

Braidotti, Rosi. 2006. *Transpositions*. Cambridge: Polity Press.

Bradbury, Malcolm. 1995. 'What Was Post-Modernism? The Arts in and after the Cold War'. *International Affairs* 71(4): 763–74.

Brand, Carina. 2021. 'A Materialist Reading of Abject Art: Performance, Social Reproduction and Capitalism'. *Open Library of Humanities* 7(1): 1–22.

Brass, Tom. 2022. *Marxism Missing, Missing Marxism: From Marxism to Identity Politics and Beyond*. Chicago IL: Haymarket Books.

Brook, Orian, David O'Brien, Mark Taylor. 2018. *Panic! Social Class, Taste and Inequalities in the Creative Industries* https://createlondon.org/wp-content/uploads/2018/04/Panic-Social-Class-Taste-and-Inequalities-in-the-Creative-Industries1.pdf

Broude, Norma. 1982. 'Degas' "Misogyny"'. In Norma Broude and Mary A. Garrard eds., *Feminism and Art History: Questioning the Litany*. New York: Harper & Row.

Bryan Wilson, Julia. 2009. *Art Workers: Radical Practice in the Vietnam War Era*. Berkeley CA: University of California Press.

Brown, Heather. 2013. *Marx on Gender and the Family*. Chicago IL: Haymarket Books.

Brown, Kate. 2017. 'These Four Artists Were Nominated for Germany's Foremost Art Prize—and Now They're Denouncing It', *Artnet News*, 10 November, https://news.artnet.com/art-world/artists-denounce-german-art-prize-1145351

Brown, Mark. 2011. 'Tracey Emin: Tories are only hope for the arts', *The Guardian*, 16 May, www.theguardian.com/culture/culture-cuts-blog/2011/may/16/art-emin

Brown, Wendy. 2024. 'Re-translating Marx's Capital: An Interview with Paul Reitter/Paul North'. *Jacobin*, 13 September, https://jacobin.com/2024/09/marx-capital-translation-value-distribution

Bruegel, Irene. 1979. 'Women as a Reserve Army of Labour: A Note on Recent British Experience'. *Feminist Review* 3: 12–23.

Buck, Louisa. 1997. 'Unnatural Selection'. In *STILLED LIVES: Helen Chadwick*. Edinburgh: Portfolio Gallery.

Buick, Kirsten. 2010. *Child of the Fire: Mary Edmonia Lewis and the Problem of Art History's Black and Indian Subject*. Durham NC: Duke University Press.

Bull, Malcolm. 2025. 'Why Is There the Amount of Art that There Is?' *New Left Review* 151 (January–February): 89–111.

Bull, Malcolm. 2007. 'Globalization and Biopolitics: Introduction to New Left Review 45'. *New Left Review* 45 (May–June): 1–2.

Bürger, Peter. 1984 [1974]. *Theory of the Avant-Garde*. Trans. Michael Shaw. Minneapolis: University of Minnesota Press.

Burke, Tanara. 2021. *Unbound: My Story of Liberation and the Birth of the Me Too Movement*. New York: Flatiron Books.

Butler, Judith. 1988. 'Performative Acts and Gender Constitution: An Essay in Phenomenology and Feminist Theory'. *Theatre Journal* 40(4): 519–531.

Butollo, Florian and Sabine Nuss, eds. 2022. *Marx and the Robots: Networked Production, AI and Human Labour*. Trans. Jan Peter Herrmann. London: Pluto Press.

Butschart, Amber. 2018. 'The Artificial Divide between Art and Textiles Is a Gendered Issue'. *Frieze*, 14 November, https://frieze.com/article/artificial-divide-between-fine-art-and-textiles-gendered-issue

Caffentzis, George. 2013. *In Letters of Blood and Fire: Work, Machines and the Crisis of Capitalism*. Oakland CA: PM Press.

Caffentzis, George. 2002. 'On the Notion of a Crisis of Social Reproduction: A Theoretical Review'. *The Commoner* 5 (Autumn): 22.

Čakardić, Ankica. 2017. 'From Theory of Accumulation to Social-Reproduction Theory: A Case for Luxemburgian Feminism'. *Historical Materialism* 25(4): 37–64.

CAMP and Nora El Qadim. 2020. 'On CAMP, Copenhagen: The Politics of Curating Art on Migration: A Conversation between Frederikke Hansen, Tone Olaf Nielsen and Nora El Qadim'. *PARSE* 10 (Spring), https://parsejournal.com/article/on-camp-copenhagen-the-politics-of-curating-art-on-migration/

Cammack, Paul. 2020. 'Marx on Social Reproduction'. *Historical Materialism* 28(2): 76–106.

Carpenter, Sara and Shahrzad Mojab. 2017. *Revolutionary Learning: Marxism, Feminism and Knowledge.* London: Pluto Press.

Carter, Christine Michel. 2025. 'Five Years Later, Working Mothers Continue to Leave the Workforce'. *Forbes*, March 29, https://www.forbes.com/sites/christinecarter/2025/03/29/five-years-later-working-mothers-continue-to-leave-the-workforce/

Cascone, Sarah. 2018. '"Black Pain Is Not for Profit": An Activist Collective Protests Luke Willis Thompson's Turner Prize Nomination'. *Artnet News*, 25 September, https://news.artnet.com/exhibitions/luke-willis-thompson-turner-prize-1356151

Charnley, Kim. 2017. 'Art on the Brink: *Bare Art* and the Crisis of Liberal Democracy'. In Gregory Sholette, *Delirium and Resistance: Activist Art and the Crisis of Capitalism*, Kim Charnley, ed. London: Pluto Press.

Chibber, Vivek. 2023. *The Class Matrix: Social Theory after the Cultural Turn.* Cambridge MA: Harvard University Press.

Child, Danielle. 2019. *Working Aesthetics: Labour, Art and Capitalism.* London: Bloomsbury.

Child, Danielle, Helena Reckitt, Jenny Richards. 2017. 'Labours of Love: A Conversation on Art, Gender and Social Reproduction'. *Third Text* 31(1): 147–68.

Chukhrov, Keti. 2020. *Practising the Good: Desire and Boredom in Soviet Socialism.* Minneapolis: University of Minnesota Press.

Chukhrov, Keti. 2014. 'On the False Democracy of Contemporary Art'. *e-flux journal* 57 (September), www.e-flux.com/journal/on-the-false-democracy-of-contemporary-art/

Chrysafis, Angelique. 2018. '"We feel very close to her": Can "fake feminist" Marine Le Pen win the female vote?' *The Guardian*, 17 March, www.theguardian.com/world/2017/mar/18/front-national-anger-marine-le-pen-female-supporters

Claire Fontaine. 2013. '"We Are All Clitoridian Women": Notes on Carla Lonzi's Legacy'. *e-flux journal* 47 (September), www.e-flux.com/journal/47/60057/we-are-all-clitoridian-women-notes-on-carla-lonzi-s-legacy/

Coin, Francesca. 2017. 'On Quitting: The Labour of Academia'. *Ephemera* 17(3) (August): 509–17.

Collinson, Patrick. 2016. 'Home Production Economy Worth £1tn a Year'. *The Guardian*, 7 April, www.theguardian.com/uk-news/2016/apr/07/home-production-economy-worth-1tn-a-year

Commons, John R. 1893. *The Distribution of Wealth.* New York and London: MacMillan & Co.

Combahee River Collective. 1977. 'The Combahee River Collective Statement'. Library of Congress, www.loc.gov/item/lcwaNo028151/

Connor, Cheryl. 2016. 'Can Artists Be Entrepreneurs? Absolutely!' *Forbes*, 23 August, www.forbes.com/sites/cherylsnappconner/2015/04/25/can-artists-be-entrepreneurs-absolutely/

Conte, Kari. 2019. 'Chiara Fumai: Art as Weapon'. In *Chiara Fumai: Less Light*. New York: International Studio & Curatorial Program/ISPC.

Cope, Zak. 2019. *The Wealth of (Some) Nations*. London: Pluto Press.

Corna, Luisa Lorenza. 2024. 'Against the Canon: The Unresolved Dispute between Carla Lonzi and Giulio Carlo Argan'. *Oxford Art Journal* 47(2): 277–90.

Corna, Luisa Lorenza and Jamila M.H. Mascat, eds. 2023. *Carla Lonzi: Feminism in Revolt – An Anthology*. Trans. Luisa Lorenza Corna, Matthew Hyland, Critina Viti. London: Seagull Books.

Coole, Diana and Samantha Frost, eds. 2010. *New Materialisms: Ontology, Agency and Politics*. Durham NC: Duke University Press.

Coote, Anna and Edanur Yazici. 2019. *Universal Basic Income: A Union Perspective*. New Economics Foundation, Public Services International.

Cox, Alyson. 2023. 'Pussy Riot's Latest Act: A Sotheby's Auction for Planned Parenthood'. *Papermag*, 14 March, www.papermag.com/pussy-riot-sothebys-auction#rebelltitem2

Cox, Judy. 2017. *The Women's Revolution: Russia 1905-1917*. London: Counterfire.

Crary, Jonathan. 2013. *24/7: Late Capitalism and the Ends of Sleep*. London: Verso.

Crenshaw, Kimberlé. 1991. 'Mapping the Margins: Intersectionality, Identity Politics, and Violence against Women of Color'. *Stanford Law Review* 43(6): 1241–99.

Crenshaw, Kimberlé. 1989. 'Demarginalizing the Intersection of Race and Sex: A Black Feminist Critique of Antidiscrimination Doctrine, Feminist Theory and Antiracist Politics'. *University of Chicago Legal Forum* 1989(1): 139–67.

Crouch, Colin. 2004. *Post-democracy*. Cambridge: Polity Press.

D'Alancaisez, Pierre. 2022. 'Universal Basic Income for Artists: A Neoliberal Con?' *ArtReview*, 7 September https://artreview.com/universal-basic-income-for-artists-a-neoliberal-con/

Dalla Costa, Mariarosa. 2010. 'Women's Autonomy and Remuneration for Care Work in the New Emergencies'. *Caring Labor*, November, https://caringlabor.wordpress.com/2010/11/10/mariarosa-dalla-costa-women%E2%80%99s-autonomy-and-remuneration-for-care-work-in-the-new-emergencies/#more-633

Danto, Arthur. 1964. 'The Artworld'. *The Journal of Philosophy*, 61(19), American Philosophical Association Eastern Division Sixty-First Annual Meeting, October 15: 571–84.

Davis, Angela, Barbara Ransby, Cinzia Arruzza, Keeanga-Yamahtta Taylor, Linda Martín Alcoff, Nancy Fraser, Rasmea Youssef Odeh, Tithi Bhattacharya. 2017. 'Beyond Lean-In: For a Feminism of the 99% and a Militant International Strike on March 8', *Viewpoint Magazine*, 3 February, https://viewpointmag.

com/2017/02/03/beyond-lean-in-for-a-feminism-of-the-99-and-a-militant-international-strike-on-march-8/

Davis, Ben. 2022. *Art in the After-Culture: Capitalist Crisis & Cultural Strategy*. Chicago Il: Haymarket Books.

Davis, Eric S. et al. 2020. 'Being a Stay-at-Home Dad (SAHD): Implication for the Mental Health Profession', *The Family Journal* 28(2): 150–8.

Day, Gail, Steve Edwards, David Mabb. 2010. '"What Keeps Mankind Alive?": The Eleventh International Istanbul Biennial. Once More Aesthetics and Politics'. *Historical Materialism* 14(4): 135–71.

Day, Meagan. 2022. 'How to Unionize the Art World', *ArtReview*, 10 August, https://artreview.com/how-to-unionize-the-artworld/

De Angelis, Massimo. 2017. *Omnia Sunt Communia: On the Commons and the Transformation to Postcapitalism*. London: Zed Books.

De Angelis, Massimo. 2013. 'Does Capital Need a Commons Fix?' *ephemera: theory & politics of organization* 13(3): 603–15.

De Duve, Thierry. 2007. 'The Glocal and the Singuniversal: Reflections on Art and Culture in the Global Art World'. *Third Text* 21(6): 681–8.

De Filippi, Primavera. 2023. 'When OONA Met ORLAN'. *Right Click Save*, 10 November, www.rightclicksave.com/article/when-oona-met-orlan-body-performance-art-interview

de Pizan, Christine. 1999. *The Book of the City of Ladies*. Trans. and with an introduction and notes by Rosalind Brown-Grant. London: Penguin.

Dean, Jodi. 2025. *Neofeudalism and the New Class Struggle*. London: Verso.

Dean, Jodi. 2005. 'Communicative Capitalism: Circulation and the Foreclosure of Politics'. *Cultural Politics* 1(1): 51–74.

Dean, Mitchell and Daniel Zamora. 2021. 'Foucault and Neoliberalism as Left Governmentality'. *Verso Blog*, 13 May, www.versobooks.com/en-gb/blogs/news/5085-foucault-and-neoliberalism-as-left-governmentality

Debord, Guy. 1970. *Society of the Spectacle*. Trans. Black & Red. Detroit: Printing Co-op.

Deepwell, Katy, ed. 2020. *Feminist Art Activisms and Artivisms*. Amsterdam: Valiz.

Delagrange, Julien. 2023. 'How much money do visual or contemporary artists make?' *Contemporary Art Issue*, 17 August, www.contemporaryartissue.com/how-much-money-do-visual-or-contemporary-artists-make/

Delistraty, Cody. 2019. 'Modernism's Debt to Black Women'. *The Paris Review*, 6 June, www.theparisreview.org/blog/2019/06/06/modernisms-debt-to-black-women/

Denning, Michael. 2010. 'Wageless Life'. *New Left Review* 66 (November–December): 79–97.

Digby, Anne. 1992. 'Victorian Values and Women in Private and Public', *Proceedings of the British Academy* 78: 195–215.

Dimitrakaki, Angela. 2024. 'Workers and Rebels: Women's Excision from History and Leda Papaconstantinou's moving Image Essays'. In Tina Pandi, ed. *Time in My Hands, Leda Papaconstantinou — A Retrospective*. Athens: EMST/National Museum of Contemporary Art.

Dimitrakaki, Angela. 2023. 'Feminism and Marxism: Questions on the Field of Struggle'. *ΚΡΙΣΗ* 13(1): 9–44.

Dimitrakaki, Angela. 2022a. 'From Space to Time: 'Situated Knowledges, Critical Curating and Social Truth'. *OnCurating* 53 (June): 8–19.

Dimitrakaki, Angela. 2022b. 'A Feminist Critique of Capitalism: Class, Gender, Work and Unrest in Women's Art after 2008'. *Oxford Art Journal* 45(2): 269–87.

Dimitrakaki, Angela. 2020. 'Movements, Borders, Repression, Art: An Interview with Zeyno Penkulu'. *Third Text Online*, March, www.thirdtext.org/ dimitrakaki-pekunlu

Dimitrakaki, Angela. 2019a. 'Masculinity, Art, and Value Extraction: An Intersectional Reading in the Advance of Capital as Post-Democracy'. In Hilary Robinson and Maria Buszek, eds. *A Companion to Feminist Art Practice and Theory*. West Sussex: Wiley-Blackwell.

Dimitrakaki, Angela. 2019b. 'Left with TINA: Art, Alienation and Anti-communism'. *Praktyka Teoretyczna*, 31(1): 25–48.

Dimitrakaki, Angela. 2018. Feminism, Art, Contradictions'. *e-flux journal* 92 (June) https://www.e-flux.com/journal/92/205536/feminism-art-contradictions

Dimitrakaki, Angela. 2017. 'Extensive Modernity: On the Refunctioning of Artists as Producers'. In Pam Meecham, ed. *A Companion to Modern Art*. Hoboken, NJ: Wiley-Blackwell.

Dimitrakaki, Angela. 2015. 'Women's Lives, Labour, Contracts, Documents: The Biopolitical Tactics of Feminist Art, Act Two and a Half'. In Angela Dimitrakaki and Kirsten Lloyd, eds., *ECONOMY: Art, Production and the Subject in the 21st Century*. Liverpool: Liverpool University Press.

Dimitrakaki, Angela. 2013. *Gender, ArtWork and the Global Imperative: A Materialist Feminist Critique*, Manchester: Manchester University Press.

Dimitrakaki, Angela. 2010. 'Curatorial Collectives and Feminist Politics in 21st Century Europe: An Interview with Kuratorisk Aktion' www.publik.dk/img/ tekster%20RR/Kuratorisk%20Aktion%20interview.pdf

Dimitrakaki, Angela. 2007. 'Materialist Feminism for the Twenty-first Century: The Video Essays of Ursula Biemann'. *Oxford Art Journal* 30(2): 205–32.

Dimitrakaki, Angela. 2004. 'Researching Cultures and the Omitted Footnote: Questions on the Practice of Feminist Art History. In Jean Fisher and Gerardo Mosquera, eds. *Over Here: International Perspectives on Art and Culture*. Cambridge MA: The MIT Press & New York: The New Museum of Contemporary Art.

Dimitrakaki, Angela. 1996–7. 'Elements of a Secret History: Women, Art and Gender in Modern Greece'. *Third Text* 37: 63–74.

Dimitrakaki, Angela and Harry Weeks. 2019. 'Anti-fascism/Art/Theory: An Introduction to What Hurts Us'. *Third Text* 33(3): 271–292.

Dimitrakaki, Angela and Kirsten Lloyd. 2015. 'Introduction: 'The Last Instance' – The Apparent Economy, Social Struggles, and Art in Global Capitalism'. In Angela Dimitrakaki and Kirsten Lloyd, eds. *ECONOMY: Art, Production and the Subject in the 21st Century*. Liverpool: Liverpool University Press.

Dimitrakaki, Angela and Kirsten Lloyd. 2015. '(Re)making the World: An Interview with Melanie Gilligan on Capitalist Exchange, Subject Formation and "Social Synthesis". In Angela Dimitrakaki and Kirsten Lloyd, eds. *ECONOMY: Art, Production and the Subject in the 21st Century*. Liverpool: Liverpool University Press.

Dimitrakaki, Angela and Lara Perry, eds., 2013. *Politics in a Glass Case: Women's Art, Exhibition Cultures and Curatorial Transgressions*. Liverpool: Liverpool University Press.

Dimitrakaki, Angela and Nizan Shaked. 2021. 'Feminism, Instituting and the Politics of Recognition in Global Capitalism'. *OnCurating* 52 (November): 11–20.

Dirik, Dilar. 2022. *The Kurdish Women's Movement: History, Theory, Practice*. London: Pluto Press.

D'Souza, Aruna. 2017. 'Can White Artists Paint Black Pain?' *CNN World*, 24 March, https://edition.cnn.com/2017/03/24/opinions/white-artist-controversial-emmett-till-painting-dsouza/index.html

Duarte, Joana das Flores. 2022. 'Mariátegui and Latin American Marxist Feminism: A Necessary Revisit'. Trans. Heather Hayes, *Latin American Perspectives* 49(4): 31–44.

Duello, Theresa M. et al. 2021. 'Race and Genetics versus "Race" in Genetics', *Evolution, Medicine, and Public Health* 9(1): 232–45.

Duffy, Nick. 2017. 'Germany's far-right AfD picks lesbian for election campaign', *Pink News*, 24 April, www.pinknews.co.uk/2017/04/24/germanys-far-right-afd-picks-lesbian-leader-for-election-campaign/

Duncan, Carol. 1993. 'Who Rules the Art World?' (1983). In *The Aesthetics of Power: Essays in Critical Art History*. Cambridge: Cambridge University Press.

Duncan, Carol. 1982. 'Virility and Domination in Early Twentieth-Century Vanguard Painting' (1973). In Norma Broude and Mary D. Garrard, eds. *Feminism and Art History: Questioning the Litany*. New York: Harper & Row.

Dyer-Witheford, Nick and Alessandra Mularoni. 2025. *Cybernetic Circulation Complex: Big Tech and Planetary Crisis*. London: Verso.

Edwards, Jim. 2013. 'Inside the Filthy Dorms Where Workers Who Make Apple's New iPhone 5C Must Sleep'. *Business Insider*, September 5, www.businessinsider.com/factory-dorms-where-workers-on-apples-iphone-5c-sleep-2013-9

Ehreinreich, Barbara and Arlie Russell Hochschild, eds. 2004. *Global Woman: Nannies, Maids and Sex Workers in the New Economy*. New York: Henry Holt & Co.

Eisenstein, Hester. 2009. *Feminism Seduced: How Global Elites Stole Women's Labor and Ideas to Exploit the World*. Boulder CO: Paradigm.

Elias, Ana Sofia, Rosalind Gill, Christina Scharff, eds. 2017. *Aesthetic Labour: Rethinking Beauty Politics in Neoliberalism*. London: Palgrave Macmillan.

Elias, Allison. 2022. *The Rise of Corporate Feminism: Women in the American Office, 1960–1990*. New York: Columbia University Press.

Endnotes. 2010. 'Crisis in the Class Relation: Yes! There Will Be Growth in the Spring'. *Endnotes* 2 (April), https://endnotes.org.uk/articles/crisis-in-the-class-relation

Faludi, Susan. 2013. 'Facebook Feminism, Like It or Not'. *The Baffler* 23 (August), https://thebaffler.com/salvos/facebook-feminism-like-it-or-not

Farris, Sara. 2017. *In the Name of Women's Rights: The Rise of Femonationalism.* Durham NC: Duke University Press.

Federici, Silvia. 2019. *Re-enchanting the World: Feminism and the Politics of the Commons.* Oakland CA: PM Books.

Federici, Silvia. 2018. 'Marx and Feminism'. *triple C* 16(2): 468–75.

Federici, Silvia. 2017. 'Foreword'. In Precarious Workers Brigade, *Training for Exploitation? Politicising Employability and Reclaiming Education.* London: Journal of Aesthetics & Protest Press.

Federici, Silvia. 2012. *Housework, Reproduction, and Feminist Struggle.* Oakland CA: PM Books.

Federici, Silvia. 2010. 'Feminism and the Politics of the Commons'. In *Uses of a WorldWind, Movement, Movements, and Contemporary Radical Currents in the United States*, edited by Craig Hughes, Stevie Peace and Kevin Van Meter for the Team Colors Collective, Oaskland: AK Press.

Federici, Silvia. 2004. *Caliban and the Witch: Women, the Body and Primitive Accumulation.* New York: Autonomedia.

Federici, Silvia. 1975. *Wages against Housework.* New York: Power of Women Collective and Falling Wall Press.

Federici, Silvia and Leopoldina Fortunati. 1984. *Il grande Calibano: Storia del corpo sociale ribelle nella prima fase del capitale* [The Great Caliban: A History of the Rebellious Social Body in the Early Phase of Capital]. Milan: Franco Angeli.

Fiocco, Fabiola. 2025. Gender, *Affect and Art's Alternative Workplaces: A Feminist Critique of Socially Engaged Art Paradigms in Europe*, PhD Thesis. Edinburgh: University of Edinburgh.

Florida, Richard. 2002. *The Rise of the Creative Class.* New York: Basic Books.

Foster, John Bellamy and Brett Clark. 2018. 'Women, Nature, and Capital in the Industrial Revolution', *Monthly Review*, 1 January, https://monthlyreview.org/2018/01/01/women-nature-and-capital-in-the-industrial-revolution/

Foster, John Bellamy. 1999. 'Marx's Theory of the Metabolic Rift: Classical Foundations for Environmental Sociology'. *AJS* 105(2) (September): 366–405.

Foster, Hal. 1985. *Recodings: Art, Spectacle, Cultural Politics.* Seattle WA: Bay Press.

Fraiberger, Samuel P. et al. 2018. 'Quantifying Reputation and Success in Art'. *Science*, 8 November, http://science.sciencemag.org/content/early/2018/11/07/science.aau7224.full

Frank, Natalie. 2018. 'In the Discussion About the Sacklers and Oxycontin, It's Important to Get the Facts Right', *Artnet News*, 22 January https://news.artnet.com/opinion/discussion-sacklers-oxycontin-facts-elizabeth-a-sackler-1203458

Franke, Anselm and Ana Teixeira Pinto. 2016. 'Post-Political, Post-Critical, Post- Internet: Why Can't Leftists Be More Like Fascists?' *onlineopen.org*, 8 September: 7 pages.

Fraser, Andrea. 2005. 'From the Critique of Institutions to an Institution of Critique', *Artforum* 44(1): 278–83.

Fraser, Andrea. 1994. 'How to Provide an Artistic Service: An Introduction' http://web.mit.edu/allanmc/www/fraser1.pdf

Fraser, Nancy. 2009. 'Feminism, Capitalism and the Cunning of History'. *New Left Review* 56 (March–April): 96–117.

Fraser, Nancy. 2000. 'Rethinking Recognition'. *New Left Review* 3 (May/June): 107–120.

Fraser, Nancy. 1997. 'Heterosexism, Misrecognition and Capitalism: A Response to Judith Butler'. *Social Text* 52/53 (Autumn–Winter): 279–89.

Fraser, Nancy. 1995. 'From Redistribution to Recognition? Dilemmas of Justice in a Post-socialist Age'. *New Left Review* I/212 (July–August): 68–93.

Fraser, Nancy and Rahel Jaeggi. 2023 [2018]. *Capitalism: A Conversation in Critical Theory*, ed Brian Milstein. London: Verso.

Fraser, Nancy and Alex Honneth. 2003. *Redistribution or Recognition? A Political-Philosophical Exchange*. London: Verso.

Frayssé, Olivier. 2014. 'Work and Labour as Metonymy and Metaphor'. *triple C* 12(2): 468–85.

Garlick, Steve. 2004. 'Distinctly Feminine: On the Relationship between Men and Art', *Berkeley Journal of Sociology* 48: 108–125.

Garrard, Mary D. 1995. 'Feminist Art and the Essentialism Controversy'. *The Centennial Review* 39(3): 468–92.

Getsy, David J. 2022. 'How to Teach Manet's Olympia after Transgender Studies'. *Art History* 45(2): 342–69.

Gibson-Graham, J.K. 1994. 'Stuffed if I Know: Reflections on Postmodern Feminist Social Research', *Gender, Place and Culture* 1(2): 205–24.

Gilbert, Elizabeth. Undated. 'The Key to a Well-Lived Life: Lighten Up', OPRAH. COM www.oprah.com/spirit/elizabeth-gilbert-on-failure-and-living-well/all

Gilligan, Carolyn and Naomi Snider. 2018. *Why Does Patriarchy Persist?* Cambridge: Polity Press.

Gimenez, Martha E. 2019. 'Women, Class and Identity Politics', *Monthly Review*, 1 September, https://monthlyreview.org/2019/09/01/women-class-and-identity-politics/

Gleeson, Jules Joanne and Elle O' Rourke, eds. 2021. *Transgender Marxism*. London: Pluto Press.

Glosswitch. 2017. 'Is Ivanka Trump the Feminist We Deserve?' *The New Statesman*, 15 May, www.newstatesman.com/politics/feminism/2017/05/ivanka-trump-feminist-we-deserve

Gompertz, Will. 2016. 'Geneva Free Port: The Greatest Art Collection No-one Can See'. *BBC News*, 1 December, www.bbc.co.uk/news/entertainment-arts-38167501

Gopinath, Gita. 2023. 'Cold War II? Preserving Economic Cooperation Amid Geoeconomic Fragmentation', 11 December, speech. International Monetary

Fund, www.imf.org/en/News/Articles/2023/12/11/sp121123-cold-war-ii-preserving-economic-cooperation-amid-geoeconomic-fragmentation

Gorecki, Julie. 2015. 'How Did This Happen? Capitalism's Double Subordination of Women and Nature', *The Feminist Wire*, 1 May, www.thefeministwire.com/2015/05/how-did-this-happen-capitalisms-double-subordination-of-women-and-nature/

Graeber, David. 2011. *Debt: The First 5,000 Years*. Brooklyn NY: Melville House.

Grant, Catherine. 2011. 'Fans of Feminism: Re-writing Histories of Second Wave Feminism in Contemporary Art'. *Oxford Art Journal* 32(2): 265–86.

Greenberger, Alex. 2017. '"The Painting Must Go": Hannah Black Pens Open Letter to the Whitney About Controversial Biennial Work'. *Artnews*, 21 March, www.artnews.com/2017/03/21/the-painting-must-go-hannah-black-pens-open-letter-to-the-whitney-about-controversial-biennial-work/

Grigsby, Darcy Grimaldo. 2015. 'Still Thinking about Olympia's Maid'. *The Art Bulletin* 97(4): 430–51.

Gringeras, Alison. 2017. 'Chiara Fumai and the Dead Feminist Society'. *affidavit*, 4 December, https://affidavit.art/articles/chiara-fumai

Grzinic, Marina and Tanja Ostojić, eds. 2008. *Integration Impossible? The Politics of Migration in the Work of Tanja Ostojić*. Berlin: Argo Books.

Grogan, Susan K. 1992. *French Socialism and Sexual Difference: Women and the New Society 1803-44*. Basingstoke and London: Macmillan.

Groys, Boris. 2014. 'On Art Activism'. *e-flux journal* 56 (June) www.e-flux.com/journal/on-art-activism/

Groys, Boris. 2002. 'From Artwork to Art Documentation: Art in the Age of Biopolitics'. In *Documenta 11, Platform 5: Exhibition Catalogue*. Ostfildern-Ruit: Hatje Cantz.

Habermas, Jürgen. 1991 [1962]. *The Structural Transformation of the Public Sphere: An Inquiry into a Category of Bourgeois Society*. Trans. *Thomas* Burger. Cambridge MA: The MIT Press.

Hadjinicolaou, Nicos. 1978. *Art History and Class Struggle*. Trans. Louise Asmal. London: Pluto Press.

Halberstam, Judith. 2000. 'The Body in Question: Transgender Images in Contemporary Visual Art'. *Make* 88 (June): 37–8.

Hall, Catherine. 2016. 'Writing History, Making Race: Slave-Owners and Their Stories'. *Australian Historical Studies* 47(3): 365–80.

Halperin, Julia. 2018. 'Turner Prize-Winner Lubaina Himid Is a Star at Art Basel—and She's Getting a Solo Show at the New Museum', *artnet news*, 12 June, https://news.artnet.com/market/lubaina-himid-oldest-turner-prize-market-takeoff-1301645

Halperin, Julia. 2017. 'The 4 Glass Ceilings: How Women Artists Get Stiffed at Every Stage of Their Careers'. *Artnet News*, 15 December, https://news.artnet.com/market/art-market-study-1179317

Hancox, Dan. 2018. '"What is Democracy?" Argues Why Political Justice Must Be Built from the Ground Up'. *Frieze*, 19 November, www.frieze.com/ko/article/what-democracy-argues-why-political-justice-must-be-built-ground

Haraway, Donna. 1988. 'Situated Knowledges: The Science Question in Feminism and the Privilege of Partial Perspective'. *Feminist Studies* 14(3): 575–99.

Haraway, Donna. 1985. 'A Manifesto for Cyborgs: Science, Technology, and Socialist Feminism in the 1980s'. *Socialist Review* 80: 65–107.

Hardt, Michael and Antonio Negri. 2009. *Commonwealth*. Cambridge MA: Harvard University Press.

Hardt, Michael and Antonio Negri. 2000. *Empire*. Cambridge MA: Harvard University Press.

Harper, Paula. 1985. 'The First Feminist Art Program: A View from the 1980s'. *Signs* 10(4): 762–81.

Harutyunyan, Angela, Aras Özgün, Eric Goodfield. 2011. 'Event and Counter-Event: The Political Economy of the Istanbul Economy and Its Excesses'. *Rethinking Marxism* 23: 478–95.

Hay, Mark. 2025. 'Soap to Supremacy: The Rise of White Wellness'. *Al Jazeera*, 2 February, www.aljazeera.com/features/longform/2025/2/2/how-white-nationalists-infiltrated-the-wellness-movement

Hartney, Stefano and Fred Morton. 2013. *The Undercommons: Fugitive & Black Study*. Brooklyn NY: Minor Compositions.

Hedlin Hayden, Malin and Jessica Sjoholm Skrubbe, eds. 2010. *Feminisms Is still Our Name: Seven Essays on Historiography and Curatorial Practices*. Newcastle: Cambridge Scholars Publishers.

Heidenreich, Stefan. 2016. 'Freeportism as Style and Ideology: Post-Internet and Speculative Realism, Part I'. *e-flux journal* 71 (March), www.e-flux.com/journal/71/60521/freeportism-as-style-and-ideology-post-internet-and-speculative-realism-part-i/

Helms, Gesa, Marina Vishmidt, Lauren Berlant. 2010. 'Affect & the Politics of Austerity: An interview Exchange with Lauren Berlant'. *Variant* 39/40 (Winter) www.variant.org.uk/39_40texts/berlant39_40.html

Hennessy, Mary. 2018. 'Photography, Subjectivity and the Politics of the Image from Helke Sander to Angela Schanelec'. *Camera Obscura* 33(3): 49–73.

Hennessy, Rosemary. 2000. *Profit and Pleasure: Sexual Identities in Late Capitalism*. New York and London: Routledge.

Hester, Helen and Alex Srnicek. 2023. *After Work: A History of the Home and the Fight for Free Time*. London: Verso.

Hewison, Robert. 2021. 'Freelance workers are the backbone of the art world—but how are they expected to survive on a pittance?'. *The Art Newspaper*, 5 March, www.theartnewspaper.com/2021/03/05/freelance-workers-are-the-backbone-of-the-art-worldbut-how-are-they-expected-to-survive-on-a-pittance

Hickel, Jason, Dylan Sullivan, Hizaifa Zoomkawala. 2021. 'Rich countries drained \$152tn from the global South since 1960'. *Al Jazeera*, 6 May, www.aljazeera.com/opinions/2021/5/6/rich-countries-drained-152tn-from-the-global-south-since-1960

Hichliffe, Emma and Nina Ajemian. 2024. 'The Share of Women Running Global 500 Companies Falls to just 5.6%'. *Fortune*, 5 August, https://

fortune.com/2024/08/05/the-share-of-women-running-global-500-companies-falls-to-just-5-6/

Higg, Edward and Amanda Wilkinson. 2016. 'Women, Occupations and Work in the Victorian Censuses Revisited', *History Workshop Journal* 81 (Spring): 17–38.

Hlavajova, Maria and Simon Sheikh, eds. 2016. *Former West: Art and the Contemporary after 1989*. Cambridge MA: The MIT Press and Utrecht: BAK.

Holborow, Marnie. 2024. *Homes in Crisis Capitalism: Gender, Work and Revolution*. London: Bloomsbury Academic.

Home, Stewart. 2025. *Fascist Yoga: Grifters, Occultists, White Supremacists, and the New Order In Wellness*. London: Pluto Press.

hooks, bell. 2013. 'Dig Deep: Beyond Lean In'. *The Feminist Wire*, 28 October, www.thefeministwire.com/2013/10/17973/

Horkheimer, Max and Theodor W. Adorno. 2002 [1947]. *Dialectic of Enlightenment*. Trans. Edmund Jephcott, ed. Gunzelin Schmid Noerr. Stanford: Stanford University Press.

Horne, Gerald. 2018. *The Apocalypse of Settler Colonialism: The Roots of Slavery, White Supremacy, and Capitalism in Seventeenth-Century North America and the Caribbean*. New York: Monthly Review.

Horne, Victoria. 2017. 'Losing Ground? A Note on Feminism, Cultural Activism, and Urban Space'. *Third Text* 31(1): 67–78.

Horne, Victoria. 2014. 'BP Spotlight: Sylvia Pankhurst and Women & Work'. *Radical Philosophy* 186 (July–August): 64–8.

Horne, Victoria and Lara Perry, eds. 2017. *Feminist and Art History Now: Radical Critiques of Theory and Practice*. London: IB Tauris.

Hu, Zoe. 2023. 'The Agoraphobic Fantasy of Tradlife'. *Dissent* (Winter), www.dissentmagazine.org/article/the-agoraphobic-fantasy-of-tradlife/

Ind, Lucas. 2023. 'Why I am a Tracey Emin Apologist', *The Courtauldian*, 27 October, www.courtauldian.com/single-post/why-i-am-a-tracey-emin-apologist

Jameson, Fredric. 2003. 'Future Cities'. *New Left Review* 21, May–June: 65–79.

Jameson, Fredric. 2002. *A Singular Modernity: Essay on the Ontology of the Present*. London: Verso.

Jameson, Fredric. 1998. '"End of Art" or "End of History"?' In *The Cultural Turn: Selected Writings on the Postmodern 1983–1998*. 1991. London: Verso.

Jameson, Fredric. 1991. *Postmodernism, or the Cultural Logic of Late Capitalism*. Durham NC: Duke University Press.

Jameson, Fredric. 1983. 'Postmodernism and Consumer Society'. In Hal Foster, ed, *The Anti-aesthetic: Essays on Postmodern Culture*. Port Townsend WA: Bay Press.

Jeanjean, Stéphanie. 2019. 'Disobedient Video in France in the 1970s: Video Production by Women's Collectives'. *Afterall* 48 (Autumn/Winter): 118–125.

Jones, Amelia. 2000. '"Post-Feminism'—A Remasculinization of Culture?' In Mira Schor and Susan Bee, eds. *M/E/A/N/I/N/G: An Anthology of Artists' Writings, Theory, and Criticism*. Durham NC: Duke University Press.

Kadri, Ali. 2024. *The Accumulation of Waste*. Leiden: Brill.

Kain, Philip J. 1993. 'Marx, Housework, and Alienation'. *Hypatia* 1(1): 121–44.

Kapstein, Ethan B. 2006. 'The New Global Slave Trade'. *Foreign Affairs* (November/December) www.foreignaffairs.com/articles/2006-11-01/new-global-slave-trade

Kelly, Mary. 1999. *Post-partum Document*. Berkeley: University of California Press.

Kelly, Mary and Griselda Pollock. 2001. 'In Conversation at the Vancouver Art Gallery' (1989). In Hilary Robinson, ed. *Feminism-Art-Theory: An Anthology 1968-2000*. Oxford: Blackwell: 369–77.

Kester, Grant. 2009. 'Lessons in Futility: Francis Alÿs and the Legacy of May '68'. *Third Text* 23(4): 407–20

Kidmose, Anne. 2024. 'Rural Kenyans Power West's AI Revolution. Now They Want More'. *Al Jazeera*, 3 February, www.aljazeera.com/features/2024/2/3/in-rural-kenya-young-people-join-ai-revolution

Kinyon, Lilly, Nives Dolšak, Aseem Prakash. 2023. 'When, Where, and Which Climate Activists Have Vandalized Museums', *npj Clim. Action* 2(1) https://doi.org/10.1038/s44168-023-00054-5

Klagge, James C. 1986. 'Marx's Realms of "Freedom"' and "Necessity"'. *Canadian Journal of Philosophy* 14(4): 769–77.

Kleiman, Kathy. 2022. *Proving Ground: The Untold Story of the Six Women Who Programmed the World's First Modern Computer*. Grand Central Publishing.

Klein, Naomi. 2023. 'AI machines aren't hallucinating. But their makers are'. *The Guardian*, 8 May, www.theguardian.com/commentisfree/2023/may/08/ai-machines-hallucinating-naomi-klein

Kokoli, Alexandra. 2023. 'Walking (to) Greenham, Again'. *Performance Research* 28(8): 34–45.

Kokoli, Alexandra. 2021. 'Aesthetic Labour of Protest, Now and Then: Women's Peace Camp at Greenham Common (1981–2000)'. In Brenda Schmahmann, ed. *Iconic Works by Feminists and Gender Activists*. London: Routledge.

Kokoli, Alexandra, ed. 2008. *Feminism Reframed: Reflections on Art and Difference*. Newcastle: Cambridge Scholars Publishers.

Kokoli, Alexandra. 2004. 'Undoing "homeliness" in Feminist Art: Feministo: Portrait of the Artist as a Housewife (1975–7)'. *n.paradoxa: international feminist art journal* 13: 75–83.

Kompatsiaris, Panos. 2015. 'Art Struggles: Confronting Internships and Unpaid Labour in Contemporary Art'. *triple C* 13(2): 554–6.

Kozlowski, Michal, Jan Sowa and Kuba Szreder, eds. 2014. *The Art Factory*. Warsaw: Free/Slow University.

Kracauer, Siegfried. 1998 [1930]. *The Salaried Masses: Duty and Distraction in Weimar Germany*. Trans. Quintin Hoare. London: Verso.

Krasny, Elke. 2017. 'Exposed: The Politics of Infrastructure in VALIE EXPORT's Transparent Space'. *Third Text* 31(1): 133–46.

Krikortz, Erik, Airi Triisberg, Minna Henriksson, eds. 2015. *Art Workers: Material Conditions and Labour Struggles in Contemporary Art Practice*. Berlin: Konst-ig.

Krumholz, Linda, Estella Lauter. 1990. 'Annotated Bibliography on Feminist Aesthetics in the Visual Arts'. *Hypatia* 5(2): 158–72.

Kumdu, Kimtee. 2024. 'The #MeToo Movement: Investigating the Lasting International Impacts'. *Harvard International Review*, 31 January, https://hir.harvard.edu/metoo-movement-international/

Kunst, Bojana. 2015. *Artist at Work: Proximity of Art and Capital*. London: Zero Books.

Kwon, Miwon. 2004. *One Place after Another*. Cambridge, MA: The MIT Press.

Laboria, Cuboniks. 2018 [online 2015]. *Xenofeminist Manifesto: A Politics for Alienation*. London: Verso.

Laclau, Ernesto and Chantal Mouffe. 2014 [1985]. *Hegemony and Socialist Strategy: Towards a Radical Democratic Politics*. London: Verso.

Lacy, Suzanne, ed. 1995. *Mapping the Terrain: New Genre Public Art*. Seattle WA: Bay Press.

Lange, Christy. 2012. '7th Berlin Biennial'. *Frieze*, 1 June, https://frieze.com/article/7th-berlin-biennale

Lebovici, Elizabeth and Giovanna Zapperi. 2018. 'Maso and Miso in the Land of Men's Rights'. *e-flux journal* 92 (June), www.e-flux.com/journal/92/205771/maso-and-miso-in-the-land-of-men-s-rights/

Lefebvre, Henri. 1968. *Le droit à la ville* [The Right to the City]. Paris: Anthropos.

Lenin, Vladimir Ilyich. 2017. *Imperialism, or the Highest Stage of Capitalism: A Popular Outline*, pamphlet, Petrograd 1917, Lenin Internet Archive 2005. https://www.marxists.org/archive/lenin/works/1916/imp-hsc/

Lenin, Vladimir Ilyich. 2015. 'Lenin's letter to Inessa Armand, 24 January 1915'. Trans. Andrew Rothstein, Lenin Internet Archive, www.marxists.org/archive/lenin/works/1915/jan/24.htm

Leslie, Esther. 2005. *Synthetic Worlds: Nature, Art and the Chemical Industry*. London: Reaktion Books.

Levine, Lucie. 2020. 'Was Modern Art Really a CIA Psy-Op?' *Jstor Daily*, 1 April, https://daily.jstor.org/was-modern-art-really-a-cia-psy-op/

Lewis, Sophie. 2025. *Enemy Feminisms: TERFs, Policewomen, and Girlbosses against Liberation*. Chicago Il: Haymarket Books.

Lewis, Sophie, 2021. *Full Surrogacy Now: Feminism against the Family*. London: Verso.

Lind, Maria. 2018. 'Soon'. *e-flux journal* 93 (September) www.e-flux.com/journal/93/213345/soon/

Lippard, Lucy. 2017a. 'Floating between Past and Future: The Indigenisation of Environmental Politics', *Afterall* 43(1): 33–7.

Lippard, Lucy. 2017b. 'From the Archives: No Regrets'. *Art in America*, 16 March, www.artnews.com/art-in-america/features/from-the-archives-no-regrets-63252/

Lippard, Lucy. 2013. 'The Anatomy of an Annual' (1978). In Angela Dimitrakaki and Lara Perry, eds. *Politics in a Glass Case: Feminism, Exhibition Cultures and Curatorial Transgressions*, Liverpool: Liverpool University Press.

Lippard, Lucy. 1997 [1973] *Six Years: The Dematerialisation of the Art Object from 1966 to 1972*. Berkeley: University of California Press.

Liss, Andrea. 2009. *Feminist Art and the Maternal*. Minneapolis: University of Minnesota Press.

Lloyd, Kirsten. 2017. 'If You Lived Here…: A Case Study on Social Reproduction in Feminist Art History'. In Victoria Horne and Lara Perry, eds. *Feminism and Art History Now: Radical Critiques of Theory and Practice. London*: I.B. Tauris.

Lloyd, Kirsten. 2012. 'Endgame? Reconfiguring the Artwork'. *Third Text* 26(5): 529–42.

Lonzi, Carla. 1977. 'Let's Spit on Hegel!' Trans. Veronica Newman. Pensiero Femminista Radicale http://femrad.blogspot.com/p/blog-page.html

Lonzi, Carla. 2012. *Autoportrait* (1969). Trans. and ed. Giovanna Zapperi. Geneva: JRP Ringier.

Lorde, Audrey. 2007 [1984]. 'The Master's Tools Will Never Dismantle the Master's House'. In *Sister Outsider: Essays and Speeches*. Berkeley, CA: Crossing Press: 110–14.

Lugones, Maria. 2010. 'Toward a Decolonial Feminism'. *Hypatia* 25(4): 742–59.

Lütticken, Sven. 2016. 'The Coming Exception'. *New Left Review* 99 (May–June): 111–36.

Luxemburg, Rosa. 1999 [1900]. 'Reform or Revolution.' Internet Archive, Trans. Integer. www.marxists.org/archive/luxemburg/1900/reform-revolution/

Lyotard, Jean-François. 1993 [1974]). *Libidinal Economy*. Trans. Iain Hamilton Grant. Bloomington and Indianapolis: Indiana University Press.

Magdoff, Fred and Harry Magdoff. 2004. 'Disposable Workers: Today's Reserve Army of Labor'. *Monthly Review*, 1 April, https://monthlyreview. org/2004/04/01/disposable-workers-todays-reserve-army-of-labor/

Mahdawi, Arwa. 2025. 'Unleash Your Masculine Energy the Mark Zuckerberg Way!' *The Guardian*, 18 January, www.theguardian.com/commentisfree/2025/ jan/18/mark-zuckerberg-masculine-energy

Majewska, Ewa. 2021. *Feminist Antifascism: Counter-publics of the Common*. London: Verso.

Majewska, Ewa. 2017. 'For a Feminist (Art) Institution: Weak Resistance as Methodology'. transit display gallery, 22 May, www.youtube.com/watch?v= c3sStWyGNls

Malabou, Catherine. 2024. 'Contemporary Political Adventures of Meaning: What Is a Floating Signifier?' *Critical Inquiry* 50(2): 306–16.

Malm, Andreas. 2019. 'Against Hybridism: Why We Need to Distinguish between Nature and Society, Now more than Ever'. *Historical Materialism* 27(2): 156–87.

Mann, Jessica. 2012. 'What do you mean, the good old days?', *The Guardian*, 28 April, www.theguardian.com/lifeandstyle/2012/apr/28/housewives-fifties-good-old-days

Marable, Manning. 2003 [2000]. '"A'n't I a Woman?", Sojourner Truth, 1851'. In Manning Marable and Leith Mullings, eds. *Let Nobody Turn Us Around: Voices of Resistance, Reform and Renewal, An African American Anthology*. Lanham, Boulder, New York, Oxford: Rowman & Littlefield.

Marshall, Colin. 2023. 'How the CIA secretly used Jackson Pollock and other Abstract Expressionists to Fight the Cold War'. *Open Culture*, 27 October, www.openculture.com/2023/10/how-the-cia-secretly-used-jackson-pollock-other-abstract-expressionists-to-fight-the-cold-war.html

Martinez, Rosa. 2010. 'Women in Art, a Politically Unbalanced Relationship'. European Institute of the Mediterranean/IEMed, August, www.iemed.org/publication/women-in-art-a-politically-unbalanced-relationship/

Marx, Karl. 1996. Karl Marx: Capital, Vol I. In *Karl Marx and Frederick Engels Collected Works Vol 35*. London: Laurence & Wishart.

Marx, Karl. 1973. 'Preface to *A Contribution to the Critique of Political Economy*'. In Karl *Marx and Fridreich Engels, Selected Works, Vol 1*. Moscow: Progress Publishers.

Marks, Steven G. 2016. *The Information Nexus: Global Capitalism from the Renaissance to the Present*. Cambridge: Cambridge University Press.

Mazur, Paul M. 1931. 'The Gold Crisis: Its Causes and Significance'. *Current History* 35(2): 167–72.

McClintock, Anne. 1995. *Imperial Leather: Race, Gender, and Sexuality in the Colonial Contest*. New York: Routledge.

McDonough, Tom. 2008. 'Invisible Cities: Henri Lefebvre's The Explosion'. *Artforum* 46(9) May, www.artforum.com/features/invisible-cities-henri-lefebvres-the-explosion-188139/

McIntyre, Niamh. 2019. 'Gender Pay Gap Figures: Debunking the Myths', *The Guardian*, 5 April, www.theguardian.com/world/2019/apr/05/gender-pay-gap-figures-debunking-the-myths

McKee, Yates. 2017. *Strike Art: Contemporary Art and the Post-Occupy Condition*. London: Verso.

McLellan, Josie. 2020. 'From the Political to the Personal: Work and Class in 1970s Feminist Art'. *Twentieth Century British History* 31(2): 252–74.

McLuhan, Marshall. 1994 [1964]. *Understanding Media: The Extensions of Man*. Cambridge MA: The MIT Press.

McMahon, Liv, Zoe Kleinman, Courtney Subramanian. 2025. 'Facebook and Instagram get rid of fact checkers', *BBC*, 7 January, www.bbc.co.uk/news/articles/cly74mpy8klo

McMillan, Kate. 2020. *Representation of Women Artists in Britain During 2020*. London: Freelands Foundation.

McMillan, Kate. 2018. *Representation of Women Artists in Britain During 2018*. London: Freelands Foundation.

McMunn, Anne, Lauren Bird, Elizabeth Webb, Amanda Sacker. 2020. 'Gender Divisions of Paid and Unpaid Work in Contemporary UK Couples'. *Work, Employment and Society* 34(2): 155–73.

McRobbie, Angela. 2010. 'Reflections on Feminism, Immaterial Labour and the Post-Fordist Regime'. *New Formations* 70: 60–76.

Medina, Maria Clara. 2023. 'The Feminisation of Resistance: The Narratives of #Ni Una Menos as Social Transformative Action'. *Journal of Political Power* 16(2): 237–53.

Meiksins Wood, Ellen. 2002 [1999]. *The Origin of Capitalism: A Longer View*. London: Verso.

Meiksins Wood, Ellen. 1995. *Democracy Against Capitalism: Renewing Historical Materialism*. Cambridge: Cambridge University Press.

Meskimmon, Marsha. 2022. *Transnational Feminisms and Art's Transhemispheric Histories Ecologies and Genealogies*. London and New York: Routledge.

Meskimmon, Marsha. 2020. *Transnational Feminisms, Transversal Politics and Art: Entanglements and Intersections*. London and New York: Routledge.

Meskimmon, Marsha and Dorothy Price, eds. 2013. *Women, the Arts and Globalisation*. Manchester: Manchester University Press.

Mies, Maria. 1986. *Patriarchy and Accumulation on a World Scale: Women and the International Division of Labour*. London: Zed Books.

Miéville, China. 2022. *A Spectre, Haunting: On the Communist Manifesto*. Head of Zeus.

Miranda, Magally and Kyle Lane-McKinley. 2017. 'Artwashing, or between Social Practice and Social Reproduction'. *A Blade of Grass*, 1 February, www.academia.edu/33913530/Artwashing_or_Between_Social_Practice_and_Social_Reproduction

MFK. 2011. *Do the Right Thing! A Manual from MFK*. Stockholm.

Mohanty, Chandra Talpade. 2003. *Feminism without Borders: Decolonizing Theory, Practising Solidarity*. Durham NC: Duke University Press.

Molesworth, Helen, ed. 2003. *Work Ethic*. University Park: Pennsylvania State University Press.

Moody, Kim. 2018. 'High Tech, Low Growth: Robots and the Future of Work'. *Historical Materialism* 26(4): 3–34.

Morrison, James Ashley. 2016. 'Shocking Intellectual Austerity: The Role of Ideas in the Demise of the Gold Standard in Britain'. *International Organization* 70(1): 175–207.

Moss, Irene and Lila Katzen. 1973. 'Separatism: The New Rip-Off', *Feminist Art Journal* 2(2): 7ff.

Mulvey, Laura. 1991. 'A Phantasmagoria of the Female Body: The Work of Cindy Sherman'. *New Left Review* I/188 (July–August): 137–150.

Mulvey, Laura. 1975. 'Visual Pleasure and Narrative Cinema'. *Screen* 16(3): 6–18.

Murray, Jenni. 2011. '20th Century Britain: The Woman's Hour', BBC, 3 March, www.bbc.co.uk/history/british/modern/jmurray_01.shtml

Murray, Ros. 2016. 'Raised Fists: Politics, Technology and Embodiment in 1970s French Feminist Video Collectives'. *Camera Obscura* 31(1): 92–121.

Myers, Matt. 2025. *The Halted March of the European Left*. Oxford: Oxford University Press.

Nascheck, Melissa. 2025. 'Why Elites Love Identity Politics: An Interview with Vivek Chibber'. *Jacobin*, 14 January, https://jacobin.com/2025/01/elite-identity-politics-professional-class

Nead, Lynda. 1992. *The Female Nude: Art, Obscenity and Sexuality*. New York: Routledge.

Neveling, Patrick. 2020. 'The Anthropology of Special Economic Zones (Free Ports, Export Processing Zones, Tax Havens)'. In Arkebe Oqubay and Justib Yifu Lin, eds. *The Oxford Handbook of Industrial Hubs and Economic Development*. Oxford: Oxford University Press: 190–205.

Neuendorf, Henri. 2016. 'Marina Abramović Says Children Hold Back Female Artists'. *Artnet News*, 25 July, https://news.artnet.com/art-world/marina-abramovic-says-children-hold-back-female-artists-575150

Nilsen, Alf Gunvald. 2020. 'Marx on Exploitation: An ABC for an Unequal World'. *Open Democracy*, 23 November, www.opendemocracy.net/en/beyond-trafficking-and-slavery/marx-exploitation-abc-unequal-world/

Nochlin, Linda and Maura Reilly, eds. 2007. *Global Feminisms: New Directions in Contemporary Art*. London: Merrell Publishers.

Noys, Benjamin. 2014. *Malign Velocities: Accelerationism and Capitalism*. London: Zero Books.

Noys, Benjamin. 2010. *The Persistence of the Negative: A Critique of Contemporary Continental Theory*. Edinburgh: Edinburgh University Press.

Novick, Ilana. 2018. 'Activists Protest at Whitney Museum, Demanding Vice Chairman and Owner of Tear Gas Manufacturer "Must Go"'. *Hyperallergic*, 9 December, https://hyperallergic.com/475198/activists-protest-at-whitney-museum-demanding-vice-chairman-and-owner-of-tear-gas-manufacturer-must-go/

Nyabola, Nanjala. 2023. 'ChatGTP and the Sweatshops Powering the Digital Age'. *Al Jazeera*, 23 January, www.aljazeera.com/opinions/2023/1/23/sweatshops-are-making-our-digital-age-work

Nyabola, Nanjala. 2018. *Digital Democracy, Analogue Politics: How the Internet Era Is Transforming Politics in Kenya*. London: Bloomsbury Academic.

O'Grady, Lorraine. 1992. 'Olympia's Maid: Reclaiming Black Female Subjectivity'. *Afterimage* 20(1): 14–15.

O'Hanian, Hunter. 2017. 'An Interview with Linda Nochlin'. College Art Association (CAA), 8 June, www.collegeart.org/news/2017/06/08/an-interview-with-linda-nochlin/

Orozco Espinel, Camila and Rebeca Gomez Betancourt. 2022. 'A History of the Institutionalization of Feminist Economics through Its Tensions and Founders'. *History of Political Economy* 54: 159–92.

Owens, Craig. 1983. 'The Discourse of Others: Feminists and Postmodernism'. In Hal Foster, ed. *The Anti-aesthetic: Essays on Postmodern Culture*. Port Townsend WA: Bay Press.

Pal, Maia and George Souvlis. 2018. 'For a Marxist Poetics of Science: An Interview with Esther Leslie'. *Verso Blog*, 5 January, www.versobooks.com/blogs/news/3550-for-a-marxist-poetics-of-science-an-interview-with-esther-leslie?srsltid=AfmBOoqslnPZP6mfM1uow6z9Ra_1t6SH4bvsnjJjVNtYa7Xh2vfbZZrq

Parker, Rozsika and Griselda Pollock, eds. 1987. *Framing Feminism: Art and the Women's Movement 1970-1985*. London: The Women's Press.

Parker, Rozsika and Griselda Pollock. 1981. *Old Mistresses: Women, Art and Ideology*. London: HarperCollins.

Pasquinelli, Matteo. 2023. *The Eye of the Master: A Social History of Artificial Intelligence*. London and New York: Verso.

Passoti, Eleonora. 2020. 'Militancy with a Twist: Fighting Art to Deter Displacement in Boyle Heights, Los Angeles'. In *Resisting Redevelopment:*

Protest in Aspiring Global Cities. Cambridge: Cambridge University Press: 301–23.

Pejic, Bojana et al., eds. 2010. *Gender Check: Femininity and Masculinity in the Art of Eastern Europe*. Cologne: Walter König.

Perlin, Nick. 2012. *Intern Nation: How to Earn Nothing and Learn Little in the Brave New Economy*. London: Verso.

Perry, Lara. 2017. 'The Artist's Housework: On Gender and the Division of Artistic and Domestic Labour in 19th-Century London'. *Third Text* 31(1): 15–29.

Petsche, Jackson. 2012–13. 'The Importance of Being Autonomous: Toward a Marxist Defense of Art for Art's Sake'. *Mediations* (Fall 2012–Spring 2013): 143–58. www.mediationsjournal.org/articles/the-importance-of-being-autonomous

Pollock, Griselda. 2021. 'Feminism and Art c. 1970: Writing (Art) Otherwise'. In Francesco Ventrella and Giovanna Zapperi , eds. *Feminism and Art in Postwar Italy: The Legacy of Carla Lonzi*. London: Bloomsbury.

Pollock, Griselda. 2015. 'Vision, Voice and Power: Feminist Art Histories and Marxism' (1988). In *Vision and Difference: Feminism, Femininity and the Histories of Art*, 3rd Edition. London: Verso.

Pollock, Griselda. 2014. 'Whither Art History?' *The Art Bulletin* 96(1): 9–23.

Pollock, Griselda, ed. 1996. *Generations and Geographies in Feminist Art*. London and New York: Routledge.

Pollock, Griselda. 1992. 'Panting, Feminism, History'. In Anne Phillips and Michele Barrett, eds. *Destabilizing Theory: Contemporary Feminist Debates*. Stanford: Stanford University Press.

Pollock, Griselda. 1987. 'Feminism and Modernism'. In Rozsika Parker and Griselda Pollock, eds. *Framing Feminism: Art and the Women's Movement 1970–1985*. London: The Women's Press.

Pollock, Griselda. 1979. 'Femininity, Feminism and the Hayward Annual Exhibition 1978'. *Feminist Review* 2(1): 33–55.

Pollack, Barbara. 2000. 'Babe Power'. *Art Monthly* 235 (April) www.artmonthly.co.uk/magazine/site/article/babe-power-by-barbara-pollack-april-2000

Portella, Elizabeth and Larry Allan Busk. 2024. 'The Formal and Real Subsumption of Gender Relations: Challenging the Transhistorical Status of Patriarchy'. *Historical Materialism* 32(3): 353–84.

Praznik, Katja. 2021. *Art Work: Invisible Labour and the Legacy of Yugoslav Socialism*. Toronto: Toronto University Press.

Prideaux, Sue. 2025. '"The Polynesians loved him": The astonishing revelations that cast Paul Gauguin in a new light'. *The Guardian*, 17 March, www.theguardian.com/artanddesign/2025/mar/17/polynesians-astonishing-revelations-paul-gauguin-syphilis-underage

Purdon, James. 2024. 'Fossil-Fuelled: The Sticky Relationship between Art and the Oil Industry'. *Apollo*, 15 May, https://apollo-magazine.com/art-british-oil-industry-shell-fossil-fuel/

Quaintance, Morgan. 2017. 'The New Conservatism: The New Conservatism and the UK Artworld's Performance of Progression'. *e-flux conversations*, October, https://conversations.e-flux.com/t/the-new-conservatism-complicity-and-the-uk-art-worlds-performance-of-progression/7200

Racjhman, John. 2009. 'Les Immatériaux or How to Construct the History of Exhibitions'. Tate Papers 12, (Autumn) www.tate.org.uk/research/tate-papers/12/les-immateriaux-or-how-to-construct-the-history-of-exhibitions

Rancière, Jacques. 2006. Hatred of Democracy. Trans. Steve Corcoran. London: Verso.

Raunig, Gerald, Gene Ray, Ulf Wuggenig, eds. 2011. Critique of Creativity: Precarity, Subjectivity and Resistance in the 'Creative Industries'. London: Mayfly Books.

Read, Jason. 2015. The Politics of Transindividuality. Leiden: Brill.

Renauld, Marie-Madeleine. 2021. 'Geneva Free Port: The World's Most Secretive Art Warehouse'. The Collector, 1 May, www.thecollector.com/geneva-free-port-the-worlds-most-secretive-art-warehouse/

Ribalta, Jorge. 2015. 'Foreword'. In Not Yet: On the Reinvention of the Documentary and the Critique of Modernism. Madrid: Reina Sofia.

Riviere, Joan. 1929. 'Womanliness as a Masquerade'. The International Journal of Psychoanalysis (10): 303–13.

Roberts, John. 2015. Revolutionary Time and the Avant Garde. London: Verso.

Roberts, John. 2007. The Intangibilities of Form: Skill and Deskilling in Art after the Readymade. London: Verso.

Robinson, Hilary. 2019. 'Witness It: Activism, Art, and the Feminist Performative Subject'. In Hilary Robinson and Maria Buszek, eds. A Companion to Feminist Art. Hoboken NJ: Blackwell-Wiley: 245–60.

Robinson, Joan. 1964 [1962]. Economic Philosophy. Hamondsworth: Penguin.

Rockhill, Gabriel. 2017. 'The CIA Reads French Theory: On the Intellectual Labour of Dismantling the Cultural Left'. The Philosophical Salon, 28 February, https://thephilosophicalsalon.com/the-cia-reads-french-theory-on-the-intellectual-labor-of-dismantling-the-cultural-left/

Rodríguez García, Magaly, Elise van Nederveen Meerkerk, Lex Heerma van Voss. 2017. 'Selling Sex in World Cities, 1600s-2000s'. In Magaly Rodríguez García, Elise van Nederveen Meerkerk, Lex Heerma van Voss, eds. Selling Sex in the City: A Global History of Prostitution, 1600s–2000s. Leiden: Brill.

Romer, Christy. 2019. 'Only a third of artists' income comes from their art, study finds'. Arts Professional, 18 January, www.artsprofessional.co.uk/news/only-third-artists-income-comes-their-art-research-finds

Rose, Barbara. 1993. 'Is it Art? Orlan and the Transgressive Act'. Art in America 81(2): 83–125.

Rosler, Martha. 1979. 'Lookers, Buyers, Dealers, Makers: Thoughts on Audience'. Exposure 17(1): 10–25.

Ross, Kristin. 2002. May '68 and Its Afterlives. Chicago: Chicago University Press.

Rottenberg, Catherine. 2018. The Rise of Neoliberal Feminism. Oxford: Oxford University Press.

Rowbotham, Sheila. 2014 [1974]. Women, Resistance and Revolution: A History of Women and Revolution in the Modern World. London: Verso.

Ruddock, Daisy. 2023. 'Art Institutions Accused of Censoring pro-Palestine Views', *The Index on Censorship*, 8 December, www.indexoncensorship. org/2023/12/art-institutions-accused-of-censoring-pro-palestine-views/

Rushkoff, Douglas. 2023. '"We will coup whoever we want!": The unbearable hubris of Musk and the billionaire tech bros', *The Guardian*, 25 November, www.theguardian.com/books/2023/nov/25/we-will-coup-whoever-we-want-the-unbearable-hubris-of-musk-and-the-billionaire-tech-bros

Sadler, Victoria. 2014. 'New Suffragettes Display at the National Portrait Gallery'. *HuffPost* 21 August, www.huffingtonpost.co.uk/victoria-sadler/new-suffragettes-national-portrait-gallery_b_5697155.html

Saltz, Jerry. 2004. 'Super Theory Woman'. *Artnet Magazine* (July), http://www.artnet.com/Magazine/features/jsaltz/saltz7-8-04.asp

Sandberg, Cheryl. 2013. *Lean In: Women, Work and the Will to Lead*. New York: Alfred Knopf.

Santoro, Suzanne. 2019. 'Then and Now / Allora e Ora', talk at Centro anti violenza, Erinna, Vt. 2019, www.suzannesantoro.com/single-post/then-and-now-allora-e-ora

Sayej, Nadja. 2017. 'What's inside Ivanka Trump's male-dominated $25m art collection?' *The Guardian*, 27 July, https://www.theguardian.com/artanddesign/2017/jul/27/ivanka-trump-jared-kushner-art-collection

Schapiro, Miriam. 1972. 'The Education of Women as Artists: Project Womanhouse'. *Art Journal* 31(3): 268–70.

Schuhrke, Jeff. 2024. *Blue Collar Empire: The Untold story of US Labor's Global Anticommunist Campaign*. London: Verso.

SDLD50. 2018. 'The Biennial of Very Fine People, on Both Sides'. *Mute*, 12 September, www.metamute.org/community/your-posts/biennial-very-fine-people-both-sides

Sefeni, Suzie. 2023. 'The Invisible Labour of Africa in the Digital Revolution'. *African Argument*, 17 March, https://africanarguments.org/2023/03/the-invisible-labour-of-africa-in-the-digital-revolution/

Sekula, Allan. 1986. 'The Body and the Archive'. *October* 39 (Winter): 3–64.

Seymour, Richard. 2024. *Disaster Nationalism: The Downfall of Liberal Civilization*. London: Verso.

Simpson, Gerry. 2016. 'James Lorimer and the Character of Sovereigns: The Institutes as 21st Century Treatise'. *The European Journal of International Law* 27(2): 431–46.

Smith, John. 2016. *Imperialism in the Twenty-First Century: The Globalization of Production, Super-Exploitation, and the Crisis of Capitalism*. New York: Monthly Review Press.

Smith, Roberta. 2007. 'They Are Artists Who Are Women: Hear Them Roar'. *The New York Times*, 23 March, www.nytimes.com/2007/03/23/arts/design/23glob.html

Smith, Roberta. 1999. 'Lee Lozano, 68, Conceptual Artist Who Boycotted Women for Years'. *The New York Times*, 18 October, www.nytimes.com/1999/10/18/arts/lee-lozano-68-conceptual-artist-who-boycotted-women-for-years.html

Shaikh, Anwar. 1990. 'Capital as a Social Relation'. In John Eatwell, Murray Milgate, Peter Newman, eds. *Marxian Economics*. London: W. W. Norton & Company.

Shaked, Nizan. 2022. *Museums and Wealth: The Politics of Contemporary Art Collections*. London: Bloomsbury.

Shaked, Nizan. 2019a. 'Looking the Other Way: Art Philanthropy, Lean Government and Econo-fascism in the USA'. *Third Text* 32(3): 375–95.

Shaked, Nizan. 2019b. 'Getting to a Base Line in Identity Politics: The Marxist Debate'. In Eddie Chambers, ed. *The Routledge Companion to African American Art History*. London and New York: 209–18.

Shaked, Nizan. 2017. *The Synthetic Proposition: Conceptualism and the Political Referent in Contemporary Art*. Manchester: Manchester University Press.

Sholette, Greg. 2017. *Delirium and Resistance: Activist Art and the Crisis of Capitalism*, Kim Charnley ed. London: Pluto Press.

Sholette, Greg. 2010. *Dark Matter: Art and Politics in the Age of Enterprise Culture*. London: Pluto Press.

Schor, Gabrielle. 2025. *The Feminist Avant-Garde: Art of the 1970s, The Verbund Collection, Vienna*. London: Prestel.

Seijdel, Jorinde and Liesbeth Melis, eds. 2009. *Open (17) A Precarious Existence: Vulnerability in the Public Domain*. NA1010 Publishers.

Sliwinska, Basia, ed. 2021. *Feminist Visual Activism and the Body*. New York: Routledge.

Sloane, Nan. 2018. *The Women in the Room: Labour's Forgotten History*. London: I.B. Tauris.

Sokolowska, Joanna, ed. 2018. *All Men Become Sisters*. Lodz: Museum of Lodz.

Solanas, Valerie. 2004 [1967]. *SCUM Manifesto*. London: Verso.

Solis, Marie. 2021. 'Koa Beck on dismantling the persistence of white feminism', NBC News, 9 January, www.nbcnews.com/news/nbcblk/koa-beck-dismantling-persistence-white-feminism-n1253555

Spivak, Gayatri Chakravorty. 2003. *Death of a Discipline*. New York: Columbia University Press.

Stabile, Carole A. 1997. 'Feminism and the Ends of Postmodernism'. In Rosemary Hennessy and Chrys Ingraham, eds. *Materialist Feminism: A Reader in Class, Difference and Women's Lives*. New York and London: Routledge.

Stacey, Frances. 2014. *Constructed Situations: A New History of the Situationist International*. London: Pluto Press.

Stallabrass, Julian. 2022. 'Contemporary art is popular – but it's still about money and power'. *Open Democracy*, 22 July. www.opendemocracy.net/en/stallabrass-contemporary-art-market-audience/

Standing, Guy. 2011. *The Precariat: The New Dangerous Class*. London: Bloomsbury.

Steel, Mark. 2013. 'Labour says the working class no longer exists, so why do 60 per cent of us claim to belong to it?' *The Independent*, 15 January, www.independent.co.uk/voices/comment/labour-says-the-working-class-no-longer-exists-so-why-do-60-per-cent-of-us-claim-to-belong-to-it-8452739.html

Stella-Sawicka, Jo. 2018. 'Social Work: A New Section dedicated to Women Who Challenged the Market'. *Frieze*, 26 June, https://frieze.com/article/social-work-new-section-dedicated-women-who-challenged-market

Steinhauer, Jillian. 2017. 'How Mierle Laderman Ukeles Turned Maintenance Work into Art'. *Hyperallergic*, 17 February, https://hyperallergic.com/355255/how-mierle-laderman-ukeles-turned-maintenance-work-into-art/

Steyerl, Hito. 2022. 'Duty-free Art'. In Sven Lütticken, ed. *Autonomy: A Critical Reader*. London: Afterall Books.

Steyerl, Hito. 2011. 'Art as Occupation: Claims for an Autonomy of Life'. *e-flux journal* 30 (December), www.e-flux.com/journal/30/68140/art-as-occupation-claims-for-an-autonomy-of-life/

Steyerl, Hito. 2010. 'Politics of Art: Contemporary Art and the Transition to Post-Democracy', *e-flux journal* 21 (December), www.e-flux.com/journal/21/67696/politics-of-art-contemporary-art-and-the-transition-to-post-democracy/

Strom, Timothy Erik. 2025. 'Exponential Abyss'. *Sidecar, New Left Review*, 18 January, https://newleftreview.org/sidecar/posts/exponential-abyss

Sulley, Steven. 2022. 'The Remarkable Resilience of Contemporary Art as an Investment'. *Forbes*, 28 September, www.forbes.com/sites/forbesbusinesscouncil/2022/09/28/the-remarkable-resilience-of-contemporary-art-as-an-investment/?sh=df153845a663

Sunkara, Bhaskar. 2024. 'The Age of Class Dealignment'. *Jacobin*, 21 November, https://jacobin.com/2024/11/dealignment-left-parties-working-class

Sweezey, Paul M. and Harry Magdoff. 1987. *Economic History as It Happened, Volume IV: Stagnation and the Financial Explosion*. New York: Monthly Review.

Tang, Jeannine. 2013. 'The Problem of Equality, or Translating "Woman" in the Age of Global Exhibitions'. In Angela Dimitrakaki and Lara Perry, eds. *Politics in a Glass Case: Feminism, Exhibition Cultures and Curatorial Transgressions*. Liverpool: Liverpool University Press.

Tebaldi, Catherine. 2024. 'Granola Nazis: Fascism in the World of Health, Fitness and Nature'. C-REX Center for Research on Extremism, University of Oslo, 29 January, www.sv.uio.no/c-rex/english/news-and-events/right-now/2024/granola-nazis.html

Teixeira Pinto, Ana. 2019. 'Capitalism with a Transhuman Face'. *Third Text* 33(3): 315–36.

Teman, Elly and Zsuzsa Berend. 2021. 'Surrogacy as Family Project: How Surrogates Articulate Familial Identity and Belonging'. *Journal of Family Issues* 42(6): 1143–65.

Temblon, Mary and Lucia Fort, eds. 2008. *Girls' Education in the 21st Century: Gender Equality, Empowerment and Economic Growth*. Washington: The World Bank.

Thatcher, Jennifer. 2013. '50/50'. *Art Monthly* 367 (June): 5–8. www.artmonthly.co.uk/magazine/site/article/50-50-by-jennifer-thatcher-june-2013

Thier, Hadas. 2020a. *A People's Guide to Capitalism: An Introduction to Marxist Economics*. Chicago Il: Haymarket Books.

Thier, Hadas. 2020b. 'The Working Class Is the Vast Majority of Society'. *Jacobin*, 13 September, https://jacobin.com/2020/09/working-class-peoples-guide-capitalism-marxist-economics

Thompson, Nato, ed. 2011. *Living as Form: Socially Engaged Art from 1991–2011*. New York: Creative Time Books & Cambridge MA: The MIT Press.

Tobin, Amy. 2023. *Women Artists Together: Art in the Age of Women's Liberation*. New Haven, Co & London: Yale University Press.

Tolokonnikova, Nadya and Slavoj Žižek. 2014. *Comradely Greetings: The Letters of Nadya Tolokonnikova and Slavoj Žižek*. London: Verso.

Tormos-Aponte, Fernando, Shariana Ferrer-Núñez and Carolina Hernandez. 2023. 'Intersectional Politics of the International Women's Strike'. *Journal of Women, Politics & Policy* 44(4): 470–85.

Toscano, Alberto and Jee Kinkle. 2014. *Cartographies of the Absolute*. Winchester UK: Zero Books.

Toss, John. 2005. 'Masculinities in an Industrialized Society: Britain, 1800-1914'. *Journal of British Studies* 44(2): 330–42.

Toupin, Louise. 2018. *Wages for Housework: A History of an International Feminist Movement*, 1972–77. Trans. Käthe Roth. London: Pluto Press.

Trodd, Tamara. 2024. 'Helen Chadwick's "Of Mutability": Visual Pleasure and Goddess Imagery in British and American Art and Theory of the 1970s and 1980s'. *Woman's Art Journal* 45(2): 25–36.

Trudell, Megan. 2017. 'The Women of 1917'. *Jacobin*, 25 May, www.jacobinmag.com/2017/05/women-workers-strike-russian-revolution-bolshevik-party-feminism

Tsianos, Vassilis and Dimitris Papadopoulos. 2015. 'DIWY! Precarity in Embodied Capitalism'. In Angela Dimitrakaki and Kirsten Lloyd, eds. *ECONOMY: Art, Production and the Subject in the 21st Century*. Liverpool: Liverpool University Press.

Tulke, Julia. 2022. 'Dear Documenta: 5 Years On: A Conversation with Eirini Efstathiou'. *Greek Studies Now Cultural Analysis Network*, 10 May, https://gc.fairead.net/dear-documenta-5-years-on

Van Goethem, Geert. 2006. 'An International Experiment of Women Workers: The International Federation of Working Women, 1919–1924'. *Revue Belge de Philologie et d' Histoire*, 84(4): 1025–47.

Varagur, Krithika. 2017. 'Revealed: Reality of Life Working in an Ivanka Trump Factory'. *The Guardian*, 13 June, www.theguardian.com/us-news/2017/jun/13/revealed-reality-of-a-life-working-in-an-ivanka-trump-clothing-factory

Varia, Nisha. 2016. 'This is how women are exploited in today's global workforce'. *World Economic Forum*, 7 March, www.weforum.org/agenda/2016/03/this-is-how-women-are-exploited-in-today-s-global-workforce/

Varoufakis, Yanis. 2024. *Technofeudalism: What Killed Capitalism*. London: Penguin.

Vishmidt, Marina. 2018. *Speculation as a Mode of Production: Forms of Value Subjectivity in Art and Capital*. Leiden: Brill.

Vishmidt, Marina. 2015. 'The Manifestation of the Discourse of the Commons in the Art Field'. Kunci Cultural Studies Center, 30 March, http://kunci.or.id/articles/marina-vishmidt-commons-in-the-field-of-art/

Vishmidt, Marina. 2013. '"Mimesis of the Hardened and the Alienated": Social Practice as Business Model'. *e-flux journal* 43 (March) www.e-flux.com/journal/43/60197/mimesis-of-the-hardened-and-alienated-social-practice-as-business-model/

Vishmidt, Marina and Neil Gray. 2011. 'The Economy of Abolition/Abolition of the Economy'. *Variant* 42 www.variant.org.uk/42texts/EconomyofAbolition.html

Visser, Jelle. 2024. 'Did Employers Abandon Collective Bargaining? A Comparative Analysis of the Weakening of Collective Bargaining in the OECD'. *Industrial Relations Journal* 55(5): 350–77.

von Osten, Marion. 2009. 'Irene ist Viele! Or What We Call "Productive" Forces'. *e-flux journal* 8 (September), www.e-flux.com/journal/08/61381/irene-ist-viele-or-what-we-call-productive-forces/

Voon, Claire. 2017. 'LGBTQ Refugee Rights Group Steals Artwork from Documenta in Athens'. *Hyperallergic*, 1 June, https://hyperallergic.com/382407/lgbtq-refugee-rights-group-steals-artwork-from-documenta-in-athens/.

Wade, Nicholas. 2010. 'Tug of War Pits Genes of Parents in the Fetus'. *The New York Times*, 13 September, www.nytimes.com/2010/09/14/health/14gene.html

Wajcman, Judy and Erin Young. 2023. 'Feminism Confronts AI: The Gender Relations of Digitalisation'. In Jude Browne, Stephen Cave, Eleanor Drage, Kerry McInerney, eds. *Feminist AI: Critical Perspectives on Algorithms, Data, and Intelligent Machines*: Oxford: Oxford University Press.

Wajcman, Judy. 2010. 'Feminist Theories of Technology'. *Cambridge Journal of Economics* 34(1): 143–52.

Wajcman, Judy. 1991. *Feminism Confronts Technology*. University Park: Pennsylvania State University Press.

Walsh, Joan. 2025. 'Kamala Haris was poised to crush the women's vote. What went wrong?' *The Nation*, 17 January, www.thenation.com/article/society/women-voters-gender-gap-kamala-harris/

Walsh, Peter William. 2022. 'Q&A: The UK's policy to send asylum seekers to Rwanda. Migration Observatory commentary'. COMPAS, University of Oxford. https://migrationobservatory.ox.ac.uk/resources/commentaries/qa-the-uks-policy-to-send-asylum-seekers-to-rwanda/

Walters, Joanna. 2018. 'Artist Nan Goldin Stages Opioids Protest at Metropolitian Museum's Sackler Wing'. *The Guardian*, 11 March, www.theguardian.com/us-news/2018/mar/10/opioids-nan-goldin-protest-metropolitan-museum-sackler-wing

Wark, McKenzie. 2017. 'Responses to Revolution at 100 Questionnaire'. The Center for Creative Ecologies (November), https://creativeecologies.ucsc.edu/revolution-at-100-mckenzie-wark/

Wark, McKenzie. 2015. 'Communicative Capitalism'. *Public Seminar*, 23 March, https://publicseminar.org/2015/03/communicative-capitalism/

Warner, Michael, undated. 'Origins of the Congress for Cultural Freedom'. CIA, www.cia.gov/resources/csi/static/origins-congress-cultural-freedom.pdf

Watkins, Susan. 2018. 'Whose Feminisms'. *New Left Review* 109 (January–February): 5–76.

Weeks, Kathi. 2011. *The Problem with Work: Feminism, Marxism, Antiwork Politics, and Postwork Imaginaries*. Durham NC: Duke University Press.

Weigand, Kate. 2001. *Red Feminism: American Communism and the Making of Women's Liberation*. Baltimore: John Hopkins University Press.

Weigel, Moira. 2019. 'Feminist Cyborg Scholar Donna Haraway: "The Disorder of Our Era Isn't Necessary" Interview'. *The Guardian*, 20 June, www.theguardian.com/world/2019/jun/20/donna-haraway-interview-cyborg-manifesto-post-truth

Weiss, Penny A., ed. 2018. *Feminist Manifestos: A Global Documentary Reader*. New York: NYU Press.

White, Edward. 2016. 'Conservatism with Knobs On'. *The Paris Review*, 2 December, www.theparisreview.org/blog/2016/12/02/conservatism-with-knobs-on/

Wiseman, Eva. 2021. 'The Dark Side of Wellness: The Overlap between Spiritual Thinking and Far-right Conspiracies'. *The Guardian*, 17 October, www.theguardian.com/lifeandstyle/2021/oct/17/eva-wiseman-conspirituality-the-dark-side-of-wellness-how-it-all-got-so-toxic

Woods Chavisa. 2019. 'Hating Valerie Solanas (and Loving Violent Men)'. *Full Stop*, 21 May, www.full-stop.net/2019/05/21/features/chavisa-woods/solanas/

Wray, Ben. 2025. 'Population Decline Will Transform Our Social World'. *Jacobin*, 7 February, https://jacobin.com/2025/02/birth-rate-decline-capitalism-migration

Wright, Robin. 2019. 'The Story of 2019: Protests in Every Corner of the Globe'. *The New Yorker*, 30 December www.newyorker.com/news/our-columnists/the-story-of-2019-protests-in-every-corner-of-the-globe

Wu, Chin-Tao. 2009. 'Biennials without Borders'. *New Left Review* 57 (May–June): 107–15.

Wu, Chin-Tao. 2003. *Privatising Culture: Corporate Art Interventions since the 1980s*. London: Verso.

Zamora, Daniel and Michael C. Behrent. 2015. *Foucault and Neoliberalism*. Cambridge: Polity Press.

Zapperi, Giovanna. 2017a. 'Challenging Feminist Art History: Carla Lonzi's Divergent Paths'. In Lara Perry and Victoria Horne, eds. *Feminism and Art History Now: Radical Critiques of Theory and Practice*. London: Bloomsbury.

Zapperi, Giovanna. 2017b. *Carla Lonzi. Un' arte della vita* [Carla Lonzi: An Art of Life]. Rome: Derive Approdi.

Zaretsky, Eli. 1976. *Capitalism, the Family and Personal Life*. London: Pluto Press.

Zarobell, John. 2020. 'Freeports and the Hidden Value of Art'. *Arts* 9, 117: 1–12.

Žižek, Slavoj. 2016. *Refugees, Terror and Other Troubles with the Neighbors: Against the Double Blackmail*. Brooklyn NY: Melville House.

Websites and Institutional Online Sources

'A Letter from Artists in the Whitney Biennial'. 2019. *ARTFORUM*, 19 July, www.artforum.com/columns/a-letter-from-artists-in-the-whitney-biennial-244155/

ActionAid. 2024. 'Unpaid Care and Domestic Work'. *ActionAid*, 23 July, www.actionaid.org.uk/our-work/womens-economic-rights/unpaid-care-and-domestic-work

American Association of University Women. 2017. *The Simple Truth about the Gender Pay Gap*. www.aauw.org/research/the-simple-truth-about-the-gender-pay-gap/

Arts Council. 2018. *Livelihoods of Visual Artists Report*. 19 December, www.artscouncil.org.uk/livelihoods-visual-artists-report

ArtReview. 2024. Power100, https://artreview.com/power-100/

Athens Biennale. No date. 'AB6: ANTI'. https://athensbiennale.org/en/ab6/

Biennial Foundation. No date. 'Antarctic Biennale'. www.biennialfoundation.org/biennials/antarctic-biennale- antarctica/

Brooklyn Museum. No date. 'Collection / Components of The Dinner Party: Curatorial Overview'. www.brooklynmuseum.org/eascfa/dinner_party/core_imagery

CAMP. No date. 'About Camp'. http://campcph.org/about-camp

Change.org. 2018. 'Response to the Belgian Art Prize Exclusionary Shortlist 2019'. 12 May, www.change.org/p/la-jeune-peinture-belge-belgianartprize-response-to-the-belgianartprice-exclusionary-shortlist-2019

Clean Clothes Campaign. 2023. 'Activists' High Profile Hoax Highlights adidas' Hypocrisy'. https://cleanclothes.org/news/2023/activists-high-profile-hoax-highlights-adidas-hypocrisy

Community Wellbeing Space. No date. https://watchthisspace.online/about/

Cultureunstained.org. 2017. 'Bad Company: BP, Human Rights and Corporate Crimes'. https://cultureunstained.org/wp-content/uploads/2017/06/bad-company-bp-human-rights-and-corporate-crimes-culture-unstained-june-20171.pdf

Directorate of Intelligence. 'France: Defection of the Leftist Intellectuals [Sanitized Copy Approved for Release 2011/05/13]'. www.cia.gov/readingroom/docs/CIA-RDP86S00588R000300380001-5.pdf

Dreaming In Public. No date. www.dreaminginpublic.com/consulting

Entry 'Sor Juana Inés de la Cruz'. No date. *Britannica*, www.britannica.com/biography/Sor-Juana-Ines-de-la-Cruz

Ethics of Collecting. No date. https://ethicsofcollecting.org/ (accessed 23 February 2025)

etoy.CORPORATION. 2007. 'Disclaimer'. http://missioneternity.org/disclaimer/

etoy.CORPORATION. 2007. 'Mission Eternity'. https://etoy.com/projects/mission-eternity/

European Business Magazine. 2024. 'How Much Is the Global Gambling Industry Worth?' 23 April, https://europeanbusinessmagazine.com/business/how-much-is-the-global-gambling-industry-worth/

Frieze. 2016. 'In Profile: Hoor Al-Quasimi'. 30 March, www.frieze.com/article/profile-hoor-al-qasimi

Fugitive Materials. No date. *Fugitive Materials Catalog 2 The Birth of a Gay Network*. New York https://ilab.org/assets/catalogues/Fugitive-Materials-Catalog-2-The-Birth-of-A-Gay-Network.pdf (accessed 28 January 2025).

Global Women's Strike. No date. https://globalwomenstrike.net/

HantleyFilmArchives. 'Advert For Brillo, 1950s — Film 99774'. www.youtube.com/watch?v=zcooHxayHKc

HKW. 2018. 'Parapolitics: Cultural Freedom and the Cold War'. https://archiv.hkw.de/en/programm/projekte/2017/parapolitics/parapolitics_start.php

Imperial War Museum. No date. 'The Women Who Took On the British Government's Nuclear Programme'. www.iwm.org.uk/history/the-women-who-took-on-the-british-governments-nuclear-programme

Institute for Health Metrics and Evaluation. 2024. 'The Lancet: Dramatic declines in global fertility rates set to transform global population patterns by 2100', 20 March, www.healthdata.org/news-events/newsroom/news-releases/lancet-dramatic-declines-global-fertility-rates-set-transform

Lean In. No date. https://leanin.org/ (accessed 3 February 2024).

Lean In. No date. Women at Work Collection, https://leanin.org/leadership-program-resources

Lean In. No date. 'Women in the Workplace 2021', https://leanin.org/women-in-the-workplace/2021/introduction

Manual Labours. No date. www.manuallabours.co.uk/about/

National Endowment for the Arts. 2005. 'Artists in the Workforce, 1990-2005: Executive Summary'. www.arts.gov/sites/default/files/ArtistsInWorkforce_ExecSum.pdf

New Museum. No date. 'Amalia Ulman: Excellences & Perfections'. www.newmuseum.org/exhibitions/view/amalia-ulman-excellences-perfections

n.paradoxa: international feminist journal at www.ktpress.co.uk/feminist-art-exhibitions.asp

ONASSIS AiR. No date. www.onassis.org/initiatives/onassis-air

'Open Letter: A Response from the "100" French Scholars.' 2020, www.opendemocracy.net/en/can-europe-make-it/open-letter-response-100-french-scholars/

ORLAN. No date. 'Petition against Death'. www.orlan.eu/en/petition/

OXFAM. 2025. *Takers Not Makers: The Unjust Poverty and Unearned Wealth of Colonialism – Executive Summary*. January, https://oi-files-d8-prod.s3.eu-west-2.amazonaws.com/s3fs-public/2025-01/English%20-%20Davos%20Executive%20Summary%202025.pdf

OXFAM. 2017. 'An Economy for the 99%'. Oxfam Briefing Paper, January, https://oi-files-d8-prod.s3.eu-west-2.amazonaws.com/s3fs-public/file_attachments/bp-economy-for-99-percent-160117-summ-en.pdf

OXFAM International. 2024. 'Wealth of five richest men doubles since 2020 as five billion people made poorer in "decade of division"'. 15 January, www.oxfam.org/en/press-releases/wealth-five-richest-men-doubles-2020-five-billion-people-made-poorer-decade-division